PIMLICO

731

THE DIARIES OF CHARLES GREVILLE

Edward Pearce, after a national newspaper career starting in 1977, still keeps his hand in with books reviews, obituaries and travel pieces. However, for several years now, he has concentrated on writing history. *The Lost Leaders* (about three near-prime ministers) was followed by *Lines of Most Resistance* (about English resistance to Irish Home Rule), *Denis Healy* (the authorised biography), and *Reform!* (about the 1832 Act). The idea of preparing a handy, abridged Greville came to him when using Volume II as a major source for that study. He lives in North Yorkshire and is currently writing the life of Robert Walpole.

THE DIARIES OF
CHARLES GREVILLE

EDITED BY
EDWARD PEARCE
WITH
DEANNA PEARCE

PIMLICO

Published by Pimlico 2006

2 4 6 8 10 9 7 5 3 1

Editorial Introduction, Selection and Arrangement © Edward Pearce 2005

Edward Pearce has asserted his right under the Copyright,
Designs and Patents Act 1988 to be identified as the editor of this work

First published in hardback in Great Britain by Pimlico in 2005

Paperback edition published by Pimlico in 2006

Pimlico
Random House, 20 Vauxhall Bridge Road,
London SW1V 2SA

Random House Australia (Pty) Limited
20 Alfred Street, Milsons Point, Sydney,
New South Wales 2061, Australia

Random House New Zealand Limited
18 Poland Road, Glenfield,
Auckland 10, New Zealand

Random House South Africa (Pty) Limited
Isle of Houghton, Corner of Boundary Road &Carse O'Gowrie,
Houghton 2198, South Africa

Random House UK Limited Reg. No. 954009

A CIP catalogue record for this book is available from the British Library

ISBN 1-8441-3757-0

Papers used by Random House UK Ltd are natural, recyclable products
made from wood grown in sustainable forests. The manufacturing processes
conform to the environmental regulations of the country of origin

Printed and bound in Great Britain by Bookmarque Ltd, Croyden, Surrey

For

David McKie
another diarist,
also a student of dedications

CONTENTS

INTRODUCTION

Charles Greville is a stranger to the reading public as Samuel Pepys is not. The Secretary to the Navy is not so much better known than the Clerk to the Privy Council because he played a more vital part in politics. Pepys's role as reformer and reorganiser of the Navy did not launch the fleet of editions, full and abbreviated, beget a West End play or exclusively inspire two outstanding biographies (by Richard Ollard and Claire Tomalin). The man fascinates, *has* fascinated, since the Reverend John Smith laboriously transcribed his short-hand in the 1820s, not because of his busy part in the politics of 1660–90, of which he recorded only the first ten years and the Tangier journal. There is empathy for Pepys through all his poutings, resentments, sexual excursions and financial adhesions, because he inspires fellow feeling. He may be more influential than us, more important, more engaged in great doings, but he is *like* us.

Pepys has a wife to quarrel with, a wife who, recalling his father's trade of tailor, calls him 'a prick louse'. He fusses delightedly all the way to the diction-aries of quotation over the new suit for which God is asked to make him able to pay. He chases women, and breaks into Spanish in the diary when he catches them. This may not *quite* be us, but we recognise the impulse. Pepys is inse-cure, not in the precious terms of some psychiatric notion, but as the rest of us recognise insecurity.

He worries about the opinion of his superiors, about money, about the trouble into which both of these might get him. Pepys at his most discred-itable, during a national crisis, bundling the tricky profits of his office into a coach, under the armed protection of a trusted servant, to his father's house in Huntingdonshire, is fugitive and vulnerable, threatened as normal men feel threatened in their delinquencies. The fact that he then turns round and, in the best contemporary way, talks the Government out of well-deserved condem-nation for the burning of the Fleet at anchor, puts him back among the great ones, but we have seen him sweat.

Pepys is not a gentleman. Not so much risen as rising, he has all the delight anyone would feel on picking a straw and seeing it drawn out beyond his imag-inings. The pride is the pride of surprise; the obligato to this life is a long, nervous whistle of surprised delight. For all his abilities and hard work, or indeed the initial jobbery from the Montague upper end of his impossibly extended family, Pepys retains the style of someone winning the pools. All of which makes him hard to resent in the way that the takers and transmitters of high caste, social command, masterful assurance and expectations of the world are resented. And this is Charles Greville's problem, his problem especially today. Greville is a toff, the grandson of a duke, someone whose niece marries the heir to another dukedom, a regular at Epsom, Newmarket and the clubs, someone comfortable (and scornful) at court.

He is not quite Godolphin Horne, who 'held the human race in scorn', but the condition of being, like Godolphin, nobly born, orders his life. He speaks of 'we' and 'all the world', meaning perhaps three thousand people of mutually acknowledged birth, connection and manners, with a fringe of the very gifted. To an age which resents Oxford and Cambridge as obviously intended 'for the sort of people who eat smoked salmon', for no greater offence than setting difficult entrance examinations, Greville, with his unblushing allusions to 'the lower orders', deflects popular acclaim. No wonder that this familiar staple to historians got no further in public awareness than having provided, decades past, the *nom de plume* of a modest *Daily Mail* gossip column.

Never mind any of that. Greville is as interesting, vivid and enchanting as Pepys. Greville can be quite wonderful. His *Diaries* run through a fascinating period from the disintegrating last days of the Pitt–Liverpool Tory dominion through Reform, where he is close spectator, minor player and vividly opinionated commentator, through turmoils like the July Days of Paris 1830, the end of the Corn Laws, the Crimean War. And, just before, clenched with gout, he wearily rolls away from diary keeping, he acknowledges the doubtfully welcome landing of Garibaldi.

His gentlemanly place as Clerk to the Privy Council brings him into friendship (and as much enmity) with every politician of weight across thirty-five years: the detested Palmerston, a Duke of Wellington he admires but finds recurringly intolerable in his settled obtuseness, Robert Peel, whose greatness slowly dawns with events and acquaintance upon the early grumbler, Prince Albert, 'King in everything but name', and finally upon Gladstone and Disraeli, both still bubbling upward with talent and frustration as his record ends in 1860. A burst of real affection for Disraeli after his kindness to tribulated friends of Greville provides a pleasant episode. This was a highly intelligent, also a complex man, something which makes the settled cool view of his aristocratic background reliably misleading. He has both prejudices and an open mind. And he is no imperialist, small wars disgust him.

Like anyone born in 1794, he sees change as dangerous. The French Revolution had, after all, been started by admirers of the Whig Settlement seeking constitutional enlargement, and had ended in the almost three thou-

sand deaths of the Terror. The 'something nasty in the woodshed' of that experience would survive among and beyond the British upper class, together with
'Jacobin', as respectively flesh-creeping legend and hostile epithet for a Fabian
incrementalist, until the Soviet Russia and 'Bolshevik' replaced them. Greville
stood at the furthest ripples of that anxiety: edgy and aware of risk, but too
open-minded and intelligent to join Wellington and the Ultras in rigid denial
of all change. He was by inheritance a Whig, and the rustic, ineducable snarl
of the High Tories brought out his contempt.

So, fascinatingly, did royalty. Being a nobleman enjoined formal deference
at court, but allowed perfect freedom for cold-eyed distaste. There 'never was
a more worthless dog' than George IV. His successor, William IV, 'may go
mad'. Certainly he 'is the silliest old gentleman dwelling his dominions', but
what can one expect 'from someone whose head is shaped like a pineapple'?
The young Victoria who 'is not clever', gets smacks and apples on different
occasions. And here is the central appeal of Greville to the reader: he is a critic
and a slashing critic at that, a critic of events and institutions, but, much more
entertainingly, of people. So William, in contrast to his sophisticated, decadent
elder brother, is complimented as 'a plain, vulgar, hospitable country gentleman
opening his doors to all the world with a frightful Queen and a posse of
bastards, a Whig Minister and no foreigners and no toad eaters at all'. Henry
Brougham, Lord Chancellor and polymath, has 'genius, eloquence, variety and
extent of information', but he is also 'base, cowardly and unprincipled and with
all the execrable judgment which, I believe, often flows from the perversion of
moral sentiment'.

At what he calls 'a dinner of clever men' Greville is snubbed by Maule KC,
a former schoolfellow under Maule's flogging uncle: 'So I set him down for a
brute like his uncle and troubled him no further. I am sure that dinners of all
fools have as good a chance of being agreeable as dinners of all clever people.'
The mind stays open to evidence. The appearance of Henry Hunt, dangerous
democrat and damning witness of Peterloo, is recognised during a long speech
as 'very good, like a country gentleman of the old school, a sort of rural dignity
about it, very civil, good humoured and respectful to the house, but dull;
listened to however and very well received'.

Greville looks, sees, jumps to conclusions and denounces, often to rescind the
denunciation handsomely: 'I was quite wrong about that' is an agreeable recur-
rence in the notes he adds on readings-through of passages years later. But
always he is downright. Neither political correctness nor restraint has any place
here. The prelatical and mile-high Tory, Phillpotts, Bishop of Exeter, 'has a desperate
countenance and looks like the man he is'. Greville's views, which we have to
remember are those of six generations ago, can sound ferocious, witness his observations on a new model county jail, equipped with a treadmill and 'admirably
kept', but where, he is assured, 'private whipping is the most effectual mode of

punishment'. But the same man, brought into contemplation by the cholera which lands there, of people six to a bed in the industrial slums of Sunderland, shudders at what lies beneath the ice on which people like him tread.

He is, too, aristocrat enough to have no problems with his own folly. Having at dinner found 'a vacant place between Sir George Robinson and a common looking man in black' he speculates that this is 'some obscure man of letters or medicine, perhaps a cholera Doctor ... [One] remark and the manner of it gave me the notion that he was a dull fellow ... so as to excite something like a sneer ... having thus settled my opinion, I went on eating my dinner when Auckland, who was sitting opposite to me, addressed my neighbour, "Mr Macaulay, will you drink a glass of wine?" I thought I should have dropped off my chair.'

And Macaulay is a touchstone for Greville. His awe at learning, scholarship and intellectual distinction is very strong. The habitual armigerous horse-owning circle contains few people he respects, but Macaulay, Sydney Smith, the serious, high-calibre people of Holland House, leave him fascinated. This outlook is accompanied by the regular self-reproach, much of it comic, of the intellectual *manqué*. At one point he quotes a length of Lucretius, not exactly Fourth Form Latin, and follows it with Dryden's translation before lamenting his failure to do real and serious reading. Again, the open mind stays open in other countries: the passages covering his jaunts to France, Italy and Germany are among his best things. The account of Naples, a place (unlike England, where the poor do badly and the rich very well), in which somehow the climate feeds and warms the poor while the weak economy keeps the rich from splendour, is very perceptive. And he adores Naples.

The *Diaries* are rich in incident and event-painting, like the glow seen by whist players at the Travellers' which turns out to be Covent Garden Theatre burning down, bringing out both the fur-collared folk from the Austrian ambassador's ball and the small thieves of Seven Dials. He can catch the fear in the nostrils at a dark moment, as with cholera, about which 'we' and 'all the world' have been insouciant until 'Mrs Smith, young and beautiful, was dressed to go to Church on Sunday morning, was seized with the disorder, never had a chance and died at eleven at night'. Mrs Smith was an Earl's daughter, but the anxiety bites very hard.

Pepys is long on sex. Greville, though he acknowledges keeping for a while an attractive girl, 'who has good manners', provided by his friend De Ros, the premier baron of England, is either indifferent or discreet about sex and Greville. He is, though, sprightly enough about sex and other people: Melbourne sued as Prime Minister for 'Criminal conversation', Lord Hertford's string of whores, the Bishop of Clogher who might have escaped from detection in sodomitical circumstances if his breeches had not been down. What he does know about from personal experience is the races! Early in the *Diaries* he is manager to the Duke of York (the one son of George III he actively likes), also an owner himself, winning a St Leger; and he perpetually laments, without ever amending it, the company he keeps: 'Jockeys, trainers and blacklegs are my companions, and it is like dram-drinking; once having entered upon it, I cannot leave it off . . .' He should, of course, be listening to Macaulay or Sydney Smith.

But such company gives us the account of John Gully ex-prizefighter, ex-keeper of a gambling hell, villain of the turf, coal speculator, supporter of radical reform and parliamentary candidate for Pontefract: 'Lord Mexborough withdrew and he was elected without opposition . . .' After which, this astute fellow 'has gradually separated himself from the rabble of bettors and blackguards, of whom he was once the most conspicuous . . .' This course would, after Greville's lifetime, lead a Gully grandson to the Speakership and a still-thriving viscountcy. There will be another, and sensational, story when that same Lord De Ros, reversing Gully's process, flees the country after a long and tortuous attempt by Greville to save him from exposure. Evidence in court will reveal the premier baron, playing only in the very best venues, as a straight-up-and-down cardsharp.

You read Greville to know the age, to pick up its vivid incident, the duel, the hanging, the gambler's suicide, and for the elegance with which his plain-spokenness is expressed, as with the friend 'who had never been vicious or profligate, but who was free from anything like severity or austerity, who began to show signs of a devout propensity and, not contented with an ordinary discharge of duties, he read tracts and sermons, frequented Churches and Preachings, gave up driving on Sundays and appeared to be in danger of falling into the gulph of Methodism'. The style is Regency a little after its time, with after-echoes of the eighteenth century and occasional flights into Victorian moralising best quietly limited. A house built well between 1825 and 1860 you would enjoy looking at and would probably enjoy living in. Readers have that opportunity now.

On a personal note, I have badgered and lobbied my publishers, notably the wise Will Sulkin, to whom gratitude and thanks, for support in putting Greville back into general circulation. I had used the first and second volumes of the *Diaries* heavily in writing my book on the Reform Act published here in 2003. And, beyond utility, I had been captivated by the man. Unfortunately, Greville has become almost exclusively the nineteenth-century specialist's library resource; he needs the public air. There have been small, half-hearted publishing episodes, but the last full edition came out, 550 sets of seven volumes, plus an eighth, as index, in 1938. A handy abridgement, putting him into readers' hands, seemed a duty. Greville is history, wit, elegance and his own age's type; with his odd mix of aristocracy and anxiety, race meeting and Holland House symposium, he is too good to be obscure, far too good to be missed.

Edward Pearce
Thormanby
North Yorks

CHARLES GREVILLE:
A BIOGRAPHICAL SKETCH

Charles Cavendish Fulke Greville was born in 1794, a grandson of the Duke of Portland. He enjoyed the education of his class, Eton and Christ Church, Oxford, after preparatory studies at a notably brutal establishment run by one Maule. His future as a younger son was taken care of with the position of Private Secretary to the Tory politician, Earl Bathurst, a close ally of the repressive Home Secretary, Viscount Sidmouth (1812–21). Greville was not, in his own opinion, either a diligent or attentive employee and failed to pursue the political career which the post might have opened up.

As a young man, apart from some amorous episodes, he was chiefly interested in the turf, becoming a fairly successful manager of the Duke of York's stables. He remained close to the duke who died in 1827 and was an owner himself, disappointed in a Derby, quarrelling furiously with the dominant figure of nineteenth-century racing, Lord George Cavendish-Bentinck, but winning a St Leger and serious money.

It was common enough for young men about town with an interest in the turf and cards, another Greville enthusiasm, to come unstuck and be financially finished off before leaving ahead of their creditors for a tightly economic existence in a French Channel port. The famous example is, of course, Beau Brummel, a visit to whom in his pitiful exile, together with a list of other fallen bucks, appears in the *Diaries* with the shudder of someone who might have joined them.

There was a streak of shrewd self-preservation about the diarist, and two appointments – the sinecure Secretaryship for Jamaica and the genuine post of Clerk to the Privy Council – had made him secure enough. And when the Jamaica sinecure was threatened by a committee of Reform Whigs in the mid-1830s, he was ruefully grateful to the Tory politicians who successfully defended a privilege he did not try to justify.

He lived a life interestingly balanced among five occupations. There was the Great House social round dance; then the world, as he put it, of 'blacklegs and bettors' (*sic*) on a variety of racecourses; politics, where he cheerfully played an active part at a high level; and the intellectual world where he delighted in the company of leading writers and artists – regular callers, like him, at the perpetual Liberty Hall and running argument which was Holland House. (He genuinely revered intelligence.) Finally, by reason of his post, which required his presence (and the sovereign's) at meetings of the Privy Council, Greville was a regular at court during three reigns, those of George IV, William IV and Victoria. Duties took him regularly to Windsor but also to Balmoral and Queen Victoria's favourite home, Osborne House on the Isle of Wight.

He engaged in backstage politics during the 1831–2 struggle for the Reform Act, serving as middleman between a group of Opposition peers seeking a compromise and members of the Cabinet. Later, he kept his political hand in through the press, having at all times an excellent line, via two successive editors, to The Times, in those days a fairly radical sheet. He had a Times leader writer, Henry Reeve, for his office junior and both made use of him and wrote himself. For example, in 1840–41, he organised a concerted campaign through the paper against Palmerston's aggressive (and successful) foreign policy in the Middle East.

His life away from the Diaries was that of an intelligent, critical-minded aristocrat who felt guilty about his dissipations, girls kept, money lost and all, but while keeping up with his temptations in a prudent fashion, not only knew the entire political, aristocratic and intellectual world, but talked, listened and made notes. He was an alert, attentive traveller in France, Germany and Italy, adding his fairly sympathetic accounts of these countries to the Diaries.

A frustrated writer with only the odd pamphlet to his credit, he made a record of his times in a split mood. He often contemplated giving up the Clerkship, looking to the big win on the horses which would let him do so. But though the big win, or, rather, run of racing luck, actually came, it was not until some time later, in 1859, that he finally resigned. As to the diaries, he often complained about the futility of writing what would never be seen. But although he stopped making entries in 1860, he took care just before his death in 1865 to see them into the hands of Reeve as literary executor. He would be furiously abused by posterity, including a hissing Queen Victoria, when they began to be issued. There was good reason. The Diaries respect no persons; they are a sardonic betrayal of his class. He was a witness, not just to the adulteries and delinquencies of nobility and Government, but to its inadequacy. He is full of sharp opinions, not least a view of Victoria which shows the Queen Empress as dull, clinging, undereducated and, effectively, Prince Albert's secretary.

But compared with her two predecessors, William IV and George IV, Victoria is gently treated. Reeve discreetly censored his edition but it created sensation enough. The full text is the record of a man who knew every Prime Minister, Royal Duke and actress and marked the cards of them all.

EDITOR'S NOTE

These *Diaries* are officially called *The Journals of the Reigns of George IV and Queen Victoria*. This is inaccurate since a few early passages relate to George III's time; and the whole reign of William IV, 1830–37, is covered, indeed contains some of the most important material. They are often known as *The Greville Papers*, though the last editors of the full text, Strachey and Fulford, present them as *The Greville Memoirs*. But at the end of a long day, they *are* diaries and have so been described here.

They begin in 1814, and forty-eight pages of the Strachey/Fulford text are taken up with pre- and post-Waterloo material, 1814–15; nothing more appears until he resumes writing in 1818. The period 1818–23, inclusive, contains exactly a hundred pages; he then goes silent, putting in an obituary of the Marquess of Titchfield to represent the whole of 1824 and skipping 1825 altogether. In 1826 he makes a declaration about unspeakable events in his private life about which he had no wish to make a record. But in 1827 he hits his stride and the diaries as we know them take off at full length, the exciting year of 1829 accumulating 118 pages. There are, over the next thirty or so years, some lapses, not least his periodic disappearances to Epsom or Newmarket in the middle of a political crisis, but then we get the racing instead. And there is a mild diminuendo, with much grumbling about being out of things in the last five years or so of the diaries. But from 1827 until he calls it a day in 1860, he is a constant and pretty regular chronicler. The full text involves seven volumes of about five hundred pages each, plus a volume-length index.

Part of that text was published in 1875 under the editorship of Henry Reeve who brought out more in 1887. Lytton Strachey began work on a full text edition in 1928 assisted by a gentler star of Bloomsbury, Ralph Partridge, who, when Strachey died in 1932, continued helping his successor, Roger Fulford. The full edition appeared in 1938; Fulford also issued a pocket abridgement in 1963.

I have worked from their text but making my own footnotes and, in the interest of a straight read, omitting all sorts of learned code for restored and amended text. The distinction between on-page notes, in square brackets, and those put to the end of the book, concerns two different functions – clarifying the narrative and adding fuller background. It is inevitably arbitrary, but essential.

I have followed Greville's orthography where it does not irritate or confuse, keeping the pleasant 'Catholicks' and 'the Publick', but changing spellings which would now be wrongly taken for Americanisms, like 'favor'. I hope I have used common sense over punctuation, broadly following Greville but not to the point of a comma after 'and' in a list. I have also indulged Greville's internal contradictions. So the 'D'Israeli' of the '30s and '70s remains, 'D'Israeli' followed by the 'Disraeli' of the '50s. The purpose has been low and practical, to give the reader a clear, easily read book.

As for the actual abridgement: in a reduction from around 1,800,000 words, any editor inevitably picks cherries and draws upon set pieces. But where Greville is covering a continuous story, however broken up – the Reform Act, Palmerston's Egyptian adventure, the early days of Albert and Victoria, Greville's odd friendship with Napoleon III, the Crimean War and the Indian Mutiny – I have tried to maintain a narrative and make clear what happened. All this nicely reflects Greville who tried to keep a story line but enjoyed himself most with amusing and explosive incidents. Despite his exalted position and privacy he wrote more than he realised for the general public.

THE DIARIES

VOLUME I

1814

February 11th

... I believe that a difference of opinion exists in the Cabinet upon the question of peace with Bonaparte. Lords Castlereagh, Liverpool, Sidmouth, Bragge, Vansittart, Buckinghamshire, Westmoreland and Mulgrave are for peace, Lords Harrowby, Eldon, Bathurst and Melville are against any peace with Bonaparte.

March 4th

The Regent was very near dying in consequence of a disgraceful debauch about ten days ago. He sent for Mr Colman[1] of the little Theatre from the King's Bench [the debtors' prison where Colman was detained for several years] and sat up the whole night with him and others of his friends drinking until he was literally dead drunk. He was saved with some difficulty by Sir W. Farquhar.

April 17th

The Baron de Weissembourg [correctly Weissenberg, Johann von, Austrian diplomat] was taken prisoner and carried with him [Bonaparte] to Fontainbleu [Fontainebleau]. He conversed with the Baron very freely on the state of his affairs, and said that he was aware that he was entirely ruined; he was aware he should be accused of having committed faults; he certainly had committed one great fault, in having married an Austrian instead of a Russian princess.

July 4th

The Emperor [of Russia, Tsar Alexander I] and King of Prussia [Frederick William III] have at length left England, and this visit, so long and anxiously looked forward to, is over. The phrensy of curiosity which pervaded all ranks to see these Great People, and the excess of impatience for their arrival was succeeded by a satisfaction as great, tho' more placid at their departure.

September 16th

... It has been much doubted whether Bonaparte was ever much addicted to Women: Sir Charles Stuart [ambassador at Paris, 1815–30] and who relates many interesting anecdotes which he has picked up there, avers that he was, and that at Berlin and other places he used to intrigue with women, going about incognito as King of Westphalia[2] or some such title, his grandeur being such that he went about incognito as a King! Sir CS also declared to us that he knew for a fact that Napoleon was clapped when he left Fontainbleu on his way to Elba.

September 26th

... I took that opportunity of asking him [Count Maximilian von Murfeldt, Austrian general] to give me an account of the interview which he had with Bonaparte when he was taken prisoner at the Battle of Leipsick [Leipzig]. He related a great deal of the conversation to me which is most curious and interesting. I wrote down all I could remember of what he told me.

[Greville's own note of 15 December 1835: I wonder what the Devil I did with his narration.]

October 27th

When the Commissioners who are appointed to examine the state of the King's health are introduced into his apartment, for that purpose, it is usual for the physicians to engage him in conversation in order to satisfy themselves of the real state of his disorder ... Upon entering the apartment the K said as usual 'What news is there Sir Henry?'[3] 'Very great news Sir.' He replied. 'Indeed' said the King 'but before you tell me, how is Lord Westmoreland?' 'He is very well sir' replied Sir H., 'and constantly enquires after your Majesty with the greatest affection.' 'Indeed,' said the King, 'asks after me still?' and he leant back and cried like a child; then said 'He is a rough man, but has an excellent heart at bottom' – 'but come' he added. 'What is the news?' 'Sir' said Sir Henry, 'the Emperors of Austria and Russia and the King of Prussia are at the head of their armies in the heart of France ... and your Majesty's army is in France also.' At this intelligence, the King appeared greatly agitated and eagerly asked 'Who commands?' 'Lord Wellington, Sir' replied Sir Hy. 'That's a damned lie.' said the King. 'He was shot two years ago' – and then he began to talk incoherently.

1815

Chatsworth January 24th 1815

Lord Stewart's[1] conduct at Vienna has excited much dissatisfaction, and it is thought impossible he can remain there after the disgraceful things which have happened to him. At a ball one night he took some liberties with (pinched) a young lady of high rank who informed her mother of what he had done ... Soon afterwards she again met Ld. S. who repeated the offence. The young lady again informed her mother who immediately declared that there was a person present who was unfit to be in society. This made a great breeze, and Ld. S. was forced to apologise, which he did in the most abject terms, at the same time accusing himself by saying 'En verité, Je suis ivre.'

February 28th 1815 London
... Mr Secretary Peel I well recollect expressed his extreme satisfaction at an event which (as he said) by accomplishing the destruction of Buonaparte[2] would consolidate the security of Europe. He considered his failure as certain, and talked confidently of his being speedily apprehended and executed ...

Friday March 10th
The news arrives of Buonaparte having landed in France between Fréjus and Antibes on the 4th inst. The whole town is thrown into extreme amazement.

Sunday March 12th
Despatches from Fitzroy Somerset are received: everything is said to be going on well. B. had not advanced further than the Gap, and had not received any assistance. All the Marshals had sworn to be loyal to the King, and the best spirit existed all over the Country.

Monday March 13th
No despatches from Paris, and nothing more known in the morning; but French Papers arrive which state that a Telegraphick message had announced that B. slept at Bourgoin on the 9th and might enter Lyons on the 10th.

Friday [March] 17th
No despatches and no certain intelligence is arrived this day. The Success of Bonaparte is considered certain, and it is thought that the King has already quitted Paris.

In the afternoon; – it is reported on the authority of Mr Rosschild [sic] that Buonaparte entered Paris in the evening of the 14th ...

Saturday [March] 18th
... the affairs of the Bourbons wear a much better aspect than was imagined. Bonaparte has not advanced beyond Lyons and his whole force does not amount to 9000 men. Paris was quiet and the King had not left it ... Genl. Drouet was arrested ... it is said that he has been executed.[3]

Sunday [March] 19th
... A report tonight says that Buonaparte has been deserted by 2000 of his troops and that he is surrounded at or near Lyons. We have no reports on which we can rely ...

Mon [March] 20th

No despatches arrived this morning, but a report pervaded the town, that Buonaparte's Rear Guard *had been defeated with great loss by M.Ney.*

Tuesday [March] 21st

Buonaparte had advanced to Auxerre on the 17th and had again quitted that place. Hitherto he has met with no opposition . . .

Wednesday [March] 22nd

There were reports in the City that Buonaparte had been defeated and killed. The stocks fell on the 22nd from 61 to 58 . . . in the evening a gentleman by the name of Morrison arrived with intelligence that the King had left Paris and retired to Abbeville . . . the people at Abbeville shouted 'Vive l'Empereur' whilst the King was there.

Thursday [March] 23rd

Intelligence has been received of Buonaparte having entered Paris on the 20th . . .

Friday March 31st

. . . I saw Sir Robert Wilson [British general][4] this morning who told me that Prince Volchonsky [a Russian courtier], who has just returned from Paris, said that the Parisians were delighted at the return of Napoleon, and that universal satisfaction and gaiety prevailed.

June 18th

All Europe has been arming for the approaching contest during the past three months and every day is now expected to bring accounts of the commencement of hostilities . . . in the House of Commons the question for peace or war was debated with great violence and carried for the latter by immense majorities . . . Mr Whitbread who is the actual, though not the nominal, head of the Opposition, has returned to his old system of interrogating and catechising Lord Castlereagh . . . It is a mode of proceeding altogether novel in Parliament and unfair and illiberal in the highest degree. It is a departure from the honourable and manly principles upon which opposition in Parliament ought always to be conducted, and besides giving rise to unbecoming personalities in discussion, displays a hostility altogether unworthy of a great party . . .

In the meantime the preparations for war have been continued with extraordinary activity . . . the Prussian Army, complete in numerical strength and military equipment, is prepared to enter France, and the Duke of Wellington with 70,000 British and Hanoverians and a considerable corps of Belgians and Dutch, is equally prepared . . . Further reinforcements have since increased the number to above 70,000 men. The Austrian, Russian and German Armies will invade France on the Western [*sic*] frontier, while the British and Prussians penetrate through the northern. The French Force is variously represented, but according to the best accounts, it appears to amount to about 350,000 men, of which 180,000 are old troops ... The Bourbons are impressed with all that confidence which has never forsaken them even in their extremist distress. The Duc de Berri reviews and manouvres the small army which he commands in Flanders, composed of 3 or 4000 men, ill-equipped, ill-armed, ill-clothed, and of the most wretched appearance. He however gallops about with a numerous État Major, all glittering with embroidery and stars and crosses and medals.

June 30th

Whilst I was writing the above, the English and French Armies were engaged, and on that day the fate of Buonaparte of France and perhaps of Europe, was decided on the plains of Waterloo ... For nine successive hours the elite of the French Army attacked the British Lines, pouring forth fresh troops again and again with a heroism which nothing but national antipathy could have excited. The French Cavalry charged the solid squares of infantry with desperate valour and, undismayed by repulse, returned again and again to the attack. Lord Wellington was everywhere and exposed his person like the meanest soldier. Buonaparte ... mounted his horse and putting himself at the head of the Imperial Guard, he made a grand assault with this whole force, Infantry, Cavalry and Artillery. After an obstinate and murderous contest, this attack was repulsed and Lord Wellington, perceiving that the Enemy was retiring in great confusion and that the Prussian corps under Genl. Bulow [(1755–1816), an outstanding Prussian general] was beginning to appear on his left, he ordered the whole British Line to move forward and attack the French Army. The attack succeeded at every point, the French were driven from their positions with immense loss and the whole of their cannon, baggage and ammunition was taken ... The news of this victory was received in England with a general joy which was considerably damped by the magnitude of the loss that was sustained ... it is supposed to amount to nearly 15,000 men. In the mean time the victory proved to be greater and more decisive than the most sanguine had expected. The French Army was completely routed and unable to rally upon any point.

1818

I began to keep a Journal some time ago and after continuing it irregularly, dropped it entirely. I have since felt tempted to resume it irregularly because having frequent opportunities of mixing in the society of celebrated men, some particulars about them might be interesting hereafter.

I have been frequently at Talleyrand's[1] who keeps an open house . . . Bonaparte once said to him that he was represented to be very rich and he wished to know how his wealth had been acquired. He replied that he had bought into the funds the 17th Brumaire [8 November][2] and sold on the 19th . . . I went once to the Chamber of Deputies – it was so uninteresting I never returned. The question was unimportant, but even on important questions I don't think it can be entertaining. There are not above seven or eight Members who are able to speak extemporaneously . . .

April 1st

I came to London on Sunday night with Berkeley Craven. The world is very dull and everything is much as it always is.

June 7th

. . . The Queen [Charlotte von Mecklenberg-Strelitz, consort of George III] was so ill on Friday evening that they expected she would die.

July 24th

The elections are carried on with great violence . . . The mob seem to have shaken off the feelings and the usual character of Englishmen, and in the brutal attacks which they have made on Captain Maxwell [a Tory candidate],[3] have displayed the savage ferocity which marked the mobs of Paris in the worst times . . . Lord Castlereagh[4] went to the hustings, and voted for Sir M. Maxwell; he was hooted, pelted and got off with some difficulty. His Lordship's judgment was not very conspicuous on this occasion; both Sir M's friends and enemies are of Opinion that Lord C's vote did him a great deal of harm and turned many men against him . . .

August 4th

I went to Oatlands [the Duke of York's estate].[5] There was a very large party . . . we played whist till four in the morning. On Sunday we amused ourselves by eating fruit in the garden and shooting at a mark with pistols and playing with the Monkeys. I bathed in the cold bath in the grotto which is as clear as crystal and as cold as ice. Oatlands is the worst managed establishment in England; there are a great many servants, and nobody waits on you, a vast number of horses and none to ride or drive.

August 16th

. . . We dine at eight and sit at table until eleven. In about a quarter of an hour after we leave the dining-room, the Duke sits down to play at Whist and never stirs from the table as long as anybody will play with him . . . The Duke of York is not clever, but he has justness of understanding which enables him to avoid the errors into which most of his brothers have fallen, and which have made them so contemptible and unpopular. Although his talents are not rated high ... the Duke of York is loved and respected. He is the only one of the Princes who has the feelings of an English Gentleman ...

Ampthill September 9th [then the home of the active Whig Lord Holland] I rode down today with Alvanley and Montron [close friend of Talleyrand] came in a chaise and four. Luttrell [poetaster, boulevardier] and Rogers,[6] the dinner was very bad because the Cook is out of humour. The evening passed off heavily ...

'Mr Fox'[7]

Lord Holland was talking to Mr Fox the day after the debate on the war (after the Peace of Amiens)[8] about public speakers and mentioned Sheridan's speech on the Begums.[9] Fox said 'You may rest assured that that speech was the finest ever made in Parlt.' Lord Holland said, 'It is very well of you to say so, but I think your speech last night was a pretty good one.' Fox said 'And that was a devilish fine speech too' ...

1819

January 28th

I went to Gorhambury [estate of the Earl of Verulam] on the 24th to shoot. The D. of York was there. We should have had a brilliant chasse, but it rained. We went out at three and killed 105 pheasants.

February 3rd

I went with Bouverie [Charles Bouverie, a fellow racing enthusiast] to Newmarket on Monday to look at the horses. On Wednesday I came to town and went on to Oatlands. We played at Whist till near 5. I had been a great loser but I won it back, and six guineas. Madame de Lieven[1] was there. This woman is excessively clever, and when she chooses, brilliantly agreeable. She is beyond all people fastidious. She is equally conscious of her own superiority and the inferiority of other people, and the contempt she has for the under-standings of the generality of her acquaintance has made her indifferent to please and incapable of taking any delight in general society ... she carried ennui to such a pitch that, even in the society of her most intimate friend, a woman in every way her equal, she frequently owns that she is bored to death ... Her manners are stately and resolved, and so little bonhomie penetrates through her dignity that few feel sufficiently attracted to induce them to try and thaw the ice in which she always seems bound.

March 5th

Geo. Lambe [successful Tory candidate at the Westminster by-election] was to have been chaired on the day he was elected, but the mob was outrageous and would not suffer it. They broke into his committee room, and he and McDonald were forced to creep out of a two pair of stairs window into the Churchyard. His partisans assembled on horseback, were attacked and pelted and forced to retreat after receiving many hard knocks. In the evening the mob paraded the town and broke the windows of Lord Castlereagh's and Lord Sefton's houses . . .

May 14th

The Newmarket meetings finished yesterday. I have won between 4 and 500 by the three weeks. There was deep play the first and second meetings . . .

June 12th

I have been to Oatlands for the Ascot party and lost about 300gns at Whist; one night I lost 420. On the course I did nothing. Ever since the Derby ill fortune has pursued me and I cannot win anywhere . . . Play is a detestable occupation; it absorbs all our thoughts and renders us unfit for everything else in life. It is hurtful to the mind and destroys the better feelings; . . . at the gaming table all men are equal; no superiority of birth, accomplishments or ability avail here; great noblemen, merchants, orators, jockeys, statesmen and idlers are thrown together in levelling confusion; the only pre-eminence is that of success, the only superiority that of temper.

July 30th

. . . the British constitution after struggling for several hundred years has reached as high a pitch of perfection as it is given to human institutions to attain. England enjoys profound repose [On 19 August there would take place the killings and maimings at Peterloo] and we have no longer to contend for our liberties. Let us take care that the spirit of party, covering itself with the specious name of patriotism, does not now sow dissensions amongst us which may gradually and imperceptibly sap the foundations of the mighty fabrick which has been planned with such wisdom, erected with such pains and cemented with so much blood. [Greville was twenty-five years old.]

December 24th

The Duke of Kent gave the name of Alexandrina to his daughter in compliment to the Emperor of Russia. She was to have had the name Georgiana, but the Duke insisted upon Alexandrina being her first name. The Regent sent for Lieven and made him a great many compliments *en persiflant* on the Emperor's being Godfather, but informed him that the name Georgiana could be second to no other in this country, and therefore she could not bear it at all. [The second name chosen for this child was Victoria.]

The frost is intense. The town is empty. I returned from Wherstead last Wednesday se'ennight [a term of seven nights, not necessarily a calendar week] and went to Oatlands on Thursday; there was nearly the same party. The Prince Leopold came and dined there on Saturday. He is very dull and heavy in his manner and seems overcome with the weight of his dignity. The Prince will not succeed here; everybody is civil to him from the interest he excited at the time of the Princess's death[2] – an interest which has not yet subsided, but his pomposity fatigues and his avarice disgusts. There seems to be no harm in him, but everybody contrasts his manners with those of the D. of York, and the comparison is not to his advantage.

1820

London January 20th. Friday

I went last Sunday se'ennight to Woburn [estate of the Dukes of Bedford]. The House, place, establishment and manner of living are the most magnificent I have seen. There is no place which gives so splendid an example of an English Lord as this. The chasse was brilliant; in five days we killed 835 pheasants, 645 hares, 59 rabbits, 10 partridges and 5 woodcocks. The Duchess was very civil and the party very gay. I won at whist and liked it very much ...

February 4th

... On Sunday last came the news of the King's death. [George III ended his long tragedy, dying on 29 January 1820.] The new King has been desperately ill. He had a bad cold at Brighton, for which he lost eighty ounces of blood; he afterwards had a severe oppression amounting almost to suffocation, on his chest. Halford was gone to Windsor, and left orders with Knighton[1] not to bleed him again till his return, Knighton was afraid to bleed him. Bloomfield sent for Tierney[2] who took it upon himself to take fifty ounces from him ... Tierney certainly saved his life, for he must have died had he not been blooded.

February 24th

The plot which has been detected had for its object the destruction of the Cabinet Ministers, and the chief actor in the conspiracy was Arthur Thistlewood ... Government received information that they were to be assembled to the number of from twenty to thirty at a house in Cato Street, Edgware Road, and that had resolved to execute their purpose last night, when the Cabinet would be at dinner at Lord Harrowby's ... The Ministers who were expected at dinner remained at Fife House, and at eight o'clock, Mr Birnie with twelve constables was despatched to Cato Street ... A man armed with a musket was standing sentry whom they secured. They then ascended a narrow staircase which led to the room in which the gang were assembled and burst the door open. The first man who entered was shot in the head, but only wounded; he who followed was stabbed by Thistlewood and killed ... The conspirators then with their swords put out the lights and attempted to escape ... [This was the Cato Street Conspiracy, high point of violent opposition in a period of intense hardship.]³

June 7th

The Queen [Caroline of Brunswick, estranged wife of George IV]⁴ arrived in London yesterday at seven o'clock. I rode as far as Greenwich to greet her. The road was thronged with an immense multitude the whole way from Westminster Bridge to Greenwich. Carriages, carts and horsemen followed, proceeded and surrounded her coach the whole way. She was everywhere greeted with the greatest enthusiasm. Women waved pocket handkerchiefs and men shouted wherever she passed. She travelled in an open landau, Alderman Wood [a prominent and aggressive radical, at whose house Caroline was staying] sitting by her side ... As she passed by White's⁵ she bowed and smiled at the men who were in the window ... It is impossible to conceive the sensation created by her arrival.

Nobody either blames or approves of her sudden return, but all ask 'What will be done next? How is it to end?' ...

June 9th

... The mob have been breaking down windows in all parts of the town and pelting those who would not take off their hats as they passed Wood's door ... Great sums of money have been won and lost on the Queen's return, for there was much betting at the clubs ... It is odd enough, Lady Hertford's windows have been broken to pieces and the frames driven in, while no assault has been made on Lady Conyngham's [respectively the King's former and present mistress].

June 27th

The Queen demanded to be heard by counsel at the bar of House of Lords. Contrary to order and contrary to expectation, the counsel were admitted, when Brougham made a very powerful speech ...

July 6th

Since the report of the Secret Committee the publick opinion is entirely changed as to the result of the proceedings against her. Everybody thinks that the charges will be proved and that the King will be divorced ... [But] it is certain hitherto that all ranks of men have been decidedly favourable to the Queen and disbelieve the charges against her. The military in London have shown alarming signs of disaffection ...

July 7th

I was in the H. of Lords the night before last to hear Brougham and Denman speak at the bar. Brougham's speech was uncommonly clever, very insolent, and parts of it very eloquent ...

July 14th

I have been at Newmarket where I had the first fortunate turn this year, I won 300. I came to Town and found half a dozen people dead. Mrs Gascoigne died the day her daughter's marriage was declared with Lord Cranborne [later 2nd Marquess of Salisbury]. The conversation about the Queen begins to subside ... London is drawing to a close, but in August it will be very full as all the Peers must be here. They say the trial will last six months.

August 11th

... I read the *Liaisons Dangereuses* through without stopping from beginning to end the other day. The author of this book is unknown [Pierre Choderlos de Laclos (1741–1803)]. It is beautifully written and not uncommonly clever, but the man who wrote it must have had the most depraved heart in the world ... The Duchess of York died on Sunday Morning of water on her chest. She was insensible the last two days. She is deeply regretted by her husband, her friends and her servants. Probably no person in such a situation was ever more really liked. She has left £12,000 [£600,000 at present values] and some children whom she had caused to be educated.

London October 8th

The Town is still in an uproar about the trial and nobody has any doubt that it will finish by the bill being thrown out ... The Queen fell asleep in the House of Lords one day which occasioned the following epigram by Ld. Holland.

> 'Her conduct at present no censure affords
> She sins not with peasants but sleeps with the Lords.'

October 15th

Since I came to Town I have been to the trial every day ... I never remember any question which so exclusively occupied everybody's attention and so completely absorbed men's thoughts and engrossed conversation ... Until the evidence of Lt. Hownam, it was generally thought that proofs of her guilt were wanting. But since his admission that Bergami[6] slept under the tent with her, all unprejudiced men seem to think the adultery proved . . . The Ministers were elated in an extraordinary manner by this evidence of Hownam's . . . They look upon the progress of this trial in the light of a campaign and upon each day's proceedings as . . . a sort of battle. The D. of Portland told me that he conversed with the D. of Wellington upon the subject, and urged as one of the reasons why this Bill should not pass the H. of Lords, the disgrace it would entail upon the K. by the recrimination that would ensue in the H. of C. His answer was 'that the King was degraded as low as he could be already.' . . . Lady Harrowby said that if the House of Lords was to suffer itself to be influenced by the opinions and wishes of the people, it would be the most mean and pusillanimous conduct, and after all, what did it signify what the people thought or what they expressed if the army was to be depended upon? . . .

December 31st Woburn

. . . I wrote to *XY* [two initials expunged] from Wandsford begging her to meet me at Sprotboro and the letter fell into the hands of her husband. He opened and read it but as he is extremely bête, she can make him believe anything et nous sommes très bien tirés de cette affaire. I staid [*sic*] at Sprotboro for some time and then went to Nun Appleton. From thence I returned to Sprotboro, and then I went to Tickhill, Welbeck, Burghley, Middleton, and I came here on the 17th. I grew horribly tired . . .

1821

Monday March 5th

Lord Chetwynd died on Wednesday morning last. I came that day from Newmarket and was informed of the event on getting out of the carriage. Thus, if I do not lose any money at play, my difficulties are at an end. [Viscount Chetwynd had held the pleasantly remunerated post of Clerk in Ordinary; on his death, it went to Greville.]

March 22nd

I was sworn in the day before yesterday and kissed hands at a Council at Carlton House yesterday morning.

May 2nd

When the Canonry of Windsor became vacant Lady C[onyngham][1] asked the King to give it to Mr Sumner who had been [her son] Mount Charles's tutor. The King agreed, the man was sent for and kissed hands at Brighton.

A letter was sent to Lord Liverpool to announce the appointment . . . As soon as Lord L. received the letter he got into his carriage and went down to the King and stated that unless he was allowed to have the distribution of this patronage without any interference, he could not carry on the Government and would resign his office if Sumner was appointed. The man was only a curate and had never held a living at all.[2] . . . Lady C lives in one of the houses on Marlboro Row . . . She rides out with her daughter but never with the King who always rides with one of his gentlemen. They never appear in public together. She dines there every day; before the King comes into the room she and Lady Elizabeth join him in another room, and he always walks in with one on each arm. She comports herself entirely as Mistress of the house but never suffers her daughter to leave her. She has received magnificent Presents and Lady Elizabeth the same; particularly the mother has strings of pearls of enormous value . . .

August 6th

For ever be this day accursed which has been to me the bitterest of my existence. The particulars will remain too deeply engraved on my memory to need being written down here. (The devil take me if I have any idea to what this alludes. I can't guess. *Feby 1836*.)

December 18th

Have not written anything for months . . . My progress was as follows, not very interesting: To Newmarket, Whersted, Riddlesworth, Caversham, Euston [ducal country house, not the railway terminal], Elveden, Welbeck, Sprotborough, Nun Appleton, Welbeck, Burghley and London. Nothing worth mentioning occurred in any of these places . . . I went to Brighton yesterday se'ennight for a Council. I lodged in the Pavilion and dined with the King. The gaudy splendour of the place amused me for a little and then bored me. The dinner was cold and the evening dull beyond dullness. They say the King is anxious that form and ceremony should be banished, and if so it only proves how impossible it is that form and ceremony should not inherit a palace.

1822

July 16th

Since I wrote last I have been continually in town. I have won the Derby [as manager to the Duke of York, not owner], my sister[1] is married and I have done nothing but make love to Georgina Lennox.[2] At the Priory I went into her room at night but was fool enough to go away without doing anything. I shall not be such a fool again . . . I have been very often bored to death by the necessity of paying some attention to keep up an interest with G. L. Having had so much trouble, I don't choose to drop it without bringing the thing to a conclusion . . . The affair of the Bishop [of Clogher][3] has made a great noise. The people of the public house have made a good deal of money by showing the place. Lord Sefton went to see the soldier in prison. He says he is a fine soldier-like man and has not the air which these wretches usually have. The Bishop took no precautions and it was next to impossible he should not have been caught. He made a desperate resistance when taken and if his breeches had not been down they think he would have got away. It seems that the soldier will be proceeded against with the greatest vigour and the magistrate is much blamed for having taken such small bail as that which he required. The Duke will not spare the soldier. Lord Lauderdale said the other day that the greatest dissatisfaction would pervade the publick mind at the escape of the Bishop and the punishment of the soldier . . .

August 13th

I went to Cirencester on Friday and came back yesterday. At Hounslow I heard of the death of Lord Londonderry [known to history by the family's courtesy title of Lord Castlereagh, Foreign Secretary (1812–22)] . . . the state of his dejection in which he appeared induced his attendants to take certain precautions which unfortunately proved fruitless. They removed his pistol and razors, but he got hold of a penknife which was in the room next to his, and on Sunday night or early on Monday morning he cut his throat with it . . . the general opinion seems to be that Canning[4] will not go to India but will be appointed in his room.

September 22nd

I went to Sprotboro on the 15th and on the 16th I won £5,700 [Theodore won at 100–1; winnings at present values represent, say, £280,000] on the St Leger . . .

November 5th

. . . Since I left London for the Doncaster races I have travelled 1200 miles. I lost £4000 at play between 1st and 3rd and the 2nd and 3rd meetings . . .

Welbeck November 16th

I have had a great deal of conversation with Titchfield [Greville's cousin, eldest son of the Duke of Portland] particularly about Canning . . . When the King had consented to receive him he wrote a letter nearly in these words to Lord Liverpool. 'The King thinks that the brightest jewel in his crown is to extend his forgiveness (I am not sure that this was the word) to a subject who has offended him[5] and he therefore informs Lord L. that he consents to Mr Canning forming a part of the Cabinet.' This letter was communicated to Canning, and upon reading it, he was indignant, as were his wife and his daughter. The consequence was that he wrote a most violent and indignant reply addressed to [Liverpool] and which was intended in like manner to have been shown to the King. As the King's letter was to him . . . Upon hearing what had passed however down came Lord Granville and Mr Ellis in a great hurry . . . [whose] arguments, vehemently urged and put in every possible shape, prevailed, and the angry reply was put in the fire and another written full of gratitude, duty and acquiescence.

1823

Sept. 17th

Near seven months since I have written any thing. What concerns myself is principally winning and losing and getting H. with child [Harriet Graham, wife of Sir Bellingham Graham Bt. who did not discover the parentage until 1824] . . .

I have been constantly in London for the last seven months doing nothing. Events there have been none.

1826

February 9th

I have written nothing for two years . . . I suppose that what has happened to me within the last two years must be so indelibly engraved on my memory that it needs not to be recorded, and as I am not going to write my life I may spare myself the pain of going over these dismal occurrences . . .

February 12th

The last three months have been remarkable for the panic in the money market which lasted a week or ten days – that is, was at its height for that time . . . The state of the City and the terror of all Bankers and Merchants, as well as of all owners of property is not to be conceived but by those who witnessed it . . . For many days the evil continued to augment so rapidly and the demands on the Bank were so great and increasing that a bank restriction was expected by everyone. So determined however were Ministers against this measure, that rather than yield to it, they suffered the bank to run the greatest risk of stopping; for on the evening of the day during which the alarm was at its worst there were only 8000 sovereigns left in the Bank.[1] . . .

February 20th

The Small Notes Bill,[2] as it is called, lowered the funds and increased the alarm among the monied men. Numerous were the complaints of the inefficacy of the measure for present relief, numerous the predictions of the ultimate impossibility of carrying it into effect. In the City, however, on Thursday afternoon things began to improve; there was more confidence and cheerfulness. On Friday evening the Chr. of the Exchr. comes down to the House and surprises everyone by abandoning part of his plan and authorising the Bank to issue one pound notes till October . . . The great evil now is a want of circulating medium, and as the immediate effect of the measure would be another run on the Bank, and that probably all the gold drawn from it would disappear – for men are now anxious to hoard gold – this evil would be increased tenfold . . . The funds rose nearly two per cent upon this alteration in the Bill before the House, on account of the prospect of an abundance of money . . . So great and absorbing is the interest which the present discussions excite that all men are become political economists and everybody is obliged to have an opinion . . .

March 22nd

Huskisson's speech on Ellice's[3] motion (the silk trade) was one of the ablest ever delivered in Parlt. Canning's the next day was very brilliant, but many people did not like it and thought it was too glittering . . . The accounts from Greece are quite dreadful of their affairs and the destitute state and despair of the Greeks[4] . . .

July 2nd

Four months since I have written anything. The D. of York has been dangerously ill, and it is still doubtful whether he will recover . . . H.M. has since been very much annoyed with the Duke, cried a great deal when he heard how bad he was, and has been twice to see him.

London December 14th

. . . The Duke of York very ill; has been at the point of death several times from his legs mortifying. Canning's speech the night before last most brilliant; much more cheered by the Opposition than by his own friends. He is thought to have been imprudent, and he gave offence to his colleagues by the concluding sentence of his reply when he said 'I called into existence the new world to redress the balance of the old.' The I was not relished.[5]

1827

Friday night January 5th half past one

I am just come from taking my last look at the poor Duke [of York]. He expired at twenty minutes after nine. Since eleven o'clock the physicians never left his room. He never moved and they repeatedly thought that life was extinct, but it was not until that hour that they found it was all over ... We went directly into the room. The Duke was sitting exactly as at the moment he died, in his great armchair, dressed in his grey dressing gown, his head inclined against the side of the chair, his hands lying before him and looking as if he was in a deep and quiet sleep ... Thus did I take my last leave of the poor Duke. I have been the minister and associate of his pleasures and amusements for some years, I have lived in his intimacy and experienced his kindness, and am glad I was present at this last sad occasion to pay my poor tribute of respect and attachment to his remains ...

February 12th

... The funeral took place a fortnight after his death. Nothing could be managed worse than it was, and except the appearance of the soldiers in the chapel which was extremely fine, the spectacle was by no means imposing; the cold was intense, and it is only marvellous that more persons did not suffer from it. As it is, the Bishop of Lincoln [The Rt. Rev George Pelham] has died of the effects of it; Canning has been dangerously ill, and is still very unwell; and the Dukes of Wellington and Montrose were both very seriously unwell for some days after ...

February 21st

Three days ago Lord Liverpool[1] was seized with an apoplectic stroke or paralytic attack. The moment it was known every sort of speculation was afloat as to the probable changes this event would make in the Ministry. It was remarkable how little anybody appeared to care about the *man*; which indifference, whether it reflects most upon the world or upon him, I don't pretend to say.

March 25th

When the King heard of Lord Liverpool's illness he was in great agitation. He sent for Peel in the night and told him he must see the Duke of Wellington. Peel endeavoured to dissuade him but in vain. The Duke was sent for, but he refused to go ...

April 13th

The King came to town a week ago. From the moment of his arrival every hour produced a fresh report about the administration; every day the new appointment was expected to be declared ... He wavered and doubted, and to his confidants with whom he could bluster and talk big, he expressed in measured terms his detestations of Liberal principles and especially of Catholick Emancipation ... On the 9th Canning went to see the King and after a long audience, he came away without anything being settled. On the 10th he went again and told HM that longer delay was impossible and that he must come to some determination. On the evening of the 10th we received a note from Lady Bathurst saying that the King had desired Canning to form an adminis- tration ... Last night it was said that the Duke of Wellington would not remain in the Cabinet, and Georgy Bathurst [Georgiana, daughter of Lord Bathurst] told my mother last night that Peel had resigned ... although Canning has gained his point – he has got the power into his hands and is nominally Prime Minister – no man ever took office under more humiliating circum- stances ... Canning, disliked by the King, opposed by the aristocracy and the nation and unsupported by the parliament is appointed Prime Minister ... he must form a Cabinet full of disunion, and he is doubtful what support he can expect from the old adherents of Government by whom he is abhorred.

Thursday night April 12th

The writ was moved for Canning today by Wynne,[2] he having accepted the office of First Commissioner of the Treasury. This morning the [Lord] Chancellor, Peel, Ld. Westmorland, and the D. of Wellington resigned [Bathurst and Melville followed shortly after].

May 12th

As soon as Canning got the King's commission he began to negotiate, and the Whigs readily enough entered into negotiation. The friends of Ministers resigned one after another and for some time it seemed very doubtful whether Canning would be able to form a Government at all. His first measure was however very judicious – that of appointing the Duke of Clarence[3] – nothing served so much to disconcert his opponents ... and after much delay it was announced that the Whigs would support the new Government ... Parliament met and the rage which had been accumulating in the minds of the seceders soon burst forth in a furious attack on the provisional arrangement. The Whigs have nearly in a body joined the Government with the exception of Lord Grey in the H. of Lords who in a speech full of eloquence attacked Canning's political life and character ... The King sees numbers of people, talks incessantly, and does nothing ...

June 17th

I was at the Royal Lodge for one night last Wednesday ... The King was very well and in excellent spirits, but very weak in his knees and could not walk without difficulty. The evening passed off tolerably owing to the Tyrolese whom Esterhazy [Austrian ambassador] brought down to amuse the King, and he was so pleased with them that he made them sing and dance before him the whole evening; the women kissed his face, the men his hands and he talked to them in German ... though this evening went off well enough, it is clear that nothing would be more insupportable than to live at this court; the dullness must be excessive and the people who compose his habitual society

are the most insipid and uninteresting that can be found. As for Lady
Conyngham, she looks bored to death, and she never speaks, never appears to
have one word to say to the King who, however, talks himself without ceasing.
Canning came the day I went away, and was very well received by H. My; he
looked dreadfully ill.

July 25th

We went all over the Castle [Windsor][4] the other day ... I don't think enough
is effected for the enormous sums expended, though it is a fine and will be a
good house; still how far (as a palace) from Versailles, St Cloud and the other
places in France! ...

August 9th

Canning died yesterday morning at four o'clock ... When he saw the King on
Monday, H.M. told him he looked very ill, and he replied that 'he did not know
what was the matter with him but he was ill all over.' ...

August 10th

... The Tories were full of hope and joy at first, but in proportion as they
were elated at first so they were dejected yesterday when they found that the
King sent for Lord Goderich [the former Chancellor, Frederick Robinson][5]
and not for the Duke of Wellington. He never seems to have thought of the
Duke at all.

Saturday December 15th

The Ministry is at an end. Goderich resigned either by letter to the King
yesterday or at the Council on Thursday. They have been going on ill together
for some time ... In the meantime I find from Mount Charles [eldest son of
Lord and Lady Conyngham] that the King is quite mad upon the Catholick
question and that his real desire is to get rid of the Whigs, take back the Duke
of Wellington and make an anti-Catholick Government ...

1828

January 2nd

About three weeks ago I passed a few days at Panshanger where I met Brougham
... Brougham is certainly one of the most remarkable men I ever met ... I
never saw any man whose conversation impressed me with such an idea of his
superiority over all others. As Rogers said on the morning of his departure,
'This morning Solon, Lycurgis, Demosthenes, Archimedes, Sir Isaac Newton,
Lord Chesterfield and a great many more went away in one post chaise.' ...

January 28th

Until the Duke of Wellington's commission as First Lord of the Treasury
appeared, many people doubted that he would take it . . .

June 12th

We have now got a Tory Government and all that remained of Canning's party
are gone.[1]

June 18th

. . . The Duke of Wellington's speech on the Catholic question is considered
by many to have been so moderate as to indicate a disposition on his part to
concede emancipation, and bets have been laid that Catholicks will sit in
Parliament next year. Many men are resolved to see it in this light who are
anxious to join his Government and whose scruples with regard to that question are removed by such an interpretation of his speech. I do not believe he
will do anything unless he is compelled to do it which, if he remains in office,
he will be . . . The march of time and the state of Ireland will effect it in spite
of everything . . .

August 16th

The Lord High Admiral [the future William IV] was turned out. The Duke
told him he must go, but that he might resign as if of his own accord. The
Duke is all-powerful. It is strongly reported that Peel will resign, that the Duke
means to concede the Catholick question and to negotiate a *concordat* with the
Pope.

London November 25th

*I have not written anything since I left town, because nothing occurred worth recording
. . . I have heard constantly from Henry* [Henry Greville, his younger brother,
private secretary to the Chief Secretary for Ireland] *from Dublin who told me
all he knew which amounted to nothing.*

December 20th

Hyde Villiers called on me ten days ago to give me an account of his visit to
Ireland . . . O'Connell[2] though opposed by a numerous party in the Association
[the Catholic Association, the organisation campaigning in Ireland for full
Catholic rights], is all powerful in the country, and there is not one person
who stands a chance of supplanting him in the affections of the great mass of
the Catholicks. For twenty-five years he has been labouring to obtain that
authority and consideration which he possesses without a rival . . . As an orator
he would probably fail in the English H. of C.; but to a mob, especially an Irish
mob, he is perfect . . . He is rich, has a large landed property, is at the head of

his profession, an admirable lawyer and manager of a cause ... He is besides, a man of high moral character ... [but] to accomplish any particular object he cares not what charges of partial inconsistency he exposes himself, trusting to his own ingenuity to exonerate him from them afterwards ... O'Connell thinks he can keep the country quiet another year certainly; Doyle [Catholic Bishop of Kildare and Leighlin],[3] thinks not.

1829

January 12th

Mount Charles came to me this morning ... he verily believed the King would go mad about the Catholic question, his violence was so great about it ... Whenever he does get on it there is no stopping him; that audience of Peel's was all about it. He asked Peel if he was as firm as ever and Peel assured him that he was. He attributes the King's obstinacy to his recollections about his father and the Duke of York and to the influence of the Duke of Cumberland ... He then talked to me about Knighton, whom the King abhors with a detestation that could hardly be described ... He says that his language about Knighton is sometimes of the most unmeasured violence – wishes he was dead and one day when his [Mount Charles's] father and mother were just coming into the room ... he said 'I wish to God somebody would assassinate Knighton'. Still it appears there is some secret chain which binds them together ... The King's indolence is so great it is next to impossible to get him to do even the most ordinary business, and Knighton is the only man who can get him to sign papers etc. His greatest delight is to make those who have business to transact with him wait for hours in an anteroom while he is lounging with Mt. Chas. or anybody talking of horses or any trivial matter ...

... This account corresponds with all I have before heard and confirms the opinion I have long held that a more contemptible, cowardly, selfish, unfeeling dog does not exist than this King, on whom such flattery is constantly lavished. He has a sort of capricious good nature, arising however out of no good principle or good feeling, but which is of use to him as it cancels often in a moment and at small cost a long score of misconduct ... There have been good and wise Kings, but not many of them. Take them one with another, they are of inferior character, and this I believe to be one of the worst of the kind. The littleness of his character prevents his displaying the dangerous faults that belong to great minds, but with vices and weaknesses of the lowest and most contemptible order it would be difficult to find a disposition more abundantly furnished.

January 25th

... Polignac is gone to Paris, [ambassador to London then – see *post* – disastrously Prime Minister to Charles X] but the Duke thinks not to be Minister. Polignac told him that he wished to return here, as he thought he could do more good here than there.

January 28th

... I met George Dawson who turned back with me and we had a long conversation about Irish affairs and I gathered from him what is to be done. The Catholic question is to be conceded, the elective franchise altered and the [Catholic] Association suppressed. The latter is, I take it, to be a preliminary measure and I suspect the Duke went to the King on Monday with the resolution of the Cabinet on the subject ... We talked a great deal about Peel, and I see clearly that he has given way; ...

February 4th Wednesday

... I returned by Oxford and called on Dr Bandinelli [Librarian of the Bodleian] ... I was surprised to find in the Bodleian a vast number of books (manuscripts) which had belonged to Pepys ... The rage and despair of the Orange papers is very amusing. I have not yet heard how the King took it all. Glad as I am that the measure is going to be carried, the conduct of those who are to assist in it (the old Anti-Catholicks) seems to me despicable to the greatest degree; having opposed it against all reason and common sense for years past, now that the Duke of Wellington lifts up a finger they all obey ...

February 5th

Went to Brooks's yesterday and found all the Whigs very merry at the Catholick news. Most of them had just come to town and had heard nothing till they arrived. The old Tories dreadfully dejected, but obliged to own it was all true; intense curiosity to see what Peel will say for himself ... York Minster has been burnt and Lord Wharncliffe says that it will take 700,000 to restore it [£35 million at current values].[1] I am very sorry for it is the finest building I ever saw ...

February 6th

Parliament met yesterday; a very full attendance and intense interest and curiosity ... Peel was very feeble and his case for himself poor and ineffective; all he said was true enough, but it was only what had been said to him over and over again for years past ... if there had been a Brunswicker [member of the Ultra wing of the Tory party][2] of any talent in the house, he might have cut it up finely; two or three of them spoke but wretchedly ill ...

Now the Duke is all-powerful, and of course he will get all the honour of the day. Not that he does not deserve a great deal for having made up his mind to the thing; he has managed it with firmness, prudence and dexterity, but to O'Connell and the Association and those who have fought the battle on both sides of the water, the success of the measure is due. Indeed Peel said as much, for it was the Clare election [in 1828, where O'Connell stood and was elected][3] which convinced both him and the Duke that it must be done and from that time the only question was whether he should be a party to it or not.

February 8th

We are now beginning to discover different people's feelings about the Catholic business, and it is clear that many of the Great Tories are deeply offended that the Duke was not more communicative to them, chiefly it seems because they have continued to talk in an opposite sense and in their old strain up to the last moment, thereby committing themselves and thus making themselves ridiculous ... The Duke of Rutland means to go to Belvoir and not vote at all. The Duke of Beaufort does not like it ... Lowther has been to the King, and it is supposed he has resigned ... In Dublin the moderate people are furious with O'Connell for his abuse of everybody. There is no getting over the fact that he it is who has brought matters to this conclusion, and but for him, the Catholic question would never have been carried; but his violence, bad taste and scurrility have made him 'lose the lustre of his former praise'. He is much too great a blackguard. Grant [Charles Grant, Canningite, later in the Grey Reform Cabinet] was in a great fright for the Duke of Newcastle brings him in and he will probably insist upon his voting against the Bill or going out.

February 11th

... A ridiculous thing happened the other day in the Lord Chancellor's Court. Sugden [Tory MP and lawyer][4] had taken a brief on each side of a case without knowing it. Horne [future Solicitor-General and Attorney-General][5] who opened on one side and was followed by another lawyer was to be answered by Sugden; but he having got hold of the wrong brief, spoke the same way as Horne. The Vice-Chancellor [Sir Lancelot Shadwell, the last holder of this office] said 'Why Mr Sugden is with you?' 'Sir' said Horne 'his argument is with us, but he is engaged on the other side.' Finding himself in the scrape, he said 'it was true he held a brief for the other party, but for no client would he ever argue against what he knew to be a clear rule of law.' But the court decided against them all.

February 22nd Sunday

Went to Newmarket last Sunday and came back on Thursday. Still the Catholick question and nothing else ... There has been nothing of consequence in either House, except the dressing which Lord Plunkett gave Lord Eldon, though that

hard-bitten old Dog shows capital fight. Peel has got a most active and intelligent committee, and they consider his election safe [Peel's opponent in the
Oxford election was Sir Robert Inglis][6] ... If Canning had lived, God knows
what would have happened, for they never would have turned round for him
as they are now about to do for the Duke ... All this has given a blow to the
aristocracy which men only laugh at now, but of which the effects will be felt
some day or other ... Peel's election is going on ill. The Convocation presents
a most disgraceful scene of riot and uproar ...

March 1st

... Peel's defeat at Oxford,[7] though not likely to have any effect on the general
measure, is unlucky because it serves to animate the Anti-Catholicks; and had
he succeeded, his success would have gone far to silence as it must have discour-
aged them. Then the King gives Ministers uneasiness for the Duke of
Cumberland has been tampering with him ... and there is nothing false or
base he would not do if he dared; but he is such a coward ...

... There never was anything so mismanaged as the whole affair at Oxford
... It appears that an immense number of parsons came to vote, of whose
intentions both parties were ignorant, and they almost all voted for Inglis.

March 4th Wednesday

Nothing could exceed the consternation which prevailed yesterday about this
infernal business. The advocates of the Bill and friends of the Govt. were in
indescribable alarm and not without good cause. All yesterday it was thought
quite uncertain whether the Duke's resignation would not take place, and the
[Lord] Chancellor [Lyndhurst] himself said that nothing was more likely
than that they would all be out ... the King pretended that he had not been
made aware of all the provisions of the Bill, that the securities did not satisfy
him, and that he could not consent to it. The Chancellor could do nothing with
him; so instead of returning to town he went on to Strathfieldsaye [more
commonly Stratfield Saye, Wellington's country home in Hampshire] ... There
he arrived at three in the morning, had a conference of two hours with the
Duke and returned to London quite exhausted to be in the H. of Lords at ten
in the morning ...

March 5th Thursday

... In the evening Mt. Chas. came and told me that everything was settled –
that as soon as the King found the Duke would really leave him unless he gave
way, he yielded directly, and that he believes that if the Duke had told him so
at first, he would not have made all this bother ...

March 6th

Peel brought on the Catholick question last night in a speech of four hours and said to be by far the best he ever made. It is full of his never-failing fault, egotism, but certainly very able, plain, clear and statesmanlike and the peroration very eloquent ... It is remarkable that attacks, I will not say upon the Church, but upon Churchmen, are now made in both Houses with much approbation ... I am convinced that very few years will elapse before the Church will really be in danger. People will grow tired of paying so dearly for so bad an article.

March 11th

... Fourteen Irish Bishops are coming over in a body to petition the King against this Bill, and most foolish they. The English Bishops may by possibility be sincere in their opposition (not that I believe they are), but nobody will believe that the Irish think of anything but their scandalous revenues. The thing must go; the only question is when and how ...

March 19th

... He [George IV] leads a most extraordinary life. Never gets up till six in the afternoon. They come to him and open the window curtains at six o'clock in the morning; he breakfasts in bed, does whatever business he can be brought to transact in bed too, he reads every newspaper quite through, dozes three or four hours, gets up in time for dinner, and goes to bed between ten and eleven. He sleeps very ill and rings his bell forty times in the night; if he wants to know the time, though a watch hangs close to him, he will have his *valet de chambre* down rather than turn his head to look at it. The same thing if he wants a glass of water; he won't stretch out a hand to get it ...

March 21st

This morning the Duke fought a duel with Lord Winchilsea. Nothing could equal the astonishment caused by the event ... they met at Wimbledon at eight o'clock. There were many people about who saw what passed; they stood at a distance of fifteen paces ... The Duke fired and missed, and then Winchilsea fired in the air ... The Anti-Catholick papers and men lavish the most extravagant encomiums on Wetherell's [Ultra Tory][8] speech and call it 'the finest oration since the second Philippic', he was drunk they say. The Speaker said 'the only lucid interval was that between his waistcoat and his breeches'. When he speaks he unbuttons his braces and in his vehement action his breeches fall down and his waistcoat runs so there is a great interregnum. He is half-mad, eccentric, ingenious with great and varied information and a coarse, vulgar mind delighting in ribaldry and abuse, besides an enthusiast.

April 4th

... The Bill [Catholic Emancipation] has been two nights in the H. of Lords. They go on with it this morning, and will divide this evening. The Chancellor made a very fine speech last night, and the Bishop of Oxford spoke very well the night before, but the debate has been dull on the whole; the subject is exhausted. The House of Lords was very full, particularly of women, every fool in London thinking it necessary to be there. It is only since last year that the steps of the throne have been crowded with ladies; formerly one or two got in who skulked behind the throne or were hid in Tyrrhwyt's [Sir Thomas Tyrwhitt, Black Rod] box, but now they fill the whole space and put themselves in front with their large bonnets without either fear or shame.

April 5th

The question was put at a little before twelve last night, and carried by 105–217 to 112 (a greater majority than the most sanguine expected) ... This tremendous defeat will probably put an end to anything like serious opposition; they will hardly rally again ...

April 9th

... I sat next to Stanley who told me a story which amused Me. M'Intosh, in the course of the recent debates, went one day to the H. of Commons, at eleven in the morning to take a place. They were all taken on the benches below the gangway, on asking the doorkeeper how they happened to be all taken so early, he said 'Oh Sir, there is no chance of getting a place, for Colonel Sibthorpe[9] sleeps at the bawdy house close by and comes here every morning by eight o'clock and takes places for all the Saints.' [evangelical group around William Wilberforce] ...

April 13th

... I went on Friday morning to the Old Bailey to hear the trials, particularly that of the women for the murder of the apprentices; the mother was found guilty and will be hanged today – has been by this time ...

June 11th

Been at Epsom for a week; the D. of Grafton, Lds Wilton, Jersey and Worcester, Russell, Anson, Irby and myself took Down Hall for the races and lived very well ... I won 800 about on the two races. Nothing particular has occurred. Lord and Lady Ellenborough are separated, and he is supposed to have behaved very handsomely to her. They say that he does not know the whole story of her intrigue with Felix Schwartzenberg[10] ... They have made Best a peer who is poor and has a family, by which another Poor Peerage will be added to the list; and he is totally unfit for the situation he is to fill – that of Deputy Speaker of the H. of Lords and to assist the Chancellor in deciding Scotch cases of which he knows nothing whatever ... The event of last week was Palmerston's speech [as an Irish peer, Palmerston sat in the Commons] on the Portuguese question which was delivered at a late hour and in an empty house but which they say was exceedingly able and eloquent. This is the second he has made this year of great merit. It was very violent against Government. He has been twenty years in office and never distinguished himself before, a proof of how many accidental circumstances are requisite to bring out the talents which a man may possess. The office he held was one of dull and dry detail and he never travelled out of it ...

June 24th

... I have set about making a reconciliation between the King and Sefton ... The cause of the quarrel is very old and signifies little enough now though rather provoking at the time. Arthur Paget [hero of Waterloo, by this time Marquess of Anglesey] was in love with Lady Sefton, and (at Stoke where the Prince and a large party were staying) the King [i.e. Prince] pimped for Arthur, by taking Sefton out on some expedition and leaving the lovers to amuse themselves ... they have been at daggers drawn ever since and Sefton has revenged himself by a thousand jokes at the King's expense, of which H.M. is well aware. Their common pursuit and a desire on the one side to partake of the good things of the palace, and on the other to be free from future pleasantries, has generated a mutual disposition to make it up, which is certainly sensible, especially as it matters very little now what happened to Lady S. twenty or thirty years ago ...

July 24th

The accounts from Ireland are all bad; nothing but massacres and tumults, and all got up by the Protestants who desire nothing so much as to provoke the Catholicks into acts of violence and outrage. They want a man of energy and determination who will cause the law to be respected and impartially administered ...

August 8th

There is a story current about the Duke of Cumberland and Lady Lyndhurst which is more true than most stories of this kind. The Duke called upon her and made a desperate attempt upon her person which she resisted and told him she did not intend he should have her. He said by God, he would; on which after a scramble, she rang the bell. He was obliged to desist and go away, but before he did, he said 'By God, madam I will be the ruin of you and your husband and will not rest till I have destroyed you both.' ...

August 28th Friday

... So busy are the French with their own politicks that even the milliners
have left off making caps. Lady Cowper told me today that Madame Maradan
complained that she could get no bonnets etc. from Paris; for they would
occupy themselves with nothing but the change of Administration. Nothing
can exceed the violence that prevails; the King does nothing but cry, Polignac
is said to have the fatal obstinacy of a Martyr, the worst sort of courage of
the *ruat caelum* sort. Aberdeen said at dinner at Madame de Lieven's the other
day that he thought him a very clever man; and that the Duke of Wellington
went further and said that he was the ablest man France had had since the
Restoration ...

August 31st

... Henry [Greville] writes me word from Ireland that Doherty conducts the
trial of the Policemen with consummate skill; the object was that the trial
should appear fair, and that the men should be acquitted. They were acquitted
and the people were furious. [What follows is the unsigned footnote in Strachey
and Fulford] 'At the fair at Borrisokane June 26th–28th 1829, eight Catholics
had been killed and by indiscriminate firing by the police and Orangemen. Four
of these policemen were tried for murder at Clonmel assizes in August and
were acquitted by Protestant juries.'

September 16th Wednesday

... I have been living at Fulham at Lord Wharncliffe's villa for six or seven
weeks, keeping a girl of whom, although she has good looks, good manners
and is not ill-disposed, I am getting tired and doubt if ever I shall take one to
live with me again. Henry De Ros who is the grand purveyor of women to all
his friends, gave her to me; I have lived here in idleness and luxury giving
dinners and wasting my time and money rather more than usual. I have read
next to nothing since I have been here; – I am ashamed to think how little –
the Odes of Horace, some of Cicero's letters, two vols of Lingard, Lord Mohun's
Belisarius, the Letters [*sic*] Provinciales, 2 or 3 novels, scraps of reviews,
Hallam (3rd time) atqua alia paucissima, in short, a most unprofitable life ...
Old Creevey[11] is rather an extraordinary character ... he was thrown upon
the world with about £200 a year or less, no home, few connections, a great
many acquaintance, a good constitution and extraordinary spirits. He possesses
nothing but his cloathes, no property of any sort; he leads a vagrant life,
visiting a number of people who are delighted to have him, and sometimes
roving about to various places as fancy happens to direct and staying till he
has spent what money he has in his pocket. He has no servant, no home, no
creditors; he buys everything he wants at the place he is at; he has no ties upon
him and his time entirely at his disposal and that of his friends. He is certainly

living proof that a man may be perfectly happy and exceedingly poor, or rather without riches for he suffers none of the privations of poverty and enjoys many of the advantages of wealth. I think he is the only man I know who possesses nothing ...

November 12th

At Roehampton at Lord Clifden's from Tuesday the 10th till today; Sir James McIntosh[12], Moore, Poodle Byng, and the Master of the Rolls. It was uncommonly agreeable. I never was in McIntosh's society for so long before, and never was more filled with admiration. His prodigious memory and the variety and extent to his information remind me of all I have heard and read of Burke and Johnson ... said he was a great reader of novels; had read [Scott's] *Old Mortality* four times in English and once in French. Ellis [Lord Clifden] said he preferred Miss Austen's novels to Scott's. Talked of the Old Novelists – Fielding, little read now, Smollett less ... Medical statistics. Curious information. England the healthiest country, Vienna the unhealthiest town in Europe. Deaths here 1 in 40, there 1 in 23, Berlin nearly as Vienna. Most suicides at Berlin. More deaths from pulmonary complaints in Paris than London ... Ellis told a story of George Selwyn [(1719–91), eighteenth-century wit and eccentric]. Somebody asked (I forget when) if Princess Emily [Amelia Sophia, second daughter of George II] was to have guards. (She was a great Wh.) He said 'Yes, Ma'am one every now and then.' ...

December 27th

At Panshanger since the 24th; Lievens, John Russell, Montrond, M. de la Rochefoucault [*sic*] F. Lamb. On Christmas Day the Princess got up a little *fête* such as is customary all over Germany. Three large trees in large pots were put upon a long table covered with pink linen; each tree was illuminated with three circular tiers of coloured wax candles – blue, green, red and white. Before each tree was displayed a quantity of toys, gloves, pocket-handkerchiefs, workboxes, books and various articles – presents made to the owner of the tree. Here it was only for the children; in Germany the custom extends to persons of all ages ...

1830

January 5th

... In the meantime all accounts concur in stating the great and increasing distress; and in such a state of things as not unnaturally produces a good deal of ill-humour, the Duke [of Wellington] is abused for gadding about, visiting and shooting while the country is in difficulty, and it is argued that he must

be very unfeeling and indifferent to all to amuse himself in this manner . . . As
to his supposed indifference to the public distress, I firmly believe that his mind
is incessantly occupied with projects for its relief . . .

Roehampton January 9th

Yesterday morning died Sir T. Lawrence after a very short illness. Few people
knew he was ill before they heard that he was dead. He was *longé primus* of all
living Painters, and has left no one fit to succeed him in the chair of the Royal
Academy. Lawrence was about sixty, very like Canning in appearance, remarkably gentleman-like, with very mild manners . . . agreeable in society, unassuming and not a great talker; his mind was highly cultivated, he had a taste
for every kind of literature . . . He is an irreparable loss; since Sir Joshua there
has been no Painter like him . . .

January 22nd

. . . Lawrence was buried yesterday; a magnificent funeral, which will have cost,
they say, £2000. The Pall was borne by Clanwilliam, Aberdeen, Sir G. Murray,
Agar Ellis and three more – I forget who. There were thirty-two mourning
coaches and eighty private carriages. The ceremony in the Church lasted two
hours. Pretty well for a man who was certainly a rogue and a bankrupt, and
probably a bugger . . .

January 26th

. . . Shee [Sir Martin Archer Shee (1769–1850), portraitist] was elected
President R.A. last night at ten o'clock. He had sixteen or eighteen votes; Sir
William Beechey six who was the nearest to Shee; Wilkie [Sir David Wilkie
(1785–1841), the only artist of distinction involved here] only two. He is an
Irishman and a Catholic, a bad painter, a tolerable poet and a man of learning
but, it is said, florid . . .

February 5th

Parliament met yesterday and there was a brisk debate and amendment in each
House on the Address. The Duke had very indiscreetly called the distress 'partial'
in the Speech, and the consequence was an amendment moved by Knatchbull
[one of the Ultras][1] declaring it to be general. The result shows the Government
has not the slightest command over the House of Commons, and that they
have nothing but casual support to rely upon . . . it is pretty clear however that
they are in no danger of being turned out, though they are wretchedly off for
speakers. Huskisson made a shabby speech enough, O'Connell his *debut*, and a
successful one, heard with profound attention; his manner good and his arguments attended to and replied to . . .

February 7th

The thaw is come after a frost unparalleled in duration and severity and in the suffering it has caused. The thermometer in Greenwich has been lower than for 90 years past . . .

February 13th

. . . Dined after with Cowper, Durham[2] and Glengall. Durham said that Lord Grey's politics were the same as his and that before Easter he thought an Opposition would be formed, and that the elements (though scattered) exist of a very strong one. I doubt it.

February 16th

Last night the English Opera House was burnt down – a magnificent fire. I was playing whist at the 'Travellers' with Ld. Granville, Auckland [George Eden (1784–1849), later Earl of Auckland and Governor-General of India] and Ross when we saw the whole sky illuminated and a volume of fire rising in the sky. We thought it was Covent Garden, and directly set off to the spot. We found the Opera House and several houses in Catherine Street on fire and though it was three in the morning, the streets filled by an immense multitude. Nothing could be more picturesque than the scene, for the flames made it as light as day, and threw a glare on the strange and motley figures moving about. There was all the gentility of London from Esterhazy's ball and all the clubs, and gentlemen in fur cloaks and pumps and velvet waistcoats mixed with objects like the *sans-culottes* in the French Revolution – men and women half-dressed, covered with rags and dirt, some with nightcaps or handkerchiefs round their heads – then the Soldiers, the firemen and the Engines and the new police [the force created by Robert Peel that same year and known for some time as the 'New Police'] running and bustling and clearing the way and clattering along, all with intense interest and restless curiosity produced by the event and which received fresh stimulus at every renewed burst of the flames as they rose in a shower of sparks like gold dust. Poor Arnold [Samuel Arnold, playwright and manager, had rebuilt the Opera House in 1816] lost everything and was not insured . . .

February 21st

Dined with the Chancellor; Granvilles, Hollands, Moore [Tom Moore, poet and biographer] . . . Lord Holland told stories of Lord Thurlow[3] whom he mimicks, they say, exactly. When Lord Mansfield [Lord Chief Justice (1756–88)] died, Thurlow said 'I hesitated a long time between Kenyon and Buller. Kenyon was very intemperate, but Buller was so damned corrupt, and I thought upon the whole that intemperance was a less fault in a judge than corruption, not but what there was a damned deal of corruption in Kenyon's intemperance.'

Lady Holland and I very friendly [original footnote reads: 'The word "friendly" has been written in at a later date over "smirking and polite"'] the first time I have met her in a company since our separation (for we have never quarrelled). She is mighty anxious to get me back for no other reason than that I won't go . . . Went to Esterhazy's ball; talked to old Rothschild who was there with his wife and a Dandy little Jew Son. The old Villain says that Polignac's Government will stand by the King's support and Polignac's own courage; offered to give me a letter to his Brother[4] who would give me any information I wanted, squeezed my hand and looked like an old rogue as he is.

February 26th

Intended to have gone to the House of Lords to hear the debate on Lord Stanhope's motion (State of the nation) but went to see Fanny Kemble in *Mrs Beverley* instead. She had a very great success – house crowded and plenty of emotion, but she does not touch me . . . ; however she is very good and will be much better.

February 27th

Dined at Ld. Lansdowne's; Moore, Rogers, J. Russell, Spring Rice, Charles Kemble . . . talked of his daughter and her success – said she was twenty, had once seen Mrs Siddons in *Lady Randolph* when she was seven years old. She was so affected in *Mrs Beverley* that he was obliged to carry her into her dressing room where she screamed for five minutes; the last scream (where she throws herself on his body) was involuntary, not in the part and she had not intended it, but could not resist the impulse.

March 2nd

Tomorrow I set out to Italy

Paris March 6th Saturday night

Left London at three o'clock on Wednesday the 3rd in a post chaise and four, undersprung and loaded with every possible comfort, arrived at Dover between twelve and one . . . a good but rather long passage – near four hours – and the day magnificent. Landed with difficulty in boats. Detained in Calais till seven. There I had a long conversation with Brummel [George Bryan 'Beau' Brummell][5] about his consulship and was moved by his account of his own distresses to write to the Duke of Wellington and asked what he could do for him.[6] He was however as gay as ever. I found him in his old lodging, distressing; some pretty pieces of furniture in the room, an entire toilet of Silver and a large green Macaw perched on the back of a tattered silk Chair with faded gilding; full of gaiety, impudence and misery.

March 8th

... Lady Keith [Baroness Keith and Nairn in her own right, married to the French Comte de Flahaut] with whom I had a long talk, told me that she did not believe it possible they [Polignac and his Ministers] could stand, that there was no revolutionary spirit abroad, but a strong determination to provide for the stability of their Institutions, a disgust at the obstinacy and pretensions of the King, and a desire to substitute the Orléans for the reigning branch which was becoming very general; that Polignac is wholly ignorant of France and will not listen to the opinion of those who could enlighten him ...

March 9th

... The battle is due to begin in the Chamber on Saturday or Monday and on the Address. Talleyrand told me that the next three weeks would be the most important of any period since the Restoration ...

Susa March 15th 9 o'clock

... Lyons is a magnificent town. It was dark when I arrived, or rather moonlight, but I could see that the quay we came along was fine, and yesterday morning I walked about for an hour, and was struck with the grandeur of the place; it is like a great and magnificent Bath; ... After crossing the Pont de Beauvoisin we began to mount the Echelles, which I did on foot, and I shall never forget the first impression made upon me by the Mountain Scenery. It burst upon me at a turn of the road – one huge perpendicular rock above me, a deep ravine with a torrent rushing down and a mountain covered with pines and ilexes on the other side, and in front another vast rock which was shining in the reflected light of the setting sun. I shall never forget it ... As I got near the top of the mountain, the road which had hitherto been excellent, became execrable and the cold intense, I left summer below and found winter above, but the scenery was inexhaustible and the cold intense. But the scenery was an inexhaustible source of pleasure.

I looked in vain for the chamois, pheasants, partridges, hares, wolves and bears, all of which I was told are found there. At last arrived at the summit, I found at the inn, Don— (I forget what) a friar, the only inhabitant of the hospice who hearing me say that I would go there (as my carriage was not yet come) offered to go with me; he was young, fat, rosy, jolly and dirty, dressed in a black robe with a travelling cap on his head, he appeared quick and intelligent and spoke French and Italian. He took me over the Hospice and showed me two very decently furnished rooms, which the Emperor Napoleon used to occupy, and two inferior apartments which had been appropriated by the Empress Marie-Louise.

Turin March 16th

Got here early and meant to sleep, but have changed my mind and am going
on. A fine but dull-looking town. Found the two Fosters [Sir Augustus and
Lady Foster][7] ... Foster told me that this country is rich, not ill governed,
but plunged in bigotry. There are near 400 convents in the King's dominions.
It is the dullest town in Europe and because it is so dull I am in a hurry to
get out of it ... I did not part from the Alps without casting many a lingering
look behind.

Genoa March 18th

... Everything bespeaks solidity, durability and magnificence. There are stupendous works which were done at the expense of individuals. In every part of
the town are paintings and frescoes which in spite of constant exposure to the
atmosphere, have retained much of their brilliancy and freshness ... The view
from my *albergo* is the gayest imaginable, looking over the harbour which is
crowded with sailors and boats full of animation ...

Evening

... The Churches have a profusion of marble and gilding and frescoes; the
Duomo of black and white marble, of mixed architecture, all highly orna-
mented – all stinking to a degree that was perfectly intolerable and the same
thing whether empty or full; it is the smell of stale incense mixed with garlic
and human odour, horrible combination of poisonous exhalations ... the
Churches are always open and, go into them when you will, you see men
and women kneeling and praying before this or that altar, absorbed in their
occupation, and who must have been led there by some devotional feeling ...
Then the Catholic Church makes no distinction between poverty and wealth
– no pews for the aristocracy well warmed and furnished, or seats set apart
for the rich and well dressed; here the Church is open to all, and the beggar
in rags comes and takes his place by the side of the lady in silks, and both
kneel on the same pavement, for the moment at least and in that place,
reduced to the same level ...

Florence March 21st

... Much as I was charmed with the mountains, I was not sorry (for a change)
to get into the rich, broad plain of Tuscany, full of vineyards and habitations along
the banks of the Arno. The voice and aspect of cheerfulness is refreshing after a
course of rugged and barren grandeur; the road is excellent and the travelling
rapid ... Tuscany seems to be flourishing and contented; the Government is absolute but mild, the Grand Duke enormously rich ... To the Pitti Palace, of which
one part is under repair and not visible, but I saw most of the best pictures. I like
pictures better than statues. It is a beautiful palace and well furnished for show.
Nobody knows what Vandyke was like without coming here.

March 26th

... Rode to Lord Cochrane's [Admiral Thomas Cochrane, later Earl Cochrane][8] villa, where we found them under a matted tent in the garden going to dinner. He talks of going to Algiers to see the French attack it. He has made £100,000 by the Greek bonds. It is a pity he ever committed a robbery; he is such a fine fellow and so shrewd and good-humoured ...

Rome March 29th

Set off yesterday morning at half past seven from Florence and arrived here at six this evening in a fine glowing sunset, straining my eyes to catch interesting objects and trying in vain to make out the different hills ...

March 30th

... In about five hours I galloped over the Forum, Coliseum, Pantheon, St John Lateran, Santa [?Maria?] Maggiore, the Vatican and several arches and obelisks ... I have already seen enough to repay me for the journey. They only who have seen Rome can have an idea of the Grandeur of it and of the wonders it contains, the Treasures of art and the records of antiquity ...

April 3rd

Went on Thursday evening to Lady M. Deerhurst's where all the English in Rome (or rather the most vulgar) were assembled ... There has been no rain here for about two months, and the clouds of dust are insupportable; as it is the town in Europe the best supplied with water (there are three aquaducts; the ancients had sixteen) so it is the worst watered ...

Evening

... The Borghese is the beau ideal of a Villa; lofty, spacious apartments, adorned with statues, busts and marbles, painting and gilding, and magnificent gardens; but deserted by its owner who has only been there once in thirty years, and untenable in the summer from malaria which is unaccountable, for it is close to Rome, high and full of trees; but nobody knows anything about the malaria. The gardens are the fashionable lounge, but after June nobody can walk there.

April 4th

To the Sistine Chapel for the ceremonies of Palm Sunday; got into the body of the Church, not without difficulty, saw La Ferronays [French Minister] in his box and got him to let us in ... but it was only on a third attempt I could get there for twice the Papal halbardiers thrust me back, and I find since it is lucky that they did not do worse; for on some occasion one of them knocked a cardinal's eye out; and when he found out who he was begged his pardon and said he had taken him for a Bishop ... The figures on ceiling and walls are very grand even to my ignorance. The music (all vocal) beautiful, the service harmoniously chanted and the responsive bursts of the Chorus sublime. The Cardinals appeared a wretched set of old twaddlers, all but about three in extreme decrepitude ...

April 6th

... At the Quirinal which was fitted up for the King of Rome [Napoleon's son] and inhabited by the Emperor of Austria, we saw everything but the Pope's apartments. It is a delightful house and commands a charming view of Rome. The Pope always goes there the last day of holy week, and stays there all the summer. Nothing can be more melancholy than his life as described by the *custode*; he gets up very early, lives entirely alone and with great simplicity. In short it shows what a strange thing ambition is which will sacrifice the substantial pleasures of life for the miserable shadow of grandeur ...

April 9th Friday

Yesterday morning to the Sistine again; prodigious crowd, music moderate. As soon as it was over we set off to see the benediction; and after fighting, jostling and squeezing through an enormous crowd, we reached the *loggia* over one side of the colonnade. The Piazza of St Peter's is so magnificent that the sight was of necessity fine, but not near so much as I had fancied. The people below were not numerous or full of reverence. Till the Pope[9] appears, the bands play and the bells ring, when suddenly there is a profound silence; the feathers are seen waving in the balcony, and he is borne in on his throne; he rises, stretches out his hands, blesses the people – URBI ET ORBI – a couple of indulgences are tossed out, for which there is a scramble, and so it ends ... Then off we scampered again through the long galleries of the Vatican to another hall where the pilgrims dine ... the whole hall was filled with people, all with their hats on, chattering and jostling, and more like a ring of blacklegs and blackguards at Tattersall's than respectable company at a religious ceremony in the palace of the Pope. There remained the Cardinals' dinner, but I had had more than enough and came away, hot, jaded and disgusted with the whole affair.

In the evening I went to St Peter's when I was amply rewarded for the disappointment and bore of the morning. The Church was crowded; there was a Miserere in the chapel which was divine, more beautiful than anything I had heard in the Sistine, and it was the more effective because at the close of it, it really was night. The lamps were extinguished at the shrine of the Apostle, but one altar – the altar of the Holy Sepulchre – was brilliantly illuminated ... The night here brings out fresh beauties, but of the most majestic character. There is a colour in an Italian twilight that I have never seen in England, so soft and beautiful and grey, and the moon rises 'not as in northern climes, obscurely bright', but with far-spreading rays around her ... The weather here half-kills me; it is like a sirocco, and so very enervating ...

At night

... I walked tonight to St Peter's to look at it by moonlight. From every point of view it is magnificent; the stillness of the night broken only by the waters of the foundations which glitter in the moonbeams like sheets of molten silver. The obelisk, the façade, the cupola and the columns all contribute to the grandeur and harmony of the scene; but everything at Rome should be seen at night. The Castle of St Angelo, the Tiber and the Bridge are all wonderfully fine in these bright nights ...

Easter Sunday

High Mass in St Peter's which was crowded. I walked about the Church to see the groups and the extraordinary and picturesque figures moving through the vast space. They are to the last degree interesting: in one place hundreds prostrate before an altar – Pilgrims, Soldiers, Beggars, Ladies, Gentlemen, old and young in every variety of attitude, costume and occupation. The benediction is much finer than on Thursday, the day magnificent, the whole piazza filled with a countless multitude, all in their holiday dresses and carriages in the background to the very end ... The Pope is dressed in white with the triple crown on his head; two great fans of feathers exactly like those of the great Mogul, are carried on each side of him. He sits aloft on his throne and is slowly borne to the front of the balcony. The moment he appears there is dead silence and every head is bared.

When he rises, the Soldiers all fall on their knees and some but only a few of the spectators. The distance is so late that he looks like a puppet and you see him move his hands and make some sign – the sign of the cross ...

The numbers who come to the benediction are taken as a test of the popularity of a Pope, though I suppose the weather has a good deal to do with it. Leo XII was very unpopular from his austerity and particularly his shutting up the wine shops. The first time he gave the benediction after that measure hardly anybody came to be blessed ...

April 12th

... I was introduced to Don Michele Gaetani, said to be the cleverest man in Rome, and had a long conversation with Monsignore Spada who is a young layman with ecclesiastical rank and costume, and a Judge. A Monsignore holds ecclesiastical rank at Rome as a Lady of the Bedchamber at Petersburg holds military, where she is a major general there is no other. He is free to marry and, I presume, to do anything else, but he must preserve a certain gravity of dress and conduct; he is a curious nondescript, about an equal mixture of the Cardinal and the Dandy ...

Velletri April 15th

Left Rome at nine o'clock this morning; at Albano procured an ancient rural cicerone, a boy and two donkeys and set out on the grand *giro* of the place ... close to Genzano we went to look at the Lake of Nemi which is very pretty, but not so grand as Albano. The peasantry are a fine race in these parts, and we met many men driving carts or riding asses who would not disgrace the most romantic Banditi ...

Started from Velletri at six in the morning ... and after a tiresome journey, got to Naples at two o'clock in the morning. Vesuvius was obliged to emit some flames as we passed by, just to show us his whereabouts. They were however his first and last while I was in Naples.

Naples April 18th

I am disappointed with Naples. I looked for more life and gaiety, a more delicious air, beautiful town and picturesque lazzaroni, more of Punch, more smoke and flame from Vesuvius. It strikes me as less beautiful and gay than Genoa, but these are only first impressions. The Bay and the Villa Reale, a garden along the sea, full of sweets and sea breezes and shade, are certainly delightful. All the people seem determined to cheat as much as they can, from the master of the Inn to the driver of the Hackney coach ...

April 19th

I retract all I said about disappointment for I have since seen Naples, and it is the most beautiful and the gayest town in the world ...

Continued on the 20th

Went by a delightful drive to the Marquis de Gallo's Villa on the Capo di Monte which far surpasses all the Villas I saw at Rome. The entrance is about half a mile from the house through a wood, one part of which is a vineyard; the vines hanging in festoons from cherry trees and corn growing underneath. The House is not large but convenient; a wide terrace runs along the whole front of it with a white marble balustrade; below this is a second terrace covered with Rose trees, below that is a third, planted with vines and oranges and myrtles ... Naples lies beneath and the bay stretches beyond with the opposite mountains and all the towns and villages from Portici to Sorrento ...

In the evening I went to a ball at the Duchess of Eboli; Very few people and hardly any English, and those not of the best—only four I think, Sir Henry Lushington, the consul, a Mr Grieve of whom I know nothing but that his father was a physician at St Petersburg and that —— killed his father at Eton by putting a cracker into his pocket on 5th November which set fire to other crackers and burnt him to death; ... but most of the Italian women were there, and I was surprised at their beauty. Acton [Sir Ferdinand Acton], [10] who introduced me to some of them, assured me that they were models of conduct which did not precisely tally with my preconceived notion of Neapolitan Society ...

Saturday [April] 22nd

Yesterday to Pompeii, far better worth seeing than anything in Italy. Who can look on other ruins after this? At Rome there are certain places consecrated by recollection, but the imagination must be stirred up to enjoy them; here you are actually in a Roman town. Shave off the upper storey of any town, take out windows, doors and furniture and it will be as Pompeii now is; it is marvellous ...

Went afterwards and drove through the Grotto of Pausilippo, that infernal grotto which one must pass through to get out of Naples on one side; it is a source of danger ... There are a few glimmering lamps always obscured by dust, and it is hardly ever light enough to avoid danger except at night; in the middle it is pitch dark ...

Salerno April 24th

Here Morier and I are going to pass the night on our way to Paestum, and as he is gone to bed (at half past eight), I must write. Yesterday morning Morier, St John, Lady Isabella and I went to Pozzuoli, embarked in a wretched boat to make the *giro* of Baiae ... I was disappointed with the country which is bare and uninteresting; but the line of coast with the various bays and promontories and the circumjacent islands is very agreeable ... The Cave of the Sybil, Lake Avernus and temple of Apollo are not worth seeing, but as they are celebrated by Virgil they must be visited, though the embellishments of Virgil's imagination and the lapse of time have made disappointment inevitable, nature indeed no longer presents the same aspect; for there is a mountain more (Monte Nuovo) and a wood less (about the lake) than in Virgil's time ... Here were all the raw materials for a romance – a splendid setting sun, mountains, convent, flock of goats, evening bell, Friars, peasants, etc. Arrived here [Salerno] delighted with the outside and disgusted with the inside of the town; the Bay of Salerno beautiful, place gay and populous, all staring at a fire balloon which was just ascending, and soon after came down in the sea. The Inns execrable. We got into one at last in which is a wide terrace looking over the sea and there we ordered our dinner to be laid; but we were soon driven, not by the cold, but the flaring of our tallow candles. We were obliged to write our names down for the Police who are very busy and inquisitive ...

Naples [April] 25th

Started at four o'clock in the morning from Salerno and got to Paestum at eight. Tormented to death by beggars and cicerone (often both characters in one) ... No excavations have ever been made here, but they talk of excavating.

There were some fine Etruscan vases found in a tomb at Paestum which we did not see. The brute of a *custode* knew nothing of it, nor should I if I had not seen the model in the Museum afterwards ... What treasures Naples possesses, and how unworthy she is of them! ...

[*April*] 26th

... The lazzaroni are very amusing. This morning five of them stripped stark naked under my window, put off in a boat and thirty yards from the shore, fished for cockle fish which they do by diving like ducks ... the creatures are amphibious; they don't care who sees them, and their forms are perfect ...

Friday May 3rd

... To Salvatore's house – Morrier, Watson and I set off to ascend Vesuvius; rode on donkeys to the bottom of the last ascent ... After infinite puffing and perspiring, and resting at every big stone, I reached the top in thirty-five minutes. It was very provoking to see the facility with which the creatures who attended us sprung up. There was one fellow with nothing on but a shirt and half a pair of breeches who walked the whole way to Resina with a basket on his head full of wine, bread and oranges, and while we were slipping and clambering and toiling with immense difficulty, he bounded up with his basket on his head, as straight as an arrow all of the time, and bothering us to drink when we had not breath to answer. I took three or four oranges, some bread and a bottle of wine from him at the top, and when I asked Salvatore what I should pay him, he said two carlins (eightpence English). I gave him three (a shilling) and he was transported ... The mountain was provokingly still, and only gave one low grumble and a very small emission of smoke and fire while we were there; it has never been more tranquil ... Salvatore has especial care of the mountain under the orders of Government, to whom he is obliged to make a daily report of its state, and he is as fond of it as a nurse of her favourite child, or a trainer at Newmarket of his best racehorse, and delights in telling anecdotes of old eruptions and phenomena, and of different travellers who have ascended it ...

... Yesterday the miracle [the 'liquifaction of the blood of San Gennaro/St Januarius'] was performed, and of course successfully ... Acton and I went together and one of the people belonging to the Church seeing us come in and judging that we wanted to see the blood, summoned one of the canons who was half asleep in a stall, who brought the blood which is contained in a glass vase mounted with silver. It liquefies in the morning, remains in that state all day, and congeals again at night ... I had thought the French had exposed and put an end to all this juggle, but not at all. They found the people so attached to the superstition that they patronised it; ... Acton told me that nobody believed it but the common people, but they did not dare to leave off ...

May 7th

In the morning to the chapel of Saint Januarius to see the blood liquefy . . . I never saw such a scene at once so ludicrous and so disgusting but more of the latter. There was the saint all bedizened with pearls on the altar and the other silver Ladies and Gentlemen all round the chapel with an abundance of tapers burning all before them . . . the Priests keep muttering and look at the blood to see if it is melting. Today it was unusually long so these old Sybils kept clamouring 'Santa Trinità!' 'Santa Virgine!' 'Dio Omnipotente!' 'San Gennaro!' in loud and discordant chorus; still the blood was obstinate. So the Priest ordered them to go down on their knees and recite the Athanasian Creed . . . This would not do, so they fell to abuse and entreaties with a vehemence and volubility and a shrill clamour which was at once a proof of their sincerity and their folly.

Such noise, such gesticulations. One woman I shall never forget with outstretched arm, distorted visage and voice of piercing sharpness . . . At last, after all the handling praying, kissing, screaming, entreating and abusing, the blood did melt; when the organ struck up they all sang in chorus and so it ended.

It struck me as particularly disgusting, though after all it is not fair to abuse these poor people who have all been brought up in the belief of the miracle and who fancy that the prosperity of their city and all that it contains is somehow connected with its due performance . . .

May 8th Evening

I have taken my last ride and last look at Naples, and am surprised at the sorrow I feel at quitting it, as I fear for ever . . . Tonight I have stood once more by the sea shore and could almost have cried to think I should never see again—'The smooth surface of this summer sea' – nor breathe this delicious air, or feast my eyes on the scene of gaiety and brilliancy and beauty around me . . . Naples, they told me, does very well for a short time, but you soon grow tired of it. To be sure I have only been here three weeks, but I liked it better every day, and am wretched at leaving it. What could I ever mean by thinking it was not gay and less lively than Genoa? Tonight as I came home from riding, the shore was covered with lazzaroni and throngs of people and dancing and singing and harpers and fiddling – all so merry and as if the open air and their own elastic spirits were happiness enough . . .

Mola di Gaeta May 9th

I have dined here on an open terrace (looking over the garden and the delicious Bay) where I have been sitting writing all evening. The moon is just rising, and throwing a flood of silver over the sea . . . I have walked over this garden [at Capua] which contains remains of one of Cicero's Villas, but they are only arched rooms like vaults and not worth seeing but for the name of Cicero . . .

Rome May 13th

To the Pantheon and walked round and round and looked, and admire; even the ragged wretches who came in seemed struck with admiration. It is so fine to see the clouds rolling above through the roof; it passes my comprehension how this temple escaped the general wreck of Rome. To St Peter's and went up to the roof and to the ball; through the aperture of which I could just squeeze, though there is plenty of room when once in it. The ball holds above thirty people, stuffed close of course. Three other men were going up at the same time who filled the narrow ascent with garlicky effluvia. It is impossible to have any idea of the Grandeur of St Peter's without going over the roof examining all the details and looking down from the galleries . . .

 . . . I read in *Galignani* [English language newspaper published abroad] the agreeable intelligence that my mare Lady Emily had beat Clotilde at Newmarket which I attribute entirely to my *ex voto* of a silver horse shoe which I vowed before I went to Newmarket, to the Virgin of the Pantheon in case I won the match; and I am resolved to be as good as my word, I have ordered the horse shoe which is to be sent on Monday, and as soon as it arrives it shall be suspended among all the arms and legs and broken gigs and silver hearts and locks of hair etc, etc . . .

NAPLES

Naples possesses a better climate and a worse Government than any country in Europe. There is no Constitution of any sort and the King is absolute. The laws are ill-administered, the Nobility are oppressed, there is no commerce, high taxation and a large Army . . . The Revenue is 28 millions of ducats (about 5 millions of money), the debt 6 millions, the interest of which is 400,000 a year. The King takes 500,000 a year for his Civil List; the great expense is the Army which amounts to 50 or 60,000 men, well equipped. It is supposed that the Neapolitan Government is compelled by some treaty with Austria to keep up this enormous force; for placed as they are at the extreme point of Europe, and with no neighbour but the Pope, it is impossible for them to go to war with any power whatever, and they have not a pretext for maintaining this enormous force but to suppress the discontent of their own subjects. Naples swarms with soldiers, and in no besieged town could there be more incessant drumming and marching than there . . . Sir Henry Lushington, our Consul, told me that nothing could be more miserable than the condition of the Country; the commerce in a state of stagnation, the soil rich and productive to the highest degree, but not producing a tenth of what it might from the oppression of the land tax and the want of any vent for their produce . . .

The Character of the Government is narrow-minded and suspicious, they are aware of their unpopularity and are always dreading plots against their authority . . . there is a constant system of espionage, and the prisons are crowded with people who are detained for political offences and often only for political opinions . . . Upon going into another Country, one is anxious to know whether it is better or worse off than our own. My view of Naples tends to confirm what I have long believed, that the rich in England are far better off and the poor far worse off than in any part of Europe. Here are none of the prodigious contrasts that strike one so forcibly at home. The climate is a great leveller; for the sun shines, the wind blows and the fruits and the flowers grow alike for all, and these are the principle luxuries and delights of Naples. The Neapolitan peasant has few wants and these are easily satisfied; the costly comforts of the English Aristocracy are by no means necessary to the Neapolitan Gentleman, and his gratifications consist rather in a little external vanity in dress and equipage than in social luxury and a splendid hospitality. The Neapolitan peasant hardly wants a house, the thin and harmless wine of the Country or iced water and water melons, fruits and vegetables are his sufficient diet; clothes he scarcely wears, his labour is not violent or unremitting; he throws himself down and sleeps through the midday heats under any shed he can find; he is always gay and merry and he dances and sings and fiddles apparently without care or sorrow. Still there are Winter months – and what they do then I have no idea. The Winter is however neither severe nor long . . . Every sort of trade at Naples is carried on *sub dio*, and sailors, shoemakers, artisans of all kinds sit working at their doors and enjoying the fresh air. Of course orthodox John Bullish travellers are full of pity mixed with indignation for a city where there is a miracle of San Gennaro and a half-naked population, and they at once pronounce the community to be plunged in ignorance, misery and vice. I don't believe there is throughout the community more vice than in England or so much misery, and the vice is of a far less disgusting character, for in England it is always based on drunkenness which exhibits in its most hideous form, whereas at Naples drunkenness is almost unknown.

[*May*] 15th [*Rome*]

The last three days have been the hottest to which Rome is subject – not much sun, no wind, but air like an oven. The only cool place is St Peter's and that is delicious . . . The post brought very bad accounts of the King who is certainly dying. I have no notion that he will live till I get home, but they tell me there will be no changes . . .

[*May*] *20th*

... To the Borghese Villa. At present I think Chiswick better than any Villa here, but they tell me that when I get home and see Chiswick and remember these I shall think differently ...

[*May*] *22nd*

... To the Pamfili Doria, a bad house with a magnificent view all round Rome; fine garden in the regular clipt style, but very shady, and the stone pines the finest here; this garden is well kept. Malaria again; Rome is blockaded by malaria and someday will surrender to it altogether; as it is, it is melancholy to see all these deserted Villas and palaces scarcely one of which is inhabited or decently kept ... The other morning the ground here was covered by a thin red powder, which was known to come from an eruption, and everybody thought it was Vesuvius, and travellers reported, but it turns out to be from Etna or Stromboli [Greville's own footnote says 'Stromboli'].

Rome must be 400 or 500 miles from Etna (not as the crow flies).

[*May*] *27th*

Went to Tivoli. The journey hotter than flames over the Campagna. It is the most beastly town I ever saw, more like the ghetto here than any other place, full of beggars and children ... we got into the heat and lost the colouring of the early morning, and those lights and shades on which the beauty of this scenery depends. I was altogether disappointed; the hills are quite bare or covered with olives, the most tiresome of trees; the falls [at the Villa d'Este] are all artificial and though the view at the foot of the largest (or as near as you can approach it) is beautiful, on the whole no part of the scenery answered my expectations ...

[*May*] *29th*

At ten Kestner called for Louvaine and me and we went to see the Pope. His court is by no means despicable. A splendid suite of apartments at the Quirinale with a very decent attendance of Swiss Guards, Guardie Nobili, Chamberlains – generally ecclesiastics – dressed in purple, valets in red from top to toe, of Spanish cut and, in midst of all, a barefooted Capuchin. After waiting a few minutes, we were introduced to the presence of the Pope by the Chamberlain who knelt as he showed us in ... His dress was white silk, and very dirty, a white silk skullcap, red silk shoes with an embroidered cross which the faithful kiss. He is a very nice, squinting old twaddle, and we liked him. He asked us if we spoke Italian and we modestly answered, a little, he began in the most desperately unintelligible French I ever heard; so that though no doubt he said many excellent things, it was nearly impossible to comprehend any of them ... He is in fact a connoisseur. Talked of quieting religious dissensions in England, the Catholic question etc.; and when I said 'Très-saint Père, le Roi mon maître n'a pas de meilleurs sujets que ses sujets catholiques' his eyes whirled round in their sockets like teetotums and he grinned from ear to ear ... After about a quarter of an hour he bade us farewell: we kissed his hand and backed out again ...

June 1st

... To the Corsini Villa, the gardens of which are some of the shadiest and most agreeable in Rome, but nobody inhabits the palace. The Corsini live at Florence, and when they come here they lodge elsewhere, for the malaria (they say) occupies their domain. Thus it is that between poverty and malaria, Rome is deserted by its great men. But the population ought to be increasing for almost every woman one meets is with child ...

June 2nd

... Called on Bunsen [Karl Christian Bunsen, Prussian Minister] ... had a long conversation with him about the expediency of appointing an English Minister or agent of some sort at Rome which he thinks very desirable and very feasible, upon the same plan upon which the relations of Prussia and Rome are conducted and which he says go on very smoothly and without embarrassment or inconvenience ... He says that Albani [Giuseppe Albani][11] is a sensible man; that the Cardinals are bigoted and prejudiced, hostile to England, and most of them forgetful of what the See of Rome owes to our country ... He thinks there is much superstition among the lower classes, little religion among any, great immorality in all; the same desire of intriguing and extending its influence which the Romish Church has always had, but with very diminished means and resources.

June 5th

Called yesterday on La Ferronays ... He is in great alarm and sorrow at the appointment of Peyronnet [Charles-Ignace Peyronnet, repressive Minister of the Interior][12] and the aspect of affairs in France ... the Government had evidently thrown away the scabbard by naming him on the eve of a general election and thus offering every sort of insult to the whole nation ... He looks to the Duke of Wellington as the only man whose authority or interference can arrest the French Ministry in the career which must plunge France into a civil war, if not create a general war in Europe ... When La Ferronays told Polignac his opinion of the course he was beginning, the other only said, 'Mon cher, tu ne connais pas le pays.'

[June] 11th

... as I do all that superstition dictates, I drank in the morning a glass of water at the Fountain of Trevi for they say that nobody ever drinks at the Fountain of Trevi without returning to Rome.

Bologna [June] 14th

... The Bolognese jargon is unintelligible. A man came and asked him [the linguist Giuseppe Mezzofanti, Librarian of the Bologna Public Library] some questions while I was there in a language that was quite strange to me, and when I asked him what it was, he said Bolognese, and that though not harmonious, it was forcible and expressive ...

Venice [June] 16th

We crossed the Po, and afterwards the Adige, in boats. The country is flat and reminded me of the Netherlands. I was asleep all night and woke in time to see some of the Villas on the bank of the Brenta. Of Padua I was unconscious. Embarked in a gondola at Fusina and arrived at this remarkable city under the bad auspices of a dark, gloomy and very cold day. It is Venice but living Venice no more. In my progress to the Inn I saw nothing but the signs of ruin and blasted grandeur, Palaces half decayed and the windows boarded up.

Two o'clock

I am just driven in by a regular rainy day and have the prospect of shivering through the rest of it in a room with a marble floor and hardly any furniture. However it is the only bad day there has been since the beginning of my expedition. The most striking thing in Venice (at least in such weather as this) is the unbroken silence. The gondolas glide along without noise or motion, and except other gondolas, one may traverse the city without perceiving a sign of life ... To the Church of St Mark and the Doge's Palace – all very interesting, antique and splendid. But the Austrians[13] have modernised some of the rooms and consequently spoilt them. They have also blocked up the Bridge of Sighs and the reason (they told me) is that all the foreigners who come here are so curious to walk over it, which seems an odd one for shutting it up ... Though the Ponte di Sospiri is no longer visible, the prisons are, and horrible places twenty-four in number, besides three others under water which the French had closed up ... There are two places in which criminals or prisoners were secretly executed; they were strangled, and without seeing their executioner, for a cord was passed through an opening which he twisted till the victim was dead ... and if they resisted, he stabbed them in the throat. The wall is still covered with the blood of those who have thus suffered. From the time of their erection, 800 years ago, to the destruction of the Republic nobody was ever allowed to see these prisons till the French came and threw them open ...

[June] 17th

The morning was fine again and everything looks gayer than yesterday. From the Rialto to the Piazza di San Marco there is plenty of life and movement, and it is exactly like Cranbourne Alley and the other alleys out of Leicester

Square. While Venice was prosperous, St Mark's must have been very brilliant, but everything is decayed. All round the Piazza are coffee houses which used to be open and crowded all night, and some of them are still open but never crowded. They used to be illuminated with lamps all round, but most of these are gone ... There is no commerce, the Government spend no money, and do nothing to benefit or enliven the town (there has not yet been time to see the effect of making it a free port). The French employed the people and spent money and embellished the place ...

... This morning I asked for the newspapers which came by the post yesterday, and found they were not yet returned from the Police and would not be till tomorrow ... At night I went to a dirty ill-lit theatre to see the *Barbiere di Siviglia* which was very ill-performed. There was a ballet but I did not stay for it.

Vicenza June 19th

... The whole road from Fusina to this place is as flat as the paper on which I am writing. I really don't believe there is a molehill, but it is extremely gay from the variety of habitations and the prodigious cultivation of all sorts. Vicenza is one of the most agreeable towns I ever saw and I would rather live in it than in any palace I have seen since Rome ... It is spacious and clean, full of Palladio's architecture ... From the Church of Santa Maria del Monte, a mile from the town, is a magnificent view, and the town itself under the mountains of the Tyrol, and the end of a vast cultivated plain, looks very inviting and gay ...

Brescia [June] 21st

This is a particularly nice town, airy, spacious and clean, and in my life I never saw so many good-looking women ... The women are excessively dressed, and almost all wear black lace veils thrown over the back of the head which are very becoming. The walks on the ramparts are shaded by a double row of trees, and command a pretty view of the mountains and country round ...

Milan June 23rd

Milan is a very fine town without much to see in it. The Duomo, Amphitheatre, Arch of the Simplon, Brera (pictures) ... I like the Duomo, but I know my taste is execrable in architecture. I don't however like the mixture of Italian with the Gothic – balustrades over the door for example – but like its tracery and laborious magnificence ...

Varese June 26th

Left Milan at six o' clock on the 24th and got to Como after dark ... Como seemed a very pretty town. The road here excellent, but very slow. Did not arrive till 1/4 past 10.

Evening, top of the Simplon ...

Breakfasted at Baveno which is the best Inn I have seen in Italy. The road
from Baveno is exceedingly beautiful, but on the whole I am rather disappointed with the Simplon, though it is very wild and grand; but I am no
longer struck with the same admiration at the sight of mountains that I
was when I entered Savoy and saw them for the first time. I walked the last
thirteen miles to the ascent of this place and found one of the best dinners
I ever tasted, or one which my hunger made appear such.

Geneva [*June*] *29th*

Got here last night and found twenty letters at least. I only think of getting
home as fast as I can. Left the Simplon in torrents of rain which lasted all day
... They tell me it has never ceased raining here, while on the other side of the
Alps hardly a drop has fallen. Only three rainy days while I was in Italy, one in
Venice, one in Rome and a couple of halves elsewhere. I wish I was at home.

Evening

Passed the whole day driving about Geneva ... a great appearance of wealth
and comfort and cultivation, no beggars and none of the houses tumbling
down and deserted. Altogether I like the look of the place though in a great
hurry to get away from it ... Mont Blanc won't show his snows, nor would
Vesuvius his fires. It was dark when I crossed the Cenis, and raining when
I descended the Simplon.

Paris July 3rd

Got here last night, after the Devil's own journey of sixty-three hours from
Geneva, only stopping two hours for breakfast; but by never touching anything
but bread and coffee I was neither heated nor tired ... Heard of the King's
death in the middle of the night. No news here.

Calais [*July*] *6th*

Voilà qui est fini. Got here last night and found the Government packet only
goes out five days a week and not today. I am very sorry it is all over but very
glad to find myself in England again – that is, when I get there ... Here is
the end of my brief but most agreeable expedition, probably the only one I
shall ever make. However this may be, I have thus gained at least –

> A consciousness remains that it has left,
> Deposited upon the silent shore
> Of memory, images, and silent thought,
> That shall not die, and cannot be destroyed.

VOLUME I ENDS

VOLUME II

1830

London July 16th

Never was elevation like that of King William the 4th. His life has been hith-erto passed in obscurity and neglect, in miserable poverty surrounded by a numerous progeny of bastards, without consideration or friends, and he was ridiculous from his grotesque ways and little meddling curiosity. Nobody ever invited him into their house or thought it necessary to honour him with any mark of attention or respect; and so he went on for above forty years till Canning [see *supra*] brought him into notice by making him High Admiral at the time of his grand Ministerial schism. In that post he distinguished himself by making ridiculous speeches, by a morbid official activity and a general wild-ness which was thought to indicate incipient insanity, till shortly after Canning's death and the Duke's accession (as is well known), the latter dismissed him. He then dropped back into obscurity, but had become by this time somewhat more of a personage than he was before. His brief administration of the Navy, the death of the Duke of York, which made him heir to the throne, his increased wealth and regular habits procured him more consideration, though not a great deal. Such was his position when George IV broke all at once and after three months of expectation, William finds himself King.

July 18th

King George had not been dead three days before everybody discovered that he was no loss, and King William a great gain. Certainly nobody was less regretted than the late King, and the breath was hardly out of his body before the press burst forth in full cry against him, and raked up all his vices, follies and misdeeds which were numerous and glaring enough ... there never was anything like the enthusiasm with which he [William] was greeted by all ranks; though he has trotted about both town and country for sixty-four years, and nobody turned round to look at him, he cannot now stir without a mob, Patrician as well as Plebeian, at his heels.

All the Park congregated round the gate to see him drive into town the day before yesterday. But in the midst of all this success and good conduct certain indications of strangeness and wildness peep out which are not a little alarming, and he promises to realise the fears of his Ministers that he will do and say too much, though they flatter themselves that they have muzzled him in his approaching progress by reminding him that his words will be taken as his Ministers', and he must, therefore, be chary of them; but at the late King's funeral he behaved with great indecency. That ceremony was very well managed and a fine sight, the military part particularly, and the Guards magnificent ... The King was Chief Mourner; and, to my astonishment, as he entered the chapel directly behind the body, in a situation in which he should have been, apparently, if not really, absorbed in the melancholy duty he was performing, he darted up to Strathaven, who was ranged on one side below the Dean's stall, shook him heartily by the hand, and then went on nodding to the right and left ...

His good nature, simplicity and affability to all about him are certainly very striking, and in his elevation he does not forget his old friends and companions. He was in no hurry to take upon himself the dignity of King, nor to throw off the habits and manners of a country gentleman. When Chesterfield went to Bushey to kiss his hand and be presented to the Queen, he found Sir John and Lady Gore there lunching, and when they went away, he called for their carriage, handed Lady Gore into it, and stood at the door to see them off. When Howe came to see him, he said the Queen was going out driving and should 'drop him' at his own house.

The Queen, they say, is by no means delighted at her elevation. She likes quiet and retirement at Bushey (of which he made her Ranger) and does not want to be a Queen. However 'L'appétit viendra en mangeant.' He says he does not want luxury and magnificence, he has slept in a cot, and he has dismissed the King's cooks 'renversé le marmite'. He keeps the stud, (which is to be diminished), because he thinks he ought to support the turf. He has made Mount Charles a Lord of Bedchamber and given the Robes to Sir C. Pole, an admiral. Altogether he seems a kind-hearted, well-meaning, not stupid, bustling old fellow, and if he doesn't go mad may make a very decent King ...

July 20th

Yesterday was a very busy day with H. Majesty who is doing much too fast, and begins to alarm his Ministers and astonish the world. In the morning he inspected the Coldstreams (dressed for the first time in his life) in a military uniform and with a great pair of gold spurs half-way up his leg like a game cock, although he was not to ride, for having chalkstones in his hands he can't hold the reins. The Queen came to Lady Bathurst's to see the review and hold a sort of drawing room when the Ministers' wives were presented to her and official men, to which were added Lady Bathurst's relations; everybody was undressed except the officers. She is very ugly with a horrid complexion, but has good manners, and did all this (which she hated) very well. She said the part as if she was acting and wished the green curtain to drop ...

... After the review the King breakfasted. Nature must have been merry when she made this Prince ... All this [a meeting of the Privy Council] was very well; no great harm in it; more affable, less dignified than the late King; but when this was over, and after so much fatigue, when he might very well have sat himself quietly down and rested, he must needs put on his plain cloathes and start on a ramble about the streets, all alone too. In Pall Mall he met Watson Taylor, and took his arm and went up St James's Street. There he was soon followed by a mob making an uproar and when he got near White's, a whore came up and kissed him.

Belfast (who had been sworn in Privy Councillor in the morning), who saw this from White's and Clinton [Robert Trefusis, 18th Baron Clinton, served in Peninsular War, at court after 1827] thought it time to interfere, and came out to attend upon him. The mob increased and always holding W. Taylor's arm, and flanked by Clinton and Belfast, who got shoved and kicked about to their inexplicable wrath, he got back to the palace amid shouting, bawling and applause ...

[July] 21st Grove Road

I hardly ever record the scandalous stories of the day unless they regard to character and events, but what relates to publick men is different from the loves and friendships of the idiots of society. Since I have been away the Chancellor [John Singleton Copley, Baron Lyndhurst][1] has had a touch of love, and for a person not less immaculate than Lady Fitzroy Somerset.[2] I met her (Lady Chancellor) at the Review Breakfast the other day and she told me all about it, Lord Worcester having previously given me an account. He [Lyndhurst] seems to have been fou – tout a fait perdu la tête – for he wrote her note after note, and some from the Bench telling her he was sitting to lawyers to whom he could not listen for all his thoughts were pre-occupied with her. Pleasant for the Suitors this, and it would make a pretty paragraph for a speech on Chancery abuses at least as an argumentum ad cancellarium. The other told me it was all true, that he had exhibited himself very ridiculously that she had remonstrated with him strongly, had told him she did not care what he did, so that he abstained from being ridiculous. He swore he had not succeeded, to which she replied so much the worse, as success would have been the best excuse for his folly that he was so in her powers that he dares not be angry with what she says or what she does. I don't know in what her power consists, but she says she can certainly unfrock him if she chuses. The fact is she is a whore and he is a knave.

July 29th

But the great event of the day was the reception of the King of France's two decrees, and the address of his Ministers who produced them; nothing could equal the universal astonishment and consternation. Falck [Dutch ambassador] told me he was reading his newspaper at his breakfast regularly through, and when he came to this, the teacup almost jumped from his hands, and he rubbed his eyes to see whether he saw correctly . . .

July 30th

Everybody anxious for news from France. A few hope and fewer think the King of France will succeed, and that the French will succeed, but the press here joins in grand chorus against the suppression of the liberty of that over the water. [Charles X of France, who had succeeded his brother Louis XVIII in 1824, had embarked with his absolutist Minister, the Prince de Polignac, upon 'the Ordonnances', a series of measures imposing press censorship and heavily reducing the powers of the National Assembly] . . . This, like everything else, will be judged by the event – desperate fatuity if it fails, splendid energies and accurate calculation of opposite moral forces if it succeeds. I judge it will fail because I can see no marks of wisdom in the style of execution, and the state paper is singularly puerile and weak in argument. It is passionate and not dexterous, not even plausible. All this is wonderfully interesting and will give us a lively autumn.

July 31st

Yesterday morning I met Matuscewicz in St James's Street who said, 'You have heard the news?' But I had not, so I got into his cabriolet, and he told me that Bulow had just been with him with an account of Rothschild's estafette [courier], who had brought intelligence of a desperate conflict at Paris between the people and the Royal Guard in which 1000 men had been killed of the former, and of the eventual revolt of two regiments which decided the business; that the Swiss had refused to fire on the people; the King gone to Compiègne, the Ministers missing, and the Deputies who were in Paris had assembled in the Chambers and declared their sittings permanent . . . unless there is a reaction, which seems improbable, the game is up with the Bourbons. They richly deserve their fate.

At night

The tri-coloured flag had been raised; the National Guard was up, commanded by old Lafayette (their chief forty years ago) who ruled in Paris . . . Rothschild had another courier with later intelligence. The King had desired to treat, and that proposals might be made to him; the Ministers escaped from Paris by a subterranean passage which led from the Tuileries to the river and were at St Cloud . . . they are all terrified to death at the national flag and colours because they see in its train revolutions, invasions and a thousand alarms . . .

. . . The [British] elections are going against Government and no candidate will avow that he stands on Government interest, or with the intention of supporting the Duke's Ministry which looks as if it had lost all its popularity.

August 2nd Evening
Soon after I got to George Street the Duke of Wellington came in, in excellent spirits and talked over the whole matter. He said he could not comprehend how the Royal Guard had been defeated by the mob, and particularly how they had been forced to evacuate the Tuileries; that he had seen English and French troops hold houses whole days not 1/4 so strong. I said that there could not be a shadow of a doubt that it was because they *would* not fight . . .

He described the whole affair as it has taken place, and said that there can be no doubt that the moneyed men of Paris (who are all against the Government) and the Liberals had foreseen a violent measure on the part of the King and had organised the resistance; that on the appearance of the edicts, the bankers simultaneously refused to discount any bills, on which the great manufacturers and merchants dismissed the workmen to the number of many thousands who inflamed the public discontent and united to oppose the military and the execution of the decrees. He said positively that we should not take any part and that no other Government ought or could. He does not like the D. of Orléans and thinks his proclamation mean and shabby, but owned that under all circumstances his election to the Crown would probably be the best thing that could happen . . .

August 3rd
I went yesterday to the sale of the late King [George IV]'s wardrobe which was numerous enough to fill Monmouth Street [known, then, as now, for fancy dress shops and theatrical costumiers] and sufficiently various and splendid for the wardrobe of Drury Lane . . . His profusion in these articles was unbounded because he never paid for them, and his memory so accurate that one of his pages told me he recollected every article of dress, no matter how old, and that they were always liable to be called on to produce some particular coat or other part of apparel of years gone by. It is difficult to say whether in great or little things that man was most odious and contemptible.

August 5th
In the afternoon met Vaudreuil [acting French ambassador] and had a long conversation with him on the state of things. He said 'My family has been ruined twice by these cursed Bourbons, and I will be damned if they shall a third time!' that he had long foreseen the inevitable tendency of Polignac's determination. He thinks that if this had not taken place, a few years must have

terminated the reign of the Bourbons and that it is only the difference between sudden and lingering death; that when he was in Paris, he had seen the dissatisfaction of the young officers in the Guards who were all Liberal; [the word 'Liberal', first given currency by François René Chateaubriand (1768–1848), was applied to the opponents of the Bourbon regime after the Restoration. Strachey and Fulford] and knowing these sentiments, what a coalition they must have been in when called upon to charge and fire on the people while secretly approving of their conduct 'entre leurs devoirs de Citoyens et de Militaires.' . . .

[*August*] 10th Goodwood

. . . I rode over the Downs three or four miles (from Petworth) and never saw so delightful a country to live in. There is an elasticity in the air and turf which communicates itself to the spirits.

In the meantime the French Revolution has been proceeding rapidly to its consummation, and the Duke of Orléans is King. Montrond who was at Stoke, thinks that France will gravitate towards a Republic, and principally for this reason that there is an unusual love of equality and no disposition to profit by the power of making *majorats*, therefore that there can never be anything like an aristocracy . . . some people are alarmed at the excessive admiration which the French Revolution has excited in England and there is very general conviction that Spain will speedily follow the example of France and probably Belgium also. Italy I don't believe will throw off the yoke; they have neither spirit nor unanimity, and the Austrian military force is too great to be resisted. But Austria will tremble and see that the great victory which Liberalism has gained has decided the question as to which principle, that of light or darkness, shall prevail for the future of the world.

August 14th London

Staid at Goodwood till the 12th; went to Brighton, riding over the Downs from Goodwood to Arundel, a delightful ride. How much I prefer England to Italy! There we have mountain and sky; here vegetation and verdure, fine trees and soft turf; and in the long run the latter are the most enjoyable . . . In the meantime our elections here are still going against Government, and the signs of the times are all for reform and retrenchment, and against slavery. It is astonishing the interest the people generally take in the slavery question, which is the work of the Methodists, and shows the enormous influence they have in the country. The Duke (for I have not seen him) is said to be very easy about the next parliament. Whereas, as far as one can judge, it promises to be quite as unmanageable as the last and is besides very ill-composed – full of Boys and all sorts of strange men.

August 20th Friday

... I called on Batchelor (he was *valet de chambre* to the Duke of York, afterwards to George IV). I was there a couple of hours and heard all the details of the late King's illness and other things ... At that time she [Lady Conyngham] was in wretched spirits and did nothing but pray from morning till night. However her conscience does not seem to have interfered with her ruling passion, avarice, and she went on accumulating. During the last illness wagons were loaded every night and sent away from the Castle, but what their contents were was not known, at least he did not say. All Windsor knew this ... Sefton in the meantime told me that Brougham and Lord Grey were prepared for a violent opposition, and that they had formed a formal junction with Huskisson, being convinced that no Government could now be formed without him. I asked him if Palmerston was a party to this junction and was told that he was, and the first thing I heard when I got to town was that there is a negotiation going on between Palmerston and the Duke, and that the former takes every opportunity of declaring his goodwill to the latter and how unshackled he is. Both these things can't be true, and time will show which is ... Brougham is to lead this opposition in the H. of C., and Ld. Grey in the Lords, and nothing is to be done but as the result of general deliberation and agreement ...

That man [Brougham], with all his talents, never can or never will *do* in any situation; he is base, cowardly and unprincipled, and with all the execrable judgment which, I believe, often flows from the perversion of moral sentiment. Nobody can admire his genius, eloquence, variety and extent of information and the charm of his society more than I do; but his faults are glaring and the effect of them manifest to anybody who will compare his means and their results ...

August 24th

... The dinner in St George's Hall on the King's birthday was the finest thing possible – all good and hot and served on the late King's gold plate. There were one hundred people at table. After dinner the King gave the D[uke] of W[ellington]'s health, as it was the anniversary of Vimiera [*sic*]; [Vimeiro, 1808, one of Wellington's chief victories during the Peninsular War] the Dukes of Gloster and Cumberland [both Dukes, sons of George III, were men of the extreme right, Ultras, embittered against Wellington for having, under the pressure of Irish events, enacted Catholic Emancipation] turned their glasses down. I can't agree with Charles X that it would be better to *travailler pour son pain* than be K. of England.

At night

Went to Lady Glengall's to meet Marmon [*sic*]. [Marshal Marmont].[3] He likes talking of his adventures ... He was very communicative about events

in Paris, lamented his own ill-luck, involved in the business against his
wishes and feelings; he disapproved of Polignac and his measures, had no
notion the *ordonnance* was thought of. In the morning he was going to St
Germain for the day when his A.D.C. brought him the newspaper with the
ordonnances. ll tomba de son haut. Soon after the Dauphin sent to him to
desire, that as there might be some *vitres cassées,* that he would take the
command of the troops. Directly after, the thing began. He had 7000 or
8000 men; not a preparation had been made of any sort, they had never
thought of resistance, had not consulted Marmont or any military man; he
soon found how hopeless the case was and sent eight estafettes to the K,
one after another during the action, to tell him so and implore him to stop
it while it was time. They never sent any answer. He then escaped to St
Cloud where he implored the King to yield. It was not until after seven
hours pressing that he consented to name M. de Mortemar Minister, but
would not withdraw the edicts.

He says that up to Wednesday night they would have compromised and
accepted M. de Mortemar and the suppression of the edicts, but the King
still demurred. On Wednesday night he yielded, but the communications
were interrupted. That night the meeting at the Palais Royal at which his
[the King's] fate was determined; and on Thursday morning when his
offers arrived, it was too late and they would no longer treat ... He says
never man was so unlucky, that he was *Maréchal de quartier* and could not
refuse to serve; – only acted on the defensive; that 2000 of the troops and
1500 of the populace were killed ...

September 9th

Came from Stoke the day after the Egham races and went to Brocket Hall on
Saturday last; returned the day before yesterday. Nothing can exceed the interest,
the excitement, the consternation which prevail here. On Saturday last the funds
suddenly fell near three per cent, no cause apparent, a thousand reports and a
panic on the Stock Exchange. At last on Monday it appeared that the Emperor
of Russia had, on the first intelligence of the revolution in France, prohibited
the tri-coloured cockade and ordered all Russian subjects to quit France ...
They [the funds] have since rallied to nearly what they were before ...

I had a long conversation with my brother-in-law [Lord Francis Egerton,
one of the family of the Duke of Bridgewater, who built the major canals in
the Liverpool and Manchester area] who is never very communicative or
talkative, but he takes a gloomy view of everything, not a little perhaps tinctured by the impending ruin which he foresees to his own property from the
Liverpool Railroad which is to be opened with great ceremony on the 15th;
but he thinks the Government so weak that it cannot stand and expects the
D[uke] will be compelled to resign.

September 10th

Henry [Henry De Ros, premier baron of England, close friend of Greville] writes me word from Arbuthnot's that the Duke is very much disturbed about the state of affairs, thinks ill of France and generally of the state of Europe. I think the alarmists are increasing everywhere, and the signs of the times are certainly portentous; still I doubt there being any great desire of change among the mass of the people of England, and prudent and dexterous heads (if there be any such) may yet steer on through the storm. If Canning were alive, I believe he would have been fully equal to the emergency if he was not thwarted by the passions, prejudices and follies of others; but if he had lived, we should not have had the Catholic question settled. [Canning on forming his brief Ministry, had reluctantly acceded to George IV's insistence that the Catholic question should not be opened] and what a state we should be in now if that was added to the rest.

September 14th

Last Saturday to Panshanger; returned yesterday. Melbourne and G. Lamb and the Ashleys. George said there would be a violent opposition in the approaching session. William [Lord Melbourne, later, from 1834, Prime Minister] told me he thought Huskisson was the greatest practical statesman he had known, the one who united theory with practice the most, but owned that he was not popular and not thought honest.

Newark, September 18th, Saturday

... came to town on Thursday, and in the afternoon heard the news of Huskisson's horrible accident, and yesterday morning got a letter from Henry with the details, which are pretty correctly given in *The Times* newspaper. It is a very odd thing, but I had for days before a strong presentiment that some terrible accident would occur at this ceremony ... It seems to have happened in this way: while the Duke's car was stopping to take in water, the people alighted and walked about the railroad; when suddenly another car which was running on the adjoining level, came up. Everybody scrambled out of the way and those who could got again into the first car. This Huskisson attempted to do, but he was slow and awkward; as he was getting in some part of the machinery of the other car struck the door by his, by which he was knocked down, run over by the other car and his leg smashed. He was taken up and conveyed by Wilton and Mrs Huskisson (who must have seen the accident happen) to the house of Mr Blackburne eight miles from Heaton. Wilton saved his life for a few hours by knowing how to tie up the artery; amputation was not possible; and he expired at ten o'clock that night. Wilton, Lord Granville and Littleton were with him to the last. Mrs Huskisson behaved with great courage. The Duke of Wellington was deeply affected, and it was with the greatest difficulty that he could be persuaded upon the progress [by railway] to Manchester; and at last he only yielded to the most pressing solicitations of the Directors and to a strong remonstrance that the mob might be dangerous if he did not appear ...

The death of Huskisson cannot fail to leave an important effect upon political events; it puts an end to his party as a party, but it leaves the survivors at liberty to join either the Opposition or the Government while during his life there were great difficulties to their doing either, in consequence of the antipathy which many of the Whigs had to him on one side and the Duke of Wellington on the other ... As to the Duke of Wellington, a fatality attends him and it is perilous to cross his path. There were perhaps 500,000 people present on this occasion, and probably not a soul besides hurt. One man only is killed, and that man is his most dangerous political opponent, the one from whom he had most to fear ...

Huskisson was about sixty years old, slouching and ignoble looking. In society he was extremely agreeable, without much animation, generally cheerful, with a great deal of humour, information and anecdote, gentlemanlike, unassuming, slow in speech and with a downcast look as if he avoided meeting anybody's gaze ... it is probable that there is no man in Parliament, or perhaps out of it, so well versed in finance, commerce, trade and colonial matters, and that therefore he is a very great and irreparable loss ...

September 27th Chatsworth

Got to Spotsboro last Sunday; rather dull; Lord Talbot and Lady Cecil, W[illia]m Lascelles, Irby, Charlotte Denison, Captain Grey. It rained all the time of the races [at Doncaster]. I won £700 by the week; very little money lost but a good deal won – sounds like a contradiction, but is not. They offered Priam to Chesterfield for £3000 before his match and he refused; he offered it after and they refused ...

Buckenham [Buckenham Castle, Norfolk] October 25th

A month since I have written a line; always racing and always idleness. Went from Chatsworth to Heaton Park; [race meeting near Manchester. Strachey and Fulford] an immense party, excellent house and living and very good sport ... in a park with gentlemen riders. All interest however was absorbed in the loves of Chesterfield [6th Earl, married her in November] and Anne Forester and George Anson and Isabella. [Anne Forester's younger sister married him the same day.] The last night the former proposed and, at the same time, asked me to go to London to break the intelligence to Mrs Fox; accordingly, I travelled up all night and in the morning went and told her. I was with her three hours, in the course of which she cried a good deal, laughed a little and talked incessantly, was full of rage, despair and wrath, partly tragical and partly comical.

She must have had a shrewd idea that he had ceased to care about her, though she says not, but she certainly was not prepared for this sudden and irrevocable overthrow. George Forester [2nd Baron] was in an agony for fear she should be greatly vexed, and his feelings together with the whole story would make a romance.

I went from thence to Newmarket and lost £400 – few people and bad sport. On the Thursday to Newsell's where I was bored to death, and on Sunday to this place till last Sunday when I returned to Newmarket and came here yesterday.

London November 8th

Parliament met, and a great clamour was raised against the King's Speech without much reason; but it was immediately evident that the Government was in a very tottering condition, and the first night of this session, the Duke of Wellington made a violent and uncalled-for declaration against Reform which has, without doubt, sealed his fate. Never was there an act of more egregious folly or one so universally condemned by friends and foes ... I came to town last night and found the town ringing with his imprudence and everybody expecting that a few days would produce his resignation.

The King's visit to the City was regarded with great apprehension, as it was suspected that attempts would be made to produce riot and confusion at night; and consequently all the troops that could be mustered were prepared, together with thousands of special constables, new Police ['new,' commonly 'New', because created the year before by the Home Secretary, Robert Peel] Volunteers, East India sailors and Marines; but last night a Cabinet council was called, at which it was definitely arranged to put it off altogether ...

November 9th

... In Downing St we met George Dawson who told us the funds had fallen three per cent and that the panic was tremendous, so much so that they were not without alarm lest there should be a run on the Bank for gold ... The King is said to be very low, hating Reform, desirous of supporting the Duke, but feeling that he can do nothing. However in the H. of Lords last night the speakers vied with each other in praising His Majesty and extolling his popularity. Lady Jersey told me that the Duke had said to her 'Lord, I shall not go out, you will see we shall get on very well.'

November 12th

We ordered Russian ships to be put under a precautionary quarantine yesterday and made a minute to record what we had done. The funds kept advancing, everything is quiet and ministers begin to take courage. The Duke means, if he has a majority of twenty on Tuesday, to stay in. It seems that this is his idea that the resolutions of Brougham [Henry Brougham, radical Whig, newly elected on a relatively democratic mandate for Yorkshire, had announced a motion proposing parliamentary reform] will be so general on purpose to obtain as many votes as he can that they will be no test of the real opinion of the House; because most of those who may concur in a general resolution in favour of Reform would disagree entirely as to specific measures, if any were introduced; but it is evident that the support of his [the Duke's] friends is getting feebler every day ...

... What they all feel is that his obstinacy will endanger everything; that by timely concession and regulating the present spirit, real improvements could be made and extreme measures avoided.

November 16th

The Duke of Wellington's administration is at an end. If he has not already resigned, he probably will in the course of the day. Everybody was so intent on the Reform question that the Civil List was not thought of and consequently the defeat of Government last night was unexpected ... The exultation of the Opposition was immense. Word was sent down their line not to cheer, but they were not to be restrained and Sefton's yell was heard triumphant in the din. The Tories voted with them. There had been a meeting at Knatchbull's when they decided to go against Government ...

November 19th

The day before yesterday Lord Grey went to the King who received him with every possible kindness and gave him *carte blanche* to form a new administration, placing even the Household at his disposal – much to their disgust. Ever since the town has been, as usual, teeming with reports, but with fewer lies than usual. The fact is that Lord Grey has had no difficulties and has formed a Government at once; only Brougham put them all in a dreadful fright. He all but declared a hostile intention to the future administration; he boasted that he would take nothing, refuse even the Great Seal [the Great Seal of England, symbol of the office of Lord Chancellor] and flourished his Reform *in terrorem* over their heads ...

November 20th

Here I was interrupted and broke off yesterday morning. At twelve yesterday everything was settled but the Great Seal, and in the afternoon the great news transpired that Brougham had accepted it. Great was the surprise, greater still the joy at a charm having been found potent enough to lay the unquiet spirit, a bait rich enough to tempt his restless ambition ... As it is the joy is great and universal; all men feel that he is emasculated and drops on the Woolsack as on his political deathbed; once in the H. of Lords, there is an end of him, and he may rant, storm and thunder without hurting anybody.

November 21st

... In the meantime, the new Government will find plenty to occupy their most serious thoughts and employ their best talents. The state of the country is dreadful; every post brings fresh accounts of conflagrations, destruction of machinery, associations of labourers and compulsory rise of wages. Cobbett [William Cobbett, the great radical journalist and crusader, author of *Rural Rides* and publisher/editor of the vastly influential *Political Register*], Carlile [Richard Carlile, extreme radical editor, soon afterwards the organiser of a political union based on the London Roundhouse] write and harangue to inflame the minds of the people who are already set in motion and excited by all the events which have happened abroad ...

... The Duke of Richmond went down to Sussex and had a battle with a mob of 200 labourers whom he beat with 50 of his own farmers and tenants, harangued them and sent them away in good humour. He is, however, very popular.

November 22nd

Dined yesterday at Sefton's; nobody but Lord Grey and his family, Brougham and Montrond, the latter just come from Paris. It was excessively agreeable. Ld. Grey is in excellent spirits, and Brougham whom Sefton bantered from the beginning to the end of dinner. Be Brougham's political errors what they may, his gaiety, temper and admirable social qualities make him delightful, to say nothing of his more solid merits, of liberality, generosity and charity ...

November 25th

The accounts from the country on the 23rd were so bad that a Cabinet sat all the morning and concerted a proclamation offering large rewards for the discovery of offenders, rioters or burners ... Anson as master of the Buckhounds was made a Privy Councillor, not usually a Privy Councillor's place, but the King said he rather liked increasing the number than not. Clanricade has a Gold Stick ... Lord Grey at the same time promised his brother, Sir Henry Grey, a Grand Cross, but Lord Hill (who as Commander in Chief has all the crosses at his disposal) was offended at what he considered a slight to him and went to the King to complain.

November 28th

... There has been nothing new within these three days, but the alarm is still very great and the general agitation which pervades men's minds unlike what I have ever seen. Reform, economy echoed backwards and forwards, the doubts, the hopes and the fears of those who have anything to lose, the uncertainty of everybody's future condition, the immense interests at stake, the magnitude and imminence of the danger, all contribute to produce a nervous excitement which extends to all classes and almost every individual. Until the Ministers are re-elected nobody can tell what will be done in Parliament and Lord Grey himself has no idea what sort of strength the Government will have in either House ... but I doubt if the Duke will ever be in a civil office again, nor do I think the country would like to see him the head of a Government unless it were one conducted in a very different manner from the last ...

Notwithstanding the great measures which have distinguished his Government such as Catholic Emancipation and repeal of the Test Acts, a continual series of systematic blunders and utter ignorance of and indifference to, public opinion have rendered the first of these great measures almost useless. Ireland is on the point of becoming in a worse state than before the Catholic question was settled; and why? Because first of all, the settlement was put off far too long, and the fever of agitation would not subside, and because it was accompanied by an insult to O'Connell [Daniel O'Connell, see *supra*] which he has been resolved to revenge and which he knows that he can.

Then instead of depriving him of half the means by paying the priests and so getting them under the influence of Government, they neglected this and followed up the omission by taxing Ireland and thus uniting the whole nation against us. What is this but egregious presumption, blindness and want of all political calculation and foresight? ... To buy O'Connell at any price, pay the Catholic Church, establish poor laws, encourage emigration and repeal the obnoxious taxes are the only expedients which have a chance of restoring order ...

December 12th

... The burnings go on and though they say that one or two incendiaries have been taken up, nothing has yet been discovered likely to lead to a detection of the system ...

Brougham leans to mercy I see. But what a curious supplementary sort of trial this is; how many accidents may determine the life or death of the culprit. In one case in this report which they were discussing before the [Privy] Council, Brougham had forgot that the man was recommended to mercy, but he told me that at the last Recorder's report, there was a great difference of opinion on one (a forgery case), when Tenterden [Charles Abbott, Baron Tenterden, Chief Justice of King's Bench, 1818–32; did not lean to mercy] was for hanging the man and he for saving him; that he had it put to the vote and the man was saved. Little did the criminal know that when there was a change of Ministry that he owed his life to it, for if Lyndhurst had been [Lord] Chancellor he would most assuredly have been hanged; not that Lyndhurst was particularly severe or cruel, but he would have concurred with the Lord Chief Justice and would have regarded the case solely in a judicial point of view, whereas the mind of the other was probably biased by some theory about the crime of forgery or by some fancy of his strange brain ...

I was agreeably surprised yesterday by a communication from Lord Lansdowne [the new (and Whig) Lord President of the Privy Council, to which Greville was Clerk] that he thought no alteration could be made in my emoluments and that he was still prepared to defend them if anyone attacked them. Still, though it is a very good thing to be so supported, I don't consider myself safe from parliamentary assaults. In these times it will not do to be idle, and I told Lord L. that I was anxious to keep my emoluments, but ready to work for them . . .

All the Russells are dissatisfied that John [Lord John Russell, later Prime Minister and Earl Russell] had not a seat in the Cabinet, and that Graham has [Sir James Graham],[4] and the more so because they know or believe that this preference is owing to Lambton [John Lambton, Baron later Earl of Durham, Grey's son-in-law] who does what he likes with Lord Grey. My mind has always misgiven me about Lord Grey, and what I have lately heard of him satisfies me that a more overrated man never lived, or one whose speaking was so far above his general abilities or who owed so much to his oratorical plausibilities. His tall, commanding and dignified appearance, his flow of language, graceful action, well-rounded periods and an exhibition of classical taste, united with legal knowledge, render him the most finished orator of his day; but his conduct has shown him to be influenced by pride, still more by vanity, personal antipathies, caprice, indecision and a thousand weaknesses generated by these passions and defects. Anyone who is constantly with him and who can avail themselves of his vanity can govern him . . .

When he had quarrelled with his old Whig friends, he began to approach the Tories, the object of his constant aversion and contempt; and what civilities passed between the Bathursts and him, and what political coquetries between him and the Duke of Wellington, and how he believed it was only George IV who prevented his being invited by the Duke to join him. Then George IV dies, K William succeeds; no invitation to Lord Grey and he plunges into furious opposition to the Duke. His vanity has all his life made him the fool of women – some years ago of Lady Blessington, when however he was not singular for she had a parcel of old statesmen who were all at her feet, Rosslyn, Lansdowne, Stranford and I forget who else.

About three years ago, the [Lord] Chancellor, Lyndhurst, was the man in the world he abhorred the most; and it was about this time that I well recollect one night at Madame de Lieven's I introduced Lord Grey to Lady Lyndhurst. We had dined together somewhere and he had been praising her beauty; so when we all met I presented him. He has been in love with her ever since, and very soon after, all his antipathies ceased and he and Lyndhurst became great friends. This was the cause of Lady Lyndhurst's partiality for the Whigs which enraged the Tory Ladies and some of their Lords so much, but which served her turn and enabled her to keep two hot irons in the fire. When the Duke went out, Grey was very anxious to keep Lyndhurst as his Chancellor and would have done so if it had not been for Brougham who, whirling Reform *in terrorem* over his head, announced to him that it must not be. Reluctantly enough, Grey was obliged to give way, for he saw that with Brougham in the H. of C. against him he could not stand for five minutes and that the only alternative was to put Brougham on the Woolsack.

December 16th

The affair at Warsaw[5] seems to have begun as a conspiracy against Constantine and four of the generals who were killed, perished in his anteroom defending him. With the smallest beginnings, however, nothing is more likely than a general rising in Poland. [Nothing was. The Poles rose, and over nine months the Tsar crushed them.]

December 23rd

. . . O'Connell had a triumphant entry into Dublin and advised that no honour should be shown to Lord Anglesey [Lord-Lieutenant]. They had an interview of two hours in London when Lord A. asked him what he intended to do. He said 'Strive *totis viribus* to effect a repeal of the Union [between Great Britain and Ireland effected largely by fraud in 1800 in reaction to the Rising of 1798]; when Lord A. told him that he feared that he should then be obliged to govern Ireland by force, so that they are at daggers drawn. There is not a doubt that Repeal is making rapid advances. Moore [Thomas Moore (1779–1852), Irish poet and balladeer] told me that he had seen extraordinary signs of it and that men in the middle classes, intelligent and well-educated, wished for it, though they knew the disadvantages that would attend a severance of their connexion with England. He said that he could understand it, for as an Irishman, he felt it himself.

December 26th Roehampton

At Lord Clifden's; Luttrell, Byng and Dudley; the latter very mad, doing nothing but soliloquise, walk about, munch and rail at Reform of every kind. Lord Anglesey has entered Dublin amidst silence and indifference, all produced by O'Connell's orders, whose entry was greeted by the acclamations of thousands; and his speeches then and since have been more violent than ever. His authority and popularity are unabated and he is employing them to make all the mischief he can, his first object being to make friends of the Orangemen to whom he affects to humble himself and he has on all occasions caused the orange ribband to be joined with the green.

We had a meeting at the [Privy] Council Office here on Friday to order a prayer 'on account of the troubled state of certain parts of the U.K.' – a great nonsense.

December 30th

I never remember times like these, nor read of such – the terror and the lively expectation which prevail and the way in which people's minds are turned backwards and forwards, from France to Ireland then range excursively to Poland or Piedmont, and fix again on the burnings, riots and executions here.

1831

January 2nd

Came up to town yesterday with the Villiers at a dinner of clever men, got up at the Atheneum, and was extremely bored . . . all men of more or less talent and information and altogether producing anything but an agreeable party. Maule was Senior Wrangler and Senior Medallist at Cambridge and is a lawyer. He was nephew to the man with [under] whom I was at school thirty years ago and I have never seen him since; he was then a very clever boy and assisted to teach the boys, being admirably well taught by his uncle who was an excellent scholar and great brute.

I have young Maule [William Henry Maule KC 1833, Baron of the Court of Exchequer 1839, member of the judicial committee of the Privy Council 1855] now in my mind's eye suspended by the hair of his head while being well caned, and recollect as if it were yesterday his doggedly drumming a lesson of Terence into my dull and recalcitrant brain as we walked up and down the garden walk before the house . . . He looked up and said 'Oh it's too long ago to talk about' and then turned back to his paper. So I set him down for a brute like his uncle and troubled him no further. I am sure that dinners of all fools have as good a chance of being agreeable as dinners of all clever people . . .

January 19th

. . . George Lamb said that the King is supposed to be in a bad state of health, and this was confirmed to me by Keate, the surgeon, who gave me to understand that he is going the way of both his brothers [George IV d.1830 and Frederick, Duke of York, d.1827]. He will be a great loss in these times; he knows his business, lets his Ministers do as they please, but expects to be *informed* of everything. He lives a strange life at Brighton with tag rag and bobtail about him and always open house. The Queen is a prude and will not let the ladies come *décolletées* to her parties. George the 4th, who liked ample expanses of that sort, would not let them be covered . . .

Roehampton January 22nd

The event of the week is O'Connell's arrest on a charge of conspiracy to defeat the Lord-Lieutenant's proclamation. Ld. Anglesey writes to Lady A. thus:- 'I am just come from a consultation of six hours with the Law Office, the result of which is a determination to arrest O'Connell, for things are now come to that pass that the question is whether he or I shall govern Ireland.' We await the result with great anxiety, for the opinion of lawyers seems divided as to the legality of the arrest and laymen can form none.

February 9th

Hunt [Henry Hunt MP][1] spoke for two hours last night; his manner and appearance are very good, like a country gentleman of the old school, a sort of rural dignity about it, very civil, good-humoured and respectful to the House, but dull; listened to, however, and very well received.

February 17th

... Went to Lady Dudley Stuart's last night, a party; saw a vulgar-looking fat man with spectacles and a mincing, rather pretty pink and white woman, his wife. The man [Napoleon-Achille Murat] was Napoleon's nephew, the woman [Catherine Murat, née Dudley, actually Washington's great-niece] Washington's granddaughter. What a host of associations, all confused and degraded! He is a son of Murat, the King of Naples, who was said to be 'le dieu Mars jusqu'a six heures du soir'. He was heir to a throne and is now a lawyer in the United States, and his wife, whose name I know not, Sandon told me, was Washington's granddaughter.

February 24th

... Neither the late nor any other Government ever cut so poor a figure as this does. Palmerston does nothing, Grant does worse, Graham does no good, Althorp a great deal of harm, Stanley alone has distinguished himself, and what he has had to do has done very well ... While the Government is thus weak and powerless the elements of confusion and violence are gathering fresh force, and without any fixed and legal authority to check them, will pursue their eccentric course till some publick commotion arrives, or till the Conservative resources of the country are called into action ...

The King went to the play the night before last; was well received in the house, but hooted and pelted coming home, and a stone shivered the window and fell into prince George of Cumberland's lap ...

February 25th

A drawing room yesterday at which the Princess Victoria made her first appearance, a short vulgar-looking child ...

Duncannon who vacated his seat on taking the Woods and Forests [a minor ministerial office of the day] is beat in Kilkenny — a nice country that and a fine people. He has been living at his estate and done more good and acquired more influence than most Irish landlords. They do justice to his merits, but O'Connell holds up his finger and not a soul dares support him; his own tenants and friends receive notice that if they vote for him their houses will be burnt and themselves murdered. They are a nation of ferocious barbarians, and the hodgepodge of ignorance and knowledge, tyranny and liberty, poverty, fanaticism, cunning, idleness and passions of every description let loose upon society have produced such a condition of things as never existed in any country in the world. They have all the evils of barbarism and of civilisation together. It is an immense furnace with O'Connell always blowing the coals and stirring the fire.

February 26th

All that history about Duncannon and his election turns out to be false, so I might have saved that eloquent tirade of indignation for some other occasion like the decorations of a play that is damned.

March 2nd

The great day at length arrived and yesterday [Lord] John Russell moved for leave to bring in his Reform Bill. To describe the curiosity, the intensity of expectation and excitement would be impossible, and the story had been so well kept that not a soul knew what the measure was (though most people guessed pretty well) till they heard it. He rose at six o'clock and spoke for two hours and a quarter – a sweeping measure indeed! much more so than anyone had imagined ... They say it was ludicrous to see the faces of the members for those places which are to be disfranchised as they were severally announced, and Wetherell [Member for Boroughbridge where the two parliamentary seats were scheduled for abolition] who began to take notes, as the plan was gradually developed, after sundry contortions and grimaces and flinging about of his arms and legs, threw down his notes with a mixture of despair and ridicule and horror ... Everything is easy in these days else how Palmerston, Goderich, Grant etc [all originally followers of Canning or Huskisson, moderate Tories] can have joined in a measure of this sweeping, violent and speculative character it is difficult to conceive; they were the disciples of Castlereagh and the adherents of Canning; but after the Duke of Wellington and Peel carrying the Catholic question, Canning's friends advocating Radical Reform and Eldon [John Scott, Earl of Eldon, Ultra Tory, Lord Chancellor 1801–27] living to see Brougham on the Woolsack, what may one not expect? ... As to this question, the greatest evil of it is that it is a pure speculation and may be productive of the best consequences or the worst, or even of none at all for all that its authors and abettors can explain to us or themselves ...

[*March*] *5th Saturday*

Thursday night the great speeches were those of Hobhouse [John Cam
Hobhouse (1786–1869), later Lord Broughton, radical Whig later in Cabinet]
on one side and Peel on the other . . . The people come into the 'Travellers'
after the debate and bring their different accounts all tinctured by their particular opinions and prejudices . . . The excitement is beyond anything I ever
saw . . .

March 7th

Nothing talked of, thought of, dreamt of, but reform. Every creature one meets
asks, What is said now? How will it go? What is the last news? What do *you*
think? and so it is from morning till night, in the streets, in the clubs and in
private houses. Yesterday morning met Hobhouse; told him how well I heard
he had spoken and asked what he thought of Peel's speech; said it was brilliant, imposing, but not much in it.

March 10th

The debate has gone on and is to be over tonight; everybody heartily sick of
it, but the excitement as great as ever. Last night O'Connell very good and
vehemently cheered by the Government, Stanley, Duncannon and all; all differences giving way to their zeal; Attwood [Mathias Attwood, Tory MP, brother
of the Radical Thomas Attwood who organised the all-important Birmingham
Political Union] the other way, good; Graham a total failure, got into nautical
terms and a simile about a ship. Sir J. York [MP and admiral, drowned May
1831!] quizzed him with great effect . . .

There is news in that the Poles have been beat and have submitted [not, in
fact, until the fall of Warsaw in September]. There is a great fall in the French
funds as they are expected not to pay their dividends. Europe is in a nice mess.
The events of a quarter of a century would hardly be food for a week nowadays.

March 11th

It is curious to see the change of opinion as to the passing of this Bill. The
other day nobody would hear the possibility of it, now everybody is beginning
to think it will. The tactics of opposition have been very bad, for they ought
to have come to a division immediately when I think the Government would
have been beat; but it was pretty certain that if they gave time to the country
to declare itself, the meetings and addresses would fix the wavering and decide
the doubtful. There certainly never was anything like the unanimity which
pervades the country on the subject . . .

March 17th

Brougham has been getting into a squabble with the military. At the drawing room on Thursday, they refused to let his carriage pass through the Horse Guards which he ordered his coachmen to force his way through, which he did ... A few days after, he drove over the soldiers in Downing Street who were relieving guard; but this time he did no great harm to the men, and it was not his fault, but these things are talked of.

Dined yesterday with General MacDonald to meet the Kembles [theatrical dynasty begun in the eighteenth century with John Philip Kemble and his sister, Sarah Siddons]. Miss Fanny is near being very handsome from the extraordinary expression of her countenance and fine eyes, but her figure is not good. She is short, hands and feet large, arms handsome, skin dark and coarse and her manner wants ease and repose.

[March] 22nd

... Tonight they will divide and after a thousand fluctuations of opinion, it is thought the Bill will be thrown out by a small majority.

March 23rd

The House divided at three o'clock this morning and the second reading was carried by a majority of *one* in the fullest House that ever was known – 303 to 302 – both parties confident up to the moment of the division; the Opposition most so and at last the Government expected to be beat. Denman [Sir Thomas Denman, Attorney-General] told somebody as they were going to divide that the question would be lost; Calcraft [who had spoken temperately against the Bill, then voted for it]² and the Wynnes going over at the eleventh hour did the business.

March 24th

The agitation the other night on the division was prodigious. The Government, who staid in the House [voting at this time in the smaller, pre-fire Commons involved only one side entering a lobby, the other remaining in the chamber to be counted] thought they had lost it by ten; and the Opposition who were crowded into the lobby, fancied from the numbers that they were sure of winning. There was betting going on all night long, and large sums had been won and lost. The people in the lobby were miscounted and they thought they had 303 ...

April 10th

At Newmarket since last Wednesday week where politics and books were laid aside, for at that place nothing ever runs in my head except a racehorse. I won £900 [say, £45,000 at present values] by a very lucky accident. Running for the Claret, St Nicholas was placed first and Amphiaraus 2nd. The horse who really came in first was Captain Arthur, but the judge did not see him. A complaint was made of crossing against St Nicholas which was tried after the races and the race given to Amphiaraus, so that the horse I backed came in 4th (for Little Red Rover was before him) and I got the money as if the horse I backed had won.

April 14th

The Reform campaign has re-opened with a violent speech from Hunt denouncing the whole thing as a delusion; that the people begin to find out they have been humbugged and that as it will make nothing cheaper, they don't care about it.

April 24th

On Monday [19th April] General Gascoyne [Isaac Gascoyne, Tory MP for Liverpool] moved that the Committee should be instructed not to reduce the members of the H. of C. and this was carried after two nights' debate by eight. The dissolution was then decided upon. Meanwhile Ld. Wharncliffe gave notice of a motion to address the King not to dissolve parliament, and this was to have come on Friday. On Thursday, Ministers were again beat in the H. of Commons on a question of adjournment, and on Friday they got the King to go down and prorogue Parliament in person the same day. The *coup d'état* was so sudden that nobody was aware of it until within two or three hours of the time and many not all. They told him [King William] that the cream-coloured horses could not be got ready, when he said 'Then I will go down with anyone else's horses.' Mash [Thomas Mash, Comptroller of Accounts to the King] went off in a carriage to the Tower to fetch the Crown ... In the H. of Commons Sir R. Vyvyan [Sir Richard Vyvyan, a young Cornish baronet identified with the Ultra faction of the Tories] made a furious speech attacking the Government on every point, and (excited as he was) it was very well done.

The Ministers made no reply but Sir F. Burdett and Tennyson [respectively Sir Francis Burdett, long-standing radical Whig MP, and the poet's uncle] disputed his opinion which enraged the Speaker, and soon after, he called up Peel for whom he was resolved to obtain a hearing ... He made a very violent speech attacking the Government for their incompetence, folly and reckless-ness, and treated them with the utmost asperity and contempt. In the midst of his speech the guns announced the arrival of the King, and at each explo-sion, the Government gave a loud cheer, and Peel was still speaking in the midst of every sort of noise and tumult when the Usher of the Black Rod knocked at the door to summon the Commons to the House of Peers.

There the proceedings were if possible still more violent and outrageous

... the Duke of Richmond endeavoured to prevent any speaking by raising points of order and moving that the Lords should take their regular places (in separate ranks) ... this put Lord Londonderry into such a fury that he rose, roared, gesticulated, waved his whip and four or five Lords held him down by the tail of his coat to prevent his flying on somebody ... While he [Lord Mansfield] was still speaking the King arrived, but he did not desist even while H.M. was entering the H. of Lords, nor till he approached the throne; and while the King was ascending the steps the hoarse voice of Lord Londonderry was heard crying 'Hear, hear, hear!'

The King from the robing room heard all the noise and asked what it all meant ... the King ought not properly to have worn the crown, never having been crowned; but when he was in the robing room he said to Lord Hastings, 'Lord Hastings, I wear the crown; where is it?' It was brought to him and when Lord Hastings was going to put it on his head he said 'Nobody shall put the crown on my head but myself.' He put it on, and then turned to Lord Grey and said, 'Now my Lord, the coronation is over.' George Villiers said that in his life he never saw such a scene, and as he looked at the King upon the throne with the crown loose upon his head and the tall, grim figure of Ld. Grey close beside him, with the sword of state in his hand, it was as if the King had his Executioner by his side, and the whole picture was strikingly typical of his and our future destinies ...

Upto the moment of the dissolution few people expected it would happen, some thinking the King would not consent, others that the Government would never venture upon it, but the King is weak and the Ministry reckless ... still I see no possibility of arresting the progress of Reform. The Government have made it up with O'Connell which is one mouthful of the dirty pudding they have had to swallow as one of their own friends said of them.

April 26th
Last night at the Queen's ball; heaps of people of all sorts; everybody talking of the elections. Both parties pretend to be confident, but the Government with the best reason. The County Members, as Sefton says, are falling like ninepins ...

[April] 29th
The night before last there was an illumination got up by the foolish Lord Mayor [Sir John Key, whose folly consisted in being a Reform Whig] which of course produced an uproar and a general breaking of obnoxious windows ... A gun (with powder only) was fired over the heads of the mob from Apsley House [Wellington's town house, known as 'Number One London'].

... O'Connell has put forth a proclamation entreating, commanding peace, order and support of the Bill's supporters ... I hear renewed complaints of

Peel, of his selfish, cold, calculating cowardly policy . . . All these things disgust people inconceivably, and it is not the less melancholy that he is our only resource, and his capacity for business and power in H. of Commons places him so far above all his competitors that, mean and shuffling and despicable as he is (in point of heart and sentiment), if we are to have a Conservative Party and if this torrent is resistible, we must look to him alone to lead it.

May 7th

At Newmarket last week. Nothing could go on worse than the elections – Reformers returned everywhere, so much so that the contest is over and we have only to wait the event and see what the H. of Lords will do. In the H. of C. the Bill is already carried.

. . . [the King] is furious with the Lord Mayor at all the riot and uproar the night of the illumination. That night the Queen went to the Ancient Concert, and on her return, the mob surrounded the carriage; she had no guards, and the footmen were obliged to beat them off with their canes to prevent their thrusting their heads into the coach . . . She was in fact terrified and as she detests the whole of these proceedings, the more depressed and disgusted . . .

May 11th

The elections are going on universally in favour of Reform; the great interests in the counties are everywhere broken and old connexions dispersed. In Worcestershire Captain Spencer [Frederick Spencer, captain RN, younger brother of Althorp, Whig leader in the Commons whom Greville at this time detested. Later 4th Earl Spencer.], who has nothing to do with the county and was brought there by his brother-in-law, Ld. Lyttleton, has beat Lygon [later Lord Beauchamp. The Lygons were the dominant family in Worcestershire.], backed by all the wealth of his family; the Manners [ducal family of Rutland] have withdrawn from Leicestershire and Cambridgeshire and Ld. Somerset from Glostershire . . . the state of excitement, doubt and apprehension which prevails will not quickly subside for the battle is only beginning; when the Bill is carried we must prepare for the second act.

May 14th

The elections still going on for Reform. They [the Government] count on a majority of 140 in the H. of C. but the Tories meditate resistance in the H. of L. which it is to be hoped will be fruitless, and it is probable that the Peers will trot round as they did about the Catholic question when it comes to the point.

June 5th

All last week at Fern Hill for the Ascot races: the Chesterfields, Tavistocks, Belfasts, G. Ansons, Montagu, Stradbroke, B. Greville etc. etc. The royal family came to the course the first day with a great cortège – eight coaches-and-four, two Phaetons, pony sociables, led horses etc. – Munster [George FitzClarence, eldest illegitimate son of the King by Dora Jordan, lately elevated to an Earldom], Augustus the parson and Frederick driving phaetons [other of William's eight illegitimate children]. The D. of Richmond was in the King's *caleche* and Lord Grey in one of the coaches. The reception was strikingly cold and indifferent, not half so good as that which the late King used to receive. He was bored to death with the races, and his own horse broke down. On Wednesday he did not come; on Thursday they came again. Beautiful weather and unprecedented multitudes ... Above forty people for dinner for which the room is not nearly large enough –

Very handsome, the dinner not bad, but the room insufferably hot ... He [the King] drinks wine with everybody, asking seven or eight at a time. After dinner he drops asleep. We sat for a short time. Directly after coffee the band began to play; a good band not numerous and principally of violins and stringed instruments ... we walked about with two or three servants carrying lamps to show the proportions, for it was not lit up. The whole thing is magnificent, and the manner of life does not appear to be very formal and need not be disagreeable but for the bore of never dining without twenty strangers ...

No longer George the 4th, capricious, luxurious and misanthropic, liking nothing but the society of listeners and flatterers with the Conyngham tribe and one or two Tory Ministers and Foreign ambassadors; but a plain, vulgar, hospitable gentleman opening his doors to all the world with a frightful Queen and a posse of bastards, [this was later amended to something more polite] a Whig Minister and no foreigners and no toad-eaters at all.

June 10th

We have been occupied these two days at the [Privy] Council Office in providing against the approach of the Cholera morbus. News came that it is got to Riga. We sent for Sir H. Halford and desired him to take some more physicians into consultation with him and make us a report. They reported it was contagious, but (as far as they could judge) not communicable by inanimate matter [cholera is carried by water]. That is the opinion of almost all the foreign practitioners who have considered the subject. We have consequently extended the quarantine to the Baltick and all the Prussian Ports, Hanse Towns etc. But we release goods, confining persons for seven days ... There are disturbances in various parts of the country, great misery in Ireland ...

June 19th

. . . Most of the authorities think it will come, but I doubt it will if it is only to be communicated by contact . . . This topic has now occupied for some days a good deal of the attention of the fine fools of this town, and the Tories would even make it a matter of party accusation against the Government only they don't know exactly how, so they say the Government ought to be impeached if it comes here.

June 23rd

The alarm about the cholera still continues but the Government are thrown into great perplexity by the danger on the one hand of the cholera and the loss on the other to trade.

June 25th

J. Russell brought his Bill in last night in, a good speech as his friends, and a dull one as his enemies, say . . . Lord Grey passed a very fine eulogium upon Lord Ponsonby [John Ponsonby, 2nd Baron, later 1st Viscount Minister at Buenos Aires 1826–8, Rio de Janeiro 1828–30, Brussels 1830–31, Naples 1831 then Constantinople 1832–7, Viscount 1839, ambassador to Vienna 1846–50]. However this was necessary as he is going as Minister to Naples, not having a guinea.

July 3rd

. . . The Reform Bill came on again last night, but it no longer excites much interest.

July 5th

. . . Lord Grey sent for me yesterday morning to talk over the coronation, for in consequence of what the D. of Wellington said in the H. of Lords the night before, he thinks there must be one. The object is to make it shorter and cheaper than the first which occupied a whole day and cost £240,000.

July 8th

Second reading carried at five in the morning by 136 majority, somewhat greater than the Opposition had reckoned on . . . People are beginning to recover from their terror of the cholera seeing that it does not come and that we are beset with alarms of a different kind, which are those of the Scotch merchants for their cargoes. All evidence proves that goods are not capable of bringing in the disorder, but we have appointed a Board of Health which is contagionist and we can't get them to subscribe to that opinion.

We don't dare act without its sanction, and we are obliged to air goods. This airing requires more ships and lazarets than we have, and the result is a perpetual squabbling, disputing and complaining between the Privy Council, the Admiralty, the Board of Health and the merchants . . .

July 10th

They have made a fine business of Cobbett's trial; [an article in his *Political Register* was the foundation of a charge of 'publishing a libel with the intention of raising discontent in the minds of labourers in husbandry'. The jury divided ten for conviction two for acquittal, and after fifteen hours were discharged.]; his insolence and violence were past endurance, but he made a fine speech . . . There is a fresh access of alarm on account of the cholera which has broken out at Petersburg and will probably spread over Germany . . . The Board of Health are however in great alarm and the authorities generally think we shall have it. From all I can observe from the facts of the case I am convinced that the liability to contagion is greatly diminished by the influence of sea air, for which reason I doubt it will be brought here across the water.

July 14th

The effects of Peel's leaving the party to shift for itself were exhibited the night before last. He went away (there was no reason why he should not, except he should have staid to *manage* the debate and keep his people in order), and the consequence was they went on in a vexatious squabble of repeated adjournments till eight o'clock in the morning when the Government at last beat them. The Opposition dwindled down to twenty-five people, headed by Stormont, Tullamore and Brudenell [later Lord Cardigan, distinguished for leading the charge of the Light Brigade](Three asses) while Government kept 180 together to the last . . .

   After these two nights it is impossible not to consider the Tory party as having ceased to exist for all the practical and legitimate ends of political association – that is as far as the House of Commons is concerned where, after all, the battle must be fought. There is still a rabble of Opposition, tossed about by every wind of folly and passion and left to the vagaries and eccentricities of Wetherell or Attwood or Sadler[3] or the intemperate zeal of such weak fanaticks as the three Lords [all three sat in the Commons as holders of courtesy or Irish titles] above mentioned . . .

July 20th

. . . Then went to St James's and had the Council, at which the King made a little speech to the effect that he would be crowned to satisfy the tender consciences of those who thought it necessary, but that he thought it his duty (as this country, in common with every other, was labouring under distress) to make it as economical as possible . . . The other day Long Wellesley [a rascally member of the Duke of Wellington's family],[4] carried off his daughter, a ward in Chancery, from her guardians and secreted her. The matter came up before the Chancellor who sent for Wellesley. He came and refused to give her up; so he committed him to the Fleet Prison. The matter was brought up next day before the H. of C. and referred to their committee of Privileges; and in the meantime Brougham has been making a great splutter about his authority and his Court, both on the Judicial bench and from the Woolsack . . .

Halford has been with me this morning gossiping (which he likes); he gave me an account of Charles I's head to which he was directed by Wood's *Athenae Oxonienses*. He says that they found Henry VIII's coffin, but that the air had penetrated and the body had been reduced to a skeleton, but by his side was Jane Seymour's coffin untouched, and he has no doubt her body is perfect . . . He says Charles's head was exactly as Vandyke had painted him.

July 26th

Fresh alarms have been raised about Cholera morbus. A man at Port Glasgow insists upon it without much apparent reason that it prevails there; so we have sent a medical man there in order to quiet people's minds and set the question at rest. Lord Grey who is credulous, believes the Glasgow man's story and spread the news in his own family who immediately dispersed it over the rest of the town, and yesterday nobody could talk of anything else; not believing it very much and not understanding it at all, for if they did they would not be so flippant.

July 31st Oatlands

The Arbuthnots, [Charles Arbuthnot, known as Gosh, a Minister in the Government of Wellington, his close friend. His wife Harriet, an uncritical admirer of the Duke, left a diary giving the Ultra Tory view of this period], Mr Loch [James Loch, an economist and MP]; walked for an hour and a half with Arbuthnot under the shade of one of the great trees, talking of various old matters and some new, principally about Canning, and his disputes and differences with the Duke of Wellington . . . Originally the King could not bear C. and he was only persuaded by the Duke to take him into the Cabinet . . . Not very long after Canning got into favour, and in this way:- Harriet Wilson,[5] at the time of her connexion with Lord Ponsonby [see 25 June 1831] got hold of some of Lady Conyngham's [see 20 August 1830] letters to him, and she wrote to Ponsonby threatening unless he gave her a large sum, to come to England and publish everything she could. This produced dismay among all the parties, and they wanted to get Ponsonby away and silence the woman. In this dilemma Knighton [see *supra*] advised the King to have recourse to Canning who saw the opening to favour, jumped at it, and instantly offered to provide for Ponsonby and anything which could relieve the King from trouble. Ponsonby was sent to Buenos Ayres forthwith and the letters were bought up. From this time Canning grew in favour which he took every means to improve and shortly gained complete ascendancy over the King ... Knighton behaved exceedingly well during the King [George IV]'s illness, and by the vigilant watch he kept over the property of various kinds prevented the pillage which Lady Conyngham would otherwise have made. She knew everything, but did not much trouble herself about affairs, being chiefly intent upon amassing money and collecting jewels ...

Long Wellesley has given up his daughter and has been released from the Fleet. I met the Solicitor-General yesterday who told me that Brougham had been in the midst of his blustering, terribly nervous about it, ...

We had a meeting on the Coronation business yesterday morning and took into consideration the estimates. That from the Chamberlain's Office was £70,000 and upwards which was referred to a sub-committee to dissect and report upon.

[*August*] *9th Tuesday*

On Sunday overtaken by the worst storm I ever saw – flashes of lightening, crashes of thunder and the rain descending the waterspout – I rode to Windsor to settle with the Queen what sort of Crown she would have to be crowned in. I was ushered into the King's presence who was sitting at a red velvet table in G. 4th's sitting room, looking over the flower garden. A picture of Adolphus FitzClarence was behind him (at full length), and one of the parson, the Rev. Augustus FitzC., [illegitimate children of William] in a Greek dress opposite ...

... She [the Queen] looked at the drawings, meant to be civil in her ungracious way to me, and said she would have none of our crowns, that she did not like to wear a hired crown, and asked me if I thought it right that she should. I said 'Madam, I can only say that the late King wore one at his coronation.' However she said 'I do not like it and I have got jewels enough, so I will have them made up myself.' The King said 'Very well then *you* will have to pay for the setting' (to me). 'Oh no' she said 'I shall pay for it all myself.'

[*August*] *11th*

... Nothing remarkable in the H. of C. but John Russell's declaration that 'this Bill would not be final if it was not found to work as well as the people desired', which is sufficiently impudent considering that hitherto they have always pretended that it was to be final and that it was made so comprehensive only that it might be so; and this has been one of their grand arguments, and now we are never to sit down and rest, but go on changing until we get a good fit, and that for a country which won't stand still to be measured. Harding, whom I found at dinner at the Atheneum yesterday, told me he was convinced that a revolution in this country was inevitable; and such is the opinion of others who support this Bill, not because they think concession will avert it, but will let it come with more gradually and with less violence ... God knows how it will all end. There has been but one man for many years past to arrest this torrent, and that was Canning; and for him the Tories – idiots that they were, and never discovered that he was their best friend – hunted to death with their besotted and ignorant hostility.

[August] 12th

Yesterday a Committee of Council to settle the coronation and submit the estimates which we brought under £30,000 instead of £240,000 which they were last time ...

Goodwood August 20th

Here I have been a week today for the races, and here I should not be now – if it were not for the gout which has laid me fast by the foot, owing to a blow. While on these racing expeditions I never know anything of politics, and though I just read the newspapers, have no anecdotes to record of Reform or foreign affairs ... The Duke [of Richmond] who has so strangely become a Cabinet Minister in a Whig Government and who is a very good sort of man and my excellent friend, appears here to advantage, exercising a magnificent hospitality, and as a sportsman, a Farmer, a Magistrate and good, simple, unaffected Country gentleman with great personal influence. This is what he is fit to be,

> 'With safer pride content
> The wisest Justice on the Banks of (Trent)'

And not to assist in settling Europe and making new constitutions ...

Stoke August 28th

... The King did a droll thing the other day. The ceremonial of the coronation was taken down to him for approval. The homage is first done by the Spiritual Peers with the Archbishop at their head. The first of each class (the Archbishop for the Spiritual) say the words, then they all kiss his cheek in succession. He said he would not be kissed by the Bishops and ordered that part to be struck out. As I expected, the Prelates would not stand it; the Archbishop remonstrated, the King knocked under, and so he must undergo the salute of the Spiritual as well as the Temporal Lords.

[August] 30th

In the evening a large party discoursed. Talleyrand ... He talked ... Of Madame de Staël and Monti; – they met at Madame de Marescalchi's Villa near Bologna and were profuse of compliments and admiration for each other. Each brought a copy of their respective works beautifully bound to present to each other. After a day passed in exchange of literary flatteries and the most ardent expressions of delight, they separated, but each forgot to carry away the present of the other, and the books remain in Madame de Marescalchi's library to this day.

August 31st

... Another Coronation committee yesterday, and, thank God, the last, for this business is the greatest of all bores. There is a furious squabble between the Great Chamberlain and the Earl Marshal (who is absent and has squabbled by deputy) about the former's box in Westminster Abbey. At the last coronation K.G IV gave Lord Gwydir *his* box in addition to his own, and now Lord Cholmondeley claims a similar box. This is resisted. The present King disposes of his own box (and will probably fill it with every sort of *cannaile*); the Lords won't interfere, the Grand Chamberlain protests and says he has been shamefully used, and there the matter stands. The Grand Chamberlain is in the wrong.

September 5th

At Gorhambury since Saturday; the Harrowbys, Bathursts, F. Lewises, Lady Jersey, Mahon, Lushington, Wortleys; rather agreeable and lively; all anti-Reformers, so no quarrelling about that, though Lord Harrowby is ready to squabble with anybody either way, but furiously against the Bill ... Read at Gorhambury *The Custom of the Country*[6] and the most indecent play I should think in any language ...

September 17th

The coronation went off well, and whereas nobody was satisfied before it everybody was after it. No events of consequence. The cholera has got to Berlin and Warsaw is taken by the Russians, who appear to have behaved with moderation ... It is remarkable that the common people at Berlin are impressed with the same strange belief that possessed those of Petersburg, that they have been poisoned and Chad [George Chad, British ambassador to Prussia] writes today that they believe that there is no such disease and that the deaths ascribed to the malady are produced by poison administered by the doctors who are bribed for this purpose; that the rich, finding the poor becoming too numerous to be conveniently governed, have adopted this mode of thinning the population which was performed with success by the English in India; that the foreign Doctors are the Delegates of a central Committee which is formed in London and directs the proceedings ...

In the meantime Reform, which had subsided into a calm for some time past, is approaching its termination in the H. of Commons and as it gets nearer the period of a fresh campaign and a more arduous, though shorter one, agitation is a little reviving. *The Times* and other violent newspapers are moving heaven and earth to stir up the country and intimidate the Peers, many of whom are frightened enough already . . .

There was a dinner of (eight I understand) at Apsley H. yesterday; the cabinet of Opposition, to discuss matters before having a general meeting (at the Duke's dinner there were sixteen or seventeen, all the chief anti-Reformers of the peers. They agreed to oppose the second reading. Dudley who was there told me it was tragedy first and farce afterwards; for Eldon and Kenyon who had dined with the Duke of Cumberland, came in after dinner. Chairs were placed for them on either side of the Duke, and after he had explained to them what they had been discussing and what had been agreed upon, Kenyon made a long speech on the first reading of the Bill in which it was apparent that he was very drunk for he talked exceeding nonsense but Eldon sense. Dudley said that it was not that they were drunk as Lords and gentlemen sometimes are, but they were drunk like Porters). Lyndhurst was not there tho' invited. He dined at Holland House [the great Whig salon, presided over by Lady Holland, wife of a member of the Cabinet]. It is pretty clear though that he will vote for, for his wife is determined that he shall . . .

Newmarket October 1st

Came here last night to my great joy to get holydays and leave Reform and cholera and politics for racing and its amusements . . . On Monday the battle begins in the H. of L. and upto this time nobody knows how it will go, each party confident, but opinion generally in favour of the Bill being thrown out.

Riddlesworth October 10th . . .

Yesterday morning the newspapers (all in black) announced the defeat of the Reform Bill by a majority of forty-one at seven o'clock on Saturday morning after five nights' debating. By all accounts the debate was a magnificent display and incomparably superior to that in the H. of Commons, but the reports convey no idea of it. The great speakers on either side:- Lords Grey, Lansdowne, Goderich, Plunket, the Chancellor and Ld. Grey in reply, for the Bill; against it, Ld. Wharncliffe (who moved the amendment), Harrowby, Carnarvon, Dudley, Wynford and Lyndhurst. The Duke of Wellington's speech was exceedingly bad; he is in fact, and has proved it in repeated instances, unequal to argue a great constitutional question. He has neither the command of language, the power of reasoning, nor the knowledge requisite for such an effort . . . the Chancellor is said to have surpassed all his former exploits, Lyndhurst to have been nearly as good and Lord Grey very great in reply . . . The majority was much greater than anybody expected, and it is to be hoped may be productive of good by showing the necessity of a compromise; for no Minister can make sixty Peers which Ld. Grey must do to carry this Bill; it would be to create another House of Lords ...

It may be hoped too that the apathy of the capital may have some effect in the country though the Unions [the Political Unions, with that of Birmingham led by Thomas Attwood, as their model which, with middle- and working-class participation, represented the first stirrings of democratic political organisation] which are so well disciplined and under the controul [sic] of their orators, will be sure to make a stir.

[*October*] *12th*

The Reformers appear to have rallied their spirits ... Ebrington's[7] resolution of confidence was carried by a great majority in the H. of C. after some violent speeches from Macaulay, [Thomas Babington Macaulay, historian] Shiel,[8] and O'Connell ... Such men as these care nothing into what state the country is thrown, for all they want is a market to which to bring their talents; but how the Miltons, Tavistocks, Althorps [all reformist heirs to great titles and estates: Fitzwilliam, Bedford and Spencer respectively] and all who have a great stake in the country can run the same course is more than I can conceive or comprehend. Party is indeed, as Swift says, 'the madness of many' when carried to its present pitch. In the meantime the Conservative party[9] are as usual committing blunders, which will be fatal to them. Lord Harrowby was to have moved yesterday a resolution pledging the House to take into consideration early in the next session the acknowledged defects in the representation with a view to make such ameliorations in it as might be consistent with the constitution. This will not be done because the Duke of Wellington objects ...

I can conceive no greater misfortune at this moment than such a disunion of that party, and to have its deliberations ruled by the obstinacy and prejudices of the Duke. He is a great man in little things, but a little man in great matters – I mean in civil affairs; in those mighty questions which embrace enormous and various interests and considerations and to comprehend which great knowledge of human nature, great sagacity, coolness and impartiality are required, he is not fit to govern and direct. [Reflecting on this comment in 1838, Greville asked himself if he had been unfair, answering 'On the whole I think not. He is not, nor ever was, a little man in anything, great or small; but I am persuaded that he has committed great political blunders though with the best and most patriotic intentions, and that his conduct throughout the Reform contest was one of the greatest and most unfortunate of them.']

[*October*] *14th*

The Town continues quiet; the country nearly so. The press strain every nerve to produce excitement, and *The Times* has begun an assault on the Bishops whom it has marked out for vengeance and deprivation for having[10] voted against the Bill . . .

I believe these measures [the Reform Bill] to be full of danger, but that the manner in which they have been introduced, discussed, defended and supported is more dangerous still. The total unsettlement of men's minds, the bringing into contempt of all the institutions which have hitherto been venerated, the aggrandisement of the power of the people, the embodying and recognition of popular authority, the use and abuse of the King's name, the truckling to the press are things so subversive of Government, so prejudicial to order and tranquillity, so encouraging to sedition and disaffection that I do not see the possibility of the country settling down . . .

A thousand mushroom orators and politicians have sprung up all over the country, each big with his own ephemeral importance and every one of whom fancies himself fit to govern the nation. Among them are some men of active and powerful minds, and nothing is less probable than that these spirits of mischief and misrule will be content to subside into their original nothingness and retire after the victory into the obscurity from which they emerged.

Newmarket October 23rd

Nothing but racing all this week; Parliament has been prorogued and all is quiet. The world seems tired and requires rest. How soon it will all begin again God knows, but it will not be suffered to sleep long.

London November 11th

Nothing written for a long time; racing; went after the second October meeting to Euston and from thence to Horsham, returned to Newmarket, was going to Felbrigg, but came to town on Tuesday last (the 8th) on account of the cholera which has broken out at Sunderland.

The country was beginning to slumber after the fatigues of Reform when it was rattled up by the business of Bristol [riots set off by the appearance of its Recorder, Sir Charles Wetherell, who had insulted the poorer freeholders of that city in the House of Commons. It lasted for some days, was destructive of property but not of the lives of citizens until extreme military measures produced the results, Greville reports] which for brutal ferocity and wanton, unprovoked violence may vie with some of the worst scenes of the French Revolution . . . it was a premature out-breaking of the thirst for plunder and longing after havoc and destruction which is the essence of Reform in the minds of the mob . . . nothing could exceed the ferocity of the populace, the imbecility of the magistracy or the good conduct of the troops. More punishment was inflicted by them than has been generally known and some hundreds were killed or severely wounded by the sabre. One body of dragoons pursued a rabble of colliers into the country and covered the fields and roads with the bodies of wounded wretches, making a severe example of them . . .

The Bristol business has done some good, inasmuch as it has opened people's eyes (at least so it is said), but if we are to go on as we do, with a mob-ridden Government and a foolish King who renders himself subservient to all the wickedness and folly of his Ministers, where is the advantage of having people's eyes open when seeing they will not perceive, and hearing they will not understand?

Nothing was wanted to complete our situation but the addition of physical evil to our moral plague, and that is come in the shape of the cholera which broke out at Sunderland a few days ago . . . Lord Lansdowne who is President of the Council, an office which for once promises not to be a sinecure, has taken the opportunity to go to Bowood [country house and estate of the Lansdownes] and having come up (sent for express) on account of the cholera the day it was officially declared really to be that disease, he has trotted back to his house in the country . . .

One good will be accomplished let what will happen, for much of the filth and misery of the town will be brought to light, and the condition of the poorer and more wretched of the inhabitants can hardly fail to be ameliorated . . . At Sunderland they say there are houses with 150 inmates who are huddled five and six in a bed. They are in the lowest state of poverty. The sick in these receptacles are attended by an apothecary's boy who brings them (or I suppose tosses them) medicines without distinction or enquiry.

I saw Lord Wharncliffe [with Lord Harrowby one of the leading Waverers, a group of Tory peers who proposed a compromised, weaker Reform Bill] last night, just returned from Yorkshire; gives a bad account of the state of the public mind; he thinks that there is a strong revolutionary spirit abroad . . .

Saturday November 19th Roehampton

Yesterday morning I called on Lord Wharncliffe [who] proceeded to give me the following account of what had passed:- A short time ago Palmerston [a member of the Whig Cabinet] spoke to his son, John Wortley, and expressed a desire that some compromise could be effected between the Government and Opposition leaders which John imparted to Lord Harrowby and his father. The overture was so well received by them that Stanley [Edward Stanley, another member of the Cabinet] went to Sandon, Lord Harrowby's place in Staffordshire . . . the two fathers and two sons discussed the matter and came to a sort of general resolution as to the basis on which they would treat which they drew up and which Wharncliffe read to me. It was moderate, temperate, embraced ample concessions and asserted the necessity of each party refraining from demanding of the other what was so pledged as to be unable to concede without dishonour. On Wharncliffe's return to town, he again saw Palmerston [who] suggested that if Government really desired this, it would be better that

Wharncliffe should see Lord Grey himself on the subject. Palmerston told Lord Grey who assented and gave Wharncliffe a rendezvous at East Sheen on Wednesday last ... when they seem to have come to a good understanding as to the principles on which they should treat.

On parting, Grey shook hands with him twice and told him he had not felt so much relieved for a long time. The next day, Lord Grey made a minute of the conversation which he submitted to the Cabinet; they approved of it [Greville's wishful thinking] ... The terms are not settled, but the general basis agreed upon seems to be this: the concession [by the Tory peers] of Schedule A[11] of representatives to the great towns and a great extension of the County representation on one side; the abandonment, or nearly so, of Schedule B, such an arrangement with regard to the £10 qualification[12] as shall have the effect of a higher rate and an understanding that the manufacturing interest is not to have preponderating influence in the country representation ... Such is the history of this curious transaction which affords a triumphant justification of the course which the Opposition adopted; ... it is likewise a great homage rendered to character, for Wharncliffe has neither wealth, influence nor superior abilities nor even popularity with his own party.

He is a spirited, sensible, zealous, honourable, consistent Country gentleman; their knowledge of his moderation and integrity induced Ministers to commit themselves to him and he will be in all probability enabled to render an essential service to his country ... Beside the prospect of a less objectionable Bill, an immense object is gained in the complete separation of the Ministry from the subversive party, for their old allies, the radicals will never forgive them for this compromise with the anti-Reformers, and they [Ministers] have no alternative but to unite with those who call themselves the Conservative Party against the rebels, republicans associators and all the disaffected in the country ...

[November] 22nd

... My satisfaction was yesterday considerably dampened by what I heard of the pending negotiations concerning Reform. Agar Ellis[13] at Roehampton talked with great doubt of its being successful which I attributed to his ignorance of what had passed, but I fear it is from his knowledge that the Government mean, in fact, to give up nothing of importance ... Richmond is exceedingly dissatisfied himself, for he has always been the advocate of the aristocratic interest in the Cabinet, and he has battled to make the Bill less obnoxious to it ... I always dreaded that Wharncliffe, however honest and well meaning, had not calibre enough to conduct such a negotiation and might be misled by his vanity. Accordingly he is 'dans la gloire de Nike' as they say and bustles about the town, chattering away to all the people he meets and I fear is both ignorant himself of what he is about and involuntarily deceiving others too; he is in a fool's paradise ...

The cholera which is going on (but without greatly extending itself at Sunderland) has excited an universal alarm which is now beginning to subside ... On Friday last, we despatched Dr Barry [Dr (later Sir) David Barry, who had witnessed cholera in St Petersburg, Deputy-Inspector of Hospitals from 1831] down to Sunderland with very ample powers and to procure information which it is very difficult to get ...

November 23rd

Dr Barry's first letter from Sunderland came yesterday in which he declares the identity of the disease with the cholera he had seen in Russia. He describes some cases he had visited, exhibiting scenes of misery and poverty far exceeding what one could have believed it possible to find in this country; but we who float on the surface of society know but little of the privations and sufferings which pervade the mass. I wrote to the Bishop of Durham, to the Chief Magistrates and sent down £200 to Colonel Creagh (which Althorp immediately advanced) to relieve the immediate and pressing cases of distress.

Saw George Bentinck [Lord George Cavendish-Bentinck, younger son of the Duke of Portland][14] in the afternoon who confirmed my apprehension that Wharncliffe had been cajoled into a negotiation which Government intended should end by getting all they want. Richmond, Grey and Palmerston were in a minority of three in the Cabinet for putting off the meeting of Parliament.[15] One of the most radical of the cabinet is Goderich [now allied with Grey]. Such a thing it is to be of feeble intellect and character, and yet he is a smart speaker and an agreeable man ...

[November] 28th

... The Duke of Wn. has written again to Wharncliffe declining altogether to be a party to any negotiation. De Ros told me that he never saw such a letter as Peel's – so stiff, dry and reserved, just like the man in whom great talents are so counteracted and almost made mischievous by the effects of his cold, selfish, calculating character ... There seems to be a constant sort of electrical[16] reciprocity of effort between us and France just now. The 'Three Days' [of May 1830] produced much of our political excitement, and our Bristol business has been acted with great similarity of circumstance at Lyons and is still going on. Talleyrand produced the *Moniteur* last night with the account ... It was begun by workpeople who were very numerous, not political in its objects, but the cries denoted a mixture of everything, as they shouted 'Henry V[17] Napoleon II, La République and Bristol'.

He was at Lady Holland's looking very cadaverous and not very talkative, talked of Madame du Barri[18] that she had been very handsome and retained some remains of beauty up to the period of her death; of Champcerie, of Luckner,[19] who was guillotined, and as the car passed on, the people cried (as they used) 'À la guillotine, À la guillotine!' Luckner turned round and said '*On y va, canaille*'.

[*November*] 30th
. . . Saw Talleyrand last night who said they had better news from Lyons, that there was nothing political in it. News came yesterday morning that the cholera had broken out at Marseilles.

December 3rd
Wharncliffe showed me his correspondence with the Duke of Wellington on this negotiation . . . I was surprised to find with what tenacity the Duke clings to his cherished prejudices and how he shuts his eyes to the signs of the times and the real state of the country. With the points at issue he would never grapple. Wharncliffe argued for concession *because* they have not the means of resistance and that they are in fact at the mercy of their opponents. The Duke admitted the force against them, but thought it would be possible to govern the country without Reform 'if the King was not against them' . . . It seems pretty clear however that he will oppose this Bill just as he did the last, and he will probably have a great many followers; but the Party is broken up, for W[harncliffe] and H[arrowby] will vote for the second reading; the Bishops will generally go with them, and probably a sufficient number of Peers . . . The men who murdered the Italian boy were tried yesterday and convicted on evidence wholly circumstantial but very conclusive. Tindal tried them. [Sir Nicholas Tindal, Chief Justice of the Court of Common Pleas.] When the verdict was announced there was a succession of tremendous shouts from the crowd who surrounded the prison so loud as to interrupt the Recorder while he gave sentence. The men were hardened to the last. A boy uncertainly identified as 'Carlo Ferrair' had been murdered, Burke and Hare-style, for dissection, by two men, John Bishop and Thomas Williams. They were hanged before a crowd of 30,000 on 5 December. [See the recent study *The Italian Boy* by Sarah Wise, Jonathan Cape 2004.]

[*December*] 8th
. . . The cholera is on the decline in Sunderland, but in the meantime our trade will have been put under such restrictions that the greatest embarrassments are inevitable. Intelligence is already come that the Manchester people have curtailed their orders, and many workmen will be out of work . . .

[*December*] 11th
. . . The cholera which for some days appeared to be subsiding at Sunderland has resumed fresh vigour, and yesterday 19 new cases were reported – the greatest number since the beginning (in any one day) – besides two others at

Newcastle.

Tomorrow Reform comes on. Some say that it will be as hotly disputed as ever and that Peel's speeches indicate a bitterness undiminished, but this will not happen. It is clear that the general tone and temper of parties is softened . . .

In the evening

G B [Bentinck] told me this evening of a scene which had been related to him by R[ichmond] that lately took place at a Cabinet dinner; it was very soon after Durham's return from abroad. He was furious at the negotiations and question of compromise . . . After dinner he made a violent *sortie* on Lord Grey (it was at Althorp's), said he would be eternally disgraced if he suffered any alterations to be made in this Bill, that he was a betrayer of the cause and, amongst other things, reproached him with having kept him in town on account of this Bill in the summer, 'and thereby having been the cause of the death of his son'. [Charles Lambton, only son of Durham and thus grandson of Grey][20] . . . They [Cabinet members present] thought it was quite certain that Durham would resign the next morning . . . However Durham did not resign; he absented himself for some days from the Cabinet and at last returned as if nothing had happened, and there he goes on as usual . . .

[December] 13th

John Russell brought on his Bill last night in a very feeble speech, a great change is apparent since the last Bill. The House was less full and a softened and subdued state of temper and feeling were evinced. Peel made an able and bitter speech, though perhaps not a very judicious one . . . In fact, Peel is now aware (as everybody else is) of the enormous fault that was committed in not throwing [the Bill] out at once before the press had time to operate and rouse the country to the pitch of madness it did.[21]

Met Melbourne [William Lamb, Viscount Melbourne, Home Secretary] at Ld. Holland's; they were talking of a reported confession to a great extent of murders, which is said to have been begun and not finished, by the Burkers, or by one of them. Melbourne said it was true, that he began the confession about the murder of a black man to a Dissenting Clergyman, but was interrupted by the ordinary [prison chaplain]. Two of a trade could not agree and the man of the Established Church preferred that the criminal should die unconfessed, and the public uninformed, rather than the Dissenter extract the truth. Since writing this I see Hunt put a question to G. Lamb [George Lamb, Melbourne's brother and under-secretary] on this point, and he replied that he knew of no other confessions – a lie. I have heard, but on no authority, that some surgeons are so disagreeably implicated that they chuse to conceal these horrors.

[December] 20th

The second reading of the Bill was carried at one o'clock on Saturday night by a majority of two to one and ended very triumphantly for Ministers who are proportionally elated and their opponents equally depressed ... [Stanley] shone the more from Peel's making a very poor exhibition. He had been so nettled by Macaulay's sarcasms the night before on his tergiversation, that he went into the whole history of the Catholic question [see Vol. I, 1829] and his conduct on that occasion which beside savouring of the egotism with which he is so much and justly reproached, was uncalled for and out of place.

1832

Panshanger January 1st

Here since Thursday. Luttrell, Melbourne, F. Lamb. Nothing new. Went all over the Jail yesterday which is admirably kept. There are four treadmills where they work – that is those who are condemned to hard labour; 130 prisoners, the greatest number there has been for a long time, but there is more poaching by a great deal since the new Game Bill and more dissoluteness and idleness since the Beer Bill. So much for legislative amelioration, but some deny that the effects proceed from the causes. The treadmill has failed to reform or terrify the prisoners, but the Jailer assured us (Luttrell, Eden and me) that private whipping was the most effectual mode of punishment, what they dreaded most – private better than public because no disgrace attaches to it, and it hurts. The prison allowance varies with different classes of offenders and with those who labour and those who do not. The lowest have two pounds of bread, soup three times a week and milk-porridge every morning. The prisoners were remarkably healthy, their cells were warm and dry; the Jailer attributes their health to the lowness of their diet ... There has been but one execution for a long time – last year a young man was hanged for copulating with a cow ... in this case the evidence was only circumstantial and the man was reprieved, and at the end of a fortnight the order came down for his execution.

Distress seems to increase hereabouts and crime with it – Methodism and saintship increase too. The people of this house are an example of the religion of the fashionable world and the charity of natural benevolence which the world has not spoilt. Lady Cowper and her family go to Church, but scandalise the congregation by always arriving half an hour late. The hour matters not; if it began at 9 or 10 or 12 or 1, it would be the same thing. They are never ready and always late – but they go ... Lady Cowper and her daughters inspect personally the cottages and condition of the poor. They visit, enquire and give; they distribute flannel, medicines, money, and they talk to and are kind to them, so that the result is a perpetual stream of flowing from a real fountain of benev-

olence which waters all the country round and gladdens the hearts of the peasantry and attaches them to those from whom it emanates.

Since I came to town I have read all the rest of Juvenal (after the first 6
books), Dryden's translations, Horace's epistles, 4th volume of Hatsell,
[*Precedents of Proceeding in the House of Commons*, four vols, new edition 1818],
some of Gibbon, of Lingard, Dover's *Life of Frederick*, various scraps . . . I begin
the New Year with a firm resolution to read a great deal more . . .

Gorhambury [*January*] 7th . . .

Had a conversation with Lady Cowper before I came away; between Palmerston,
Frederick Lamb and Melbourne; she knows everything, and is a furious anti-
Reformer . . . Palmerston and Melbourne, particularly the latter, are now heartily
ashamed of the part they have taken about Reform. They detest and abhor the
whole thing, and they find themselves unable to cope with the violent party
. . . I told her that nothing could justify their conduct and their excuses were
good for nothing; but that there was no use in resigning now . . . As to Lord
Grey, it is exceedingly difficult to understand his real sentiments and to reconcile his present conduct with the general tenor of his former professions, that
he was averse to so violent a measure I have no doubt — his pride and aristocratic principles would naturally make him so — but he is easily governed,
constantly yielding to violence and intimidation . . .

London [*January*] 20th Friday

. . . Yesterday morning he [Wharncliffe] came to me again, very desponding.
He had found Harrowby in a state of despair, uncertain what he should do and
looking upon the game as lost, and he had been with the Duke of Wellington
who was impenetrably obstinate, declaring that nothing should prevent his
opposing a Bill which he believed in his conscience to be pregnant with certain
ruin to the country . . . he was resolved to do his utmost to throw it out
without regard to consequences.

In the evening went to Lady Harrowby's where I found him and Haddington.
We staid there until nearly two, after which Wharncliffe and I walked up and
down Berkeley Square. He was in much better spirits having had a long conversation with these two Lords, both of whom, he said, were now resolved to sail
along with him, and he contemplates a regular and declared separation from
the Duke *upon this question*. In the morning he had seen Lyndhurst who appeared
very undecided and rather leaning toward the Duke, but I endeavoured to
persuade him that Lyndhurst was quite sure to adopt on consideration the line
which appeared most conducive to his own interest . . . that with him consistency, character and high feelings of honour and patriotism were secondary
considerations; that he relied upon his great talents to render himself necessary to an administration . . . if other people are made to understand that they

can separate from the Duke *on this occasion* without offending or quarrelling with him or throwing off their general allegiance to him as their Political Leader, many will be inclined to do so ... On the whole, things look as well as such an infernal thing can look.

[*January*] 25th

We met at Ld. Harrowby's last night – Wharncliffe, Harrowby, Haddington and Sandon – and I found their minds were quite made up. Wharncliffe is to present a petition from Hull, and to take that opportunity of making his declaration, and the other two are to support him ... Ld. Harrowby saw the Archbishop who would not pledge himself, but appeared well disposed and they think they can count upon nine Bishops ... News came last night that the cholera had got within three miles of Edinbro, and to show the fallacy of any theory and the inutility of the prescribed precautions, at one place (Newport I think), one person in five of the whole population was attacked though there was no lack of diet, warmth and clothing for the poor ...

February 4th

Called on Lord Harrowby in the morning; found him in very bad spirits as well he might be, for all the invitations he had written to peers, he had received either refusals or no reply, so he augurs ill of their attempt. Carnarvon and Talbot refused; these besotted, predestinated Tories *will* follow the Duke; the Duke *will* oppose all Reform because he said he would ...

[*February*] 6th

Dined yesterday with Lord Holland; came very late, found a vacant place between Sir George Robinson and a common looking man in black. As soon as I had time to look at my neighbour, I began to speculate (as one usually does) as to who he might be, and as he did not for some time open his lips except to eat, I settled that he was some obscure man of letters or medicine, perhaps a cholera Doctor ... [One] remark and the manner of it gave me the notion that he was a dull fellow, for it came out in a way which bordered on the ridiculous, so as to excite something like a sneer ... having thus settled my opinion, I went on eating my dinner when Auckland [George Eden][1] who was sitting opposite to me, addressed my neighbour, 'Mr Macaulay, will you drink a glass of wine?' I thought I should have dropped off my chair. It was Mr Macaulay, the man I had been so long most curious to see and to hear, whose genius, eloquence, astonishing knowledge and diversified talents have excited my wonder and admiration for such a length of time and here I had been sitting next to him, hearing him talk and setting him down for a dull fellow ...

[*February*] 7th

... Wharncliffe wrote a long and very conciliatory letter to the Duke ... to which the Duke replied by a long letter, written evidently in a very ill-humour and such a galimathias as I never read, angry, ill-expressed and confused, and from which it was difficult to extract anything intelligible but this, 'that he was aware' of the consequences of the course he should adopt himself and wished the H. of Lds to adopt, viz. the same as last year, but that be those consequences what they might, the responsibility would not lie on his shoulders, but on those of the Government; acknowledged that a creation of Peers would swamp the H. of Lds and by so doing destroy the Constitution, but the Government would be responsible, not he, for the ruin that would ensue; that he was aware some Reform was necessary (in so far departing from his former declaration of November 30) but he would neither propose anything himself, nor take this measure, nor try and amend it. In short he will do nothing but talk nonsense, despair and be obstinate ... He really has accomplished being a Prophet in his own country, not from the sagacity of his predilections, but from the blind worship of his devotees ...

[*February*] 13th

On Saturday evening I found Melbourne at the Home Office in his lazy, silent, listening humour, disposed to hear everything and to say very little; told me that Sefton and Dover were continually at the Chancellor to make peers and that they both, particularly the latter, had great influence with him ...

In the evening I got a message from Palmerston to beg I would call on him which I did at the Foreign Office yesterday. He is infinitely more alert than Melbourne and more satisfactory to talk to ... He then talked of the expediency of a declaration from Ld. H., and how desirable it was that it should be made soon and be supported by as many as could be induced to come forward; that Grey had said to him very lately that he really believed he should be obliged to create Peers. I said that my persuasion was that it would be quite unnecessary to do so *to carry the second reading* ... [and] that I could not believe Lord Grey would allow himself to be bullied into it by such despicable means and by the clamour of such men as Duncombe [Sir Thomas Duncombe, Whig MP][2] and O'Connell, urged on by friends of his own. He said this was very true, but the fact was they could not risk the rejection of the Bill again; that he knew from a variety of communications that an explosion would inevitably follow its being thrown out on the second reading ...

In the meantime the cholera has made its appearance in London, at Rotherhithe, Limehouse and in a ship off Greenwich – in all seven cases. These are among the lowest and most wretched classes, chiefly Irish, and a more lamentable exhibition of human misery than that given by the medical men who called at the Council Office yesterday I never heard. They are in the most abject state of poverty, without beds to lie upon. The men live by casual labour, are employed by the hour, and often get no more than four or five hours work in the course of a week ... We have sent down members of the Board of Health to make preparations and organise boards; but if the disease really spreads, no human power can arrest its progress ... when this human misery offers itself to the plague like stubble to the fire.

[*February*] *14th*
... The cholera is established and yesterday formal communications were made to the Lord Mayor and to the Secretary of State for Foreign affairs that London was no longer healthy.

[*February*] *17th*
... The cholera has produced more alertness than alarm here; in fact at present it is a mere trifle — in three days twenty-eight cases. Nothing like the disorders which rage unheeded every year and every day among the lower orders. It is its name, its suddenness and its frightful symptoms which terrify ... A man came yesterday from Bethnal Green with an account of that district. They are all weavers, forming a sort of separate community; there they are born, there they live and labour and there they die. They neither migrate nor change their occupation; they can do nothing else. They have increased in a ratio at variance with any principle of population, having nearly tripled in twenty years from 22,000 to 62,000. They are, for the most part, out of employment and can get none. 1100 are crammed into the poor house, five and six in a bed; 6000 receive parochial relief. The Parish is in debt; every day adds to the number of claimants ... We asked the man who came what could be done for them. He said 'employment' and employment is impossible.

[*February*] *20th*
Ld. Grey was much pleased with the result of his interview and expressed unbounded reliance on Ld. Harrowby's honour ... the Archbishop is with us one day, and then doubts, though I think we shall have him at last ...

By way of an episode, news came last night of an insurrection of the Slaves in Jamaica in which fifty-two plantations had been destroyed. It was speedily suppressed by Willoughby Cotton, [Major Sir Willoughby Cotton, Governor-General 1829–34] and the ringleaders were executed by martial law.

February 23rd
... Melbourne said that the King is more reconciled to the measure [creation of peers to carry the Bill] i.e. that they have got the foolish old man in town and can talk him over more readily. A discussion last night about the propriety of making a declaration today in the H. of Lords when the Duke of Rutland

presents a petition against Reform. The Archbishop will not decide; there is no moving him. Curious that a Dr Howley, the other day Canon of Christ Church, a very ordinary man, should have in his hands the virtual decision of one of the most momentous matters that ever occupied public attention. There is no doubt that his decision would decide the business so far. Up to this time certainly Harrowby and Wharncliffe have no certainty of sufficient number for the second reading; but I think they will have enough at last.

[*February*] *24th*

... As the business develops itself and the time approaches communication becomes more open and frequent; the Tories talk with great confidence of their majority, and the Ultra Whigs are quite ready to believe them; the two extreme ends are furious. Our list upto this day presents a result of forty-three votes and thirty-seven doubtful, out of which it is hard to see a majority cannot be got. I have no doubt now they will take a very early opportunity of making a declaration. Peel in the other House is doing what he can to inflame and divide and repress any spirit of conciliation. Nothing is sure in his policy but that it revolves around himself as the centre, and is influenced by some view which he takes of his own future advantage, probably the rallying of the Conservative Party as they calls themselves who are throwing everything into confusion and sinking everything by their obstinacy) and his being at the head of it. He made a most furious and mischievous speech two nights ago and was cheered with enthusiasm by his followers.

February 29th

... My old aversion for the High Tories returns when I see their conduct on this occasion. The obstinacy of the Duke, the selfishness of Peel, the pert vulgarity of Croker and the incapacity of the rest are set in constant juxtaposition with the goodness of the cause they are defending but which they will mar by their way of defending it. A man is wanting, a fresh man with vigour enough to govern and who will rally round him the temperate and the moderate of different parties – men unfettered by prejudices, connexions and above all by pledges ...

March 9th

Went to Lord Holland's the other night and had a violent battle with him on politics. Nobody so violent as he and curious as exhibiting the opinions of the Ultras of the party. About making peers – wanted to know what Harrowby's real object was. I told him none but to prevent what he thought an enormous evil.

What did it signify (he said) whether peers were made now or later? That the present House of Lords never could go on with a Reformed Parliament, it being opposed to all the wants and wishes of the people, hating the abolition of tithes, the press and the French Revolution and that to make it harmonise with the Reformed Parliament it must be amended by an infusion of a more liberal cast ... what he means ... is to add some fifty or sixty men who may be willing to accept peerages upon the condition of becoming a bodyguard to this Government ...

[*March*] *26th*

Ten days since I have written anything here ... The events have been the final passing of the Bill [in the Commons] after three nights debate by a majority of 116, ended by a very fine speech from Peel who has eminently distinguished himself through this fight. It is a pity he is such a man ... The conduct of the Ultra Tories has been so bad and so silly that I cannot wish to bring them in, though I have a very great desire to turn the others out. As to a moderate party, it is a mere dream for where is the moderation?

This day John Russell brings his Bill into the H. of Lords, and much indeed depends upon what passes there. Harrowby and Wharncliffe will make their speeches and we shall, I conclude, have the Duke and Lord Grey ... I should not fear Harrowby but that he is petulant and sour; Wharncliffe is vain and has been excited in all this business, though with very good and disinterested motives, but he cannot bear the abuse and the ridicule with which both the extreme ends endeavour to cover him ... There was another breeze in the H. of Lords about Irish education, the whole Bench of Bishops in a flame and except Maltby who spoke *for*, all declared against the plan – Philpot [*sic*] [Henry Phillpotts, Bishop of Exeter][3] in a furious speech. What celestial influences have been at work I know not, but certain it is that the world is going mad, individually and collectively. The town has been more pre-occupied with Dudley's extravagances than the affairs of Europe. He in fact, is mad, but is to be cupped and starved and disciplined sound again. The public appetite and love of news is as voracious as a shark and likes, loves best what is grossest and most disgusting; anything relating to personal distress is greedily devoured by the monster ...

As to madness, Dudley has gone mad in his own House, Perceval[4] in the House of Commons, and John Montague in the Park, the two latter preaching, both Irvingites[5] and believers in 'tongues'. Dudley's madness took an odd turn: he would make up all his quarrels with Lady Holland to whom he had not spoken for sixteen years, and he called on her and there were tears and embraces and God knows what. Sydney Smith told her she was bound in honour to set the quarrel up again when he comes to his senses and put things in statu quo ante pacem ...

[*March*] *28th*

There appear to have been as many different opinions as of people in the discussion of the House of Lords when the Bill was brought up, and it seems paradoxical but is true, that though it was on the whole, satisfactory, nobody was satisfied. Lord Grey complained to me that Lord Harrowby was too stiff; Ld. Harrowby complained that Lord Grey was always beating about the bush of compromise, but would never commit himself fairly to concession ... The Ultra Tories are outrageous 'that He [*sic*] gave up everything without reason or cause; the Ultra-Whigs equally furious' that he had shown how little he was disposed to go in Committee; his object was to turn out the Government etc and what is really comical, neither party will believe that Harrowby is so obnoxious to the other party as he is said to be ... If ever there was a man whose conduct was exempt from the ordinary motives of ambition and who made personal sacrifices in what he is doing, it is Lord Harrowby, and yet there is no reproach that is not cast upon him, no term of abuse that is not applied to him, no motive that is not applied to him ...

April 1st

... In the meantime the tone of the other party is changed. Dover who makes lists, manages proxies and does all the little jobbing, whipping-in, busy work of the party, makes out a clear majority, and told me he now thought the Bill would get through without peers. The Government are however all agreed to make the peers if it turns out to be necessary; and especially if the Bill is thrown out, it seems clear that they would by no means go out, but make the peers and bring it in again; so I gather from Richmond and he who is the most violently opposed of the whole Cabinet to peer-making, is now ready to make any number if necessary ...

At the Duchess of Dino's [mistress/companion of Talleyrand] ball the night before last, I had a very curious conversation with Melbourne about it all. He said that 'he really believed there was no strong feeling in the country for the measure ... [and asked] What difficulty can they have in swallowing the rest after they have given up the rotten boroughs? That is, in fact, the essential part of the Bill, and the truth is *I do not see how Government is to be carried on at all without them ...'* These were, if not his exact words, the exact sense, and a pretty avowal for a man to make at the eleventh hour who has been a party concerned in this Bill during the other ten ... Let it end as it may, the history of the Bill and the means by which it has been brought forward, supported and opposed will be most curious and instructive. The division in the Lords must be very close indeed ...

I have refrained for a long time from writing down anything about the cholera because the subject is intolerably disgusting to me and I have been bored past endurance by the perpetual questions of every fool about it. It is not however devoid of interest. In the first place what has happened here proves that 'the people' of this enlightened, reading, thinking, reforming nation are not a whit less barbarous than the serfs in Russia ... The disposition of the public was (and is) to believe that the whole thing was a humbug and accordingly plenty of people were found to write in that sense and the press lent itself to propagate that idea.

The disease however kept creeping on, the Boards of Health which were everywhere established immediately became odious, and the vestries and parishes stoutly resisted all pecuniary demands for the purpose of carrying into effect the recommendation of the Central Board or the Orders of the Privy Council ... there is no end to the scenes of uproar, violence and brutal ignorance that have gone on, and this on the part of the lower orders, for whose benefit all the precautions are taken, and for whose relief large sums have been raised and the resources of charity called into activity in all parts of the town. The awful thing is the vast extent of misery and distress which prevails and the evidence of the rotten foundation on which the whole fabrick of this gorgeous society rests, for I call that rotten which exhibits thousands upon thousands of human beings reduced to the lowest stage of moral and physical degradation ...

Can such a state of things permanently go on? Can any reform ameliorate it? ... it has not always been and it certainly need not be, that the majority of the population should be in great difficulty, struggling to keep themselves afloat, and what is worse, in uncertainty and in doubt whether they can earn subsistence for themselves and their families. Such is the case at present and I believe a general uncertainty pervades every class of society, from the highest to the lowest; nobody looks upon any institution as secure or any interest as safe and it is only because these universal feelings of alarm, which are equally diffused throughout the mass but slightly affect each individual atom of it, that we see the world go on as usual, eating, drinking, laughing and dancing and not insensible to the danger, though apparently indifferent about it.

April 4th

Charles Wood [Secretary to the Prime Minister, later Chancellor of the Exchequer (1846–52) and Viscount Halifax] came to see me yesterday ... principally to get me to speak to Harrowby about a foreseen difficulty. The first clause in the Bill enacts *that fifty-six Boroughs be disfranchised.* This gave great offence in the H. of C. was feebly defended but carried by the majority ... I told him Harrowby had an invincible repugnance to it, and the effect would be very bad if they split upon the first point ... He [Wood] said if that clause was omitted, a suspicion would immediately arise that there was an intention of altering Schedule A ... and it ended by my promising to talk to Lord Harrowby about it. This I did last night and he instantly flew into a rage. He said 'he would not be dragged through the mire by these scoundrels. It was an insolence that was not to be borne; let them make their peers if they would, not Hell itself should make him vote for fifty-six; he would vote for sixty-six or any number but that, that he would not split with the Tories on the first vote; ... if the Government brought this forward, no consideration on earth should prevent his opposing it ...'

[April] 6th

... I saw Wood [Grey's secretary] ... We finally agreed that I should ask Lord H. if Ld. Grey of his own accord proposed to leave out the words *fifty-six*, but with an expression of his own opinion that this must be the number, he, (Lord H.) would meet him with a corresponding declaration that he objected to the specification of the number in the clause without objecting to the extent of the disfranchisement, it being always understood that what passes between us is unauthorised talk and to commit nobody – 'without prejudice' as the lawyers say.

I heard yesterday from Keate who is attending me (and who is the King's surgeon and sees him when he is in town) that he saw H.M. after the Levee on Wednesday, and that he was ill, out of sorts and in considerable agitation; ... that he enquired of him about his health when the K said that he had much to annoy him and that 'many things passed there (pointing to the Cabinet), out of which he had just come which were by no means agreeable and that he had more than usual to occupy him that morning'. Keate said he was very sure from his manner that something unpleasant had occurred. This was, I have since discovered, the question of a creation of peers again brought forward, to which the King's aversion has returned, so much so that it is doubtful that he will consent to a large one. It seems that unless the peers are made (in the event of the necessity arising) Brougham and Althorp will resign ...

[April] 8th

I went to see Sheridan Knowles's [(1784–1862) distant relation of R.B. Sheridan, also a playwright] new play *The Hunchback*, very good and a great success, Miss Fanny Kemble acted really well – for the first time in my opinion, great acting. I have not seen anything since Mrs Siddons (and perhaps Mrs O'Neill) so good.

[April] 9th

Saw Harrowby yesterday morning. He can't make up his mind what is best to be done, whether to go into committee or not. He rather wishes to get through Schedule A, but won't vote against the Tories if they divide on adjourning. Then went to Wood and told him there would be no difficulty about *fifty-six*. Lord Grey came in and talked the whole thing over, list etc. He said he was ill, knocked up – that in his speech today he should be as moderate and tame as anybody could wish . . .

[April] 11th

The day before yesterday Lord Grey introduced the Reform Bill [in the Lords] in a speech of extreme moderation; as promised, it was very 'tame'. The first night's debate was dull; yesterday was better . . . Harrowby spoke well; Wharncliffe ill. Nothing can equal the hot water we have been in – defections threatened on all sides and doubts rising, betting nearly even . . . As to our business, it is 'la mer à boire' with nobody to canvass or whip in, and not being a party . . .

[April] 14th

The Reform Bill (second reading) was carried this morning at seven o'clock in the House of Lords by a majority of nine. The House did not sit yesterday. The night before, against the Bill, Phillpot[ts], the Bishop of Exeter, made a grand speech, full of fire and venom, very able. It would be an injury to compare this man with Laud [William Laud, Charles I's Minister, Archbishop of Canterbury and failed absolutist, executed on attainder 1645]; he more resembles Gardiner [Stephen Gardiner, Catholic Bishop of Winchester and Lord Chancellor under Mary I, an instigator of the burnings of Protestants in that reign]; had he lived in those days he would have been such another, boiling with ambition, an ardent temperament and great talents. He has a desperate and a dreadful countenance, and looks like the man he is.

The last two days gave plenty of reports of changes either way, but the majority has always looked like from seven to ten. The House will adjourn on Wednesday and go into committee after Easter; and in the meantime what negotiations! And what difficulties to get over! The Duke of Wellington and Lord Harrowby have had some good-humoured talk and the former seems well-disposed to join in amending the Bill, but the difficulty will be to bring these extreme and irritated parties to any agreement as to terms. The debate in the Lords, though not so good as last year, has been as usual much better than that in the Commons.

The accounts from Paris of the cholera are awful, very different from here. Is it not owing to our superior cleanliness, draining and precautions? There have been 1300 sick in a day there, and for some days an average of 1000; here we have never averaged above fifty and, except the squabbling in the newspapers, we have seen nothing of it whatever; there many of the upper classes have died of it . . .

[April] 15th

The debate in the H. of Lords was closed by a remarkable reply from Lord Grey, full of moderation and such as to hold out the best hopes of an adjustment of the question – not that it pacified the Ultra Tories who were furious . . . The tone of the violent supporters of Government is totally changed; at Lord Holland's last night they were singing a very different note, and now, if the counsels of the Lords are guided by moderation and firmness, they may deal with the Bill *almost* as they please but they must swallow Schedule A. The difficulties however are great; the High Tories are exasperated and vindictive . . .

The debate on Friday was good but very inferior to the last. Phillpotts got a terrific dressing from Lord Grey, and was handled not very delicately by Goderich and Durham, though the latter was too coarse. He had laid himself very open and, able as he is, he has adopted a tone and style inconsistent with his lawn sleeves, and unusual on the Episcopal Bench. He is carried away by his ambition and his alarm and horrifies his Brethren who feel all the danger (in these times) of such a colleague. The episode of which he was the object was, of course, the most amusing part of the whole.

Newmarket [April] 22nd

Ill and laid up with the gout for this week past. Came here on Friday 20th. The carrying of the second reading seems to have produced no effect. Everybody is gone out of town, the Tories in high dudgeon . . . It is a long time – probably not since the days of Charles II – that this place (Newmarket) has been the Theatre of a political negotiation and concealing the importance of the subject, the actors are amusing – Richmond, Graham [see *supra*], Wharncliffe and myself . . .

London May 12th

Nothing written for a long time, nor had I anything to write until a few days ago. From the time of Wharncliffe's departure I heard nothing but I bitterly regret not having been in town last week. The Committee [stage of the Bill] stood for Monday; on Friday se'ennight I was in Buckenham when the Duke of Rutland told me he was going to London, that they meant to divide on Monday on a proposal to postpone Schedule A and B till after C and D [Schedules C and D listed the redistributions of seats disfranchised for double-seat disfranchisement (Schedule A) and single-seat loss (Schedule B)] . . . On arriving in town . . . I went to Boodle's where I found him [Wharncliffe] and he immediately began his case. He said that on his return to town he saw Lord Grey . . . and he said that there was one point for which Lord Grey should be prepared and that he knew that the Tories were much bent upon proposing the postponement of Schedules A and B. Ld. Grey said that this would be productive of the greatest possible embarrassment, that it would be a thing he could not agree to, and he hoped he would do all in his power to prevent it. Wharncliffe said that he would endeavour, but he believed they were very eager about it . . .

Lyndhurst told him [Wharncliffe] that the Tories were so irrevocably bent upon this and that they were so difficult to manage and so disposed to fly off that it was absolutely necessary to give way to them ... upon which Harrowby and Wharncliffe gave in and agreed to support it. One of them (Haddington, I think) suggested that Wharncliffe ought to communicate this intention to Lord Grey, to which however Lyndhurst objected, said that the Tories were suspicious, had already taken umbrage at the communications between Wharncliffe and Grey, and that it must not be. To this prohibition Wharncliffe, fatally for his own character, submitted and accordingly not a word was said by anybody till the afternoon of the debate, when just before it began Wharncliffe told Richmond who of course told Lord Grey ... The debate came on; the proposition [to postpone the first clause, the one identifying fifty-six seats] was made in a very aggravating speech by Lyndhurst and on its being carried, Lord Grey threw up the Bill and the Government in a passion ...

The day after the debate Grey and Brougham went down to Windsor and proposed to the King to make fifty peers. They took with them a minute of Cabinet signed by all the members except the Duke of Richmond. Palmerston proposed it in Cabinet and Melbourne made no objection. H.M. took till the next day to consider when he accepted their resignations which was the alternative they gave him. At the Levee the same day, nothing occurred; the King hardly spoke to the Duke, but he afterwards saw Lyndhurst (having sent for him). This was not well done, for besides the character of the man which makes him the least fit to form an administration, it was a sort of insult to his ex-Ministers to send at once (?) for the person who had been the immediate instrument in turning them out. I do not know what passed between them, but the Duke of Wellington was soon sent for. The Duke and Lyndhurst endeavoured to prevail on Peel to take the Government upon himself, and the former offered to act in any capacity in which he could be useful, but Peel would not ... When Peel finally declined, the Duke accepted, and yesterday at three o'clock he went to St James's full dressed and kissed hands. [The Duke of Wellington did not ceremonially kiss the King's hands as Prime Minister, something Greville corrects in a footnote, Vol. II, p. 294.] ...

The first act of the Duke was to advise the King to reject the address of the Birmingham Union[6] which he did, said he knew of no such body ...

The position of the respective parties is curious. The Waverers undertook a task of great difficulty with slender means, and they accomplished it with complete success ... but having been in communication with both parties, they have contrived mortally to offend both and to expose themselves to odium from every quarter and to an universal imputation of insincerity and double-dealing ... The Tories, who have exhibited nothing but obstinacy and unreasonableness and who thwarted the Waverers by every means they could devise, have reaped the benefit of their efforts.

The Town is perfectly quiet. What is odd is that the King was hissed as he left London the other day and the Duke cheered as he came out of the palace . . . there will probably be a good deal of bustle and bluster here and elsewhere; but I do not believe in real tumults, particularly when the rabble and the unions know that there is a Government which will not stand such things . . . not but what much dissatisfaction and much disquietude must prevail . . . The Duke's worshippers (a numerous class) call this the finest action of his life, though it is difficult to perceive in what the grandeur of it consists or the magnitude of the sacrifice . . .

Nothing more was known yesterday, but everybody congregated at the clubs, asking discussing and wondering . . . It is supposed this *coup* has been preparing for some time. All the royal family, bastards and all, have been incessantly *at* the King and he has probably had more difficulty in the long run in resisting the constant importunity of his *entourage* and of his womankind particularly, than the dictates of his Ministers . . .

London May 17th Thursday

The events of the last few days have passed with a rapidity which hardly left time to think upon them – such sudden change and transitions from rage to triumph on one side and foolish exaltation to mortification and despair on the other. The first impression was that the Duke of Wellington would succeed in forming a Government with or without Peel. The first thing he did was to try to prevail upon Peel to be Prime Minister, but he was inexorable. He then turned to Baring [Alexander Baring (1774–1848) from the banking family, later created Baron Ashburton] who after much hesitation agreed to be Chancellor of the Exchequer. The work went on but with much difficulty, for neither Peel, not Goulburn nor Croker would take office. They tried the Speaker [Charles Manners-Sutton (1780–1845), later Viscount Canterbury] who was mightily tempted to become Secretary of State but still doubting and fearing, and requiring time to make up his mind. At an interview with the Duke and Lyndhurst at Apsley House he delivered his sentiments on the existing state of affairs in a speech of three hours to the unutterable disgust of Lyndhurst who returned home, flung himself into a chair and said that he would not endure to have anything to do with such a *damned tiresome old bitch* . . .

On [Monday] evening ensued the memorable night in the H. of Commons which everybody agrees was such a scene of violence and excitement as never had been exhibited within those walls . . . The House was crammed to suffocation; every violent sentiment and vituperative expression was received with shouts of approbation, yet the violent speakers were listened to with the greatest attention. Tom Duncombe made one of his blustering Radical harangues which was received with immense applause, but which contrasted with an admirable speech full of dignity, but also of sarcasm and severity from John

Russell – the best he ever made. The conduct of the Duke in taking office *to carry the Bill* which was not denied but which his friends feebly attempted to justify, was assailed with the most merciless severity by moderate men and Tories, such as Inglis [Sir Robert Harry Inglis, an Ultra but a notably intelligent one, replaced Peel as member for Oxford University after Peel had changed course to support Catholic Emancipation] and D(avies) Gilbert [Davies Gilbert, MP for Bodmin, also a topographer and President of the Royal Society]. Baring, who spoke four times, at last proposed that there should be a compromise and that the ex-Ministers should resume their seats and carry the Bill . . . After the debate Baring and Sutton went to Apsley House and related to the Duke what had taken place, the former saying he would face a thousand devils rather than such a House of Commons. From that moment the whole thing was at an end, and the next morning (Tuesday) the Duke repaired to the King and told him he could not form an administration. This communication, for which the debate of the previous night had prepared everybody, was speedily known and the joy and triumph of the Whigs was complete . . . Yesterday morning Lord Grey saw the King; up to the present moment the matter stands thus: the King at mercy of the Whigs, just as averse as ever to making peers, the violent wishing to press him, the moderate wishing to spare him, all parties railing at each other, the Tories broken and discomfited and meditating no further resistance to the Reform Bill . . .

Peel who has kept himself out of the scrape is strongly suspected of being anything but sorry for the dilemma into which the Duke has got himself . . . Nothing can be more certain than that he is in high spirits in the midst of it all and talks with great complacency of its being very well as it is, and that the salvation of character is everything. This from him, who fancies he has saved his own and addressed to those who have forfeited theirs, is amusing.

The joy of the King at what he thought to be his deliverance from the Whigs was unbounded. He lost no time in putting the Duke of Wellington in possession of everything that had taken place between him and them on the subject of Reform, and with regard to the creation of peers admitting that he had consented, but saying that he had been subjected to every species of persecution. His ignorance, weakness and levity put him in a miserable light and prove him to be one of the silliest old gentlemen in his dominions . . . From the account of the King's levity throughout these proceedings, I strongly suspect that (if he lives) he will go mad. While the Duke and Lyndhurst were with him, at one of the most critical moments (I forget now at which) he said 'I have been thinking that something is wanting with regard to Hanover. Pray remember this; I should like to have a slice of Belgium which would be a convenient addition to Hanover. Pray remember this', then resumed the subject they were upon.

[*May*] *19th*

The night before last the Duke made his statement. It was extremely clear, but very bald and left his case just as it was as he did not say anything that every-body did not know before ... The debate, however interesting, left the whole matter in uncertainty; and the next day the whole question began again. What was to be done — peers or no peers? A Cabinet sat nearly all day, and Lord Grey went once or twice to the King [who] tried an experiment (not a very constitutional one) of his own by writing to a number of peers, entreating them to withdraw their opposition to the Bill ... in the meantime the Duke of Wellington, Lyndhurst and other peers had given the desired assurances to the King which he communicated to Lord Grey ...

On Thursday in the H. of Commons Peel made his statement, in which, with great civility and many expressions of esteem and admiration for the Duke, he pronounced as bitter a censure of his conduct while apparently confining himself to the defence of his own, as it was possible to do, and as such it was taken.

[Greville was at the races when the Birmingham barricades were going up, the banks, following Francis Place's poster campaign, drained of gold, and civil war contemplated.]

May 31st

Since I came back from Newmarket there has not been much to write about. A calm has succeeded the storm. Last night Schedules A and B were galloped through the [Lords] Committee, and they finished the business. On Thursday next (the day of the Derby) the Bill will probably be read a third time. In the House of Lords some dozen Tories and Waverers have continued to keep up a little skirmish and a good deal of violent language has been bandied about, in which the Whigs, being the winners, have shown the best temper. In society the excitement has ceased, but the bitterness remains ...

June 18th

The Bills are jogging on and there is a comparative calm. The Whigs swear that the Reformed Parliament will be the most aristocratic we have ever seen, and Ellice told me that they cannot hear of a single improper person likely to be elected for any of the new places. The Metropolitan districts [the seats granted against strenuous Tory opposition to districts of London] want rank and talent. The Government and their people have found out what a fool the King is, and it is very amusing to hear them on the subject ... When Normanby [Constantine Phipps, Marquess of Normanby, later Colonial and Home Secretary] went to take leave of him on going to Jamaica, he pronounced a harangue in favour of the slave trade, of which he has always been a great admirer, and expressed sentiments for which his subjects would tear him to pieces if they heard him. It is one of the great evils of the recent convulsion that the King's imbecility has been exposed to the world, and in his person the regal authority has fallen into contempt . . .

I thought I had something to say when I sat down to write, but I find I have nothing. Walter Scott is arrived here dying. A great mortality among great men: Goethe, Perier, Champollion, Cuvier, Scott, Grant, McIntosh [*sic*] all dead within weeks [Casimir Perier, French Prime Minister; J-F. Champollion, decipherer of hieroglyphics; Georges Cuvier, naturalist; Sir William Grant, former Master of the Rolls; Sir James Macintosh, Liberal political thinker, see *supra*].

June 25th

At Fern Hill all last week; a great party, nothing but racing and gambling; then to Shepperton, and to town on Saturday. The event of the races was the King's having his head knocked with a stone. It made very little sensation on the spot, for he was not hurt, and the fellow was a miserable-looking ragamuffin. It however produced a great burst of loyalty in both Houses, and their Majesties were loudly cheered at Ascot . . .

July 12th

Written nothing for a long time – nothing to say. The Suttee case[7] was decided at the Privy Council [as judicial body] on Saturday last and was not uninteresting . . .

The cholera is here, and diffuses a certain degree of alarm. Some servants of people well known have died, and that frightens all the other servants out of their wits, and they frighten their masters; the death of any one person they are acquainted with terrifies people much more than that of twenty of whom they knew nothing . . . when they hear that Lady Such a one's nurse or Sir Somebody's footman is dead, they fancy they see the disease actually at their own door.

July 15th

The debate [on the Irish Church] the night before lasted till four o'clock . . . John Russell spoke out what ought to have been said long ago, that the Church cannot stand, but that the present Clergymen must be paid . . . The truth is (as I told him) [Russell] that they are with respect to Ireland, in the situation of a man who has got an old house in which he can longer live, not tenable; various architects propose this and that alteration, to build a room here and pull down one there, but at last they find that all these alterations will only serve to make the house habitable a little while longer, that the dry rot is in it and that they had better begin as they will be obliged to end, by pulling it down and making a new one . . . By casting lingering looks at the old system and endeavouring to save something here and there, by allowing the Church to remain in the rags and tatters of its old supremacy, we shall foster these hostile feelings which it is essential to put down for ever, and leave the seeds of grievance and hatred to spring up in a future harvest of agitation and confusion.

July 25th

Nothing of moment has occurred lately; the dread of cholera absorbs everybody. Mrs Smith [Elizabeth Smith, twenty-nine, daughter of Lord Forrester, married to heir of Lord Carrington], young and beautiful, was dressed to go to Church on Sunday morning, was seized with the disorder, never had a chance of rallying, and died at eleven at night. This event, shocking enough in its suddenness and the youth and beauty of the person, has excited a terrible alarm; many people have taken flight, and others are suspended between their hopes of safety in country air and their dread of being removed from metropolitan aid. The disease spreads gradually in all directions in town and country, but without appearing like an epidemic; it is scattered and uncertain; it brings to light horrible distress . . .

August 8th

. . . I dined at Holland House yesterday; a good many people, and the Chancellor came in after dinner, looking like an Old Clothesman and dirty as the ground . . . Lord Holland told some stories of Johnson and Garrick which he had heard from Kemble. Johnson loved to bully Garrick from a recollection of G's former impertinence. When Garrick was in the zenith of his popularity and grown rich and lived with the great and while Johnson was yet obscure, the Dr used to drink tea with him, and he would say 'Davy, I do not envy you your money or your fine acquaintance, but I envy you your power of drinking tea such as this.' 'Yes' said Garrick 'it is very good tea, but it is not my best, not that which I give to my Lord this and Sir somebody t'other.' . . .

August 12th

. . . Dined yesterday at Holland House; the Chancellor, Lord Grey, Luttrell, Palmerston and Macaulay. The Chancellor was sleepy and would not talk; he uttered nothing but yawns and grunts. Macaulay and Allen [John Allen, librarian and amanuensis to Lord Holland, famous as the only man in the Holland House circle willing to stand up to the dragonish Lady Holland] disputed history, particularly the character of the Emperor Henry VI, and Allen declared himself a Guelph [Guelph and Ghibelline were respectively the papal and imperial parties of the long medieval dispute] and Macaulay a Ghibelline. Macaulay is a most extraordinary man, and his astonishing knowledge is every moment exhibited, but (as far as I have seen of him, which is not sufficient to judge) he is not *agreeable*.

September 28th

At Stoke from the 22nd to the 26th then to the Grove, and returned yesterday ... I came up with Melbourne from London. He is uneasy about the state of the country – about the desire for change and the general restlessness that prevails ... agreed that John Russell had acted unwarrantably in making the speech he did the other day at Torquay about the Ballot, which, though hypothetical, was nothing but an invitation to the advocates of the ballot to agitate for it; this too from a Cabinet Minister! ... Melbourne is exceedingly anxious to keep Lord Hill [Rowland Hill, 1st Baron, successful general in the Peninsular War and at Waterloo, Commander-in-Chief since 1828; had successfully resisted an attempt by Hobhouse, Secretary at War, to abolish flogging in the army] and Fitzroy Somerset at the head of the army, and does not wish to tamper with the service or play any tricks with it. It is curious to see the workings and counterworkings of his real opinions and principles with his false position, and the mixture of bluntness, facility, shrewdness, discretion, levity and seriousness which, colouring his mind and character by turns, make up the strange compound of his thoughts and actions. [Melbourne, at this time Home Secretary, had entered the coalition as a moderate Tory which he would essentially remain after becoming Prime Minister in 1834.]

Euston October 26th

Went to Downham on Sunday last; ... I picked up a good deal from Gosh (Arbuthnot who was very garulous) of which the most curious and important was the entire confirmation of (what I before suspected) the Ill-blood that exists between the Duke of Wellington and Peel; though the interests of party keep them on decent terms, they dislike one another, and the Duke's friends detest Peel still more than the Duke does himself. He told me all that had passed at the time of the blow-up of the present Government which I had never heard before, and his story exhibits Peel in a very odious light ...

[The case] may be summed up to this effect: that Peel, full of ambition, but of caution, animated by deep dislike and jealousy of the Duke (which policy induced him to conceal, but which temper betrayed) thought to make Manners-Sutton (see May 17th 1832) play the part of Addington [Henry Addington (1757–1844), later Lord Sidmouth, had vacated the Speaker's chair to become Prime Minister (1801–4) as stand-in for the Younger Pitt after his problems with George III over Ireland], while he would be another Pitt; rejoiced at the scrape into which he saw the Duke was getting himself, he fancied he could gain in political character by an opposite line of conduct, all that the Duke would lose; and he resolved that a Government should be formed, the existence of which would depend upon himself. Manners-Sutton was to be his creature; he would have dictated every measure of Government; he would have been their protector in the House of Commons; and as soon as the fitting moment arrived, he would have dissolved this miserable Ministry and placed himself at the head of affairs. All this craft, these deep-laid schemes and constant regard of self form a strong contrast to the simplicity and heartiness of the Duke's conduct and make the two men appear in a very different light from that which they did at first. Peel acted right from bad motives, the Duke wrong from good ones. [This sub-paranoid view held by the Duke's faction is dealt with and discounted in Professor Norman Gash's *Sir Robert Peel*, Vol. II, Longman, 1972, pp. 33–4.]

November 7th Wednesday

... Lord Tenterden[8] died on Sunday night, and no time was wasted on appointing Denman [Whig MP and, from 1830, Attorney-General][9] as his successor ... Denman is an honourable man and has been a consistent politician; latterly, of course, a Radical of considerable vehemence, if not of violence ... Lyndhurst will be overwhelmed with anguish and disappointment at finding himself for ever excluded from the great object of his ambition ... When he was made Chief Baron [of the Court of Common Pleas, a lesser court], a regular compact was made, a secret article that he should succeed on Tenterden's death to the Chief Justiceship; which bargain was of course cancelled by his declaration of war on the Reform question and his consequent breach with Lord Grey; ...

November 15th

Sheriffs' business at the Exchequer Court on Monday; saw Lyndhurst and Denman meet and shake hands with much politeness and grimace.

November 20th

Dined at Holland House the day before yesterday; Lady Holland unwell, fancies she must dine at five o'clock and exerts her power over society by making everybody go out there at that hour ... The Tableau of the House is this: Before Dinner, Lady H. affecting illness and almost dissolution, but with a very respectable appetite, and after dinner in full force and vigour; Lord H., with his chalkstones and unable to walk, lying on his couch in very good spirits and talking away; Luttrell and Rogers walking about, ever and anon looking despairingly at the clock and making short excursions from the drawing room; Allen surly and disputatious, poring over the newspapers and replying in monosyllables (generally negative) to whatever is said to him ...

Talleyrand generally comes at ten or eleven o'clock and stays as long as they will let him. Though everybody who goes there finds something to abuse or ridicule in the Mistress of the House or its ways, all continue to go; all like it more or less; and whenever, by the deaths of either, it shall come to an end, a vacuum will be made in society which nothing will supply. It is the house of all Europe; the world will suffer by the loss; and it may with truth be said that it will 'eclipse the gaiety of nations'.

Brighton December 14th Friday

Came here last Wednesday week; Council on the Monday for the dissolution [of Parliament]; place very full, bustling, gay and amusing. In De Ros' house with Alvaney, Chesterfields, Howes, Lievens, Cowpers, all at Brighton and plenty of occupation in visiting, gossiping, dawdling, riding and driving; a very idle life and impossible to do anything. The court very active, vulgar, hospitable; King, Queen, Princes, Princesses, Bastards and Attendants constantly trotting about in every direction: the Election noisy and dull – the court candidate beat and two Radicals elected . . . Lord Howe devoted to the Queen and never away from her. She receives his attentions but demonstrates nothing in return; he is a boy in love with this frightful spotted Majesty, while his delightful wife is laid up with a sprained ankle and dislocated joint on a couch.

Brighton December 17th

The borough elections [parliamentary elections for the borough rather than the longer-to-count county seats] are nearly over and have satisfied the Government. They do not seem too bad on the whole: . . . Some very bad characters have been returned; among the worst Faithful [George Faithful, elected at Brighton] here; Gronow [the memoirist and man about town, Count Gronow] at Stafford; Gully, Pontefract; Cobbett, Oldham; though I am glad that Cobbett is in Parliament.

Gully's history is extraordinary. He was taken out of prison twenty-five or thirty years ago by Mellish [as we would say (and Greville would not), a fight promoter] to fight Pierce [*sic*] [Henry Pearce, otherwise the 'Game Chicken', the leading prizefighter of the early days of the nineteenth century] . . . he fought him and was beat. He afterwards fought Belcher (I believe) and Gregson [Tom Belcher and Bob Gregson (the 'Lancashire Giant'), leading fighters of the period] . . . He then took to the turf, was successful, established himself at Newmarket where he kept a Hell and began a system of corruption of trainers, jockies and boys which put the secrets of Newmarket at his disposal and in a few years made him rich . . .

Having become rich, he embarked in a great coal speculation which answered beyond his hopes, and his shares soon yielded immense profits. His wife, who was a coarse, vulgar woman, in the meantime died, and he married again the daughter of an innkeeper at Easingwold who proved as gentlewomanlike as the other had been the reverse and who is pretty besides. He now gradually withdrew from the betting ring as a blackleg . . . bought a property near Pontefract and settled down at Ackworth Park as John Gully Esq., a gentleman of fortune . . . Latterly, he has taken great interest in politics, was an ardent Reformer and a liberal subscriber for the advancement of the cause. When Parliament was about to be dissolved he was again invited to stand for Pontefract by a numerous deputation; . . . Lord Mexborough withdrew and he was elected without opposition . . . he has gradually separated himself from the rabble of bettors and blackguards, of whom he was once the most conspicuous, and tacitly asserted his own independence and acquired gentility without ever presuming towards those whom he has been accustomed to regard with deference. His position is now more anomalous than ever, for a Member of Parliament is a great man, though there appear no reasons why the suffrages of the blackguards of Pontefract should place him in different social relations with us than those in which we mutually stood before. [Gully sat for one parliament. His grandson, William Gully, became Speaker of the Commons in 1895, and in 1905, was made Viscount Selby. The Family subsists, has an estate in Scotland, and the 5th Viscount appears in *Who's Who*.]

Brighton December 31st

. . . Two nights ago there was a great assembly after a dinner for the reception of the Turkish ambassador, Namik Pasha . . . He is twenty-eight years old, speaks French well and has good manners; his dress very simple – a red cap, black vest, trousers and boots, a gold chain around his neck . . . He admired everything and conversed with great ease. All the stupid, vulgar Englishwomen followed him about like a lion with offensive curiosity.

1833

January 11th

Manners-Sutton is to be again Speaker. Althorp wrote him a very flummery letter and he accepted. The Government wants to be out of the scrape they are in between Abercrombie and Littleton, and Sutton wants his peerage. [He got it: Viscount Canterbury, 1835.] Everything seems prosperous here. The Government is strong, the H. of C. is thought respectable on the whole and safe, trade is brisk, funds rising, money plentiful, confidence reviving, Tories sulky . . . The King has been delighting the Whigs and making himself more ridiculous and contemptible by the most extravagant civilities to the new Peers – that is *to* Western and about Ld. Stafford. He now appears to be very fond of his ministers. [Poor old idiot!]

Sunday [January] 26th

. . . It seems that the Government project (or perhaps only the fact that they have one) about W(est) I(ndian) Emancipation has got wind, and the W. Indians[1] are of course in a state of great alarm. They believe that it will be announced, whatever it is to be, in the King's speech . . . Of all political feelings and passions – such this rage for emancipation is, rather than a consideration of interest – has always struck me as the most remarkable and extraordinary.

There can be no doubt that a great many of the Abolitionists are actuated by very pure motives; they have been shocked by the cruelties which have been and still are very often practised toward Slaves, their minds are imbued with the horrors they have read and heard of, and they have an invincible conviction that the state of slavery under any form is repugnant to the spirit of the English Constitution and the Christian religion and that it is a stain upon the national character which ought to be wiped away.

These people, generally speaking, are very ignorant concerning all the various difficulties which beset the question; their notions are superficial; they pity the Slaves whom they regard as injured innocents and hate their masters whom they regard as cruel barbarians. Others are animated in this cause purely by ambition and by finding that slavery is a cheap and easy species of benevolence ... Taylor [Sir Henry Taylor, Senior Colonial Office civil servant, who ruled over half the West Indies in the Colonial Office] ... said that he was well aware of the consequences of emancipation both to the Negroes and the Planters. The estates of the latter would not be cultivated; it would be impossible for want of labour; the Negroes would not work – no inducement would be sufficient to make them; they wanted to be free merely that they might be idle. They would, on being emancipated, possess themselves of ground, the fertility of which in those regions is so great that trifling labour will be sufficient to provide them with the means of existence, and they will thus relapse rapidly into a state of barbarism; ...

[*January*] *30th*

The intentions of the Government with regard to the West Indies ... having got wind, the consternation of the West India body is great. A deputation, headed by Sir Alexander Grant [MP since 1812, Chairman of Committees] waited upon Lords Grey and Goderich [Colonial Secretary] the other day and put questions to them ... To all their questions he [Grey] gave vague answers refusing to communicate anything except that nothing was decided ...

February 1st

The Reformed Parliament opened heavily (on Tuesday) as Government think satisfactorily. Cobbett took his seat ... He was very twaddling and said but one good thing, when he called O'Connell the Member for Ireland.

February 10th

... Opinions are of course very various upon the state of the House and the character of the discussion. The anti-Reformers, with a sort of melancholy triumph, boast that their worst expectations have been fulfilled ... Everybody agrees that the House of Commons was very different – the number of strange faces; the swagger of O'Connell walking about incessantly and making signs to, or talking with, his followers in various parts; the Tories few and scattered; Peel no longer surrounded with a stout band of supporters, but pushed from his usual seat which is occupied by Cobbett, O'Connell and the Radicals; he is gone up near the Speaker.

The whole debate turned upon Ireland. O'Connell pronounced a violent but powerful phillipic which Stanley answered very well. Macaulay made one of his brilliant speeches on the second night and Peel spoke the third. It was not possible to make a more dextrous and judicious speech than he did; for finding himself in a very uncomfortable position, he at once placed himself in a good one and acknowledging that his position was altogether different from what it had been, he contrived to transfer to himself personally much of the weight and authority, which he previously held as the organ and head of a great and powerful party, ...

[*February*] *14th*

The night before last Althorp brought in his plan of Irish Church Reform with complete success. He did it very well ... nobody opposing except Inglis and Goulburn and Peel in a very feeble speech ... It is clear that Peel, who is courting the House and exerting all his dexterity to bring men's minds round to him, saw the stream was too strong for him to go against it, so he made a sort of temporising, moderate, unmeaning speech which will give him time to determine on his best course and did not commit him ... He, in fact, means to open a House to all comers and make himself necessary and indispensable. Under that placid exterior, he conceals, I believe, a boundless ambition; and hatred and jealousy lurk under his professions of esteem and political attachment ... He came into life the child and champion of a political system which had been for a long time crumbling to pieces; ... He has hitherto been encumbered with embarrassing questions and an unmanageable party. Time has disposed of the first and he is divorced from the last; if his great experience of and talents have a fair field to act upon, he may yet, in spite of his selfish and unamiable character, be a distinguished and successful Minister.

February 22nd

... Last night Lord Grey introduced his coercive measures in an excellent speech, though there are some people who doubt his being able to carry them through the House of Commons. If he can't of course, he goes; and what next? The measures are sufficiently strong it must be owned – a *consommé* of insurrection-gagging Acts, suspension of Habeas Corpus, martial law and one or two other little hards and sharps. The House of Commons however proved how unruly it is on Hume's [Joseph Hume, reformer and radical MP, close associate of Francis Place] motion. The Government has no power over it – positively none. But they say it was the appointment of Munster and F.

FitzClarence that gave all the disgust. [These illegitimate and unloved sons of William had been given salaried and unmerited places not long after the passing of the Reform Act.]

London February 22nd

Stephen [James][2] who is one of the great apostles of emancipation . . . owned that he had never known so great a problem nor so difficult a question to settle. His notion is that compulsory labour may be substituted for slavery . . . and admits that if this does not answer the slaves will relapse into barbarism . . . The public appetite for discussion and legislation has been whetted and is insatiable; the millions of orators and legislators who have sprung up like mushrooms all over the kingdom, the bellowers, the chatterers, the knaves and the dupes who make such an universal hubbub must be fed with fresh victims and sacrifices. The Catholic question was speedily followed by Reform in Parliament, and this has opened a door to anything.

In the meantime the Reformed Parliament has been sitting for a fortnight or so and begins to manifest its character and pretensions . . . these fellows behave themselves as if they had taken it by storm and might riot in all the insolence of victory. There exists no party but that of the Government; the Irish act in a body under O'Connell to the number of about forty; the Radicals are scattered up and down without a leader, numerous, restless, turbulent, and bold: Hume, Cobbett and a multitude of blackguards such as Roebuck [John Arthur Roebuck (1801–79), radical politician long identified with Sheffield], Faithfull, Buckingham [James Silk Buckingham (1780–1855), journalist and MP, expelled from India for criticising its Government] and Major Beauclerk [Aubrey Beauclerk, hardly a blackguard, grandson of Dr Johnson's aristocratic young friend Topham Beauclerk, and, as a descendant of the Duke of Marlborough, quite Greville's social peer] . . . bent upon doing all the mischief they can and incessantly active; the Tories without a head, frightened, angry and sulky . . . The evil of this is that we are now reduced to the alternative of Lord Grey's Government or none at all; and should he be defeated on any great measure, he must either abandon the country to its fate or consent to carry on the Government upon the condition of a virtual transfer of the executive power to the House of Commons. If this comes to pass the game is up, for this House, like animals who have once tasted blood, if it ever exercises power such as this and finds a Minister consenting to hold office on such terms, will never rest till it has acquired all the authority of the Long Parliament and reduced that of the Crown to a mere cipher . . .

February 27th

Frederick FitzClarence has been compelled to resign the situation at the Tower which the King gave him; they found it very probable that the H. of

C. would refuse to vote the pay of it – a trifle in itself, but a sign of the times and the total want of consideration for the King, not certainly that he personally deserves much. O'Connell made a speech of such violence at the Trades Union the other day – calling the House of Commons six hundred scoundrels . . . The sense of insecurity and uneasiness evidently increases; the Government assumes a high tone, but is not at all certain of its ability to pass the Coercive Bills unaltered . . .

Yesterday morning the Duke of Wellington came here upon some private business, after discussing which he entered upon the state of the Country . . . I told the Duke what Macaulay had said . . . 'that if he had to legislate he would instead of this Bill have suspended the laws for five years in Ireland, given the Lord-Lieutenant's proclamation the force of law and got the Duke of Wellington to go there . . .'

March 4th
Sir T. Hardy told my brother he thought the King would certainly go mad; he was so excitable, *loathing* his ministers, particularly Graham, and dying to go to war. He has some of the cunning of madmen who fawn upon their keepers when looked at by them and grin at them and shake their fists when their backs are turned . . .

March 13th
I have been again laid up with the gout and unable to attend to anything. The world which takes a livelier interest in scandals, has been occupied with the affair of Baring Wall accused of indecency with a policeman and with Dudley's will. In the former case a stout phalanx of friends have thrown their shields over him. The story is a strange one and there is a chance of his getting over it [Charles Baring Wall, a Conservative MP, was acquitted], though nobody can be plunged into such mire without smelling of it more or less ever after . . . Poor Dudley is dead and has left Lady Lyndhurst [they had been conducting an affair since 1827] £2000 a year . . .

London April 28th
Came to town last night from Newmarket and the intervening week at Buckenham. Nothing but racing, gaming, hawking; a wretched life, that is a life of amusement, but very unprofitable and discreditable to anyone who can do better things . . .

May 16th
Stanley's plan for slave emancipation . . . produced rage and fury among both West Indians and Saints [the name, attaching originally to the Evangelical Clapham Sect to which William Wilberforce, the best-known abolitionist,

belonged, was applied derisively to abolitionists generally], being too much for the former and not enough for the latter, and both announced their opposition to it ... Howick had previously announced his intention of opposing Stanley, and accordingly he did so in a speech of considerable vehemence and force which lasted two hours. He was not however well received. His father and mother had in vain endeavoured to divert him from his resolution [Henry Grey, Viscount Howick, later 3rd Earl Grey, was always more radical than his father, the Prime Minister. He was opposing the indentures with which Stanley, as a sop to the planters, was replacing open slavery. They failed.]; but though they say his speech was clever, he has damaged himself by it. His plan is immediate emancipation ...

May 19th

... The West Indian question is postponed. The Duke of Wellington told me that he thought it would pass away for this time and that all parties would be convinced of the impracticability of any of the plans now mooted. I said that nothing could do away the mischief of what had been done by broaching it ...

May 27th

All last week at Epsom, and now thank God these races are over. I have had all the trouble and excitement and worry, and have neither won nor lost; nothing but the hope of gain would induce me to go through this demoralising drudgery ... Jockeys, trainers and blacklegs are my companions, and it is like dram drinking; having once entered upon it, I cannot leave it off ... Let no man who has no need, who is not in danger of losing all he has and is not obliged to grasp at every chance, *make a book* on the Derby. While the fever it excites is raging and the odds are varying, I can neither read nor write nor occupy myself with anything else ...

June 2nd Sunday

A family affair. Went on Thursday to Margate by the Steam Boat which was full of passengers, a furious east wind blowing, so that nothing could be colder or more disagreeable. In a hack chaise from Margate to Dover where I went to see my old uncle to endeavour to prevail upon him to make it up with his son. A more extraordinary character I never saw ... Under his roof resides with him the wife of his son Algernon who ran away with a French actor from Boulogne, and he has taken her and her bastard child to live with him; and there is reason to apprehend that he will leave her the greatest part of his enormous property. Amassing wealth is his only object and delight; and Lathom the barber told me he thought he laid by 30,000 a year ... I made not the faintest impression and totally failed to soften the obdurate heart or bend the stubborn purpose of the old wretch . . . His mind appears saturated with hatred, and venom and ferocity are perpetually distilled from it. He curses his children and never deviates into the semblance of affection for anyone . . . destitute of all human interests and affections with no passion but that of universal hatred which has survived all others, he says he is, and I believe he is, content, and that he actually enjoys life. He fancies himself very religious and has a sermon read to him every evening . . . Certainly a more execrable old man or a more melancholy development of the vices of old age in an odious character I never beheld.

June 3rd

The Government are in high spirits. The Saints have given in their adhesion to Stanley's plan, and they expect to carry the West Indian question. The Bank question has satisfied the Bank and most people except Peel . . . Melbourne says 'Now that we are as much hated as they were, we shall stay in for ever.' . . .

The House of Lords is paralysed; it exists upon sufferance and cannot venture to throw out or materially alter any Bill (such as the India, Bank, Negro, Church Reform, etc) which may come up to it without the certainty of being instantly swamped and the measures, however obnoxious, being crammed down its throat . . .

June 19th

I had a long conversation with Sir Willoughby Cotton on Sunday about Jamaican affairs. He is Commander-in Chief just come home and just going out again. He told me what he had said to Stanley which was to this effect: that the compensation would be esteemed munificent, greater by far than they had expected . . . but that the plan would be impracticable and that sugar could not be cultivated after Slavery ceased; that the Slave would never understand the system of modified servitude by which he was to be nominally free and actually kept to labour and that he would rebel against the magistrate who tried to force him to work more fiercely than against his master; that the magistrates would never be able to persuade the Slaves in their new character of apprentices to work as heretofore, and the military would be called in to assist them could but do nothing. He asked Stanley if he intended, when the military were called in, that they should fire on or bayonet the refractory apprentices. He said no, they were to exhort them. He gave him to understand that in his opinion they could do nothing, and that the more the soldiers exhorted the more the Slaves would not work. With regard to my own particular he was rather encouraging than not, thought they would not molest me any more, that the Assembly might try and get me out, but that the council considered it matter [sic] of loyalty to the King not to force out the Clerk of his Privy

Council, but if anything more was said about it and I went out to Jamaica, I might be sure of getting leave again in a month or six weeks. [It is worth reproducing here the original footnote made by his Council colleague and first editor, Henry Reeve: 'This refers to Mr Greville's holding the office of Secretary of the Island of Jamaica with permanent leave of absence. The work of the office was done by a deputy who was paid by a share of the emoluments which were in the shape of fees.']

June 29th
I am going, if not too lazy, to note down the everyday nothings of my life and see what it looks like . . .

July 3rd
Nothing to put down these last two days unless I go back to my old practice of recording what I read, and which I rather think I left off because I read nothing and had nothing to put down: but last two days, read a little of Cicero's *Second Philippic*, Voltaire's *Siècle de Louis XVI*, Coleridge's [not Samuel, but his nephew Henry] *Journey to the West Indies*; bought some books, went to the opera to hear Bellini's *Norma*, thought it heavy, Pasta's [Giuditta Pasta was only thirty-five at this time but she retired two years later from her Parisian/London career to live on Lake Como] voice not what it was . . .

July 12th
Went to Newmarket on Sunday, came back yesterday, got back at half past nine, went to Crockfords and heard on the steps that poor Dover had died that morning [George Agar Ellis, see *supra*] . . . He occupied as large a space in Society as his talents (which were by no means first rate) permitted; but he was clever, lively, agreeable, good-tempered, good-natured, hospitable, liberal and rich, a zealous friend, an eager political partisan . . . He got into the House of Commons but never was able to speak, never attempted to say more than a few words, and from the beginning, gave up all idea of oratorical distinction . . . Soon after his marriage, Ellis, who had never been vicious or profligate but who was free from anything like severity or austerity, began to show signs of a devout propensity and, not contented with an ordinary discharge of religious duties, he read tracts and sermons, frequented Churches and Preachings, gave up driving on Sundays and appeared in considerable danger of falling into the gulph of Methodism; but this turn did not last long, and whatever induced him to take it up, he apparently became bored with his self-imposed restrictions and after a little, threw off his short-lived sanctity and resumed his worldly habits . . . He devoted himself to literature, politics and society; to the two first with greater success than would be expected of a man whose talents for composition were below mediocrity, and for public speaking none at all . . . Without

a strong understanding, destitute of fancy or imagination and with neither eloquence nor wit, he was a remarkably agreeable man ...

I have had a quarrel with Lady Holland about some nonsense, but she was insolent so I was fierce, and then she was civil as she usually is to those who won't be bullied by her ...

July 15th

Yesterday came the news of Captain Napier [Charles Napier, later Admiral, cousin of the better known army Napiers, serving here in the Portuguese Navy] having captured the whole of Don Miguel's Fleet to the great delight of the Whigs and equal mortification of the Tories. [The Whig Government had been supportive of Queen Maria against the absolutist claimant, Don Miguel.] It appears to have been a very dashing affair and very cowardly on the part of the Miguelites. The day before the news came, Napier had been struck out of the British Navy.

Met Duncannon in the morning ... He talked much of the Irish Church and of the abominations which had been going on under his own eyes. One case he mentioned of a man who holds a living of £1000 a year close to Bessborough, whom he knows. There is no house, no church, and there are no Protestants in the parish. He went there to be inducted and dined with Duncannon at Bessborough the day after. D. asked him how he had managed the necessary form and he said he had been obliged to borrow three Protestants from a neighbouring Parish and had read in the morning and evening service to them within the ruined walls of the old Abbey, and they signed a certificate that he had complied with the forms prescribed by law ... he was still persuaded that the Opposition meant to throw out the Bill ... The Duke [of Wellington] after his extraordinary speech in the House of Lords when he mounted the old broken down hobby of the Coronation Oath, [a standard defence against Catholic Emancipation used by Georges III and IV, that the Coronation Oath expressly forbad acknowledgement of rights for Catholics] and cut a curvet that alarmed his friends and his enemies, assembled the Tories at Apsley House and there, resuming his own good sense, though not very consistently, made them a speech and told them that some such measure must be passed for nothing else could save the Irish Church ...

July 18th

There seems every probability of Stanley's West India Bill being thrown out. The Saints, who at first had agreed to support it, object to pay the twenty million [a billion sterling at current values] for [Slave] emancipation to take place twelve years hence, and the present condition of the question seems to be that all parties are dissatisfied with it, and there is nearly a certainty that it will be received with horror by the Planters, while the Slaves will no longer work when they find the fiat of their freedom (however conditional or distant the final consummation may be) has at length gone forth . . .

July 25th–26th

. . . Stanley was nearly beat on the apprenticeship clause in the West Indian Bill on Wednesday night, Macaulay opposing him; so yesterday morning he came down to the House and gave it up . . . I dined the day before yesterday with old Lady Cork [the Countess of Cork (1746–1840)] to meet the Bonapartes. There were Joseph, Lucien, Lucien's daughter, widow of Louis Bonaparte, Hortense's son, the Dudley Stuarts [in-laws of Lucien Bonaparte], Belhavens, Rogers, Lady Clarendon, Lady C. Fitzroy, Lady Davey and myself; not very amusing but curious to see these two men, one of whom would not be a King [Lucien Bonaparte, who, though serving his brother very effectively, retained republican sentiments] when he might have chosen almost any title he pleased – conceive for instance having refused the Kingdom of Naples – and the other who was first King of Naples and the King of Spain, [Joseph Bonaparte] commanded armies and had the honour of being defeated once or twice by the Duke of Wellington, who once trampled on all Europe and at whose feet, the potentates of the earth bowed, two simple, plain-looking, civil, courteous, smiling gentlemen. They say Lucien is a very agreeable man, Joseph nothing . . . Lucien looked as he had once been like him [Napoleon] that is his face in shape is like the pictures of Napoleon when he was thin and young . . . There was not the slightest affectation of royalty . . . everything regal that he [Lucien] ever had about him seemed to have merged in his American Citizenship, and he looked more like a Yankee Cultivator than a King of Spain and the Indies . . .

The Duke of Sutherland is dead, a Leviathan of wealth.

Wednesday August 7th

At Goodwood from Saturday se'ennight to Saturday last. Magnificent weather, numerous assemblage, tolerable racing, but I did not win the great cup which I ought to have won, and should have won 1500 upon it, a most vile piece of ill-luck, but good fortune seems to have deserted me, and the most I can do is not to lose. While we were there news came of the capture of Lisbon [by Don Pedro in the name of Dona Maria Da Gloria, at once proclaimed Queen], at which of course the Whigs are delighted and the Tories the reverse . . .

[August] 8th

Met Lord Grey in the street; he said this session had nearly done him up, and he must have repose; talked of Portugal, of the desirableness of getting rid of Pedro, and of putting Palmella at the head of the Government . . . I said he must take care they did not establish too liberal a Government. He replied that the Portuguese certainly were not fit for any such thing, and that the constitution had undoubtedly done all the mischief; ...

August 20th Tuesday

To Stoke [Stoke Farm, Stoke Poges, home of the Whig politician Lord Sefton] – Creevey [generally thought to be the illegitimate brother of Sefton, to whom he was very close] and Lemarchant, [correctly, Denis Le Marchant (1795–1874), also biographer of Brougham, later Clerk of the Commons] the Chancellor's Secretary ... Lemarchant told me that the cause of Sugden's [Later Lord Chancellor. See *post*] inveterate animosity toward Brougham was this – that in a debate in the H. of C. Sugden in his speech took occasion to speak of Mr Fox, and said that he had no great respect for his authority, at which Brougham merely said, loud enough to be heard all over the House, and in that peculiar tone which strikes like a dagger, 'Poor Fox.' The words, the tone, were electrical, everybody burst into roars of laughter, Sugden was so overwhelmed that he said afterwards that it was with difficulty he could go on, and he vowed that he never could forgive this sarcasm ...

After dinner on the Sunday, Brougham talked of the Reform Bill and its first appearance in the H. of Commons. He said that once allowed to take root there, it could not be crushed, and that their only opportunity had been thrown away by the Tories. Had Peel risen at once and declared that he would not even discuss such a measure, that it was revolution, and opposed its being brought in, he would have thrown it out, and if he had then come down with a moderate measure, it would have satisfied the country *for a time*.

September 6th

Yesterday the announcement of Lord Wellesley's [Wellington's brother, Richard, Marquess Wellesley, formerly Governor-General of India] appointment to be Lord-Lieutenant of Ireland was received with as great astonishment as I ever saw. Once very brilliant, probably never very efficient, he is now worn out and effete. It is astonishing they should select such a man, and one does not see why, because it is difficult to find a good man, they should select one of the worst they could hit upon. It is a ridiculous appointment ...

September 10th

At Gorhambury on Saturday till Monday. Dined on Friday with Talleyrand, a great dinner to M. Thiers,[3] the French Minister of Commerce, a little man about as tall as Shiel, and as mean and vulgar-looking, wearing spectacles and with a squeaking voice. It is said that he is a man of great ability and a good speaker, more in the familiar English than the bombastical French style ...

The Young Queen of Portugal goes to Windsor today. The King was at first very angry at her coming to England, but when he heard that Louis Philippe had treated her with incivility, he changed his mind, and resolved to treat her with great honours. He hates Louis Philippe and the French with a sort of Jack Tar animosity. The other day, the King gave a dinner to one of the regiments at Windsor and as usual he made a parcel of foolish speeches, in one of which after descanting about their exploits in Spain against the French, he went on: 'Talking of France, I must say that whether at peace or at war with that country, I shall always consider her as our natural Enemy, and whoever may be her King or *ruler* I shall keep a watchful eye for the purpose of repressing her ambitious encroachments.' If he was not such an ass that nobody does anything but laugh at what he says, this would be very important. Such as he is, it is nothing. 'What can you expect' (as I forget who said) 'from a man with a head like a pineapple?' It is just of that shape.

London November 13th
Nothing written for nearly two months ... to Buckenham where I met Sir Robert Peel. He is very agreeable in society, it is a toss up whether he talks or not, but if he thaws and is in good humour and spirits, he is lively, entertaining and abounding in anecdotes which he tells extremely well ... On Saturday to Robarts at Southampton, and on Sunday dined with Rogers, Moore, Sydney Smith, Macaulay. Sydney less vivacious than usual and somewhat overpowered and talked down by what Moore called the flumen sermonis [river of discourse] of Macaulay. Sydney calls Macaulay 'a book in breeches'. All that the latter says, all that he writes exhibits his great powers and astonishing information, but I don't think he is agreeable. It is more than society requires, and not exactly of the kind; his figure, face and manner are all bad; he astonishes and instructs, he sometimes entertains, seldom amuses, and still seldomer pleases ... He told me that he had read *Sir Charles Grandison* [novel by Henry Richardson],[4] fifteen times ...

November 14th
Dined with Sefton yesterday; after dinner came in the Chancellor in good humour and spirits; talked of Lord Wellesley; since he has been in Ireland has astonished everybody by his activity and assiduity in business. He appeared before he went in the last stage of decrepitude and had no idea the energy was in him; but they say he is quite a new man, and it is not merely a splash, but real and bona fide business that he does ...

December 2nd Monday
I went yesterday to Irving's chapel[5] to hear him preach and witness an exhibition of the tongues ... the seats behind Irving's chair are evidently appropriated to the higher class of devotees for they were the best dressed of the

congregation. The business was conducted with decency and the congregation
was attentive. It began with a hymn, the words given out by one of the assistant preachers and sung by the whole flock. This, which seems to be common
to all dissenting services, is always very fine, the full swell of human voices
producing a grand effect; ... After this, Irving delivered a prayer in a very
slow, drawling tone, rather long and not at all striking in point of language
or thought. When he had finished, one of the men sitting beside him, rose and
read a few verses from the Bible, and discoursed thereon. He was a sorry fellow
and was followed by two others not much better. After these *Spencer Perceval*
[son of the like-named Prime Minister (1809–12), the religious maniac who
had induced an embarrassed Commons to declare a day of fasting during the
Reform struggle] stood up ... He appeared about to touch on politics, and
(as well as I recollect) was saying 'Ye trusted that your institutions were unal-
terable, ye believed that your loyalty to your King, your respect for your
nobility, your' – when suddenly a low moaning noise was heard, on which he
instantly stopt, threw his arm over his breast, and covered his eyes in an attitude of deep devotion, as if oppressed by the presence of the Spirit. The voice
after ejaculating three 'O's, one rising after another in tones very musical, burst
into a flood of unintelligible jargon which, whether it was English or gibberish
I could not discover. This lasted five or six minutes, and as the voice was
silenced, another woman, in more passionate and louder tones, took it up; this
last spoke in English and words, though not sentences were distinguishable
... She was well dressed, spoke sitting under great apparent excitement and
screamed on till from exhaustion, as it seemed, her voice gradually died away
and all was still. Then Spencer Perceval, in slow and solemn tones, resumed
not where he had left off, but with an exhortation to hear the voice of the Lord
which had just been uttered in the congregation ... and then Irving preached.
His subject was 'God's Love' upon which he poured forth a mystical incom-
prehensible rhapsody with extraordinary vehemence of manner and power of
lungs. There was nothing like eloquence in his sermon ... but there is undoubtedly something in his commanding figure and strange, wild countenance, his
vehemence and above all the astonishing power of voice, its compass, intona-
tion and variety which arrests attention and gives the notion of a great Orator.
I dare say he can speak well, but to waste real eloquence on such an auditory
would be like throwing pearls to swine ...

December 4th

Bankes [William Bankes, a Tory Ultra with standing at what we would call
Opposition front bench level] was tried and acquitted the day before yesterday.
It was a lame business and nobody can read the trial [R v Bankes and Flowers,
a charge of attempting an unnatural crime in the grounds of Westminster
Abbey] without being convinced of his guilt ... Denman [Lord Chief Justice]

merely read the evidence and did not comment on it. The Foreman said 'He left the court without a stain' – 'on his shirt' said Alvanley when he was told the verdict. But the Chief Justice said nothing.

December 9th

Went yesterday with Frederic Elliot and Luttrell to hear Fox[6] a celebrated Unitarian preacher at a Chapel in South Place ... he cannot pronounce the s. His sermon was, however, admirable and amply repaid us for the trouble of going so far. He read the whole of it, the language was beautiful, the argument clear and unembarrassed, the reasoning powerful and there were occasional passages of great eloquence ... I like the simplicity of the Service: a hymn, a prayer and the Sermon; still I think a short liturgy preferable – our own much abbreviated would be the best ...

December 18th

... In the evening dined with Moore at the Poodle's [Poodle Byng, a contemporary society figure]. He told a good story of Sydney Smith and Leslie the Professor [of Mathematics at Edinburgh, Sir John Leslie]. Leslie had written about the North Pole; something he had said had been attacked in the *Edinburgh Review* in a way that displeased him. He called on Jeffrey [Francis Jeffrey, editor of the *Edinburgh Review*] ... [and] began with a grave complaint on the subject which Jeffrey interrupted with 'Oh, damn the North Pole'. 'It was very bad' said Sydney 'but do you know I am not surprised about it for I have heard him speak very disrespectfully of *the Equator*.'

VOLUME II ENDS

VOLUME III

1834

Belvoir Castle January 6th

After many years of delay I am here since the 3rd to assist at the celebrations of the Duke of Rutland's birthday. The party is very large and sufficiently dull: the Duke of Wellington, Esterhazy [Austrian ambassador], Matucewitz [senior Russian diplomat], Rokeby, Miss d'Este, and the rest a rabble of fine people without beauty or wit among them . . . The Duke lives here for three or four months from the end of October till the end of February or March, on and off, and the establishment is kept up with extraordinary splendour. In the morning we are roused by the strains of martial music, and the Band (of his regiment of militia) marches round the Terrace, awakening or quickening the guests with lively airs. All the men hunt or shoot. At dinner there is a different display of plate every day and in the evening play at whist or amuse themselves as they please . . .

I have had snatches of talk with the Duke of Wellington, and yesterday he retired with Matucewitz, and had a long conference with him. The absolute courts have a great hankering after him, though their Ministers here can hardly look for his return to office . . . Arbuthnot, who is here, told me (and he hears these things from the Duke) that Matucewitz had expressed the greatest contempt for Palmerston and not less for Lord Grey; and that with the latter he had been much struck with his ignorance . . .

Burghley January 28th

. . . I had almost forgot the house, which is surprisingly grand in all respects, though the living rooms are not numerous or good enough. I just missed Peel who went to Belvoir yesterday. I heard wonderful things of railroads and steam when I was in Staffordshire . . . Stephenson, the great Engineer, told Lichfield that he had travelled on the Manchester and Liverpool railroad for many miles at the rate of a mile a minute, that his doubt was not how fast his Engines could be made to go but at what pace it would be proper to stop, that he could make them travel with greater speed than any bird can cleave the air, and he had ascertained that 400 miles an hour was the extreme velocity which the human frame could endure at which it could move and exist.

February 1st

Wharncliffe has been here and is gone. He, like Harrowby, is very dismal about the prospects of the country, and thinks we are gravitating toward a revolution ... He says that he has received greater marks of deference and respect in his own county, and especially at Sheffield, where a short time ago he would have been in danger of being torn to pieces, than he ever experienced, but that he could no more bring in a son for Sheffield than he could fly in the air ... Sir John Beckett is just gone to stand for Leeds and certainly the catechism to which he was there forced to submit is very ominous. A seat in the House of Commons will cease to be an object of ambition to honourable and independent men if it can only be obtained by cringing and servility to the rabble of great towns and when it shall be established that the Member is to be a Slave, bound hand and foot by pledges and responsible for every vote he gives to masters who are equally tyrannical and unreasonable ...

February 13th

It is observed that there never was a session of Parliament which opened with such an appearance of apathy as this. After the violent excitement which has almost incessantly prevailed for the last years or more, men's minds seem exhausted, and all the undergrowl of political rancour is still heard, and a feeble cry of 'the Church in danger', on the whole there is less bitterness and animosity and a tolerably fair promise that things will go in a smooth and even course ...

... Madame de Lieven told me that it was impossible to describe the contempt as well as dislike which the whole corps diplomatique had for Palmerston, and, pointing to Talleyrand, who was sitting close by, 'surtout lui' ... He spends his time in making love to Mrs Petre whom he takes to the House of Commons to hear speeches which he does not make, and where he exhibits his conquest, and certainly it is the best of his exploits, but what a successor to Canning, whom by the way he looks to imitate. What would be Canning's reaction if he could look from the grave and see these new Reformers who ape him in his worst qualities, and who blunder and bluster in the seat which he once filled with such glory and success ...?

February 14th

Last night at Miss Berry's met Mrs Somerville, [Mary Somerville (1780–1872) published a study of the spectrum and wrote on Laplace] the great mathematician ... I could not then take my eyes off the woman with a feeling of surprise and something like incredulity, all involuntary and very foolish, but to see a mincing, smirking person, fan in hand, gliding about the room talking nothing and nonsense, and to know that Laplace was her plaything and Newton her acquaintance, was too striking a contrast not to torment the brain ...

February 22nd

Went to the H. of Commons last night where I have not been for many years. A great change, a thorough set of blackguards, and hardly a human whose face I knew ... Stanley made a wretched speech; O'Connell very bad, affecting to be moderate, was only dull. Peel spoke very shortly but very well indeed. Peel's is an enviable position; in the prime of life, with immense fortune, *facile Princeps* in the House of Commons, unshackled by party connection and prejudices, universally regarded as the ablest man, and with, on the whole, a very high character, free from the cares of office, able to devote himself to literature, to politics or idleness as the fancy takes him. No matter how unruly the House, how impatient or fatigued, the moment he rises, all is silence and he is sure of being heard with profound attention and respect. This is the enjoyable period of his life, and he must make the most of it for when time and the hour shall bring about his return to power, his cares and anxieties will begin, and with whatever success his ambition may hereafter be crowned, he will hardly fail to look back with regret to this holyday time of his political career.

March 12th

... Weather like Summer, nothing particularly new, a long debate on the Corn Laws, which being called an open question, the Ministers voted different ways – that is all the Cabinet voted one way, but the underlings took their own course. Half the Ruralists are furious with Government for their indecision and way of acting on this question, but I am so totally ignorant I cannot enter into their indignation or exactly understand from what it proceeds. It was pretty to see Graham and Pow Thompson [Poulett Thompson][1] like two game cocks pecking at and spurring one another. Everybody agrees the debate was very dull, and that is all they do agree upon ...

March 14th

... [Peel] and Stanley met at Madame de Lieven's Ball, and Peel said to him why did you let that appointment take place etc? [Lord Plunkett, Lord Chancellor of Ireland, had appointed his son Thomas to the Deanery of Down, something lovingly proclaimed by Daniel O'Connell] Stanley said 'I could not give the true and only defence for Plunkett viz., that I had signed the report, but had never read it.' Peel said, 'you had better give him some other deanery and cancel this appointment.' They talked for a long time, but this tone and advice exhibit a state of sentiment by no means incompatible with a future union, when matters are ripe for it. [Greville was being shrewd. In 1834, Stanley resigned from the Government for moving too far in Ireland and he eventually entered Peel's Cabinet in 1841, only to resign in 1845 in protest at abolition of the Corn Laws.] ...

April 3rd

Yesterday I was forty years old, an anniversary much too melancholy to think of; and when I think how intolerably these forty years have been wasted, how unprofitably spent, how little store laid up for the future, how few the pleasurable recollections of the past, a feeling of pain and humiliation comes across me that makes my cheeks tingle and burn as I write . . .

William Ponsonby, whom I met the other evening, told me he had just returned from the assizes at Dorchester where the men had been convicted of illegal association. [The Tolpuddle Martyrs, sentenced to fourteen years transportation.] On the event of this trial, he said, the lower and labouring classes had their eyes fixed, and the conviction was thus of great consequence; any relaxation of the sentence would have been impossible under the circumstances and though a great disposition was evinced partly by the press, by petitions and by some speeches in Parliament to get them off more easily, Melbourne very wisely did not wait for more manifestations, but packed them off, and they are gone . . .

April 25th

Yesterday the Privy Council met to hear the London University petition, praying for a charter and the counter-petitions of Oxford and Cambridge and the medical bodies . . .

May 11th

. . . The King has been exhibiting some symptoms of a disordered mind, not however amounting to anything like actual derangement, only morbid irritability and activity – reviewing the Guards and *blowing up* people at court. He made the Guards, both horse and foot, perform their evolutions before him; he examined their barracks, cloaths, arms and accoutrements, and he had a musket brought to him that he might show the way to use it in some new sort of exercise he wanted to introduce; in short, he gave a great deal of trouble and made a fool of himself . . .

May 23rd

Newmarket, Epsom and so forth. Nothing remarkably new. In the H. of Commons the Poor Law Bill has been going smoothly; in the H. of Lords little of note but one of Brougham's exhibitions. Old Wynford brought in a very absurd Bill for the better observance of the Sabbath (an old sinner He, who never cared three straws for the Sabbath) which Brougham attacked with excessive virulence and all his powers of ridicule and sarcasm. His speech made everybody laugh very heartily, but on a division the Bishops all voting with Wynford, the latter carried the second reading by three in a very thin House . . .

On Monday last I went down to Petworth and saw the finest *fête* that could be given. Lord Egremont has been accustomed for some time in the winter to feed the poor of the adjoining parishes ... he had it arranged in the open air, and a fine sight it was: fifty-four tables, each fifty feet long, were placed in a vast semi-circle on the lawn before the house. The tables were all spread with cloths and plates and dishes; two great tents were erected in the middle to receive the provisions which were conveyed in carts like ammunition. Plum puddings and loaves were piled like cannonballs, and innumerable joints of boiled meat and roast beef were spread out while hot joints were prepared in the kitchen ... The Old Peer could not endure that there should be anybody hungering outside his gates and he went out himself and ordered that the barriers be taken down and admittance given to all. They think 6000 were fed ...

May 27th

There is the devil to pay with the Government which is on the very brink of dissolution. The Irish Church Bill is the immediate cause, Stanley and Graham standing out against the majority of the Cabinet with regard to the Appropriation clause. [It was proposed in an amendment, moved by Henry Ward, that the incomes of ten sees due to be closed should be alienated.] ... They attribute all the present bother to Graham who pleads conscience and *religious feelings*. It is impossible to guess how it will end, and there is a terrible turmoil ... (His colleagues, or their friends at least), suspect that Graham kicks up this dust with ulterior views, and they think he aims at a junction with Peel – Stanley of course included – and coming into office with a moderate mixed party.

May 28th

On returning from Epsom I heard that Stanley, Graham and Richmond had resigned and it was supposed that Ripon [Goderich translated], would follow their example. [He did].

June 1st

... The general opinion is this Cabinet so amended cannot go on long; but as they clearly mean to throw themselves upon the H. of Commons, and as the House will at all events support them for the present, they will probably last some time longer ... [Graham] contends that it is not expedient, that the connexion between the two countries is mainly held together by the Protestant Church, and that any meddling with the establishment will inevitably lead to its downfall. He stands upon religious grounds. I confess myself to be lost in astonishment at the views they take on this subject; that after swallowing the camel of the Reform Bill, they should strain at the gnats which were perched upon the camel's back, that they should not have perceived from the first that such reforms as these must be consequent upon the great measure, and, above all, that the prevalence of publick opinion, abstract justice and the condition of Ireland all loudly call for their adoption ...

June 7th

... The Government is now reformed and will scramble and totter on for some time. Things are not ripe for a change, but people will continue more and more to look for a junction between Peel and Stanley. God forbid however that we should have two parties established upon the principles of a religious hostility to each other; it would be the worst of evils, and yet the times appear to threaten something of the sort. There is the gabble of 'the Church in danger', the menacing and sullen disposition of the Dissenters, all armed with new power and the restless and increasing turbulence of the catholicks, all hating one another, and elements of discord stirred up first by one then another ...

June 27th

... Miraflores [Spanish ambassador] paid a droll compliment to Madame de Lieven the other night. She was pointing out the various beauties at some ball, and among others, Lady Seymour, and asked him if he did not admire her. He said 'Elle est trop jeune, trop fraîche' and then with a tender look and squeezing her hand, 'J'aime les femmes un peu passées.' ...

July 6th

... I had not read Stanley's speech [he had compared Ministers and their reforms of the Irish Church with pea and thimble operators at racecourses] ... I do not know when I have heard so virulent and coarse an invective, and it is rather disgusting than anything else to see one fired off at the men with whom he has been acting for some years (up to three weeks ago), with whom he declared his entire concurrence on every other question ... The Tories cheered him lustily; and what must he on reflection think of such cheers, and of his position in the House – to be halloo'd on by the party which he has hitherto treated with the greatest contempt and which he thinks the very essence of bigotry and prejudice, at least on all secular matters, against his old friends and colleagues ... he will never inspire real confidence or conciliate real esteem. I entertain this opinion with regret, and could have wished he had cut a better figure. It is clear that his talents are of a higher order than his qualities.

I dined with a Tory at the Travellers' yesterday and he said 'Of course we cheered him as loudly as we could; we want to get him, but I must own that it was a very injudicious speech, very blackguard and unbecoming.' ...

July 10th

Came to town last night from Newmarket and found things in fine state. Althorp had resigned three days ago; his resignation was accepted, on which

Lord Grey resigned too. Both of them explained in Parliament last night, Lord Grey as they tell me, in a very moving and gentlemanlike speech, admirably delivered. The Duke of Wellington made a violent attack upon him in reply which it is thought he might as well (the Duke's speech gave great disgust to many even of his own party). Nobody knows what is to happen. The King sent for Melbourne, and his nephew, John Ponsonby, told me last night he believed he would endeavour to carry on the Government; but whether he does or not it can't last; the Whig Government is virtually at an end . . .

July 15th

This interval of feverish activity has ended by formation of an Administration being entrusted to Lord Melbourne . . . Nobody thinks the Government will last long, and everybody wonders how Melbourne will do it. He is certainly a queer fellow to be Prime Minister, and he and Brougham are two wild chaps to have the destinies of this country in their hands. I would not be surprised if Melbourne was to rouse his dormant energies and be excited by the greatness of his position to display the vigour and decision in which he is not deficient. Unfortunately his reputation is not particularly good; he is considered lax in morals, indifferent in religion and very loose and pliant in politicks . . .

July 19th

Two angry debates in the Lords last night and the night before; I was present at the last but not at the first. On Thursday Wicklow made a virulent attack on the Government, the D. of Buckingham was coarse, the Chancellor rabid and a disgraceful scene of confusion and disorder arose.

August 5th

At Goodwood for the races . . . Stanley at Goodwood, absorbed in racing, billiards and what not; nobody would have guessed that this rough and rustic gaiety covered ambition, eloquence and powers which must make him one of the most eminent men, though his reputation is not what it was . . .

August 6th

To my office, then to the House of Lords and heard a discussion on foreign politics; not very amusing; Melbourne not so good as Grey would have been . . . Walked from the House with Lord Carnarvon who is an intelligent man, but an alarmist and very desponding; thinks we are going on step by step to an utter subversion of all interests and institutions.

August 16th

. . . The Chancellor went down and, in presence of the Ladies, attired in his golden robes and especially before Mrs Petre to whom he makes love, gave a judgment in some case in which a picture of Nell Gwynne was concerned, and he was very proud of the *delicacy* of his judgement. There never was anything like his exhilaration and good humour. I don't know what has come to him, except it be that he has scrambled through the session and got Lord Grey out. He wound up in the H. of Lords by the introduction of his Bill for a Judicial Committee there, which he prefaced by a speech exhibiting his own judicial acts, and undoubtedly making a capital case for himself as to diligence and despatch if it be all true (which I see no reason to doubt), and passing a great eulogium upon the House of Lords as an institution, and drawing comparison between that House and the House of Commons much to the disadvantage of the latter, expressing many things which are very true and just and of a highly conservative tendency. He is a strange Being whom, with all his inconsistencies and his knavery, one cannot but admire; so varied and prodigal are his powers. Much more are these lines applicable to him than to his predecessor on the Woolsack [Lord Lyndhurst] –

> Great wits are sure to madness close allied
> And thin partitions do their bounds divide.
> [Dryden, *Absalom and Achitophel*, part 1, lines 163–4]

... Le Marchant told somebody that his most difficult employment was to correct and copy out the Chancellor's Greek epigrams to Lord Wellesley, his Greek orthography being even worse than his English ...

August 19th

... The Chancellor had intended to go junketing on the Rhine with Mrs Petre, and this project was only marred by discovering that he could not leave the country without putting the Great Seal in commission at a cost (to himself) of £1400. This was a larger price than he was prepared to pay for his amatory trip, so he went off to Brougham [his house in Westmorland] instead ...

September 4th

... At court yesterday. The King came to town to receive the address of the City on the Queen's return – the most ridiculous address I ever heard. The Queen was too ill to appear. Her visit to Germany knocked her up, and well it might, considering the life she led – always up at six and never in bed till twelve, continual receptions and in a state of representation. Errol told me she showed them her old Bedroom in the Palace (as they call it)[2] at Meiningen – a hole which an English housemaid would think it a hardship to sleep in ...

... When [on Grey's resignation], the King sent for him [Melbourne] said to Young [Thomas Young, his secretary, known as 'Ubiquity Young'] he thought it a damned bore, and he was in many minds what he should do – be Minister or no. Young said 'Why damn it, such a position was never occupied by any Greek or Roman, and if it only lasts two months, it is well worth while to have been Prime Minister of England.' 'By God, that's true' said Melbourne 'I'll go.' ...

September 19th

Yesterday at Holland House; nobody there but Melbourne. We were talking of Reform, and Ld. Holland said 'I don't know if we were right about Reform, but this I know, that if we were to propose it at all, we were right in going to the lengths that we did, and this was Canning's opinion.' Melbourne said 'Yes I know it was, and that was mine, and that was the reason I was against Reform.' ...

London November 13th

For two months nearly that I have been in the country I have not written a line, having had nothing worth recording to put down ... My own history is shortly told. Went to Newmarket the last day of September; to Buckenham after the First October meeting; was laid up with the gout between the Second and Third; after Houghton to Euston, then to Cromer Hall, to Newmarket for a day, and to town yesterday. Won about £1600 by the three Meetings and terminated the year by winning about £7000 [£350,000 today]; the best year but one I ever made on the turf, and better on the whole, because then I lost nearly all of it at play, and now I am wiser and warier and have lost nothing in that way. Still all the success has not prevented frequent disgusts, and I derive anything but unmixed pleasure from the pursuit even when successful ...

Sunday November 16th

Yesterday the town was electrified by the news that Melbourne's Government was at an end ... Thus it befell: on Thursday Melbourne went to Brighton to make the arrangements necessary on Lord Spencer's death. [Earl Spencer was the father of Lord Althorp who succeeded to the peerage, vacating the leadership of the Commons.] ... Nothing more passed that night, and the next day when Melbourne saw the King, H. My. placed in his hands a letter containing his determination. It was couched in terms complimentary to Lord Melbourne, but he said that having lost the services of Lord Althorp as Leader of H. of C., he could feel no confidence in the stability of his Government when led by any other member of it; that they were already a minority in one H. of Parliament, and that he had every reason to believe that the removal of Lord Althorp would speedily put them in the same situation in the other; that under such circumstance he felt other arrangements were to be necessary, and that it was his intention to send for the Duke of Wellington ...

It is very evident that the King has long determined to seize the first plausible pretext he could find for getting rid of these people whom he dislikes and fears, and that he thinks (justly or not remains to be proved) that the transla-tion of Althorp affords him a good opportunity ... All the Ministers (except Brougham) read the account of their dismissal in *The Times* the next morning ... This morning Lord Lansdowne wrote me word that the Duke had accepted, but it is probable that nothing can be done till Peel returns from Italy. He will accept no other post but that of Prime Minister, though the King would prefer to put the Duke there if he would take it.

November 17th

On the Friday night, Melbourne with a party of his colleagues – Mulgrave, Ben Stanley, Pow.[lett] Thomson and one or two more – were at the play just opposite to me; the piece was *The Regent* and it was full of jokes about dismissing Ministers and other things very applicable, at which Melbourne at least (who does not care a button about *office* whatever he may do about power) was heartily amused.

Five o'clock

Just returned from St James's ... After greeting them all and desiring them to sit down [the King] began a speech nearly as follows: 'Having thought proper to make a change in my Government, at the present moment I have directed a new commission to be issued for executing the office of Lord High Treasurer, at the head of which I have placed the Duke of Wellington, and his grace has kissed hands upon that appointment ...' [Robert Peel was in Italy!]

... Thus ended this eventful day; just four years ago I witnessed the reverse of the picture. I think the Whigs upon this occasion were much more angry and dejected than the Tories upon that. They had perhaps some reason, for their case is one of rare occurrence – unceremoniously kicked out, not resignations following unsuccessful negotiations or baffled attempts at arrangements, but in the plenitude of their fancied strength, and utterly unconscious of danger they were discarded in the most positive, summary and peremptory mode. Great therefore is their indignation, mortification and chagrin, and bitter no doubt will be their opposition.

They think the new Government will have no chance of getting a House of Commons that will support them, and certainly if they do not, and if the Tories are compelled after a fruitless struggle to resign, miserable will be the condition of the King and House of Lords, and not very enviable that of any Government that may succeed them ...

[November] 19th

... The Duke, I find, after the Council on Monday (losing no time), repaired to the Home Office and ordered the Irish papers to be brought to him, then to the FO where he asked for the last despatches from Spain and Portugal, and so on to the Colonial where he required information as to the size of the Department.

I have no doubt he liked this, to play the part of Richelieu for a brief period, to exercise all the functions of administration. They complain however and not without reason of the unceremonious and somewhat uncourteous mode in which without previous notice, he entered into the vacant office, taking actual possession, without any of the usual civilities to the old occupants ...

Powell, a Tory solicitor and *âme damnée* of the Speaker's has just been here; he declares that the Tories will be 420 strong in the new Parliament, which I mention for the purpose of recording their expectations and being able to compare them hereafter with the event. They have already put themselves in motion, despatched messengers to Hertford and Lowther, and probably if they could ever be induced to open their purse strings and make sacrifices and exertions they will do it now ...

November 26th

I walked home with Duncannon[3] last night ... He is thoroughly convinced that the present appearances of indifference and tranquillity in the country are delusive, that the elections will rouse a dormant spirit, and that the minor differences of Reformers and Liberals of all denominations will be sunk in a determined hostility to the Government of Peel and the Duke ...

November 27th

... The Duke told Wharncliffe that both he and the King were fully aware of the importance of the step that H.M. had taken – that this is, in fact, the Conservative last cast – and that he (the King) is resolved to neither flinch nor falter, but having embarked with them, to nail his flag to the mast and put forth all the Constitutional authority of the Crown in support of the Government he is about to form. I am strongly inclined to think that this determination when properly ascertained will have considerable influence and that provided a respectable and presentable Cabinet be formed and Liberal measures adopted, they will succeed. Though the Crown is not so powerful as it was, there probably remains a great deal of attachment and respect to it, and if the King can show a fair case to the country, there will be found, both in Parliament and out, a vast number of persons who will reflect deeply upon the consequences of coming to a serious collision with the Throne, and consider whether the exigency is such as to justify such extremities ... I walked home with Duncannon at night, and I told him this; he seemed struck by this, but still maintained that Parliament would, in his opinion, not accept the new Ministry on any terms. If Peel makes a High Tory Government and holds High Tory language, I think so too, and I can scarcely hope that it should be otherwise. My mind, I own, misgives me about Peel; I hope everything from his capacity and dread everything from his character.

November 28th

This morning I got a letter from my uncle, the Duke of Portland, complaining of the Weights and Measures Bill and begging that if possible an order in Council might be passed suspending the operation of the Act ...

December 1st

Went to St Paul's yesterday evening to hear Sydney Smith preach. He is very good, manner impressive, voice sonorous and agreeable, rather familiar, but not offensively so, language simple and unadorned, sermon clear and illustrative. The service is exceedingly grand, performed with all the pomp of a Cathedral and chaunted with beautiful voices; the lamps scattered few and far between throughout the vast empty space under the dome, making darkness visible and dimly revealing the immensity of the building, were exceedingly striking. The Cathedral service thus chaunted and so performed is my beau ideal of religious worship – simple, intelligible and grand, appealing at the same time to the reason and the imagination. I prefer it infinitely to the Catholic service, for though I am fond of the bursts of music and the clouds of incense, I can't endure the undistinguishable sounds with which the priest mumbles over prayers ...

December 6th

The Chancellor [Lyndhurst] called on me yesterday about getting young d'Israeli into Parliament (through the means of George Bentinck) for Lynn. I had told him G. wanted a good man to assist in turning out Billy Lennox and he suggested the above named gentleman, whom he called a friend of Chandos's. His political principles must however be in abeyance, for he said Durham was doing all he could to get him by the offer of a seat and so forth; if therefore he is undecided and wavering between Chandos and Durham [Lord Chandos was the heir of the Duke of Buckingham and, like him, a Tory Ultra. Lord Durham was a dedicated radical], he must be a mighty impartial personage. I don't think such a man will do, though just such as Lyndhurst would be connected with.

December 7th

... George [Bentinck] sent to Sturges Bourne to know if he would come in for Lynn, but he would not hear of it ... d'Israeli he won't hear of.

December 8th

I read J. Russell's speech at Totnes last night; it was a very masterly performance, suitable to the occasion and effective ... He endeavoured to establish these points: first that the Duke of Wellington had continually opposed all Reform measures and had been the enemy of Reform principles; secondly, that they (the late Government) had done a great deal, and thirdly that there really had occurred no circumstances in the Cabinet or with the King to account for their summary dismissal. There is no doubt that his first position is incontrovertible that he makes out a very fair case for the second, and his argument on the third throws great doubt on the matter in my mind, having previously thought that the King had a good case to show to the world. It is not so much the Duke's opposition to this or that particular measure, but the whole tenor of his conduct and opinions which it puts one in despair to look at ... I am persuaded that he deludes himself by some process of extraordinary false reasoning, and that the habits of intense volition, jumbled up with party prejudices, old association and exposure to never-ending flattery have produced the remarkable result we see in his conduct; not withstanding the enormous blunders he has committed and his numerous and flagrant inconsistencies, he has never lost his confidence in himself and what is more curious, has contrived to retain that of a host of followers.

December 10th

Sir Robert arrived yesterday morning at eight o'clock. Great was the bustle among his clan; there were Rosses, Plantas [Party Hacks] and all of them pacing before his door while he was still closeted with the Duke ...

December 14th

Lord Wharncliffe to his great joy, was sent for by Peel yesterday and very civilly invited to join the new Cabinet ... Stanley and Graham will support the Government [both had been at some time members of the Grey and Melbourne Cabinets], and it now appears that the Duke of Wellington is the real obstacle to their joining. To Peel, Stanley has no objection; he has spoken of him in the highest terms; but after the speech which the Duke made when Lord Grey went out, in which he attacked him and his Government with a virulence which gave great disgust at the time, Stanley feels that he could not with regard for his own honour and compatibly with his respect and attachment for Lord Grey, form a part of this Government ...

[December] 16th

A great field day at court yesterday; all the new Ministers sworn in, except the Colonial Secretary who is not yet appointed and some subordinate offices ...

December 20th

Peel's letter to his constituents [this was the famous Tamworth Manifesto, the first party political appeal to the public] has appeared as his manifesto to the country; a very well written and ingenious document, and well calculated to answer the purpose, if it can be answered at all ...

December 24th

Dined yesterday at the Mansion House; never before having seen a Civic Feast, thought this a good opportunity. The Egyptian Hall is fine enough; the other rooms miserable. A great company and all Tories almost . . . A few days ago I fell in with Hobhouse and he walked with me to my office. He told me that He and his fellow Committee men at Ellice's [Edward Ellice was the Whig Chief Whip], astonished at the confident expectations of the Carltonians [the Carlton Club, headquarters and resort of all Tories, had been established in 1832] as to the result of a dissolution, went over the list scrupulously and jealously and resolved to know the worst; that after making every allowance they could and excluding all doubtful places and all Stanleyites, they found themselves with a majority of 195 votes, and deducting from that 50 men who might be Waverers and on whom it might not be safe to count, they still found 150 . . .

December 27th

Yesterday I met Munster [eldest, and most disreputable, illegitimate son of William's long sojourn with Dora Jordan] who told me long histories of the squabbles in the R. Family, that is between the King and his good for nothing bastards. I have frequently advised Munster to make it up with his father which he never can be persuaded to do, always maintaining that by holding out he shall make better terms – money being his object; . . . from his own injuries he proceeded to the misdeeds of his Brothers, for the motes in his Brothers' eyes he can see very clearly: how Frederic who had received and spent thousands, had sent in a bill of £12,000 debt; that the King had told him he might sell his house to liquidate the debt, and he would make up any deficiency between the sums; that F. had disdained to answer this, and had flounced off with eight or 10 of the King's horses, half a dozen Servants and 3 carriages without a word of notice . . .

1835

January 1st

Parliament dissolved at last, and all speculation about the elections will be settled in certainty. It is remarkable what confidence is expressed by both sides . . . Yesterday I dined with Robarts and after dinner he gave me an account of the state of his borough (Maidstone) and as it is a tolerably fair sample probably of the real condition of the generality of boroughs and of the principles and dispositions of their constituencies, I will put it down. There are 1200 voters; the Dissenters are very numerous and of every imaginable sect and persuasion. He has been member seventeen years; the place very corrupt. Formerly (before the Reform Bill) when the Constituency was less numerous, the matter was easily and simply conducted; the price of votes was as regularly fixed as the price of bread – so much for a single vote and so much for a plumper, [one voting for both candidates of a party in a two-seat borough] and this he had to pay.

After the Reform Bill he resolved to pay no more money, as corruption was to cease. The consequence was that during his canvass, none of the people who had formerly voted for him would promise him their vote. They all sulked and hesitated, and, in short, waited to see what would be offered them. I asked him what were the new constituency. 'If possible worse than the old.' The people are generally alive to public affairs – look into the votes and speeches of members, give their opinions, but are universally corrupt. They have a sour feeling against what are nick-named abuses, rail against *sinnicures*, as they call them, and descant upon the enormity of such things while they are forced to work all day long and their families have not enough to eat. But the one prevailing object among the whole community is to make money of their votes . . . Power has been transferred to a low class of person; so low as to be dissatisfied and malignant, high enough to be half-instructed; so poor that money is an object to them, and without any principle which should deter them from getting it as they can: they may, on the whole, be considered disaffected towards existing institutions . . . but as their immediate wants are uppermost, their votes are generally at the disposal of the highest bidder, whatever his politics may be . . .

January 7th
Just as might have been expected, the Conservative candidates in the City are defeated by an enormous majority. Pattison, Governor of the Bank having been proposed by Lloyd [otherwise Loyd, of Jones, Loyd and Co., later London and Westminster], the richest Banker in the City and perhaps the richest man in Europe.

January 8th
On the whole, the returns yesterday presented a gain to Government of about 10 votes, many elections turning out contrary to expectation both ways and some very severe contests . . . At dinner yesterday at Chesterfield's I met the Chancellor [Lyndhurst] whom I have not seen for some time. After dinner we talked about things. 'Well' he said 'will it do?' I said 'I don't know what to think, but I am disposed to think it will *not* do. I don't see how you are to get on.' . . .

He asked me if I thought the Opposition meant to refuse the Supplies. I said I had no doubt they did. 'Then we must go.'

January 9th

Dined at the Hollands; they are satisfied with the elections. Mulgrave said that out of the present return they had to add thirty to their list, and to deduct thirteen of their original calculations, giving them seventeen, more than they expected . . . the rabid spirit of disaffection to Government and rule bears down every other consideration and these 'enlightened electors' (as their flatterers always call them) are frantick with passion against everything belonging to what they call 'the Aristocracy' of the country . . .

January 11th

. . . The contests are curious from their closeness . . . in that of Rochester it is more remarkable from the accident by which the election was lost. There were two ships in quarantine, one of which had one voter on board and the other two; they had both sailed the same day from the port they had left, but one had been longer on the voyage. The ship with one voter had a right to be released on the 9th, the last day of the election, the other not till three days later. As the circumstances are the same, Sir J. Marshall, the Superintendent, suggested that both might be released together, but I did not dare relax the severity of the restriction [a question for the Privy Council, exercised by the Clerk, Charles Greville] . . . as if the election should turn upon it, we should never hear the last of it . . .

January 17th

The Middlesex election terminated in the return of that ruthless blackguard Hume [Joseph Hume, opponent of flogging in the Navy, the press gang, imprisonment for debt, bars to workmen travelling abroad for employment and supporter of free trade with India!] . . . It would have been a capital thing to turn out Hume, but I never expected it.

January 20th

. . . On the other hand, Palmerston beat in Hants, at which everybody rejoices, for he is marvellously unpopular; they would have liked to illuminate the Foreign Office . . .

February 8th

My brothers [Algernon Greville was secretary to Wellington] tell me that the Duke is bored to death with the King. Who thinks it is necessary to be giving advice and opinions upon different matters, always to the last degree ridiculous and absurd. He is just now mightily indignant at Lord Napier's affair in Canton [Napier had been ordered to leave Macao by the Chinese Governor] and wants to go to war with China. He writes in this strain to the Duke who is obliged to write long answers, very respectfully telling him what an Old

Fool he is . . . He thinks his present Ministers do not treat him well inasmuch as they do not tell him enough. The last, it seems, constantly fed him with scraps of information which he twaddled over, and probably talked nonsense about; but it is difficult to imagine anything more irksome for a Government beset with difficulties like this than to have to discuss the various details of their measures with a silly, bustling old fellow who can by no possibility comprehend the scope and bearing of anything.

February 14th

There has been a wonderful lull for some time past, and though we are said to be, and I believe we in fact are, on the eve of a crisis of great importance, perfect tranquillity prevails universally (except of course in Ireland), and men go about their daily occupations without any sign of apprehension . . .

February 15th

. . . I went yesterday to see the two houses of parliament [the temporary settings after the fire of 1834 while Charles Barry's work on the present building continued]; the old H. of Lords (now H. of C.) is very spacious and convenient; but the present H. of Lords is a wretched dog-hole. The Lords will be very sulky in such a place and in a great hurry to get back to their own place or have another. For the first time there is a gallery in the H. of Commons reserved for Reporters which is quite inconsistent with their standing orders, and the prohibition which still in form exists against publishing the debates. It is a sort of public and avowed homage to opinion, and a recognition of the right of the people to know through the medium of the press all that passes within those walls.

Johnny [Russell] said to me, 'Do you remember last year, when we were talking, I told you I thought the H. of Lords would throw out some measure or other – that there would be a change of Government, a dissolution; and then we should have a Parliament returned with which *nobody* could govern the country. You see we have reached that point.' . . .

February 19th

The important day is arrived, and it dawns in Sunshine and South wind. In a few hours the question of the Speakership will be decided, and there will be at least the gain (wherever the loss may fall) of getting rid of a subject which has become so intolerably tiresome . . .

[February] 20th

The great battle is over and the Government defeated, 316 to 306 [Abercrombie, candidate of the Whigs, defeated the incumbent Tory, Manners-Sutton] . . . The elation on one side and the depression on the other were naturally considerable . . . Much money was won and lost; everybody betted, I won £55, for on the whole I thought (though rather a toss-up) that the chances were in favour of Abercrombie . . . Peel and the Duke dined at Lord Salisbury's, [the 2nd Marquess, father of the Prime Minister. Professor Norman Gash, better informed, tells us that Peel didn't go!] and all the Tories were invited there in the evening, with the intentions probably of celebrating their anticipated victory; and if so, their merry meeting must have been changed to dismal alarms, for there is no denying or concealing that it is a very serious disaster. The moral effect of beginning with a defeat is bad; it discourages the wavering and timid who might have felt half disposed to support the Government . . . and though there are none among the majority who will support Government, there are some among the minority who will oppose them . . . Nothing can be more clear than that the present Ministers are in a minority, and that all the other parties in the House united can beat them when they will . . .

[February] 21st

I never was so struck as yesterday by the vulgarity of Peel. In all his ways, his dress, his manner, he looks more like a vulgar shopkeeper than a Prime Minister. He eats voraciously and cuts cream and jellies with his knife. [The Earl of] Jersey pointed this out to me. And yet he has genius and taste, and his thoughts are not vulgar though his manners are to such a degree . . .

March 14th

Last night was a terribly damaging night to the Government and fully justifies what I, in common with almost everybody else, thought of that miserable appointment of Londonderry [to be ambassador in St Petersburg]. Sheil [often at odds with O'Connell] brought it forward and a storm burst from every side . . . Peel spoke cleverly, as usual, but fighting under difficulties, and dodging about and shifting his ground with every mark of weakness. The result is that Londonderry cannot go and must either resign or his appointment be cancelled . . .

[March] 17th

Londonderry made a good speech in the H. of Lords last night, gentlemanlike and temperate. He got a good deal of empty praise in both Houses in lieu of the solid pudding he is obliged to give up . . . The man is utterly unfit and ought never to have been appointed, but the case against him (such as it appears in their hands) is quite insufficient to warrant the interference of Parliament. It is however impossible to forgive the Duke or Peel for not foreseeing all this . . .

. . . Sugden has resigned the Chancellorship of Ireland because his wife is not received at court. [He threatened to resign, but was persuaded to withdraw.] He might have ascertained very easily beforehand what would happen, or have contrived to keep her away from Dublin, but he has acted like a great fool. Lady Sugden was his Kitchenmaid, and after having two or three children by her, he married her and begot divers others. It was understood when he took the Great Seal that he declined being made a Peer on account of the illegitimacy of his eldest son. Half the World had never heard of Lady Sugden ... and as She is an excellent woman, charitable and kind-hearted, I fancy She has moved without obstruction in his natural circle of society. He went to Ireland before any Lord-Lieutenant was named, and Lady Sugden was received as a matter of course.

When Lady Haddington [wife of the Lord-Lieutenant] was apprised of her origin and history, She foresaw the difficulty, and asked the Queen what She was to do. H.M. told her to do what she pleased, but that certainly she could not be received at court here. The Lady-Lieutenant therefore was compelled to decline receiving her, for all Ireland would have been affronted had she received at the Castle a Lady not presentable at St James's ...

[March] 26th Thursday

... It is very obvious that Peel cannot go on; and I doubt very much if he could even were he to obtain a majority on Monday [the vote on the Irish Tithes Bill]. His physical strength would not suffice for the harassing warfare that is waged against him, the whole brunt of which he bears alone ... He must be in continual danger of defeats upon minor or collateral questions or suddenly started points. His party is in great part constituted of the rich and fashionable who are constantly drawn away by one attraction or another, and whose habitual haunts are the clubs and houses at the west end of the Town; and it is next to impossible to collect his scattered forces at a moment's notice. The Opposition contains a dense body of fellows who have no vocation out of the walls of the House of Commons; who put up in the vicinity; either do not dine at all or get their meals at some adjoining chop house, throng the benches early and never think of moving till everything is over ... In old times the placemen and immediate hangers-on of Government who made it their business to attend in order to carry the public business through, afforded a regular certain Majority for the Ministers of the day; but now this household phalanx is outnumbered by these blackguards, the chief of whom are O'Connell's tail and the lower Radicals ...

April 3rd

They divided at I know not what hour this morning – 321 to 289 ...

[April] 4th

I told Jonathan Peel [the Prime Minister's brother] last night that Stanley and Graham blamed Sir R. Peel for not resigning at once. He said that Sir R.

would, as far as his own feelings were concerned, have preferred resigning long ago, but that vast numbers of his supporters were furious at the idea of resigning at all, and wanted him to persist at all hazards ... He then told me (which I certainly did not attach the slightest credit to) that he should not be surprised if his brother did not now resign from public life.

[April] 5th

I understand now what Jonathan Peel meant by talking of the possibility of his Brother's retiring from public life. He is no doubt heartily disgusted with his own associates ... It is very evident that many of them are desirous (if Peel does resign) of continuing the fight under the Duke of Wellington, if they could prevail on him to try it, and to dissolve Parliament and get up a 'No Popery' cry. They say that 'the Country', by which they mean their own faction, looks up to the Duke, and that Peel has no real interest there. The fact is that they cannot forgive him for his Liberal principles and Liberal measures, and probably they never believed that he was sincere in the professions he made, or that he really intended to introduce such measures as he has done ... Peel sees and knows all this, and cannot fail to perceive that he is not the Minister for them and they no longer the party for him.

April 7th

Each day elicits some new proof of what I have written above – the totally altered feelings and expressions of all conditions of politicians about Sir Robert Peel. It would seem as if his friends were suddenly converted into his Enemies and his Enemies into his friends. The Tories still cling to the expectation that he will hold on to his office; they say he abandons his party, abandons the King. They call to mind Pitt in '84. 'Very slippery' said one to me yesterday, when I read to him Peel's answer to the City address. On the other hand, Mulgrave was last night enthusiastic in his praise; owned that He had done admirably – given proofs of his perfect sincerity and had acted in accordance with all his declarations and professions ... and then to make the whole thing ridiculous (if any thing so serious can be ridiculous), the Tories who abuse him lustily, are moving heaven and earth to retain him, by violence almost, in his place; the Whigs and Radicals, who laud him up to the skies, are striving with might and main to turn him out.

[April] 9th

Yesterday the Ministers resigned. Peel announced it to the H. of Commons in a short but admirable speech, by all accounts, exactly suited to the occasion and to his principle object – that of setting himself right with his own supporters, who begin to acquiesce, though rather sulkily, in the course he has pursued ...

April 11th

... [The King] has given Melbourne *carte blanche* to form a Government, and he is proceeding in the task. Notwithstanding the good face which the King contrives to put upon the matter in his communications with the hated new-old Ministers and masters, he is really very miserable; and the Dss. of Gloster, to whom he unbosoms himself more than to anybody, told Lady G. Bathurst that he was with her in the most pitiable state of distress, constantly in tears, and saying that 'he felt his Crown tottering on his head'.

[April] 13th

Nothing positively known yesterday, but the thing is settled in some way. Clustering and congregatings of Whigs about Brooks's, audiences with the King, and great doubt whether Grey took office, and the Foreign Office.

[April] 14th

... I certainly never remember a great victory for which Te Deum was chaunted with so faint and joyless a voice. Peel looks gayer and easier than all Brooks's put together, and Lady Holland said, 'Now that we have gained our object I am not so glad as I thought I should be,' and that I take to be the sentiment of them all ...

Buckenham April 29th

... The last day of Parliament was distinguished by a coarse attack [the phrase was 'bloated buffoon, a liar, a disgrace to his species and heir-at-law of the thief who died upon the cross'] of O'Connell upon Alvanley for what he had said the day before in the H. of Lords. Alvanley has sent him a message through Dr Damer [Lionel Damer-Dawson MP (1835–47)] demanding an apology or satisfaction, and the result I don't yet know. He, De Ros writes me word of it.

London May 17th

... all the newspapers are full of the details ... there was a meeting at De Ros's house of De Ros, Damer, Worcester and Duncombe to consider what was to be done on receipt of Morgan O'Connell's [Daniel's son] letter and whether A. should fight him or not. Worcester and Duncombe were against fighting, the other two for it. Alvanley at once said the boldest course was the best, and he would go out ... so Damer was despatched to Colonel Hodges [the referee, by profession a diplomat!] and Alvanley was ready to meet Morgan O'Connell.[1] 'The next morning' Hodges suggested. 'No, immediately.' The parties joined in Arlington Street and went off in two hackney coaches; Duncombe, Worcester and De Ros with Hume in a third. Only Hume went on the ground, for Damer had objected to the presence of some Irish friend of O'Connell's so that Alvanley's friends could only look on at a distance.

The only other persons who came near them were an old Irishwoman and a Methodist Parson, the latter of whom exhorted the contestants in vain to forego their sinful purpose, and to whom A. replied 'Pray sir, go and mind your own affairs, for I have enough to do to think now of mine.' 'Think of your soul' he said. 'Yes' said Alvanley 'but my body is now in the greatest danger.' The Irishwoman would come and see the fighting, and asked for some money for her attendance. Damer seems to have been a very bad second and probably lost his head; he ought not to have consented to the third shots upon any account. Alvanley says he execrated him in his heart when he found he had consented to it. Hodges acted like a ruffian, and had anything happened he would have been hanged. It is impossible to know if the first shot [by O'Connell] was fired by mistake or not. The impression on the minds of Alvanley's friends is that it was *not*, but it is difficult to believe that any man would endeavour to take such an advantage. However no shot ought to have been fired after that. The affair made an amazing noise.

Saturday May 30th
Wednesday last went to Charles Kemble's in the evening; singing and playing; Mr Arkwright, Miss Strutt, old Liverati (horrible squalling) and Miss Adelaide Kemble.

Thursday night
To Horace Twiss's[2] to what he called a 'Judy party' – a supper and jollification where all were expected to contribute to the amusement of the company who possessed wherewithal. The Contributors were Twiss himself, Mrs Arkwright, Miss Cooke,[3] Dance [an actor], Miss Dance, Planché,[4] Mrs Blood, Mrs Groom, Theodore Hook,[5] Billy something ... I staid till two, and they went on till three. It was sufficiently amusing altogether though noisy and vulgar; company very miscellaneous, but everybody ready to amuse and be amused.

Friday
Committee of Council on matter of London University; Brougham of course, the great performer ... there were Melbourne, Lansdowne and certain of his Colleagues, Brougham and Lyndhurst ... Richmond, Ripon, Stanley and Graham ... Brougham proposed a resolution 'that the K. should be advised to grant a charter making the petitioners an University, the regulations and restrictions to be determined hereafter'. The Bishop of London objected on behalf of King's College to any advantages being conferred on the London University which would place the latter institution in a better condition than the former. After much tedious discussion, the words 'University etc' were omitted and the resolution moved was to '*grant a charter.*' The Duke of Richmond formally opposed

it, his principal objection being the insolvent state of the concern. Brougham sat in contemptuous silence for a few minutes while the Duke spoke, and then replied.

There was a squabble between them and an evident inclination on the part of the majority present to refuse the charter, but the address of the Commons with the King's answer were read which presented a very different case to answer upon. The King's answer amounted very nearly to an engagement to grant a charter; ... Brougham, after much ineffectual discussion, said in a tone of sarcastic contempt that 'their hesitations and their scruples were ridiculous, for the House of Commons would step in and cut them both short and settle the question.' ...

June 14th

Taken up with Epsom since I last wrote ...

I did not attend the second meeting at the Privy Council on the London University question ... it ended by a report to the King, requesting he would dispense with the advice of the Council; so the matter remains with the Government. It is clear they would have advised against granting the Charter but for the answer which the King made to the address of the H. of Commons which was in fact *a promise* to grant it. The promise was the work of Peel and Goulburn, and I can't imagine what induced them to put such a one into H.M.'s mouth when they might have so properly made him say that He had referred the matter to the Privy Council, and was waiting for their report.

June 19th

At Stoke [Poges] for Ascot races ... Alvanley there – nobody else remarkable; fine weather and great luxury. Riding to the course on Wednesday, I overtook Adolphus FitzClarence [another child of Dora Jordan] in the Park who rode with me and gave me an account of his Father's habits and present state of mind. The former are as follows: He sleeps in the same room with the Queen, but in a separate bed; at a quarter before eight every morning his *valet de chambre* knocks at the door, and at ten minutes before eight exactly, he gets out of bed, puts on a flannel dressing gown and trousers, walks into his dressing room, and goes at once to the water closet. Let who will be there, he never takes the slightest notice of them till he emerges from that temple, when (like the *malade imaginaire*) he accosts whoever may be present with a cheerful aspect. He is long at his ablutions, and takes up to an hour and a half in dressing.

At half past nine he breakfasts with the Queen, the ladies and any of his family; he eats a couple of fingers and drinks a dish of coffee. After breakfast he reads *The Times* and *Morning Post*, commenting aloud on what he reads in very plain terms, and sometimes they hear 'That's a damned lie' or some such remark without knowing to what it applies. After breakfast he devotes himself with Sir H. Taylor [Herbert Taylor, secretary of George IV and William] to business till two, when he lunches (two cutlets and two glasses of sherry); then he goes out and drives till dinner; at dinner drinks a bottle of sherry – no other wine – eats moderately and goes to bed soon after eleven. He is in dreadfully low spirits; the only interval of pleasure he has had lately was during the Devonshire election when he was delighted at John Russell's defeat. He abhors all his Ministers, even those whom he used to like, but hates Johnny most of all. When Adolphus told him that a dinner ought to be given for the Ascot races, he said 'You know I cannot give a dinner; I cannot give dinners without inviting the Ministers and I would sooner see the Devil than any one of them in my house.'

July 1st

. . . I went to St James's to swear in Sir C. Grey[6] and Chas. Fitzroy Privy Councillors when we had a most peculiar burst of eloquence from His Majesty. This is the first time I have seen him and his present Ministers together, and certainly they do not strike me as exhibiting any mutual affection. After Sir Charles Grey was sworn, the King said to him . . . 'I desire you however to bear in mind that the Colony to which you are about to proceed has not, like other British colonies, been peopled from the Mother Country – that is not an original possession of the Crown, but that it was obtained *by the sword.* You will take care to assert those undoubted prerogatives which the crown there possesses and which I am determined to enforce and maintain, and I charge you by the oath which you have just taken, strenuously to assert that prerogative, of which persons who ought to have known better have dared even in my presence to deny the existence.' . . . The silence was profound, and I was amused at the astonishment depicted on the faces of the Ministers . . .

July 7th

I can't deny that many persons have shown a very kind disposition to assist me in this business of my Jamaica place, [Greville's Secretaryship of Jamaica, wholly a sinecure, was under threat, like Mr Harding's Wardenship, from the current wave of administrative reform] of different political persuasions, and with most of whom I have but a very slight personal acquaintance, none more so than Gladstone and Lord Lincoln[7] . . . A placeman is in these days an odious animal, and as a double placeman, I am doubly odious, and I have a secret kind of whispering sensation that these very people who good-naturedly enough assist me must be a little shocked at the cause they advocate . . . The funds from which I draw my means do not somehow seem a pure source; formerly these things were tolerated, now they are not . . .

July 17th

Today Baring's committee meets to decide upon my case . . . [Baring] owned that he was the only person in the Government who was not disposed to uphold my place. Thus although he is the *exception* he is permitted to have his own way against the opinion of all the others including the Prime Minister . . .

. . . Tavistock told me a day or two ago that H.M.'s Ministers are intolerably disgusted at his treatment of them and at his studied incivility to any one connected with them. The other day, the Speaker was treated by him with shocking rudeness at the drawing room. He not only took no notice of him, but studiously overlooked him while he was standing opposite to him and called up Manners-Sutton and somebody else to mark the difference by extreme graciousness to the latter . . . Since he has been Speaker the King has never taken the slightest notice of him. It is monstrous, equally undignified and foolish. [James Abercrombie (see entry 20 February 1834), had been elected speaker as the Whig candidate.]

July 18th

Yesterday I sat all day at my office wondering why I heard nothing of the Committee, till at past four o'clock Graham and Lincoln came in with smiling faces that announced good news. They had held a debate of three hours duration. Baring moved that holding my office was against the spirit of the Act of Parliament. Graham argued that holding it with the leave of absence was in accordance with the Act and the division was nine to seven . . . I owe this victory to the zealous assistance of the Conservatives, for not one Whig or radical voted with me . . . it is really amusing to see the joy with which news of Baring's defeat has been hailed by every member of his own family [This Baring, Francis, was the only notable Whig in a Tory family.] and all others who have heard of it. The goodwill of the world (a very inert but rather satisfactory feeling) has been exhibited towards me, and there is mixed up with it, in all who are acquainted with the surly reformer who is my adversary, a lively pleasure at his being baffled and mortified.

August 9th

On Wednesday last at the levée the King made a scene with Lord Torrington, one of the Lords of his Bedchamber, and a very disgraceful scene. A card was put into Torrington's hands of somebody who was presented, which he read 'So and so, *Deputy Governor*'. 'Deputy Governor?' said the King 'Deputy Governor of what?' 'I cannot tell Y.M.' replied Torrington, 'as it is not upon the card.' 'Hold your tongue sir' said the King; 'you had better go home and learn to read'; and shortly after, when some Bishop presented an address against (I believe) the Irish Tithe Bill, and the King was going as usual to hand the papers to the Lord in waiting, he stopt, and said to Torrington who advanced to take them, 'No, Lord Torrington; these are not fit documents to be entrusted to your keeping.' His habitual state of excitement will probably bring on sooner or later the malady of his family. Torrington is a youth [b. 1812] without a guinea and unable to take his own part, or he ought to have resigned instantly and publicly as the insult was publicly offered . . .

Burghley September 21st
I did lose the St Leger, and did not care; idled on at Doncaster to the end of the week, and came here on Saturday to meet the Dss. of Kent . . .

London September 27th
The dinner at Burghley was very handsome; hall well lit; and all went well, except that a pail of ice was landed in the Duchess's lap which made a great bustle . . . The papers are full of nothing but O'Connell's progress in Scotland, where he is received with unbounded enthusiasm by enormous crowds, but by no people of rank, property or character . . .

November 17th
. . . all other sensations are absorbed in that which the Emperor of Russia's speech at Warsaw has produced and which indicates an excitement or ferocity, very like insanity. [Nicholas I, visiting Poland for the first time since the rising of 1830, told the Warsaw municipality that if it should happen again he would lay the city in ruins.] Melbourne mentioned at dinner on Sunday that it was not only correctly reported rather – *understated* – but that after he had so delivered himself, he met the English Consul on the street, took him by the arm, walked about with him for an hour, and begged him not to be *too hard* upon him in his report to his Government . . . evincing on the part of the Autocrat, in the midst of the insolence of unbridled power, a sort of consciousness of responsibility to European opinion and a deferential dread of that of England in particular.

December 4th
Lord Segrave has got the Gloucestershire Lieutenancy, and this appointment, disgraceful in itself, exhibits all the most objectionable features of the old Boroughmongering systems, which was supposed to be swept away. He was in London as soon as the breath was out of the D. of Beaufort's body, went to Melbourne and claimed this appointment on the score of having three members which was more than any other man in England now returned . . . The man is an arrant blackguard, has figured disreputably in more than one Court of Justice, purchased another man's wife (Mrs Burn) with whom he openly lives at Berkeley Castle [one who] for years acted on the Cheltenham stage . . . and is notorious for general worthlessness . . .

December 16th

Dined with Sefton the day before yesterday to meet the Hollands; sat between Allen and Luttrell ... Luttrell was talking of [Thomas] Moore and [Samuel] Rogers – the poetry of the former so licentious, that of the latter so pure; much of its popularity owing to its being so weeded of everything approaching to indelicacy; and the contrast between the *lives* and the *works* of the two men – the former a pattern of conjugal and domestic regularity, the latter of all the men He had ever known, the greatest sensualist.

1836

February 1st

Howick gave me an account yesterday of Spencer Perceval's communications to the Ministers and other Privy Councillors. He called on Howick ... Perceval began 'You will probably be surprised when you learn what has brought me here.' Howick bowed. 'You are aware that God has been pleased in these latter times to make especial communication of his will to certain chosen instruments, in a language not intelligible to those who hear it nor always by those by whom it is uttered: I am one of those instruments, to whom it has pleased the Almighty to make known his will, and I am come to declare to you. etc ...' and he went on in a rhapsody about the degeneracy of the times and the people falling off from God ... he specifies all the great acts of legislation for the last five years (beginning with the repeal of the Test and Corporation Acts and finishing with the Corporation Bill) as the evidence of a falling off from God or as the causes of a divine anger ...

His different receptions by different people are amusing and very characteristic. Howick listened to him with patient civility. Melbourne argued with and cross-questioned him. He told him that 'he ought to have gone to the Bishops instead of him' ... Stanley turned him out at once. As soon as he began he said 'There's no use Mr Perceval in going on this way with me. We had therefore better put an end to the subject and I wish you a good morning.' He went to Lord Holland and Lady Holland ... John Russell who happened to be in the house ... begged to be excused alleging that he had already had his interview. So at last she let Lord H. be wheeled in, but ordered Edgar and Harold, the two Pages, to post themselves outside the door and rush in if they heard Lord Holland scream ...

February 5th

Parliament met yesterday; the King received with great apathy. The Tories have not begun very well. After boasting of their increased numbers and of the great things they had accomplished by elections during the recess, they

got beat on a division [on an amendment to the Irish Corporation Bill] by 41
... The Tories are always hot for dividing, and the silly idle creatures who
compose the bulk of their party apologise for their continual absence by saying,
'Oh you never divide, so what's the use of coming up' as if divisions must be
got up for them when it suits their convenience to quit the hunting and
shooting and run upto town ...

February 9th

... [Macaulay] can repeat all Demosthenes by heart and all Milton, a great
part of the Bible, both in English and (the New Testament) in Greek ... Far
superior to Brougham in general knowledge, in fancy, imagination and in the
art of composition, he is greatly inferior to him in those qualities which raise
men to social and political eminence. Brougham, tall, thin and commanding in
figure with a face which, however ugly, is full of expression, and a voice of
great power, variety and even melody ... is an orator in every sense of the
word. Macaulay, short, fat and ungraceful, with a round, thick, unmeaning face
and with rather a lisp, though he has made speeches of great merit and of a
very high style of eloquence in point of composition, has no pretensions to be
put in competition with Brougham in the House of Commons ...

May 11th

Great talk about the adjournment of Parliament on the 20th and about
Melbourne's affair with Mrs Norton, [Caroline Norton, granddaughter of
Sheridan, wife of George Norton, a barrister and Tory, for whom Melbourne
found employment at £1000 a year as a police magistrate] which latter if it
is not quashed by a handsome douceur to Norton, will be inconvenient. John
Bull fancies himself vastly moral, and the court is mighty prudish and between
them our off-hand Premier will find himself in a ticklish position ... I said [to
the Duke of Wellington] 'Would M. resign?' 'O Lord no! Resign? Not a bit of
it. I tell you all these things are a nine days wonder; it can't come into Court
before parliament is up. People will have done talking of it before that happens;
it will all blow over, and won't signify a straw.' So spake his Grace. I doubt
not that Prime Ministers, ex and in, have a fellow feeling and sympathy for
each other, and like to lay down the principle of such things 'not mattering'.

May 25th

The Epsom races ... This year there has been a miserable catastrophe. Berkeley
Craven deliberately shot himself after losing more than he could pay. It is the
first instance of a man of rank and station in society making such an exit. He
had originally a large landed estate strictly entailed, got into difficulties, was
obliged to go abroad, compromised with his creditors and returned, fell into
fresh difficulties, involved himself inextricably in betting, and went on with a

determination to shoot himself if his speculations failed, and so he did. He was very popular, had been extremely handsome in youth and was a fellow of infinite humour and good humour . . .

June 27th

The town has been full of Melbourne's trial; great exultation at the result on the part of his political adherents, great disappointment on that of the mob of Low Tories, and a creditable satisfaction among the better sort . . . but there is a determination in many quarters to run down the woman . . . Nobody ever imagined that she was a pattern of propriety and decorum, and the question was not whether she was refined and scrupulous in her manners, but whether she was chaste in her conduct . . . But such are the ways of the world; malignity must fasten upon something, and if the man escapes they have nothing left for it but to turn upon the woman.

July 1st

At Stoke for three days; divine weather, profusion of shade and every luxury; nobody there of any consequence.

July 24th

. . . The King is evidently waiting with the greatest impatience for the moment when his Ministers must resign. He complained bitterly of my brother-in-law's going abroad, and said it was a time when every Conservative ought to be at his post, which means that every opponent of his Ministers should strive with ceaseless zeal to drive them to the wall. He is a true King of the Tories, for his impatience fully equals theirs.

August 7th Sunday

. . . there seems to have been an end to all notion of any compromise or any giving way on the part of the Government about the clauses in the Tithes Bill, and John Russell held very strong language. The debate presented nothing remarkable . . . The whole thing went off tamely enough; everybody in Parliament knew what was to happen, and out of doors people don't care. While revenue presents an excess of two millions, political excitement is impossible. The Lords continue to throw out Bills, and many complaints are made of their evident determination to reject as many of the Commons' measures as they can . . .

August 21st

The King at his last levée received [Dr Joseph] Allen to do homage for [the Bishopric of] Ely, when he said to him 'My Lord, I do not mean to interfere in any way with your vote in Parliament except on one subject, *the Jews*, and I trust I may depend on your always voting against them.'

November 7th

... [The King] was very angry at Leopold's[1] coming here ... and on occasion exhibited a rudeness even to brutality. It seems he hates water-drinkers; God knows why. One day at dinner Leopold called for water, when the King asked 'What are you drinking Sir?' 'Water Sir.' 'God Damn it!' rejoined the other King, 'Why don't you drink wine? I never allow anyone to drink water at my table.' Leopold only dined there, and went away in the evening. All this is very miserable and disgraceful ...

When I got to London I found it all ringing with De Ros's affair to which I have never been able to bring myself to allude ... To have one's oldest and most intimate friend convicted of being a cheat and a swindler, to be compelled to believe that for a long course of years he has been practising this nefarious trade, and that I have been not infrequently myself one of his victims, while his accusers are also my intimate friends and near relations is quite enough to cloud the most cheerful prospect. He is now threatening to return here and meet charges which must overwhelm him; God knows how it will end ...

November 30th

All London is occupied with this affair of De Ros's gradually becoming more publicly discussed. As usual there is no end to *cancan*, no end to lies, statements and misstatements that are current.

December 25th

... It was in the month of March (I think) that Brooke Greville [first cousin to Charles] came to me and told me that H [Henry De Ros] had been detected marking cards at Graham's Club, but that when first informed of it he disbelieved the story, but had at length been compelled to admit its truth. He then detailed to me all the evidence; the detection at Brighton by the two Higginses, a Mr Holmes and Fancourt [Charles St John Fancourt, later Governor of British Honduras]; the resolution of the parties not to expose him, and the restoration of a sum of money (£50 I believe) by Holmes to Fancourt on the ground that it had not been fairly won ... he added that he had gone to the Travellers' to see what he was doing there and found by personal examination and by the evidence of the card accountant (Brown) that he had likewise (on one occasion if not more) marked the cards there.

He had ordered (for the purpose of convincing my incredulity) that one of the packs so marked should be sealed up and sent to me, which was done. I opened it and found the marks as he had described them ... Cumming confirmed all Brooke had told me, and assured me that there was not a shadow of doubt of the fact, I at once told him that my first impulse was, if it were still possible, to save him, by turning him from difficult courses ... we resolved that an anonymous letter should be written to him warning him of his danger and telling him that a cessation from play could alone save him ... A short time after, Cumming came to me and told me that the letter had taken effect, that he had not indeed left off playing, but that he had left off marking the cards, that he was convinced he had abandoned the practice entirely, so much so that he would dismiss from his mind the past and prevent (as far as he could) anything being said by those who were in the secret ...

From this time I was generally in the country and occupied with racing, and I know not how long it was afterwards, but Brooke and Cumming came to me and informed me that H. had resumed the practice at Graham's ... that the indignation at the Club was with difficulty restrained from breaking out and that his ultimate exposure was inevitable ... Nothing in particular occurred from that time (nobody ever speaking to me on that subject and I to nobody) till the beginning of July, when at one of the Dss. of Buccleuch's breakfasts G. Anson for the first time broached it to me and told me how miserable he had been at what had occurred, adding how incredulous he had been, but how convinced he now was; and he then told me the history of Payne's sortie at Graham's, an incorrect version of which later appeared in the *Satirist*. (At the whist table Payne who had been apprised of De Ros's playing unfairly, but who nevertheless did not abstain from playing with him, broke out on one occasion and said something which plainly indicated his suspicion that he was cheated) ...

I still maintained a hope that the reluctance to expose him which had been so extensively manifested (and which so many persons still felt) would prove his security, and as the termination of the London season was at hand, if the thing did not ooze out immediately, there was still a chance that it might blow over. In August H. went abroad [to Germany] ... and it seemed as if the world at large knew nothing about it ... About the middle of September I first heard from De Ros on the subject.

He wrote to say that he had just heard that there were such reports; that he had received certain anonymous warnings and threats which he had disregarded; protested his entire innocence; treated the reports as absurd and not deserving attention; desired further information and threatened to call the propagators of the story to a severe account ... I wrote him a very long letter in which I told him everything I knew ... In the evening I wrote a memorandum, discussing the different alternatives that were open to him ... : he should do one of two things, come over here and boldly face the charges, courting an investigation, or repair to Italy and take the chance of the thing blowing over either wholly or partially ...

In the meantime, however, certain circumstances had occurred which considerably complicated the affair. An article had appeared in the *Satirist* newspaper, giving a long and detailed (but incorrect) account of what Payne had said and done at Graham's, with all the names at full length ... Brooke made no secret

of his own belief in the delinquency of De Ros, and Payne, who was asked as
to the truth of the story in the *Satirist*, while he denied its *accuracy*, admitted
that it *had a foundation*. These circumstances confirmed my original opinion
that it was impossible De Ros could return here and *do nothing*; and that his
friends in point of fact could not, if they would, pull him through . . . I wrote
to Henry . . . and entreated him to go to Italy and bide his time . . . I then went
to London (about the 3rd November) and in a very few days Wm. De Ros and
Henry Wellesley [brother and brother-in-law respectively] arrived and sent
for me . . .

I found Wellesley very imperfectly acquainted with the facts of the case and
under the influence of those prejudices in Henry's favour which William thought
it useful to his Brother to impress upon everybody to the best of his ability. I
talked over the whole matter with them, and I told them both my opinions
with the same openness and undisguise that I had always used in my communications with William. Nothing could shake their opinion that his return here
was the most advisable course; accordingly, in about a week from that time, he
arrived in London and it was speedily known that his intention was to bring
an action against the *Satirist*, and *to do no more*.

He protested to me with every mark of earnestness and sincerity that he
was wholly innocent of the charges, and said that he was strongly advised by
high authority, more especially the Duke of Wellington, to take the course
which he had now resolved to pursue and no other . . .

Notwithstanding my efforts to steer a neutral course, and to avoid the
expression of any opinion, it was very well known that I was not only no party
to De Ros's line of conduct but that I disapproved of it; and the very reserve
of my language and my behaviour to his Antagonists were sufficient to show
that if I did not join in the general cry of condemnation, it was not because I
held him to be guiltless that I refrained: and accordingly, all those determined
friends and adherents who were either influenced by the Duke of Wellington
and William [the former having, from the first, taken a very violent part in
his defence] or who in total ignorance of the nature and amount of the evidence,
were resolved to believe him innocent, poured forth all the phials of their indignation, not only upon his Accusers, but upon those of his friends who failed to
come forward in his support and above all upon me . . .

1837

London January 2nd

. . . Henry has continued vehemently and solemnly to assert his innocence . . .
The Duke and others believe him, and believing it themselves, they are very
indignant with those who doubt it . . . Alvanley writes to him [De Ros] 'that

his [Greville's] friends seem to have deserted him'. F. Lamb [Frederick Lamb, the rakish brother of Melbourne] writes him a tirade against me, general and particular. The Duke writes in a tone of contumelious reproach, somewhat difficult of endurance. Wilton chatters in echo of the Duke . . . [Henry] tells me that his greatest consolation is to open himself to me, to ask my advice, and he implores me to task my invention for devising some means of helping him out of his dreadful situation. By an inconsistency which perhaps his situation accounts for, while still adhering to his plea of innocence or rather not abandoning it, he betrays in his alarm and his struggles all the consciousness of guilt. He clings to a hope that Cumming will have mercy on him, and owns that if C. is resolved to bring all the evidence against him that he can, he has no resource and his ruin is inevitable . . .

Dover, January 12th

In the meantime there has been a great uproar in consequence of the reconstitution of Graham's Club, and the omission of the names of Brooke, G. Anson, Higgins and several others which Graham insisted upon . . . Brooke asked me to speak to Graham and demand of him the reasons for this exclusion. This I did. No reasons of any plausibility even were to be had from him, and they appealed to the Committee from whom with some difficulty they obtained redress. The night before last I received to my great astonishment a furious note from De Ros complaining bitterly of my having spoken to Graham on behalf of Brooke and adding that 'I must make an option between them.' . . . The dissolution of the oldest and most intimate friendship I had is naturally painful to an extreme degree, but all things considered, it is perhaps better it should come to this at once.

February 19th

. . . I shall bring down my narrative of De Ros's trial, for that is what it was to the present time. I had received at Paris [Greville had spent three weeks in France] a letter from Cumming informing me that I must appear at the trial, my testimony having been rendered indispensable (in consequence of the imputations cast upon them by De Ros in order to prove their animus towards him) . . .

On Saturday evening when I was dining with Richard Greville at Boulogne when they came and told me that an English courier had arrived with letters for me . . . There was one letter from himself [De Ros] and one from Wm. De Ros entreating me not to return to England nor to appear on the approaching trial – the one threatening me with the loss of his friendship and the other with the indignation of society if I did. These letters did not however turn me from my purpose. I felt that I was bound in honour to go and the next morning I went . . .

... I went on the eventful morning to my office where I resolved to wait until I was sent for, and a more miserable day I never passed. A nervous horror crept over me and made me more restless and uneasy as each succeeding hour passed away ... and when at last about 5 o'clock the messenger really did come to fetch me, it was almost a relief and I went with a sort of desperate satisfaction that it would soon be over. The Court [in Westminster Hall] however adjourned and I was informed that I should be put into the box the next morning – but at this period it mattered very little, for the trial appeared to be virtually over.

In the middle of the day they had brought me word that Thesiger[1] had made a terrific speech, and the close of the first day's proceedings, an impression universally prevailed that De Ros had little or no chance of a verdict. Brooke Greville's evidence (on which he had hoped to make so powerful an assault, and whose character he had so confidently predicted that he should irretrievably damage) was boldly and successfully given ... The Court was crowded and there appeared to be but one opinion as to the result ...

The next morning I was put in the box where very few questions were asked me, but to my great vexation, the very first related to the cards. It was the Judge however who asked me if they were marked and subsequently the foreman of the Jury asked me some question about the marks ... My evidence finished, I went away. I was told that Alvanley shed tears when I appeared and that my own agitation and reluctance were apparent to the whole auditory. Indeed Denman [Chief Justice] ... said [to Lord Brougham] that 'I need not mind it, as my evidence was only "a drop of water in a vessel already overflowing".' The most important witnesses were Payne and Hy Bentinck ... Edward Villiers came into my room between 5 and 6, with the intelligence that the Jury after a few minutes' deliberation had found a verdict for the Defendant.

The verdict was received with the general concurrence of the Lawyers and of society. After the evidence of Bentinck and Payne, Alvanley gave it up, and long before the conclusion of the trial he desired De Ros to prepare himself for the worst and made him go home ... De Ros had destroyed everything like compassion or sympathy for himself by the atrocity of the defence he had set up ... The next day (Sunday) I went to Alvanley who had sent for me. He said that under erroneous impressions he had censured my conduct together with that of others, and he was desirous of making all the reparation he could by owning he had been wrong and saying so to all those whom he had ever said anything to the contrary: he then asked me to go to De Ros with him. We went and found him in a very miserable plight and very obstinate. He refused to take his name out of any of the Clubs as we advised him, and we found out as it has since turned out, that He is anything but aware of his situation, by no means regards it as hopeless, and thus, kicked down as he is, from the top to the bottom of the tree, he is meditating by what means and how soon he may begin to climb again ...

He never would listen to advice. He always fancied that by dexterity and artifice he should find means of steering through the difficulties that surrounded him ... I entered the room brimful of pity, feeling ashamed for him and melted to entire softness, but before I had been there 5 minutes, in spite of his agony, which was apparent, I felt hard as iron, for I saw that his suffering did not proceed from a source calculated to excite compassion or tender regret.

February 25th

I was interrupted while writing [on 22 February], and since I began, the division of eighty in favour of the [Irish] Corporation Bill seems to have settled that question, and at the same time, those of dissolution and change. At the beginning of the session the Tories were (as they are always ready to be) in high spirits, and the Government people in no small alarm ... Nothing was talked of but a dissolution, of Peel's taking office, and many people confidently predicted that a new election would produce a Tory majority ... In the midst of all these deliberations the debate came on. It was exceedingly feeble on the part of the Opposition. Stanley, Graham and Peel successively spoke, and none of them well ... Shiel made a grand declamatory tirade, chiefly remarkable for the scene it produced ... there was a blackguard ferocity in it which would have disgraced the National Convention or the Jacobin Club ... At length they divided, and there was a majority of eighty; sixteen more than on the same question last year.

The next morning (yesterday) Wharncliffe called on, and I found they were prodigiously depressed at this defeat ... Sir G. Noel remained in the House till twelve o'clock, and then went to bed [he *was* seventy-eight years old]; Ld. John Scott went out of town in the morning of the division because he was engaged to dine somewhere; and young Lefroy turned back from the [Dublin] steamboat because it blew hard and he said his mother would be alarmed for his safety ...

May 28th

The King prayed that he might live till the Princess Victoria was of age, and he was very nearly dying just as the event arrived. He is better, but supposed to be in a very precarious way. There has been a fresh squabble between Windsor and Kensington [home of Victoria and her mother] about a proposed allowance to the Princess.

June 2nd

The King has been desperately ill, his pulse down at thirty; they think He will now get over it for this time ...

June 11th

... On Wednesday it was announced for the first time that the King was alarmingly ill, on Thursday the account was no better, and in the course of Wednesday and Thursday his immediate dissolution appeared so probable that I concerted with Errol that I should send to the Castle at nine o'clock on Thursday evening for the last report that I might know whether to go to London directly or not ... It is in this state of things, with the prospect of a new reign and a dissolution ... that Lyndhurst comes down to the H. of Lords and fires off one of his violent speeches and at his bidding the IMCB [Irish Municipal Corporations Bill] has been again postponed. All this is very disgusting to me and I am at a loss to comprehend why such men as the Duke and Peel lend themselves to such courses ...

Met Melbourne in the Park, who told me he thought the King would not recover ...

June 13th

Bad accounts of the King yesterday. Melbourne desired I would get everything ready *quietly* for a Council.

June 16th Friday

On Wednesday the King was desperately bad, yesterday he was better, but not so as to afford any hope ...

... What renders speculation so easy and events so uncertain is the absolute ignorance of everybody, without exception, of the character, disposition and capacity of the Princess. She has been kept in such jealous seclusion by her Mother (never having slept out of her bedroom, nor been alone with anybody but herself and Baroness Lehzen) that not one of her attendants at Kensington, not even the Duchess of Northumberland, her Governess, have any idea of what She is or what she promises to be ...

The Tories ... prognosticate, according to their custom, all sorts of dismal consequences, none of which, of course, will come to pass. *Nothing* will happen, because in this country *nothing* ever does.

June 18th

The King lingers on; yesterday he sent for the AB of Canterbury to administer the sacrament to him.

June 19th

Yesterday the King was sinking fast ... he said 'This is the 18th of June; I should like to live to see the sun of Waterloo set.' ...

June 21st

The King died at twenty minutes after two yesterday morning, and the young Queen met the Council at Kensington Palace at eleven ... She bowed to the Lords, took her seat then read her speech in a clear, distinct and audible voice and without any appearance of fear and embarrassment ... She was quite plainly dressed and in mourning ... She went through the whole ceremony (occasionally looking at Melbourne for instruction when she had any doubt what to do, which hardly ever occurred) with perfect calmness and self-possession, but at the same time with a graceful modesty and propriety particularly interesting and ingratiating ...

No contrast can be greater than that between the personal demeanour of the present and the late Sovereigns at their respective accessions. He was a man who, coming to the throne at the mature age of sixty-five, was so excited by the exaltation that he nearly went mad and distinguished himself by a thousand extravagances of language, and though he was shortly afterwards sobered down into more becoming habits, he always continued something of a blackguard and something more of a buffoon ...

June 25th

... the most remarkable foible of the late King was his passion for speechifying, and I have recorded some of his exhibitions in this way. He had considerable facility in expressing himself, but what he said was generally useless or improper. He never received the homage of a Bishop without giving him a lecture; and the custom he introduced of giving toasts and making speeches at all his dinners was more suitable to a tavern than to a Palace ...

July 9th

Yesterday I went to the late King's funeral who was buried with the same ceremonial as his Predecessor this time seven years. It is a wretched mockery after all, and if I was King, the first thing I would do should be to provide for being committed to the earth with more decency and less pomp ... A soldier's funeral which I met in the morning – the plain coffin slowly borne along by his comrades, with the cap and helmet and sword of the dead placed upon it – was more impressive, more decent, more affecting than all this pomp with pasteboard crowns and Heralds scampering about ...

... the procession moving slowly through the close ranks of Horse and Foot Guards, holding tapers and torches in their hands while at intervals the bands played a dead march, had a very imposing effect. The service was intolerably long and tedious, and miserably read by the Dean of Windsor ...

Knowsley July 18th

Tired of doing nothing in London and of hearing about the Queen and the elections, I resolved to vary the scene and run down here to see the Birmingham railroad, Liverpool and Liverpool races. So I started at five o'clock on Sunday evening, got to Birmingham at half past five on Monday morning and got upon the railroad at half past seven. Nothing can be more comfortable than the vehicle in which I was put, a sort of chariot with two places, and there is nothing disagreeable about it but the occasional whiffs of stinging air which it is impossible to exclude altogether ... the velocity is delightful. Town after town, Park and *Château* after another, are left behind with the rapid variety of a moving panorama, and the continual bustle and animation of the changes and stoppages make the journey very entertaining ... Considering the recency of its establishment there is very little embarrassment, and it certainly renders all other travelling tedious by comparison ...

Just before I left London, the Proclamation of the King of Hanover[2] appeared, by which he overthrew the new Constitution ... it is great folly in the Opposition, and the Journals belonging to them, not to reject at once and peremptorily, all connexion with the King of Hanover ... Though we have nothing to do with Hanover, this violence will no doubt render him still more odious here than he was before. And it would be an awful thing if the Crown were, by any accident, to devolve upon him.

July 25th

I remained at Knowsley till Saturday morning when I went to Liverpool, got on the train at half past eleven, and at five past four arrived in Birmingham with an exact punctuality which is rendered easy by the reserved power of acceleration, the pace at which we travelled being moderate and not above one half the speed at which they do occasionally go; one Engineer went at the rate of forty-five miles an hour, but the Company turned him off for doing so ...

July 28th

... From the beginning [the Queen] resolved to have nothing to do with Sir John Conroy, but to reward him liberally for his services to her mother. Whether she secretly suspects the nature of her mother's connection with him, or is only animated by that sort of instinctive aversion which is frequently engendered without any *apparent* cause, it is difficult to discover. She began however by making him a Baronet, and she has given him a pension of £3000 a year; but he has never once been invited to the Palace or distinguished by the slightest mark of personal favour ... The Queen has been extremely civil to the Queen Dowager, but she has taken no notice of the King's children, good, bad or indifferent.

August 25th

Nothing of any moment has occurred for some time, and all the world has been occupied with the Elections as long as they lasted.

... After much disputing between the two parties as to the actual result, it appears by an impartial examination of the returns that the Ministers will have a majority of 30, and possibly a little more ...

August 30th

... She is upon terms of the greatest cordiality with Melbourne, and very naturally. Everything is new and delightful to her. She is surrounded with the most exciting and interesting enjoyments; her occupations, her pleasures, her business, her court, all present an increasing round of gratifications. With all her prudence and discretion, She has great animal spirits, and enters into the magnificent novelties of her position with the zest and curiosity of a child.

No man is more formed to ingratiate himself with her than Melbourne. He treats her with unbounded consideration and respect, he consults her tastes and her wishes, and he puts her at her ease by his frank and natural manners while he amuses her by the quaint, queer, epigrammatic turn of his mind and his varied knowledge upon all subjects.

October 23rd

... having asked G. Bentinck to try my horse Mango before Doncaster, we went down one night to Winchester racecourse and saw him tried. He won the trial and we resolved to back him. This was accomplished more successfully than we expected, and ten days after he won the St Leger and I won £9000 upon it, the first *great* piece of good fortune that ever happened to me. I was highly elated at the moment and the prospect afforded to me of being able to pay the greater part of my debts is a source of very reasonable satisfaction ...

November 23rd

... Upon the address Wakley[3] and others thought fit to introduce the topic of the Ballot, upon which John Russell spoke out and declared that he would never be a party to Ballot, and would not reform the Reform Bill ... At this moment it is pretty clear that the people care very little about speculative questions and only want peace and tranquillity. It is also said that there is a growing Anti-Catholic and Anti-Irish spirit which the Conservatives do their best to excite and extend ...

December 8th

D'Israeli [just elected at Shrewsbury] made his first exhibition this night, beginning with florid assurance, speedily degenerating into ludicrous absurdity, and at last being put down by inextinguishable shouts of laughter ...

December 24th

News of the insurrection in Canada arrived the day before yesterday and produced a debate of some animation in the H. of Commons ... This is a fine occasion for attacking the Government and placing them between two fires, for the Radicals abuse them for their tyrannical and despotic treatment of the Canadians, and the Tories attribute the rebellion to their culpable leniency and futile attempts at conciliation by concessions which ought never to have been made and were only made out of complaisance to the radicals here. As generally happens when there are charges of an opposite nature and incompatible with one another, neither of them are true ...

The Queen went to the House yesterday without producing any sensation. There was the usual crowd to look at the finery of carriages, horses, Guards etc, but not a hat raised or a voice heard: the people of England seem inclined to hurrah no more.

VOLUME III ENDS

VOLUME IV

1838

Burghley January 2nd

... Yesterday morning left town and slept at Newmarket, saw the horses and
rode out on Warren Hill and came here to dinner; twenty-two people, the D.
of Wellington and Aberdeen, Salisburys, Wiltons and a mob of fine people;
very miserable representatives of old Burghleigh [Elizabeth I's Minister,
commonly 'Burghley'], the two insignificant looking Marquesses [2nd of
Salisbury and 2nd of Exeter] who are his lineal descendants, and who display
no more of his brains than they do of his beard ...

Belvoir Castle January 4th

Coming here yesterday, all the party (almost) migrating and many others coming
from various parts to keep the Duke of Rutland's birthday. We are nearly forty
at dinner but it is no use enumerating the people. Last night the Duke talked
of Hanover but said that neither Wm 4th nor George 4th had ever talked to
him on the subject or he must have made himself acquainted with it; that the
Duke of Cumberland had written him word that he had never had any notion
of adopting the measures as he has since done[1] till he was going over in the
packet with Billy Holmes ... when the late King had evidently only a few days
to live, the Duke of Cumberland consulted the Duke [Rutland] as to what he
should do. 'I told him the best thing he could do was to go away as fast as he
could: Go instantly' I said, 'and take care that *you don't get pelted.*' ...

... Today we went to see the House Mr Gregory is building five miles from
here. He is a gentleman of about £12,000 a year who has a fancy to build a
magnificent house in the Elizabethan style and he is now in the middle of his
work, all the shell being finished except one wing. Nothing can be more perfect
than it is both as to the architecture and the ornaments; but it stands on the
slope of a hill upon a deep clay soil with no park round it, very little wood
and scarcely any fine trees. Many years ago when he first conceived this design,
he began to amass money and lived for no other object He travelled into
Europe collecting objects of curiosity, useful or ornamental, for his projected
Palace, and he did not begin to build until he had accumulated money enough
to complete his design. The grandeur of it is such, and such the tardiness of
its progress, that it is about as much as he can do to live until its completion;

and as he is not married, has no children and dislikes the heir on whom his property is entailed, it is the means and not the end to which he looks for gratification . . .

. . . The Duke of Rutland is as selfish a man as any of his class – that is. He never does what he does not like, and spends his life in a round of such pleasures as suit his taste, but he is neither a foolish nor a bad man, and partly from a sense of duty, partly from inclination, he devotes time and labour to the interest and welfare of the people who live and labour on his estate. He is a Guardian of a very large Union [Poor Law Union] and he not only attends regularly the meeting of Poor Law Guardians every week or fortnight and takes an active part in their proceedings, but he visits those paupers who receive outdoor relief, sits and converses with them, invites them to complain if they have anything to complain of, and tells them that he is not only their friend but their representative at the Assembly of Guardians, and that it is his duty to see that they are nourished and protected . . .

. . . Melton January 7th (Wilton's house)

Came here today from Belvoir. Last night the Duke [Wellington] narrated the battle of Toulouse and other Peninsular recollections. All the room collected round him, listening with eager curiosity, but I was playing whist and missed it . . .

Beaudesert [Lord Angelesey's house near Burton-on-Trent] January 12th Friday

On Monday went to Sutton; nobody there but Mr Hodgson [Francis Hodgson (1781–1852), later Provost of Eton], formerly my tutor at Eton, the friend of Byron, author of a translation of Juvenal – a clever, not an agreeable man. The house at Sutton is unfurnished, but handsome enough. Came here on Wednesday; a magnificent place indeed and a very comfortable house. A good many people, nobody remarkable; very idle life. Read in the newspaper that Colburn [publisher of the diaries of Pepys and Evelyn] gave Lady C. Bury [Lady Charlotte Bury, formerly lady-in-waiting to Caroline of Brunswick as Princess of Wales] £1000 for the wretched catchpenny trash called *Memoirs of the Time of George IV* which might set all the world what Scott calls 'gurnelising', for nobody could possibly compile or compose anything more vile or despicable. My trash is at least better and less *trashy* than that, but I much doubt if any future Colburn will give £1000 for all my MS . . .

Badminton [home of the Duke of Beaufort] January 23rd

. . . Lord Eldon died last week full of years and wealth. He had for some time quitted the political stage, but his name was still venerated by the dregs of that party to whom consistent bigotry and intolerance are dear . . . As a politi-

cian he seems to have been consistent throughout, and to have offered a determined and uniform opposition to every measure of a Liberal description. He
knew of no principles but those (if they merit the name of principle) of the
narrowest Toryism and of High Church, and as soon as larger and more
enlightened views began to obtain, he quitted (and forever) public life ... I
suppose he was a very great Lawyer, but he was certainly a contemptible
Statesman ...

February 18th Sunday

On Thursday night came on the Ballot and its advocates divided as they said
they should, 200. John Russell, though ill, came down and spoke against it.
Peel made a good speech and complimented John on his conduct. All the
Cabinet Ministers voted against it except Poulett Thompson who staid away.
The result is the creation of a strong impression that the Ballot will eventually be carried; Brougham says in five years [not until 1872, during the first
ministry of Gladstone, at this time a Tory] ... On Friday night, Brougham
announced to the Lords that they must make up their minds to the Ballot after
the division of the preceding night, and yesterday morning when we were assembled in my room before going into court (Parke, [James Parke, chief baron of
the Court of Exchequer] Erskine, Bosanquet and himself), he gave us his
speech in high glee. Parke, who is an alarmist, had just before said that he had
never doubted when the Reform Bill had passed that England would become
a republic and when Brougham said that he gave the Ballot five years for
accomplishment, Parke said 'And in five years we shall have a republic', on
which Brougham gave him a great cuff and with a scornful laugh said 'A
republic! Pooh, nonsense! Well, but what if there is? *There are judges* in a
republic, and very well paid too.' ... He is in extraordinary good humour; in
a state of furious mental activity, troubled neither with fear nor shame, and
rejoicing in that freedom from all ties which renders him a sort of Ishmael.
His hand against everybody and everybody against him, and enables him to
cut and slash, as fancy or passion move him, at Whig or Tory in the H. of
Lords ...

February 20th

Though the adherents of Government put on as bold a front as they can, there
is a very considerable impression that the days of the Whig Cabinet are
numbered; however, I don't think they will go just yet.

I made no allusion to the death of Creevey ... He was appointed to one of
the Ordnance offices by Lord Grey and subsequently, by Melbourne, Treasurer
of Greenwich Hospital with a salary of £600 a year and a house. About five
years ago he took into keeping a girl whom he picked up in St James's Street,
and who had long been on the nocturnal pavement under the name of Emma.

It was a very good joke among his friends at the time but he did not care for their jests and kept her upto the time of his death ... It was found that he left this woman, his sole executrix and residuary legatee, and She became entitled to all his personalty [personal property] (the value of which was very small, not more than £300 or £400) and to all the papers which he left behind him. These are exceedingly valuable for he had kept a copious diary for at least thirty-six years, had kept all his own and Mrs Creevey's [Elinor Creevey, d. 1818] letters, and copies or originals of a vast miscellaneous correspondence. Among other things there is a correspondence between Mrs Creevey and the Duchess of Devonshire (who were intimate friends) in which the whole history of the Duchess's intrigue with Lord Grey is developed with many details concerning the child who was the fruit of it ...

... Then there is Creevey's correspondence with Brougham which evidently contains things B. is very anxious to suppress for he has taken pains to prevent the papers from falling into the hands of people likely to publish them and he has urged Vizard [a solicitor once serving Queen Caroline] to get possession of them either by persuasion or purchase or both ... It is clear they propose to deceive her of the value of these papers, and to conclude a bargain with her before She becomes enlightened in this respect. The most extraordinary part of the affair is that the woman has behaved with the utmost delicacy and propriety, has shown no mercenary disposition, but expressed her desire to be guided by the wishes and opinions of Creevey's friends and connexions and to concur in whatever measures may be thought by them with reference to the character of Creevey, and the interests and feelings of those who might be affected by the contents of the papers ... It would be a hundred to one against any individual in the ordinary ranks of society and of average good character acting with such entire absence of selfishness, and I cannot help being struck by the contrast. Between the motives and the disposition of those who want to get hold of these papers and of this poor woman who is willing to give them up ... I have no doubt Colburn or Bentley [Publishers] would give £2000 or £3000 for Creevey's papers ...

... We have had Brougham every day at the Council Office, more busy writing review of Lady Charlotte Bury's book [see entry for 12 January 1838] than with the matter before the Judicial Review Committee ... His talk (for conversation is not the word for it) is totally unlike that of anybody else I ever heard. It comes forth without the slightest effort provided he is in spirits and disposed to talk at all ... he treads the ground with so elastic a step, he touches everything so lightly and so adorns all that he touches, his turns and breaks are so various unexpected and pungent that he not only interests and amuses, but always exhilarates his audience so as to render weariness and satiety impossible. He is now coquetting a little with the Tories, and especially expresses great deference and profound respect for the Duke of Wellington; his sole object in politics for the moment is to badger, twit and torment the Ministers, and in this he cannot contain himself within the bounds of civility . . . He calls this the Thompson Government from its least considerable member. [Poulett Thompson: see entry for 18 February 1838] . . .

March 8th

. . . On Tuesday night Brougham made another great slavery speech in the H. of Lords and as usual, very long, eloquent, powerful; but his case overstated, too highly overwrought and too artificial. It was upon the Order in Council by which Coolies were brought into Antigua from India. He made out a case of real or probable abuse and injustice, and his complaint was that the Government had not sufficiently guarded against the contingency by regulations accompanying the order. He was supported by several of the Tory Lords; but the Duke of Wellington refused to support him, provided Melbourne was prepared to agree to adopt certain rules . . . He and the bulk of his followers joined with the Government; they had a large majority, but Ellenborough, Lyndhurst, Wharncliffe and the Bishop of Exeter and a few more voted with Brougham, and the whole party would have been very glad to do so if the Duke would have let them . . . he [Brougham] will certainly gain a great deal of reputation and popularity by his agitation on the Anti-slavery question for it is a favourite topic in the country. Wharnclife told me he walked away with him from the House after the debate on Tuesday, and some young men who had been with him below the bar saluted him as he went by with 'Bravo Brougham!' . . .

March 11th

I dined yesterday at the Palace, much to my surprise for I had no expectation of an invitation . . . The dinner was like any other great dinner. After the eating was over the Queen's health was given by Cavendish [Duke's grandson, equerry] who sat at one end of the table, and everybody got up to drink it, a vile vulgar practice, and however proper it may be to drink her health elsewhere, it is bad taste to have it given by her Officer at her own table which, in fact, is the only table it is never drunk at. However it has been customary for the last two reigns. George 3rd never dined but with his family, never had guests and a dinner *party*.
. . . When we went into the drawing room and huddled about the door in the sort of half-shy, half-awkward way people do, the Queen advanced to meet us, and spoke to everybody in succession and if every body's 'palaver' was as interesting as mine it would have been worthwhile to have had Gurney to take it down in short hand. As the words of Kings and Queens are precious and as a fair sample of an after-dinner colloquy, I shall recall my dialogue with accurate fidelity.

Q. 'Have you been riding today Mr Greville?'

G. 'No Madam, I have not.'

Q. 'It was a fine day.'

G. 'Yes ma'am a very fine day.'

Q. 'It was rather cold though.'

G. (like Polonius). 'It *was* rather cold, Madam.'

Q. 'Your sister, Ly. Francis Egerton rides, I think, does not She?'

G. 'She does ride sometimes Madam.'

(A pause when I took the lead through adhering to the same topic.)

G. 'Has your Majesty been riding today?'

Q. (with animation) 'O yes, a very long ride.'

G. 'Has your Majesty a nice horse?'

Q. 'O, a very nice horse.'

Gracious smile and inclination of head on part of Queen, profound bow on mine, and then She turned again to Lord Grey. Directly after I was (to my satisfaction) deposited at the whist table to make up the Duchess of Kent's party, and all the rest of the party were arranged about a large round table (the Queen on the sofa beside it) where they passed about an hour and a half in what was the smallest possible talk . . . She looks and speaks cheerfully; there is nothing to criticise, nothing particularly to admire. The whole thing seemed to be dull, perhaps unavoidably so but still so dull that it is a marvel how anybody can like such a life . . . I had a few words with Lord Grey, and soon found that the Government are in no very good odour with him. He talked disparagingly of them and said (in reference to the recent debate) that 'He thought Peel could not have done otherwise than He did.'

March 17th

Went to the Royal Institution last night in hopes of hearing Faraday[2] lecture, but the lecture was given by Mr Pereira[3] upon crystals, a subject of which he seemed to be master to judge by his facility and fluency; but the whole of it was unintelligible to me. Met Dr Buckland and talked to him for an hour, and he introduced me to Mr Wheatstone,[4] the inventor of the electric telegraph of his progress in which he gave me an account . . . There is a cheerfulness and activity, an appearance of satisfaction in the conversation and demeanour of scientific men that conveys a lively notion of the *pleasure* they derive from their pursuits.

March 20th

Met Croker on Sunday, who came to speak to me about the picture of the Queen's first Council on her accession which [Sir David] Wilkie is painting. He is much scandalised because the Lord Mayor is introduced, which he ought not to be, and Croker apprehends that future Lord Mayors will found upon evidence of this picture claims to be present at the Councils of future Sovereigns on similar occasions. I wrote to Lord Lansdowne about it and told him that it so happens that I caused the Lord Mayor to be ejected who was lingering on in the room after the Proclamation had been read. Landseer [Sir Edwin Landseer (1802–73), celebrated painter of sentimental animal subjects] asked Sydney Smith to sit for him for his picture, and he replied 'Is thy servant *a dog* that he should do this thing?' . . .

March 30th

. . . On Wednesday afternoon I found Downing Street thronged with rival deputations of West Indians [Planters] and Quakers which had both been with Melbourne. Out of Brougham's flaming speeches on Anti-Slavery a tempest has arisen which threatens the West Indies with sudden and unforeseen ruin in the shape of immediate emancipation. [A Commons motion was moved on 30 March 1838 to end the apprenticeships devised at the time of abolition to extend slavery under an alias. It was defeated by 269 to 205.] It is always easy to get up anti-slavery petitions and to excite a benevolent indignation against Slavery in any shape, and Brougham has laid hold of this easy model of inflaming the public in his usual daring, unscrupulous, reckless style, pouring forth a flood of eloquent falsehoods and misrepresentations which he knows will be much more effective than any plain, matter-of-fact statements that can be urged on the other side. The West Indians had no idea they were in any danger . . . They went to Melbourne who said he agreed with them and that the Government was determined to support them . . . The Leaders of the Opposition equally took their part but the question is whether the tails will not beat the heads . . . The petitions are innumerable and men are disposed to gratify their constituents by voting as they please on this question, not caring a fig for either the Slaves or the West Indians, and reconciling it to their consciences to despoil the latter by assuming that they were overpaid with the twenty millions they got by the Emancipation Act . . .

April 2nd

. . . The Ministers got a pretty good majority (all things considered) on Friday. Gladstone[5] made a first-rate speech which places him in the first rank in the H. of C. . . . ; he converted or determined many adverse or doubtful votes . . .

April 12th

Dined with Lord Anglesey yesterday to meet Wolff [Joseph Wolff (1795–1862), missionary and explorer] . . . He illustrated the truth of the Scriptures by examples drawn from his personal observation and the habits, expressions and belief of the present inhabitants of Palestine, and he spoke with evident sincerity and enthusiasm. He sang two or three hymns as specimens of the psalmody now in use at Jerusalem ... He subsequently gave us a second lecture upon the Millennium, avowing his belief that it is near at hand; 'he hoped and believed it would take place in 1847' and he proceeded to show that this was to be inferred from the prophecies of Daniel ... He told us that he had learnt fourteen languages and had preached in nine.

May 7th

For three weeks entirely engrossed by Newmarket ... I won £2000 by the two weeks, and if I meet with no reverse am rapidly acquiring the means of paying off my debts ... I hope as I become rich (and if I get out of debt I shall be rich) I may not become grasping and avaricious and acquire a taste for hoarding money merely for hoarding's sake. When I see how insensibly and with what plausible pretexts this passion steals upon others, I tremble lest I should become a victim of it myself ...

May 18th

At Newmarket all the week past. Sad life, *there* I cannot do anything, it is useless to try. I take down books but never look into them, and the day glides along in active idleness, split into fragments in a way that renders all reading, even of the lightest kind, impracticable. It is a life utterly unworthy, not merely of a man of sense but of a reasonable being; and yet though I know, feel and think this still I go on – such is the force of inveterate habit ...

May 23rd

Talleyrand is dead ... No name was once held in greater detestation in England than that of Talleyrand. He was once looked upon universally as a sink of moral and political profligacy ... A debauched Abbot and Bishop, one of the champions and then one of the victims of the Revolution, afterwards (after having scrambled through the perilous period of the Revolution discarding his clerical character, he became the Minister of the Consulate and the Empire, and was looked upon all over Europe as a man of consummate ability, but totally destitute of principle either moral or political. Disgraced by Napoleon, he re-appeared at his fall and was greatly concerned in the restoration of the Bourbons. The years he spent here ... served to create for him a reputation altogether new ... His age was venerable, his society was delightful, and there was an exhibition of Conservative wisdom of 'moderate and healing counsels' in all his thoughts, words and actions very becoming to his age and station, vastly influential from his sagacity and experience, and which presented him to the eyes of men like Burleigh or Clarendon for prudence, temperance and discretion.

May 27th

I dined yesterday at Lambeth, at the Archbishop's public dinner, the handsomest entertainment I ever saw. There were nearly a hundred people present, all full-dressed or in uniform. Nothing can be more dignified or splendid than the whole arrangement and the dinner was well served and very good. The Archbishop [William Howley] is a very meek and quiet man, [according to his school friend, Sydney Smith, he once knocked Smith down with a wooden chessboard] not dignified, but very civil and attentive. It is excessively worth seeing . . .

May 29th

Just going to Epsom. A year ago was going with the hope of making a fortune and the certainty of winning a great deal of money; now with the great probability of losing a good deal, but I hope and trust *for the last time* . . .

June 1st

Back from Epsom (Marble Hill) yesterday having lost £1400. Very glad it is all over, and hope to keep clear for the future though as long as I have horses (and there is no getting rid of them) I shall never be able to avoid doing as others do . . .

June 21st

Soult [Nicolas-Jean, Duc de Soult, one of Napoleon's marshals and Wellington's most effective opponent in the Peninsula: at this time, ambassador extraordinary of King Louis Philippe] arrived yesterday. Croker meets him with an offensive article in the *Quarterly* brought out on purpose and emanating from his spiteful and malignant temper . . .

June 29th

Coronation (which, Thank God, is over) went off very well. Day fine without heat or rain – the innumerable multitude which thronged the streets orderly and satisfied. The appearance of the abbey was beautiful, particularly the benches of the Peeresses who were blazing with diamonds. The entry of Soult was striking. He was saluted with a murmur of curiosity and surprise as he passed through the Nave and nearly the same as he walked along the choir. His appearance is that of a veteran warrior and he walked alone . . . The Queen looked very diminutive, and the effect of the procession was spoilt by being too crowded; there was not enough interval between the Queen and the Lords and others going before her . . . the different actors in the ceremonial were very imperfect in their parts and had neglected to rehearse them. John Thynne [Sub-Dean of Westminster] told me that nobody knew what was to be done except the Archbishop and himself (who had rehearsed), Lord Willoughby (who is experienced in these matters) and the Duke of Wellington, and consequently there was a continual difficulty and embarrassment and the Queen never knew what she was to do next ...

... She said to John Thynne 'Pray tell me what I am to do, for they don't know;' and at the end, when the Orb was put into her hand, she said to him 'What am I to do with it?' 'Y.M. is to carry it, if you please, in your hand.' 'Am I?' she said 'It is very heavy.' The ruby ring was made for her little finger instead of the fourth on which the form prescribes it should be put. When the A.B. was to put it on, she extended the former, but he said it must be on the latter. She said it was too small and that she could not get it on, He said it was right to put it on there and as he insisted she yielded, but had first to take off her other rings, and then this was forced on, but it hurt her very much and as soon as the ceremony was over she was obliged to bathe her finger in iced water in order to get it off ... Lord Rolle who is between eighty and ninety fell down as he was getting up the steps of the throne. Her first impulse was to rise and when afterwards he came again to do homage she said 'May I not get up and meet him?' and she rose from the throne and advanced one or two of the steps to prevent his coming up, an act of graciousness and kindness which made a great sensation ... The Procession was very handsome and the Extraordinary Ambassadors produced some gorgeous equipages. This sort of procession is incomparably better than the old ceremonial ... In fact the thing best worth seeing was the town itself, and the countless multitudes through which the procession passed ... It is said that a million have had a sight of the show one way or another ... I went into the Park where the Fair was going on; a vast multitude but all of the lower orders; not very amusing. The great merit of this coronation is that so much has been done for the people; to amuse and interest *them* seems to have been the principal object.

July 3rd

At the Ball at court last night, to which hundreds would have given hundreds to go, and from which I would have gladly staid away: all very brilliant and tiresome.

July 24th

High Church has been recently reading lectures to her Majesty the Queen in the shape of two sermons preached at the Chapel Royal by Mr Percival [Arthur Percival, Fellow of All Souls, Oxford, royal chaplain] and Mr Hook [William Hook, later Dean of Chichester] ... Hook's sermon seems to have been the strongest of the two. He told the Queen that the Church would endure what would happen to the throne. On her return to Buckingham House, Normanby who had been there at the chapel, said to her, 'Did Y.M. not find it very hot?' She said, 'Yes, and the sermon was very hot too.'

August 8th

Stephen [effective permanent Head of the Colonial Office, see *supra*] yesterday was talking to me about Macaulay. He came to him soon after his return from India, and told him that when there he used to get up at five every morning (as everybody else did), and till nine or ten read Greek and Latin and went through the whole range of classical literature of every sort and kind; that one day in the Government library he had met with the works of Chrysostom, fourteen Greek folios, and that he had taken home first one folio and then another till he had read the whole through ... His project now is to devote himself to literature, and his present project, to write a History of England for the last 150 years ... [Stephen] said that he [Macaulay] had first of all the power of abstraction, of giving his undivided attention to the book and the subject on which he was occupied; then as other men read by syllables or by words, he had the faculty, acquired by use of swallowing, as it were whole paragraphs at once, and thus he infinitely abbreviated the mere mechanical part of study ... so with the acquired habit of devouring at a glance a vast surface of print, so that like the dragon of Wantley, to whom

> 'Houses and churches
> Were like geese and turkeys,'

he can discuss a Greek folio while an ordinary man is dawdling or boggling over a pamphlet or a newspaper.

September 7th

Nothing to record of any sort or kind: London a desert; went today to Windsor for a Council; was invited by the Queen (through Melbourne) to stay and dine; but made an excuse on the score of business, and luckily had a plausible one to make. It is too much of a good thing to cool one's heels for some 4 hours and $\frac{1}{2}$ in order to be bored for 3 more in the evening, and then end with a nocturnal jaunt to town. To sit at the Royal table and play shilling whist with the Duchess of Kent are great honours. But le jeu ne vaut pas la chandelle. The King and Queen of the Belgians are there.

September 12th

G. Villiers, who came from Windsor on Monday, told me He had been exceedingly struck with Melbourne's manner to the Queen and hers to him: his so parental and anxious but always so respectful and deferential; hers, indicative of such entire confidence, such pleasure in his society. She is continually talking to him; let who will be there, he always sits next to her at dinner, and evidently by arrangement, because he always takes in the lady-in-waiting which necessarily places next her, the etiquette being that the lady-in-waiting sit next but one to the Queen . . . There are, however, or rather may be hereafter, inconveniences in the establishment of such an intimacy, and in a connexion of so close and intimate a nature between the young Queen and her Minister; for whenever the Government which hangs by a thread, shall be broken up, the parting will be painful, and their subsequent relations will not be without embarrassment to themselves, nor fail to be the cause of jealousy in others . . .

Yesterday I went to Battersea and dined with Robert Eden the Rector [later Bishop of Bath and Wells and 2nd Earl of Auckland] . . . He gave me a curious account of the state of his parish; there is no middle class of tradesmen in good circumstances; they are divided between the extremes of wealth and poverty, Masters and Operatives; but amongst the latter there is a considerable amount of knowledge, though their minds are ill-regulated and their principles perverted . . . Some were reclaimed and came to Church, but the greater part, who required some powerful excitement, sought it in politics and became deeply imbued with the most pernicious principles of hatred against all institutions, against the higher orders, and against property. The fountain from which they draw their opinions is a Sunday paper called the *Watchman* which is universally and greedily read; it is cleverly written, accommodated to their taste, and flatters all their worst propensities. Few people know these things and are aware of the poison that is circulating through the veins, and corrupting the blood of the social mass . . .

October 26th

A blank month; to Newmarket, to Buckenham, to Cromer (fine wild, bleak coast); Buckenham again, Newmarket, London, Norman Court and here again heard nothing, learnt nothing, altogether unprofitable . . . I met the Doctor who attended young Sam Day (who won the St Leger for me on Mango) when he got the fall of which he died, and he gave me a striking account of the deathbed scene, the Actors in which, albeit of an humble and unpolished class, displayed feelings not the less intense from the simplicity of their expression and the total absence of that morbid or conventional sensibility which gives a sort of dramatic dignity to the grief of great ones . . .

December 2nd

While I was in the country, Sefton's[6] long illness came to a close . . . having sought for amusement in hunting, shooting, racing, gaming 'beside ten thousand freaks that died in thinking', he plunged with ardour into politics, and though he had no opinions or principles, but such as resulted from personal predilections and none of that judgment which can only be generated by the combination of knowledge and severe mental discipline he was able by the force of circumstances and an energetic will, to acquire political intimacies and to a certain degree to play a political part: . . . He was absolutely devoid of religious belief or opinions, he despised all religious observances but without any ostentatious mockery, but he left to all others the unquestioned liberty of rendering that homage to religion from which he gave himself a plenary dispensation. His general conduct was stained with no gross immorality, and as he was placed far above the necessity of committing dishonourable actions, his mind was habitually imbued with principles of integrity. They sat however lightly upon him as regarded the conduct of others . . .

December 15th Saturday

. . . The court is certainly not gay, but it is perhaps impossible that any court should be gay where there is no social equality; where some ceremony and a continual air of deference and respect must be observed, there can be no ease and without ease there can be no real pleasure. The Queen is natural, good humoured and cheerful. But still she is Queen, and by her must the social habits and the tone of conversation be regulated, and for this she is too young and inexperienced. She sits at a large round table; her guests around it and Melbourne always in a chair beside her where two mortal hours are consumed in such conversation as can be found which appears to be and really is, very up-hill work . . . He is at her side for at least six hours every day – an hour in the morning, two on horseback, one at dinner and two in the evening. This monopoly is certainly not judicious; . . . Month after month he remains at the Castle, submitting to this daily routine . . . and never was such a revolution seen in anybody's occupations and habits. Instead of indolently sprawling in all the attitudes of luxurious ease, he is always sitting bolt upright; his free and easy language interlarded with 'damns' is carefully guarded and regulated with the strictest propriety, and he has exchanged the good talk of Holland House for the trivial, laboured and wearisome inanities of the royal circle.

1839

January 1st

. . . As to public matters, the year opens in no small gloom and uncertainty. On the surface all is bright and smooth enough; the country is powerful, peaceful and prosperous, and all the demands of wealth and power are increasing; but the mind of the mass is disturbed and discontented and there is a continual fermentation going on, and separate and unconnected causes of agitation and disquiet are in incessant operation . . . they are the mere aspirings of a fierce democracy who have been gradually but deeply impregnated with sentiments of hatred and jealousy of the Upper classes and with a determination to level all political distinctions and privileges . . . it is idle to suppose that men of this stamp care anything for abstract political theories, or have any definite object but that of procuring the means of working less, and eating and drinking more. The account of the Chartists (as they are called) [radical MPs in partial sympathy with the extra-parliamentary Chartist movement] at and about Manchester, represent them to be collected in vast bodies, associations of prodigious numbers, meeting in all the public houses, collecting arms universally and constantly practising by firing at a mark, openly threatening, if their demands are not complied with, to enforce them by violence. In the mean time there is no military force in the country at all adequate to meet these menacing demonstrations; the Yeomanry have been reduced, and the Magistracy are worse than useless, without consideration, resolution or judgment.

February 14th

... The Corn Law question which appeared so formidable before Parliament met, has lost much of its terrors; and an error made by one of its Champions, (Mr Wood of Preston) greatly assisted to damage it. Peel turned against him certain admissions which he made of the prosperity of trade with extraordinary dexterity and effect ... This and the strong demonstration in favour of the existing system the first night, the divided opinions and indifference of the Government and the diversion made by the Chartists, have placed the Corn Laws in perfect security for this Session at least.

February 17th

Dined at Lady Blessington's yesterday ... There was that sort of strange *omnium gatherum* party which is to be met with nowhere else, and which for that reason alone is curious. We had Prince Louis Napoleon [later Napoleon III] and his ADC. He is a short, thickish, vulgar-looking man without the slightest resemblance to his Imperial Uncle or any intelligence in his countenance. Then we had the ex-governor of Canada [Lord Durham], Captain Marriott [the novelist Frederick Marryat (1792–1848), better known as Captain Marryat], the Count de Vigny [Alfred de Vigny, major French poet] (author of Cinq-Mars etc), Sir Edward Lytton Bulwer [Bulwer-Lytton (1803–73), historical novelist], and a proper sparkling of ordinary persons to mix up with these celebrities ... Lady Blessington's existence is a curiosity ... there is no end to the men of consequence who go there occasionally – Brougham, Lyndhurst, Abinger, Canterbury, Durham and many others; all the *minor* Poets, *literati*, and journalists without exception including some of the highest pretensions ... Her house is furnished with a luxury and splendour not to be surpassed; her dinners are frequent and good ... There is a vast amount of coming and going, and eating and drinking, and a corresponding amount of noise, but little or no conversation, discussion, easy quiet exchange of ideas and opinions, ... The reason for this is the woman herself, who must give the tone to her own society, and influence its character, is ignorant, vulgar and commonplace. Nothing can be more dull and uninteresting than her conversation which is never enriched by a particle of knowledge or enlivened by a ray of genius or imagination. The fact of her existence as an author is an engima, poor as her pretensions are; for while it is very difficult to write good books, it is not easy to compose bad ones ... and though I never met with any individual who had read one of her books (except the *Conversations with Byron* which are too good to be hers) they are unquestionably a source of considerable profit, and she takes her place confidently and complacently as one of the literary celebrities of her day ...

March 2nd

It appears that Lady Flora Hastings, the Duchess of Kent's lady-in waiting, has been accused of being with child. It was at first whispered about and has since swelled into a report, and finally into a charge ... Medical examination was either demanded of by her or submitted to, and the result was satisfactory to the virtue of the accused damsel. Then naturally exploded the just indignation of insulted honour. Her brother, Lord Hastings, came up to town, saw Melbourne who is said to have endeavoured to smother the affair ... it was too late since all the world has begun to talk of it, and he demanded and obtained an audience with the Queen ... the court is plunged in shame and mortification at the exposure, that the Palace is full of bickerings and heart-burnings, while the whole proceeding is looked upon by society at large as to the last degree disgusting and disgraceful. It is really an exemplification of the saying that 'les Rois et les Valets' are made of the refuse clay of creation, for though such things sometimes happen in the servants hall, and Housekeepers charge still-room or kitchen-maids with frailty or pregnancy, they are unprecedented and unheard of in good society, and among people in high or even in respectable stations ...

March 25th

... The Country is beset with difficulties on all sides if not with danger; besides the ever rankling thorn of Ireland there are the chartists, and the Anti-Corn Law agitators to say nothing of the minor reformers in England ... we have a Cabinet in which there is not one man who inspires confidence, and in which with the exception perhaps of John Russell (who is broken in health and spirits) [Russell after serving twice as Prime Minister, died in 1878] there is not one deserving to be called a Statesman ... nobody appears to care for anybody; nobody cares for the Queen, her popularity has sunk to zero and loyalty is a dead letter ... But Melbourne seems to hold office for no other purpose but that of dining at Buckingham House and he is content to rub on from day to day letting all things take their chance; Palmerston, the most enigmatical of Ministers, who is detested by the *Corps Diplomatique*, abhorred in his own office, unpopular in the H. of Commons, liked by nobody, abused by everybody,

still reigns in his little kingdom of the Foreign Office, and is impervious to
any sense of shame ...

March 29th

Poor De Ros [see Vol. III] expired last night after twelve after a confinement
of two or three months from the time he returned to England ... In him I
have lost (half lost before), the last and greatest of the friends of my youth,
and I am left a more solitary and a sadder man ...

April 7th

Besides what I have recorded Tavistock [Lord John Russell's elder brother,
later Duke of Bedford] gave me an account of Lady T.'s share in the Palace
affair ... When she got to the Palace She found the ladies all in a hubbub.
Lady Flora had returned from Scotland with an abdominal protuberance and
Sir Jas. Clarke [physician to royalty and to John Keats] had pronounced ...
that it had the appearance of her being with child; the Ladies of the Palace
reported this to Lady T. (*through some one of them whom Lady T. will not give
up*) and begged her to take some steps to protect their purity from this contam-
ination. Lady T. accordingly sent for Melbourne ... Melbourne did not put
an extinguisher upon it as he might and ought to have done, and it is in point
of fact, all his fault that the scandal has become so flagrant ... After a great
deal of violence and much angry correspondence, they (H. [Hastings] and
his advisers) thought that they had found out that Lady T.'s original infor-
mant was the Baroness [Baroness Lehzen, a confidante of the Duchess of
Kent, the Queen's mother], and they resolved to publish some letter or letters
in which this would have been insinuated; But in point of fact it was not the
Baroness ... At the Palace at least, the matter has now blown over and all is
harmony ...

April 21st

... [Tavistock] afterwards told me a great deal about the Hastings affair
which has been rendered much worse and more mischievous by the publication of the correspondence between Lady Hastings [the Countess, Flora's
mother] and Melbourne (by the former). The letters are very bad productions
on both sides; the lady's ill-written, intemperate and rhapsodical, the Minister's
rude and unbecoming. The whole affair has done incredible harm, and has
played the devil with the Queen's popularity and cast dreadful odium and
discredit on the court ... Lord Portman [his wife was accused of letting the
physician, Clarke, know that he suspected pregnancy] called on the Prime
Minister yesterday and entreated him to see the Duke. 'Why damn it' said
Melbourne 'I can't see him now, I am shaving and then I am going to a
Cabinet.' ... the young lady is said to have acted with great duplicity, for while

she was affecting amicable feelings at the Palace and to have made it up with everybody, she was writing to her uncle those statements which he afterwards published and preparing for the explosion which eventually took place . . .

May 10th

I left town on Monday, having in the morning seen Le Marchant (who knows better than anybody the numbers and details of divisions); and he told me they should have majority of twenty: little therefore was I prepared to hear on Tuesday morning that they had been left with only a majority of five . . . On Tuesday the Government met and decided to resign. The Queen had not been prepared for this catastrophe and was completely upset by it. Her agitation and grief were very great. In her interview with John Russell she was all the time dissolved in tears . . . Peel went to the Palace (in full dress according to etiquette) and received her commands to form a government. She received him (though she dislikes him) extremely well, and he was perfectly satisfied.

[While] the Tories were waiting in perfect security for the tranquil arrangement of the new government, a storm suddenly arose which threatens to scatter to the winds the new combinations . . . The Queen insisted upon keeping the Ladies of her household, and Peel objected, but without shaking her determination . . . When the Duke and Peel saw her and endeavoured to persuade her to yield this point, they found her firm and immoveable, and not only resolved not to give way but prepared with answers to all they said and arguments in support of her determination . . . The Ministers were collected from all quarters (Hobhouse from dinner at Wilton's, Morpeth from the Opera), and Melbourne laid before them a letter from the Queen. Written in a bitter spirit such as Elizabeth might have used. She said, 'Do not fear that I was not calm and composed. They wanted to deprive me of my Ladies, and I suppose they would deprive me next of my dressers and my housemaids; they wished to treat me like a girl, but I will show them that I am Queen of England.' . . . The end was that a letter was composed for her in which she simply declined to place the ladies of her household at Peel's discretion. This was sent yesterday morning when Peel wrote an answer resigning his commission into H.M. hands; but recapitulating everything that had passed . . . The Radicals, who had for the most part been terribly alarmed at the result of their own defection, instantly made overtures to the Whigs . . . In the Duke's first interview with the Queen, he had entreated her to place her whole confidence in Peel and had then said that though some changes might be necessary in the Household, she would find him in all the arrangements anxious to meet her wishes and consult her feelings. But she had already conceived a lively aversion to Peel and though her manner was civil, her heart was full of bitterness looking back with regret and forward with reluctance and dismay . . . She exhibited the talent of a clever but rather thoughtless and headstrong girl . . .

May 12th

The Cabinet met yesterday and resolved to take the Government again; they hope to interest the people in the Queen's quarrel, and, having made it up with the Radicals, they think they can stand ... [The Duke of Wellington] told my brother this afternoon that '... they must do what they could to help that poor little thing out of the difficulty in which she is placed'. He looks to the Crown of England and not to the misguided little person who wears it ...

June 10th

[The Government] have to their eternal disgrace succumbed to the Radicals and have been squeezed into making Ballot an open question ... I rode with Howick [Grey's heir, in the Government] yesterday for a long time and talked it over with him ... [he] sees all the danger – not so much from the Ballot itself as from its inevitable train of consequences – and still consents to abandon the contest. I asked him if he was not conscious that it was only like buying off the Picts and Scots and that fresh demands would speedily follow with redoubled confidence; and he owned that he was – and these are *Statesmen* and this is a *government* and here we have a beginning of the evils that the caprice and folly of the Queen, backed as it were by the wickedness of the Whigs were certain to entail ...

June 24th Ludlow Monday

Left London on Friday last by railroad, went to Wolverhampton (the vilest-looking town I ever saw) and in my carriage from thence to this place where I only arrived at a quarter past nine. The journey takes (losing no time) about eleven and a half hours – one hundred and fifty miles – of which thirty-four by land. The road from Bridgenorth to Ludlow is very striking and commands exceedingly fine views.

    ... The continuation of the violent and libellous articles in the *Morning Post* about Lady Flora Hastings and the unappeased wrath of Hastings again stirred the question of explanations and apologies; and now Brougham mixed himself up in it as the Adviser of Hastings ... Brougham thought he would be satisfied if Melbourne would make some apology to Lady Hastings ... and the Duke agreed with him that M. might and ought to do this ... but M. convinced the Duke that it would be better not to write an apology or explanation to Lady H. ... So the matter stands and meantime they are in a great fright lest Lady Flora should die; because She is very ill; and if She should die the public will certainly hold an inquest on her body and bring in a verdict of wilful murder against Buckingham Palace. As if one scandal of this sort was not enough there has been another, not so serious but unbecoming and disreputable concerning the Duchess of Montrose and Lady Sarah Ingestre who were said to have hissed the Queen from Erroll's stand at Ascot as H.M. drove up the course ... The fact, however, in spite of the indignant denials of the Ladies, is true. These two foolish vulgar women (for such they are) at a moment of great fury (for it was shortly after the grand scompiglio) did by some not decorous or feminine noises, testify their contempt, not probably of the Queen herself, but of the general contents of the procession. And this was so openly, even ostentatiously done ...

I am greatly delighted with this country which is of surpassing beauty and the old castle at Ludlow, a noble ruin and 'ruinous perfection' ... Yesterday I walked and rode over the hills above Ludlow, commanding a panoramic prospect of the Country round, and anything more grand and picturesque I never beheld ...

July 7th

Came to town yesterday from Basingstoke by railroad; found that Lady Flora Hastings was dead, and a great majority against the Education [the creation of a Committee on Education was petitioned against by vote of the Lords on 5 July because of its secular concerns] ... Lady Flora said to have died of dropsy in the womb, which also accounts for the appearance of pregnancy ... she suffered dreadfully in mind and body ... The libels in the *Morning Post*, so far from being stopped, have only been more venomous since her death, and this soi-disant Conservative paper daily writes against the Queen with the most revolting virulence and indecency ... It is just the sort of feeling that predominated in the time of Queen Caroline ... The world, foolish, meddling and ignorant, always likes to have an object to run up or run down, and here they have both.

July 14th

There have been angry debates in the Lords about the Birmingham riots, chiefly remarkable for the excitement (so unlike his usual manner) exhibited by the Duke of Wellington, who assailed the Government with a fierceness which betrayed him into much exaggeration and some injustice. Tavistock, who although a partisan, is a fair one and who has great esteem and respect for the Duke, told me that he had seen and heard him with great pain and that his whole tone was alarmingly indicative of a decay of mental power ... The Tories, with whom nothing goes down but violence, were delighted with his angry vein, and see proofs of vigour in what his opponents consider as evidence of decay; his bodily health is wonderfully good, which is perhaps alarming rather than reassuring as to the safety of his mind.

September 5th

Among other bad signs of the times, one is the decay of *loyalty* in the Tory party; the Tory principle is completely destroyed by party rage. No Opposition was ever more rabid than this is, no people ever treated or spoke of the Sovereign with such marked disrespect . . . This reproach does not apply to the Leaders of the Party who are too wise and too decorous to hold such language or approve of such conduct; but it is the *animus* which distinguishes the tail and the body and they take no pains to conceal it. [An original footnote refers to a Conservative dinner at Ashton-under-Lyne on 30 October where one John Roby MP stated, 'Virgin innocence is banished from the palace while vice riots rampant at the Royal board.']

September 14th

Brougham has sent to the press a letter to the Duke of Bedford on Education, of which he thus speaks in a note to Tavistock . . . 'My whole heart was in it, both from affection and to your excellent Father and to the subject. I hope it will do good, for the time is going away from under me . . .' The production will probably be very good in its way and very eloquent, but the note is characteristic – a mixture of pride and humility, humbugging and self-deceitful. What cares he for the Duke of Bedford, whom he scarcely sees from one end of the year to the other, and why should he care? . . . a more uninteresting, weak-minded, selfish man does not exist than the Duke of Bedford. He is a good-natured, plausible man, without enemies, and really (though he does not think so) without friends . . . Vast property, rank, influence and station always attract a sentiment which is dignified with the name of friendship . . . It is a farce to talk of friendship with such a man, on whom, if he were not Duke of Bedford, Brougham would never waste a thought.

September 17th

. . . [The Duke of Wellington] told me what Brougham had said of Macaulay (whom he hates with much cordiality) when somebody asked if he was to be Secretary at War. 'No, [nevertheless Melbourne appointed Macaulay Secretary at War] Melbourne would not consent to it; he would not have him in the Cabinet, and could not endure to sit with ten parrots, a chime of bells and Lady Westmoreland.'

September 21st

. . . I dined at Holland House last night where among others Alava [Don Miguel Ricardo De Alava (1771–1843), Spanish general, fought with Wellington, opposed to absolutist party in his country] and Hobhouse, the first in high glee at the termination of the war in Spain, and the last at the success of the Indian expedition. [A footnote by Reeve, first editor, begins 'This was the expedition to replace Shah Sooja on the throne of Afghanistan which was so auspiciously commenced and so deplorably terminated.']

November 8th

Jemmy Bradshaw's speech at Canterbury has attracted the liveliest attention, and he has been for many days the hero of newspaper discussion. The speech, which was a tissue of folly and impertinence but chiefly remarkable for a personal attack of the most violent and indecent kind upon the Queen, was received with shouts of applause at a Conservative dinner and reported with many compliments and some gentle reprehension by the Tory press . . . Peel is to be pitied for having to lead such an unruly and unprincipled faction.

November 26th

The Queen wrote to all her family and announced her marriage to them. When she saw the Dss. of Gloster in town, and told her she was to make her declaration the next day, the Dss. asked her if it was not a nervous thing to do. She said 'Yes; but I did a much more nervous thing a little while ago.' 'What was that?' 'I proposed to Prince Albert.' . . .

November 27th

The Queen settled everything about her marriage herself, and without consulting Melbourne at all on the subject, not even communicating to him her intentions . . . If she has already shaken off her dependence on Melbourne, what will she not do when she is older and has to deal with Ministers whom she does not care for, or whom she dislikes.

December 31st

We are arrived at the end of the year, and the next will begin with the Chartist trials, [concerning the Chartist riots at Newport and elsewhere which Greville failed to record].

1840

January 17th

Parliament met yesterday. Queen well enough received – much better than usual – as she went to the House. The Speech was harmless. Some had wished to have something about the Corn Laws in it, but this was overruled by the majority . . . Bradshaw and Horsman went out yesterday [to fight a duel], the former called out the latter on account of a speech at Cockermouth, in which in allusion to the famous Canterbury *Victorippick*, he had said that he had the tongue of a traitor and the heart of a coward. Though six weeks had elapsed between the speech and the challenge, H. did go out, and they exchanged shots; after which Bradshaw made a sort of stingy apology for his insult to the Queen, and the other an apology for his offensive expressions . . .

January 22nd

... The Judges are much censured for their behaviour at Newport [this refers to trials following the Chartist riots at Newport]; first, for not themselves deciding the point that was raised; next, for not asking the Jury their reasons of their recommending the criminals to mercy; and the Chief Justice's charge to the Jury was thought a very weak and poor performance ...

January 29th

On Monday night the Government were beat by 104 on the question of reducing the Prince's allowance from £50,000 to £30,000 ...

January 30th

The great debate [a motion of no confidence proposed by the Tory back-bencher, Sir John Yarde-Buller] in the H. of Commons has now lasted for two nights without being very interesting ... Last night Macaulay failed. He delivered an essay not without merit, but inapplicable and not the sort of thing that is wanted in such a debate. He had said that he should not be of use to them and he appears to have judged correctly. The Tories affected to treat his speech with contempt, and to talk and laugh, which was a rudeness worthy of the noisy and ignorant knot which constitutes the tail of that party ...

February 4th

After four nights' debate and division, at five in the morning, Government got a majority of twenty-one, just what was (at last) expected. Peel spoke for three hours and so elaborately as to fatigue the House, so that his speech probably seems much better to the reader than to the hearer of it ... But the most important part of his speech was his declaration of the principles by which he meant to be governed in office or out; and his manly and direct announcement to his followers, that they must support him on his own terms, and that if they did not like them, he was sorry for it, and they must look elsewhere for a leader if they chose it. There can be no doubt that it was wise and bold thus to cast himself on public opinion, and to put forth a manifesto which leaves no doubt of his future conduct, and from which there is no retreat for him, and by which all his adherents must be equally bound ...

February 13th

The Wedding on Monday went off tolerably well. The day before was glorious and Albert was driving about the town with a mob at his heels. Tuesday, Wednesday and today all beautiful days; but Monday as if by a malignant influence, was a dreadful day – torrents of rain and violent gusts of wind ... She had been as wilful, obstinate and wrongheaded as usual about her invitations, and some of her mischievous and foolish courtiers were boasting that out of above 300 in the chapel there would only be five Tories.

February 15th Saturday

The Duke of Wellington had a serious seizure on Thursday . . . He went to Lady Burghersh, and when he came away, the footman told the groom he was sure His Grace was not well and advised him to be very attentive to him . . . when he got to his own door, he found he could not get off his horse. He felt his hand chilled. This has been the first symptom in each of his three attacks. He was helped off. Hume was sent for, came directly and got him to bed. He had a succession of violent convulsions, was speechless, and his arm was affected. They thought he would have died in the night. The Doctors came, physicked, but did not bleed him and yesterday morning he was better. He has continued to mend ever since but it was a desperate blow and offers a sad prospect . . . [Lyndhurst] said the Duke ought now to retire from public life and not expose himself to any appearance of an enfeebled understanding . . . He owned that nobody could replace the Duke or keep the Party in order, and he said that the consequence was that it would break up, that *there are many who would be glad of an opportunity to leave it*.

    . . . It is a sad to see him almost insulted by the court, just as his sun is about to set. It turns out to be quite true that it was with great difficulty that the Queen was induced to invite him to her wedding, and at last only when it was hinted to her that if he was not there would very likely be some unpleasant manifestation of public opinion . . . He is well aware of this and he told Lord Lyndhurst (who told me) that she said 'I won't have that Old rebel' – not however that I believe she said this. This is one of the inventions I have no doubt of the busy mischief-makers and angry Tories who make bad as much worse as they can.

February 19th

Went yesterday to Apsley House. Duke going on well, but his people indignant that while all the royal family have been sending continually to enquire after him, and all London has been at his door, the Queen alone has never taken the slightest notice of him. This afflicted me and I resolved to speak to Melbourne . . . He sat down, wrote a note and sent it off directly. I said 'I suppose she will send now' – 'Oh yes, she will send now,' he replied. He then talked about her; said she was very resentful . . . I said 'Depend upon it she will get into a great scrape. The people of England will not endure that she should treat the D. of Wn. with disrespect; and it is not the mere act of sending or not that will make an impression of itself, but the whole of her conduct will, and does, produce an impression of the badness of her heart and disposition. Everybody knows her Father was the greatest rascal that ever went unhung, and they will say that it is the bad blood coming out in her.' ...

February 26th
Called on the D. of Bedford [the old Duke having just died, this was Greville's great friend, the former Marquess of Tavistock] yesterday morning and had a long talk about the court when he told me several things (in great confidence) about Prince Albert's position, how little to be envied and possibly hereafter to be pitied, taken from his family who adored him, and from his country and habits, and put down in the midst of a grandeur which is so very heavy and dull and which, unless something is done to improve the social gaiety of the court, must end by fatiguing and disgusting him. The Duchess of Bedford's impression is that the Queen is excessively in love with him, but he not a bit with her.

March 12th
... The Duke of Wellington has reappeared in the H. of Lords, goes about and works as usual, but everybody is shocked and grieved at his appearance ... He dined at the Palace on Monday and was treated with the greatest civility by the Queen. Indeed ever since the omission she has endeavoured to repair it by every sort of attention and gracefulness to which he is by no means insensible ...

April 3rd
I saw Prince Albert for the first time. He is exactly like the drawing of him (and the Queen); rather a slouching air, and though tall, clumsily made; but without speaking to him or hearing him speak, it is difficult to judge of his looks. Everybody speaks well of him.

April 13th
The China debate [concerning British hostilities with China] went off on the whole well enough for the Government, though they only got a majority of 9, owing in great measure to the number of casualties on their side. Poyntz died the night before the division and the breath was hardly out of his body before an express was despatched by a Tory whipper-in, to desire that nobody would on any account pair with Captain Spencer (his son-in-law). In this nice balance of parties, human life seemed only to be of interest as votes are influenced by it.

May 15th
... Just after I got back from Newmarket intelligence arrived of the extraordinary murder of Lord Wm. Russell which has excited a prodigious interest

and frightened all London out of its wits. Visionary servants and air-drawn razors or carving knives dance before everybody's imagination, and half the world go to sleep expecting to have their throats cut before morning. The circumstances of the case are certainly most extraordinary, and though everyday produces some fresh cause for suspecting the Man Courvoisier [François Courvoisier, a Swiss valet, was convicted of the murder of Lord William on 20 June 1840 and hanged on 6 July before a crowd of 20,000 people] both the fact and the motives are still enveloped in great mystery. People are always ready to jump to a conclusion ... I had the curiosity to go the day before yesterday to Tothill Fields Prison [close to the Houses of Parliament] to see the man who had just been sent there. He is rather ill-looking, a baddish countenance, but his manner was calm though dejected, and he was civil and respectful and not sulky. The people there said he was very restless and had not slept and that he was a man of great bodily strength.

[*May*] *17th*

... though I believe him to be guilty, I could not on such a case as there yet is find him so if placed on a jury ... Lord Ashburton, when we were talking of this told me an anecdote of General Maitland (Sir Thomas). Which happened at some place in the West Indies or South America. He had taken some town and the Soldiers were restrained from committing violence on the inhabitants when a shot was fired from a window and one of his men killed. They entered the House, went to the room from the window of which the shot had been fired and found a number of men playing at billiards. They insisted on the culprit being given up, when a man was pointed out as the one who had fired the shot. They all agreed as to the culprit and he was carried off. Sir Thomas, considering that a severe example was necessary, ordered the man to be tied to the mouth of a cannon and shot away. He was present but turned his head away when the signal was given for blowing this wretches body to atoms. The explosion took place when to his amazement the man appeared alive, but with his hair standing quite literally 'like frills upon the fretful porcupine' [*sic*], with terror. In the agony of the moment he had contrived to squeeze himself through the ropes which were loosely tied and get on one side of the cannon's mouth, so that the ball missed him. He approached Maitland and said 'You see General, that it was the will of heaven my life should be spared; and I solemnly assure you that I am innocent.' Maitland would not allow him to be executed after this miraculous escape, and it turned out after further enquiry that he was innocent and that it was some other man who had fired the shot.

August 24th

Passed the greater part of last week at the Grove where Clarendon talked to me a great deal about the Eastern question, Palmerston's policy and showed me several of his (P's) private letters. Palmerston, it seems, has had for many years as his fixed idea the project of humbling the Pasha [Mehemet Ali].[1] In the Cabinet He has carried everything his own way ... except Lord Holland and Clarendon who did oppose with all their strength Palmerston's latest treaty, but quite ineffectually ... Palmerston, in fact, appears to exercise an absolute despotism at the Foreign Office and deals with all our vast and complicated questions of diplomacy according to his own views and opinions without the slightest controul [sic] and scarcely any interference on the part of his colleagues ... I never was more amazed than at reading his letters, so dashing, bold and confident is their tone.

Considering the immensity of the stake for which he is playing and that he *may* be about to plunge all Europe into a war, and that if this war does ensue, it will be all his doing, it is utterly astonishing that he should not be more affected than he appears to be with the gravity of the circumstances ... Everything may turn out according to his expectations [everything did]. He is a man blessed with extraordinary good fortune, and his motto seems to be that of Danton, 'De l'audace, encore de l'audace, et toujours de l'audace.' But there is a flippancy in his tone, an undoubting self-sufficiency and a levity in discussing interests of such tremendous magnitude which satisfies me that this is a very dangerous man to be trusted with the uncontrolled management of foreign relations.

September

On arriving in town this morning, I found a note from M. Guizot [François Guizot, French ambassador, soon after Prime Minister, also a distinguished historian] begging I would call on him ... Accordingly I went and am just returned. His object was to put me in possession of the actual state of affairs and to read me a letter he had just received from Thiers ... Thiers' letter expressed considerable alarm ... [Mehemet Ali] had engaged not to move forward or take any offensive course ... unless compelled to do so by violence offered to him ... But if any European troops were to advance against him ... then he would cross the Taurus and taking all consequences, commence offensive operations. In that case, said Guizot, Constantinople might be occupied by the Russians and the British Fleet enter the Sea of Marmora; and if that happened he could not answer for the result in France ... He had seen Palmerston this morning and read Thiers' letter to him. I asked if it had made any impression on P. He said 'Not the slightest'; that he had said 'Oh! Mehemet Ali cédera; il ne fait pas s'attendre qu'il céde à la première sommation; mais donnez lui quinze jours, et il finira par céder.' ... Guizot however did not take the trouble to send for me merely to tell me all this and to talk the matter over with me, but to revive the energies of *The Times* ... and to get me to set that great engine again to work, especially to make them *show up* Palmerston by exhibiting the mistakes [*les mécomptes*] which he has already made. I told him I would not fail to see Barnes [Thomas Barnes (1785–1841), editor of *The Times* . . . I think (now that it is so near) that the French Government would avoid war at almost any cost; but the great evil of the present state of affairs is that the conduct of the question has escaped out of the hands of Ministers and statesmen and henceforward must depend upon the passions and caprice of the Pacha [*sic*], and the discretion of the commanders of the numerous Fleets now gathered in the Mediterranean . . . As Guizot said [peace] was at the mercy 'des incidents et des subalterns' . . .

September 10th

The day after I saw Guizot I told Clarendon all that had passed when he told me that Melbourne was now become seriously alarmed so much so that he had written word to John Russell, 'he could neither sat, drink or sleep' so great was his disturbance. John [Russell] was also extremely alarmed, and both he and Melbourne had been considerably moved by a letter the former had received from the D. of Bedford enclosing one from Lord Spencer [Lord Althorp, pilot of the Reform Bill] in which he . . . said that it was his earnest desire to support the Government in all their measures, but that it would be contrary to his judgment and his conscience to support them in their policy on this question. This appears to have made a great impression upon them, but not the least upon Palmerston who is quite impenetrable . . .

September 29th

I went to Clarendon's house on Monday evening, but he did not come home till 7 o'clock, the Cabinet having sat for so long. His account of what passed was to the last degree amusing, but at the same time *pitoyable* . . . they met, and as if all were conscious of something unpleasant in prospect, and all shy, there was for some time a dead silence. At length Melbourne, trying to shuffle off the discussion, but aware that he must say something, began 'We must consider about the time to which Parliament should be prorogued.' Upon this John [Russell] took it up and said 'I presume we must consider whether Parliament should be called together or not, because, as matters are now going on, it seems to me that we may at any moment find ourselves at war, and it is high time to consider the very serious state of affairs. I should like' he added, turning to Melbourne, 'to know what is your opinion on the subject.' Nothing however could be got from Melbourne, and there was another, long, pause which was not broken until Palmerston pulled out of his pocket a whole parcel of letters and reports from Ponsonby [Lord Ponsonby, British ambassador at Constantinople and an extreme advocate of war]. Hodges [Consul-General in Egypt] and others, and began reading them through, in the middle of which operation Clarendon happened to look up and perceived Melbourne fast asleep in his Armchair . . .

October 1st

Saw Clarendon yesterday. No progress made, everything in *statu quo* ... The next day they all dined at Holland House. There he had some talk with P. himself, amicable enough but leading to nothing; to what C. said himself about breaking up the Government P. said not a word ... Melbourne of course hopped off to Windsor the moment the Cabinet was over, and instead of remaining here, trying to conciliate people and arrange matters, he left everything to shift for itself.

Evening

The Cabinet went off far better than could have been expected. It seems pretty clear that M. had contrived to effect some arrangement with Palmerston ... A great deal more discussion then ensued and the result was that Palmerston is to see the Ministers of the Conference (either separately or together) tomorrow, and to propose to them that he should make a communication to France ...

October 2nd

Last night it was decided [in Cabinet] that Palmerston should call the Conference [the representatives in London of Prussia, Austria and Russia] together and propose to them to make a conciliatory advance to France. All Europe is looking with anxiety for the result of the Cabinet held yesterday; and this morning the *Morning Chronicle* puts forth an article having every appearance of being written by Palmerston himself (as I have no doubt it was) most violent, declamatory and insulting to France ...

October 4th

... I received a note from Guizot desiring to see me, and I went. I told him the article was abominable, but that so far from its being a true exposition of the views of the Cabinet, they had resolved upon the attempt at conciliation which Palmerston had himself agreed to make ... He promised to make the best of it with his Government, and, making them comprehend that there was a strong peace party in the Cabinet, work in conjunction with that party here to keep matters quiet ... It was not however until this morning that I knew the subject of their discussion. On arriving in town, indeed, I heard that Beyrout [Beirut] had been bombarded and taken by the English Fleet, and a body of Turkish troops had been landed ... Guizot arrived at my house in a great state of excitement [and] produced his whole budget of intelligence, being the bombardment of Beyrout, the landing of 12,000 Turks and the deposition of Mehemet Ali. He also showed me a letter from Thiers in which he told him of all this, said he would not answer for what might come of it, that he had had one and should have another meeting of the Cabinet; but Guizot said that he would very likely end by convoking the Chambers ...

October 7th Tuesday

... It is now quite clear that Palmerston has gained his point. The peace party in the Cabinet are silenced, their efforts paralysed. Clarendon agreed with me that P. had triumphed and John succumbed. The Cabinet are again dispersed, P. reigns without let or hindrance at the Foreign Office. No attempt is made to conciliate France; the war on the coast of Syria will go on with redoubled vigour ...

October 9th

Everything looked black these last two days, funds falling and general alarm ... In the afternoon I saw Guizot whom I found very reasonable, full of regret for the violence in Paris ... then he said that he still did not despair of peace if we would only do something to pacify and conciliate France; that some concession in return for hers she must have and without which her government had not the power to maintain peace ...

October 10th

The Cabinet met this afternoon. John Russell was to have taken the lead and developed his conciliatory notions, but a new turn was given to affairs by a note which Guizot placed in Palmerston's hands just before the Cabinet which he only received from Paris this morning. He called on Palmerston and gave it him, but without any observations. Palmerston brought it to the Cabinet where it was read and, to the extreme surprise of everybody, was to the last degree moderate and evincing a desire to be very easily satisfied ... Palmerston immediately showed a disposition to haggle and bargain, and make it a pretext for extorting from France the best terms she could be got to yield, and all this in the spirit of a Pedlar rather than of a Statesman ... When I asked Guizot how it was all to be accounted for, he told me that the truth was it was owing to dissension in the French Cabinet, and the determination of the King [Louis Philippe] ... With that wonderful sagacity which renders him the ablest man in France, and that tact and discernment with which he knows when to yield and when to make his stand, he allowed Thiers to have his full swing and to commit himself with the nation, the King himself all the time consenting to put the country in a formidable attitude, but making no secret of his desire for peace; and then at the decisive moment, when he found there was a division in the Cabinet, throwing all his influence into the pacifick scale ...

Downham October 23rd

... This morning I learnt (by reading it in the *Globe*) the sudden death of Lord Holland after a few hours' illness, and whom I left not a fortnight ago in his usual health and likely to live many years ... Never was popularity so great and so general, and his death will produce a social revolution, utterly extinguishing not only the most distinguished, but the only great house of reception and constant society in England. [Holland House had been open to a great circle of writers, poets, historians and serious politicians of a liberal outlook, inspiring references to 'the Holland House Radicals'] ... The event may be said with perfect truth 'to eclipse the gaiety of nations' for besides being an irreparable loss to the world at large, it turns adrift, as it were, the innumerable habitués who, according to their differing degrees of intimacy or the accidents of their social habits, made H.H. their regular and constant resort ... and there cannot be a sadder sight than to see the curtain suddenly fall upon a scene so brilliant ...

Since this I have had a letter from Clarendon (from Windsor) giving the same deplorable account of Melbourne, who is frightened at France, hopeless of success in Syria, sick to death of the scrape we have got into, but not knowing what to do and only thinking of letting matters take their course ... If the Queen was not a spoilt child only intent upon the gratification of her social predilections, if she was sensible of the great duty she owes to the country and of the peril in which it is placed ... she would see the necessity of meeting the dangers and difficulties of our position by firmness, capacity and union ...

Newmarket October 27th
At Downham laid up with the gout, and now here. Heard of Thiers' resignation on Sunday and nothing since; ...

London November 5th
... Guizot left London pretty well determined to take the Government; and after some little discussion everything was settled, and the new Cabinet proclaimed. The press instantly fell upon him with the greatest bitterness, and the first impression was that he had no chance of standing, but the last accounts held out a better prospect [Guizot held office as Prime Minister until 1848].

London November 5th
... Palmerston wrote to Melbourne in a tone of the greatest contempt for all that was saying and doing in France, and of course elated by the recent successes in Syria which with his usual luck have happened at this crucial moment and certainly do appear to be decisive ... John [Russell] however resolved upon action and ultimately determined to propose the recall of Ponsonby as the *sine qua non* of his continuation in office. The violence of these disputes, and the peril in which the existence of the Government seemed to be placed, brought Melbourne up to town, and John came to meet him and

imparted to him his intentions. Just in the nick of time however arrived the news of the Emir's flight[2] which seemed to be almost conclusive of the Syrian question. On this, Palmerston took courage and no longer insisting upon supporting Ponsonby *à tort et travers* entreated that a damp might not be cast upon the enterprise just as the final success was at hand . . .

November 7th

. . . But although such is the disposition of both Austria and Prussia, though the Queen is earnestly desirous of seeing tranquillity and security restored, and almost all, if not quite all, the Cabinet are in favour of an accommodation with France, and France herself is prepared to accept the slightest advance offered in a conciliatory spirit. The personal determination of Palmerston will probably predominate over all these opinions and inclinations . . . The most extraordinary part of the whole affair is that a set of men should consent to go on with another in whom they not only have no confidence, but whom they believe to be politically dishonest and treacherous, and that they should keep gravely discussing the adoption of measures with a full conviction that he will not fully carry them out. It is like Jonathan Wild and his companions playing together in Newgate . . .

Friday November 13th

. . . Events have so befriended Palmerston that he is now in the right, and has got his colleagues with him; but where he is and always has been in the wrong is in his neglect of forms; the more *fortiter* he is in *re*, the more *suaviter* he should be in *modo* . . . Guizot will now be cast on his own resources and must try whether the language of truth and reason will be listened to in France . . . It is clear enough to me that if he cannot . . . no concession we could make would save him from downfall or save Europe from the consequences of this moral deluge.

December 4th

In the course of the last three weeks, and since I last wrote, a great change has taken place; we have seen the capture of St Jean d'Acre and the debate in the French Chambers. Palmerston is triumphant; everything has turned out well for him . . . and it must be acknowledged that he has a right to plume himself on his success. His colleagues have nothing more to say; and as Guizot makes a common cause with him in the chamber and Thiers makes a case for himself by declaring objects and designs which justify Palmerston's policy and acts, and as the Pacha [*sic*] is now reduced to the necessity of submission, the contest is at an end.

1841

January 9th

[Palmerston] has no intimacy, no interchange of thought and complete open-ness with anybody, and all they know is (and that only as soon as he sees fit to impart it) his notions with regard to each particular question as its exigen-cies become pressing. His position, however, is a remarkable one. Belonging to a government almost every member of which dislikes or distrusts him, he has acquired by recent events a great reputation, and is looked upon generally as a bold, able and successful statesman. In the event of a dislocation of parties, he is free to adopt any course and to join with any party ...

January 21st

I dined with Lady Holland yesterday. Everything there is the same as it used to be, excepting only the person of Lord Holland who seems pretty well forgotten. The same talk went merrily round, the laugh rang loudly and frequently and but for the black and the mob-cap of the Lady, one might have fancied he had never lived or had died half a century ago ...

January 30th Saturday

Parliament opened on Tuesday last with a very meagre speech, on which no amendment could be hung ... At present everything promises a very easy session, and the Conservatives are confessedly reduced to look to the chapter of accidents for some event which may help them to turn out the Government and get hold of their places ...

February 4th

Yesterday all the Tories were in high glee at their success at the Canterbury and Walsall elections, the former not having been expected by either party and nevertheless they had a majority of 165 votes. It is certainly curious for the Government has a right to be popular or at least to expect that no tide of unpopularity should run against them;

February 12th

The other day I met Howick and had a talk with him about the Irish ques-tions now pending ... He approves of Stanley's registration and Morpeth's definition of the franchise not binding himself to *amount*, but not objecting to that proposal ...

February 14th

The day before yesterday I met Graham by accident at Boodle's, so I took the opportunity of talking to him about these Bills and I soon found that there is no possibility of any compromise ... he said that he had never seen Stanley so determined, and that he and Peel were both entirely agreed with him; that he could not understand how John Russell or indeed any member of Lord Grey's Government could consent to such a violation of the principle of the Reform Bill and to the granting of a new franchise which, if granted, must entail similar concessions in England and Scotland; that the intention of the Reform Bill was that in the Counties, property and not numbers should have influence and that the effect of this Bill would be to transfer influence from property to numbers ... When I urged the importance of settling affairs in Ireland and not leaving unsettled such a question as this to unite all the country against them, if they came in again and revive the great power of O'Connell ... and of the great danger that might arise from Ireland in the present unsettled state of Europe, he said rather than consent to such a measure as this, he was prepared to encounter every difficulty and danger; he would never consent to transfer power from the landed interest to the multitude; and as long as the Priests interfered in Irish Elections, it could not be expected that Landlords would not counteract that influence by diminishing as much as they could the numbers of those who were made to act under it; that the old saying that Cromwell had confiscated too much or exterminated too little was the truth; he saw no way of pacifying the country, and as to concessions, they must have a limit, every concession had been made that could be reasonably desired, and he would do no more.

February 27th
The debate lasted four nights on Morpeth's Bill and Ministers got a majority of five, both sides bringing down the sick and the dying without remorse.

March 14th
The other night Peel, who has been a good deal nettled by the attacks on him in a series of letters signed 'Catholicus' in *The Times*, made a very striking speech upon the education and recreation of the people. Which was enthusiastically cheered by the Whigs, but received in silence by the Tories. He made a sort of reply in his speech to the charges of irreligion, etc insinuated in those letters and took the opportunity of expressing those liberal sentiments which mark his own identification with the progress of society and which render him from their liberality and wisdom, the object of such suspicion, fear and dislike with the Tory democracy who reluctantly own him for their Leader.

March 16th Tuesday
On Friday last after the H. of Lords was over, the Ministerial Lords gathered on the bench and held a sort of Cabinet, a practice in which Melbourne takes

pleasure. Clarendon held forth about the state of the Eastern question and said all he thought without reserve. He worked up Lansdowne to a considerable amount of zeal and resolution to bestir himself. The next day L. called on Melbourne, and he owned to Clarendon that he was shocked and surprised to find that M. never had any communication with Palmerston on the subject, and, in point of fact, knew very little about what was going on. The next day there was a Cabinet, when both Lansdowne and Clarendon expressed their opinions with vivacity complaining of the proceeding at Constantinople [scene of the negotiations for protocols for peace] and urging the necessity of some decisive step being taken here to correct its effects. I asked what Melbourne and John Russell had said. The former never opened his lips; the latter was asleep the whole time. Palmerston knocked under; that is, he made no defence and no resistance, and ostensibly acquiesced in the opinions expressed and promised to act in conformity with them ...

May 2nd

... In the world of politics we have had an interval of repose till after the recess when Government suffered two defeats on the Irish Registration Bill [Morpeth's Bill was then withdrawn] and Walter came in for Nottingham on an Anti-Poor Law cry and by the union of Chartists and Tories to defeat the Whig candidate ... [Clarendon] admitted the Tory chances had advanced prodigiously and that Peel's language was quite that of determination and of a man ready to take the Government ...

May 3rd

Great agitation yesterday at the clubs and excessive interest and curiosity about coming events on which hang the existence of the Government. The Tories are talking of a vote of want of confidence and wish to follow up their successes by this decisive blow. There is the greatest difference of opinion among the Whigs as to the necessity of resigning, the propriety and, above all, as to a dissolution. The event of the day was the resignation of Gordon [Secretary of the Treasury] who could not stand the Corn alteration that is threatened. Nobody thinks Ministers will carry their budget and that will probably be their *coup de grâce*.

May 8th

Barnes [editor of *The Times*] died yesterday morning, suddenly, after having suffered an operation ... The vast power exercised by *The Times* renders this a most important event, and it will be curious to see in what hands the regulating and directing power will hereafter be placed ... it is personally to me a very great loss, for the connexion which I had accidentally established and which has now lasted so many years was exclusively and personally with

Barnes; and it would be almost impossible for me to renew it with any person who may occupy his place. [Not true: as Greville says in one of his occasional catch-up notes added much later, he would strike up with Barnes's successor as editor at *The Times*, Thaddeus Delane, an even better relationship.]

May 9th

The debate began on Friday night by an extraordinarily good speech from John Russell, as was admitted by his opponents who qualified the praise as usual by calling it a *good party* speech ... The certainty of a majority against Government is now generally admitted, and it is expected to be large. The strong supporters of Government are more and more urgent, and they say that they must chuse between the dissolution of Parliament or the dissolution of the party; ...

May 11th

The question of dissolution is still contested and the Whigs of Brooks's and the young and hot-headed are making such a clatter, and talking with so much violence and confidence that they have created a strong impression that the measure is intended ... I learnt that Melbourne is in a state of great agitation and disquietude labouring under a sense of the enormous responsibility which rests upon him, embarrassed on the one side by the importunities of his friends, and, on the other, alarmed at the danger of taking so desperate a step; ... I rode with the Duke [Wellington] yesterday, and had a little, but very little talk with him about the present crisis. He does not talk as he used to do, and he struck me as miserably changed ...

May 16th

The debate was again adjourned on Friday night, having lasted a week, very languidly carried on, and up to the present time with very few good speeches since John Russell's; Sir G. Grey, the Chancellor of the Exchequer, and Labouchere on one side; Gladstone and Stanley the best on the other ...

May 25th

... Nothing was said but all the Tories were desirous of doing something ... and yesterday Peel convened a meeting at his house, made them a speech in which he told them all the objections there were to meddling with the supplies and proposed the resolution [a motion of no confidence] of which he gave notice last night which was hailed with general satisfaction ...

June 6th

The division took place on Friday night, and there was a majority of one against the Government ... The Government people now want them to bring on a debate about Corn and John Russell is to announce tomorrow what he means to do ...

June 12th

... On Monday John Russell very properly announced that after the vote last week he should not go on with any business but that which was indispensable ... All the world is now preparing for the elections and all (as usual) sanguine in their expectations of the result, but I don't believe the Government really expect much gain, and they feel their days are numbered ...

June 18th

The Queen went to Nuneham last week for Prince Albert's visit to Oxford when he was made a Doctor. Her name was well received and so was the Prince himself in the [Sheldonian] Theatre; But her Ministers, individually and collectively, were hissed and hooted with all the vehemence of Oxonian Toryism ...

Chester, June 24th

Parliament having been dissolved yesterday, all the world are off to their elections, and I resolved to set to start upon an excursion to North Wales which I have long been desirous of seeing ...

Plas Newydd Sunday June 27th

Left Chester at half past eleven on Friday morning having stopt to hear service at the Cathedral, a poor building – very Ancient – Saxon – fine chanting which I particularly liked. A rainy day, nothing particular in the road till Conway, where the Castle is very fine, a most noble ruin and the old walls of the town, with their numerous towers, so perfect that I doubt if there is anything like them to be seen anywhere ... From Conway a fine and striking road along the seashore, and round the base of Penmaen Mawr, a mountain nearly as high as Snowdon: crossed the Menai Bridge at dusk. But with light enough to see the wonderful work and arrived at this place between ten and eleven o'clock. Nobody here; Lord Anglesey not yet arrived in his yacht which was beat about on her passage by stormy weather. A most delightful place on the margin of the Menai Strait with the mountains in full view ...

Tuesday 29th

Sunday we all went down in the boats of Lord Anglesey's cutter to Bangor to attend the service in the Cathedral under the Menai Bridge ... A poor Church at Bangor, Cathedral service but moderate musick. The Church is divided into two, half for the English, half for the Welsh; the Nave is made the parish Church, and there the service is done in Welsh. There were very few, if any, of the common people in the English afternoon service; in fact, few of them speak anything except Welsh. It has an odd effect to see the women with their high-crowned, round hats on in Church; the dress is not unbecoming. After Church we were followed by a mob to our boats, and they cheered Lord A. when he embarked.

Monday

... We then went to the ferry and got a boat in which we sailed over to Beaumaris and went up Baron's Hill (Sir Richard Bulkeley's) with which I was delighted. The House is unfinished and ugly but the situation and prospect over the bay of Beaumaris are quite beautiful. Nothing can be more cheerful [*sic*], and the whole scene round, sea, coast and mountains, indescribably beautiful. They compare this bay to the Bay of Naples, and I do not know that there is any presumption in the comparison ...

Friday July 2nd

... The road from Beddgelert is perfectly alpine in character and the peasantry neither speak nor understand anything but Welsh ... The women are generally good looking, with a vigorous frame and a healthy, cheerful aspect; and all the common people are decent in their appearance and particularly civil and respectful in their manner ... The Welsh are generally poor and wages are low; their food consists principally of potatoes and buttermilk; the average wages of labour is about nine shillings a week. The people however are industrious, sober, contented and well-behaved; they do not like either change or locomotion, and this makes them indifferent about learning English.

Sunday July 11th

Find London rather empty and tolerably calm. The elections are sufficiently over to exhibit a pretty certain result ... The Whigs give the whole thing up as irretrievably lost ... The Whigs complain bitterly of the apathy and indifference that have prevailed and cannot recover from their surprise that their promises of cheap bread and cheap sugar have not proved more attractive ...

August 4th

... [The Queen] dislikes the whole Tory Cabinet *en masse* because they are to be the Cabinet. She hates Peel from old recollections, and she can never forgive him because she is conscious that she behaved ill to him ...

August 10th

Peel's mind is not made of noble material, but he has an enlarged capacity and has had a vast experience of things, though from his peculiar disposition, a much more limited one of men ...

August 12th

The day before yesterday I met at dinner Dr Wiseman [Nicholas Wiseman, effective head of the Roman Catholic Church in Britain, later Cardinal Archbishop of Westminster in the restored hierarchy] a smooth, oily, agreeable Priest. He is now head of the College at Oscott near Birmingham, and a Bishop (in partibus) and accordingly he came in full Episcopal costume, purple stockings, tunic and gold chain. He talked religion, Catholicism, Protestantism and Puseyism almost the whole time ... talked much of Pusey, and Newman and Froude [founders of the Oxford Movement, from which developed the Anglo-Catholic tradition in the Church of England] ... [he] gave us to understand not only that their opinions are very nearly the same, but that the great body of that persuasion, Pusey himself included, are very nearly ripe and ready for reunion with Rome, and he assured us that neither the Pope's supremacy nor transubstantiation would be obstacles in their way ...

August 25th

The D. of Bedford just come here with an account of the H. of Lords last night. Spencer good, Ripon [formerly Goderich, now at odds with Melbourne's Whigs and moving an amendment to the address] very good indeed, the best speech he ever heard him make. The amendment was admirably composed most skilful and judicious. Melbourne was miserable; he never heard so bad a speech mere buffoonery and without an attempt to answer Ripon ... Brougham very bitter, voted with the Government, but attacked Melbourne ...

August 28th

The House divided last night, a majority of ninety-one, almost all the Conservatives attending and some of the others being absent. Peel seems to have spoken out and have announced to friend and foe that he will resolutely take his own course. If he adheres to this and takes a bold flight, he may be a great man ...

September 1st Wednesday

On Monday morning Peel went down to Windsor. He was well enough satisfied with his reception. The Queen was civil, but dejected ... If Peel had any occasion for his assistance he [Francis Egerton, Greville's brother-in-law] would readily afford it, but he apprehended that his difficulty would rather be found in the abundance than the lack of candidates. Peel shook his head and said that it was so indeed, and added that he had not had a single application for office from anybody who was fit for it ...

September 4th

Went yesterday to Claremont for the Council, at which the new Ministers were appointed — a day of severe trial for the Queen who conducted herself in a manner which excited my greatest admiration and was really touching to see. All of the old Government who had Seals or Wands to surrender were there (not Melbourne), and in one room; all the new Cabinet and new Privy Councillors were assembled in another, all in full dress. The Household were in the Hall. The Queen saw the Ex-people one after another (having already given audience to Peel) ... She looked very much flushed and her heart was evidently brim full, but she was composed and throughout the whole of the proceedings, when her emotion might very well have overpowered her, she preserved complete self-possession, composure and dignity ... [Peel] has in fact, deeply offended and mortified a great many expectants of office, and first and foremost, the D. of Beaufort, who, after having received the Queen at his house and been distinguished with rather peculiar marks of favour, fully expected that he would have been selected as one especially agreeable to H.M. instead of finding himself in a manner proscribed, he cannot tell why. The Irish Lords, Glengall and Charleville, are also furious, and consider Ireland, – that is Orange Ireland – insulted and neglected in their persons; the Beauforts are only sulky. Wilton, another disappointed aspirant, is in profound melancholy; the Irish Lords are open-mouthed and abusive ... With regard to Peel and his conduct, I think he is doing well and acting a fair, manly and considerate part ... However he has never before been in possession of real and great power. His course has been impeded and embarrassed by all sorts of obstructions and difficulties. It remains to be seen how he will act in his new capacity, and whether he will assert his independence to its fullest extent; above all, whether he will elevate his moral being to 'the height of his great argument'.

September 6th
Yesterday I called on Melbourne ... We had a great deal of talk about things and people connected with the court about the appointments and exclusions which were producing so much heartburning. He said he thought the Prince must be at the bottom of these; that he was extremely strait-laced and a great stickler for morality. Whereas she was rather the other way and did not much care about such niceties of moral choice.

September 7th
I fell in with the Duke of Wellington yesterday coming from Cabinet [Wellington was a member without specific office] and walked home with him ... I had some talk with him about the appointments when he told me in confirmation of what Melbourne had said that it was the Prince who insisted upon spotless character (the Queen not caring a straw about it), and who had put his veto on Beaufort etc.

September 17th Friday

Council at Windsor on Wednesday, the first since the change ... The Queen was very gracious and good humoured. At dinner she had the Duke next to her (his deaf ear unfortunately) and talked to him a good deal ... Talked for some time to Peel who could not help putting himself into his accustomed attitude of a dancing master giving a lesson. She would like him better if he could keep his legs still ... She has no conversation whatever, has never been used to converse with anybody but Melbourne, and with him either on business or on trifles.

September 22nd

The appointments are most of them completed, except the diplomatic which are still uncertain, and the Governor-General of India. This was offered to Haddington who refused it, and it is a curious circumstance that a man so unimportant, so destitute, not only of shining but of plausible qualities, without interest or influence, should by a mere combination of accidental circumstances, have had at his disposal three of the greatest and most important offices under the Crown, having actually occupied two of them and rejecting the greatest and most brilliant of them all. He has been Lord-Lieutenant of Ireland, he refuses to be Governor-General of India and he is First Lord of the Admiralty ...

September 29th

Mellish [senior Foreign Office clerk] gave me an account last night of Palmerston's last doings at the Foreign Office. He created five new attachés without the smallest need and all within a few days of his retirement ... all foul jobbing at the public expense ... Mellish told me another anecdote of Palmerston, that eleven thousand pounds [half a million sterling today] (I put it in letters because in figures some error might have been suspected) has been spent in *one year* at the Foreign Office in chaises-and-four conveying messengers to overtake the mail with his private letters which were never ready in time. Nothing ever equalled the detestation in which he is regarded in that office, and they say he is 'a Bully, a blackguard and a Coward'; still they do justice to his ability and say that any change of Government which could take place must include him in the new arrangement.

November 8th

Above a month since I have written anything in this book. In this interval my history is very brief and uninteresting. The principal events consist of the affair at Canton and the failure of the Spanish Christina plot,[1] the Exchequer business, the burning of the Tower, and now we are preoccupied with the approaching delivery of the Queen and the probable death of the Queen Dowager ... In the Spanish business Louis Philippe has been intriguing up to the chin ... It is a marvellous thing that so wise a man can't be a little honest, and (as has been remarked) a striking fact that notwithstanding his great reputation for sagacity, he is constantly engaged in underhand schemes in which he is generally both baffled and detected ...

November 11th

The Queen was delivered of a son [later Edward VII] at forty-eight minutes after ten on Tuesday morning the 9th. From some Crotchet of Prince Albert's they put off sending intelligence of H.M. being in labour till so late [sic] that several of the Dignitaries, whose duty it was to assist at the birth, arrived after the event had occurred, particularly the Archbishop of Canterbury and the Lord President of the Council.

November 27th

On Thursday dined with Millman [Church historian, later Dean of St Paul's], Macaulay, Sydney Smith, Babbage [Charles Babbage (1792–1871), mathematician, pioneer of the computer]; pretty equal partition of talk between Sydney and Macaulay.

November 30th

A correspondence has appeared in the papers between the Duke of Wellington and the Paisley deputation which is exceedingly painful to read ... This deputation is come up to represent the distress prevailing at Paisley, and they ask for an interview to lay the case before the Duke. He refuses to see them and writes a letter much in the style of his circulars [Wellington sent lithographed notes of non-communication to unknown correspondents] alleging that he has no time, holds no office and has no influence ... it is a complete delusion he is under; he has nothing to do and he has boundless influence ...

December 6th

Ellenborough's Proclamation [Ellenborough was now Governor General of India] which came out a week ago is the principal topic of conversation ... The general and impartial opinion is that he is quite right to have withdrawn the army from Afghanistan and to have announced a pacific policy for the future, but that he is much to blame in having adopted such a tone as the paper is couched in, to have cast an indirect slur on the policy of Auckland, and condemned in such unqualified terms men who are not alive to defend themselves or of the survivors who are going to be tried by a Court of enquiry ...

December 8th

I saw Emily Eden yesterday, and found they were full of bitterness against Ellenborough, and no wonder. In the first place he and Auckland had always been friends ... On his arrival in Calcutta, he was Auckland's guest for the first three days (till he was sworn in) and then Auckland was his ... He lived with them morning, noon and night on terms of the greatest cordiality, and repeatedly expressed his regret that they were going away. This renders his Proclamation particularly odious and the more because she told me that during the last months of his government, Auckland had done everything he could not to compromise his successor ... I am not so surprised at Ellenborough's *animus* since my brother told me the other day that he had told him when he was at the Board of Control [the office later superseded by the Secretaryship for India] that he never lost an opportunity of letting the Queen know his opinions as to the errors and blunders of his predecessor and his colleagues.

Bowood December 20th

... Found a very different party here from what I left at Woburn [Greville's previous excursion]. There are nothing but idle, ignorant, ordinary people, among whom there was not even an attempt at anything like society or talk; here, though not many, almost all distinguished more or less ...

December 23rd

Three days passed very agreeably, Moore sang some of his own melodies and Macaulay has been always talking. Never certainly was anything heard like him. It is inexhaustible, always amusing and instructive about everybody and everything ... The drollest thing is to see the effect upon Rogers who is nearly extinguished and can neither make himself heard nor find an interval to get in a word ... [Macaulay] said it was a mistake to impute to him either such a memory or so much knowledge; Whewell [William Whewell (1794–1866), Master of Trinity, Cambridge] and Brougham had more universal knowledge than he had, but that what he did have was the ready (perhaps too ready) use of all he knew. I said what surprised me most, his having time to read certain books over and over again; e.g. he said he had read *D. Quixote* in Spanish five or six times, and I had been afraid to say how often he had read *Clarissa*. He said that he read no modern books, none of the novels or travels that come out day after day. He had read *Tom Jones* repeatedly, but *Cecil, a Peer* not at all ...

December 26th

Macaulay went away the day before Christmas Day, and it was wonderful how quiet the house seemed after he was gone, and it was not less agreeable.

VOLUME IV ENDS

VOLUME V

1842

January 2nd Sunday

On Monday last I left Bowood (Rogers and I together) and went to Badminton [home of the Duke of Beaufort] where I found a party and habits as diametrically opposite as possible from that which we left behind. The stable and kennel formed the principal topic of interest. On Saturday came to town.

January 19th Wednesday

Went on Friday to Woburn ... The House had been very nearly burnt down the night before and was saved by a miracle. It happened in a maid's room. A gown was ignited (as they suppose); the chair on which it hung was burnt, but the fire did not reach bed or window curtains ... The smoke was so dense they could not penetrate into the room, but the servants threw buckets of water in, which by accident went to the right place and extinguished the fire ... John [Russell] was there in great force. He is arranging the Bedford papers for publication, but he has persuaded the Duke not to let the Duchess of Marlborough's correspondence be published because it is so personal and abusive, which is very superfluous piece of squeamishness, for it is just what people enjoy ...

February 1st

For the last week the King of Prussia[1] and his activity have occupied the world. He has made a very favourable impression here. In person he is common-looking, not remarkable in any way; his manners are particularly frank, cordial and good humoured. He is very curious and takes a lively interest in all he sees, and has, by all accounts, been struck with admiration at the conduct and bearing of the people as well as the grandeur and magnificence of the court and elsewhere. Whether the order, and more especially the loyalty he has witnessed, will induce him to entertain with more complacency the idea of a free constitution for his own Kingdom [they didn't] remains to be seen, not that what he finds here ought necessarily to imply that results equally happy would follow the concession of liberal institutions to Prussia ...

Sunday February 5th

Parliament met on Thursday: a great crowd and the Queen well enough received. The K. of Prussia went down in state, and sat in the H. of Lords on a chair near the Woolsack. On Friday he went away, having made a short but uncommonly active visit . . .; splendid entertainments from the rich and hearty acclamations from the poor . . .

The Queen's speech was much like all others, but derived an interest from the notice about Corn. The secret of the measure has been so well kept that upto this time nobody knows what they are going to propose . . . what is now going to happen is another exemplification of what I have long seen to be an established fact in politics – viz. that the Tories only can carry Whig measures. The Whigs work, prepare, but cannot accomplish them; the Tories directly or indirectly, thwart, discourage and oppose them till public opinion compels them to submit, and then they are obliged to take them up, and to do that which they can, but the Whigs cannot do.

February 11th Friday

On Wednesday night Peel produced his Corn Law in an elaborate speech (which bored everybody very much) of nearly three hours long. His plan was received with coldness and indifference by his own people and derision by the Opposition . . . There are however a great many very different opinions on the subject . . . That inasmuch as it satisfies the landed interest, it will keep Peel in office, but that eventually repeal, either total or with a fixed duty, must come, but in how many years must depend upon a chapter of accidents, the course of events and the temper of the people . . .

February 16th

I read yesterday a letter from Mrs Sale at Cabul [Kabul] to her husband, the general, with an account of the events there and the heroic conduct of Captain Sturt . . . The agony of apprehension apparent in the despatches and the pressing entreaties to Sale to march back to their relief show the magnitude of the danger they were in.

February 19th

. . . I went on Wednesday with Lord and Lady John, C. Howard and Macaulay to the Battersea schools, R. Eden's and Kay's. We put forward Macaulay to examine the boys in history and geography . . . They answered in a way that would have put to shame most of the fine people's children. These schools are admirable and the wonderful thing is that when people see what can be done by good management at small expense and by setting about the work of education in earnest, they do not turn their thoughts to the adoption of a similar scheme for the upper classes who go through a certain process miscalled education. Which leaves boys at the end of it nearly as ignorant as at the beginning, with the exception of rudiments of Greek and Latin. At Eden's school they learn reading, writing, arithmetick, drawing, history, geography and certain matters connected with statisticks. At Kay's the same things with the higher branches of mechanicks and especially musick in which they are great proficients.

March 5th

Nothing written for many days, principally because I had nothing to say . . . The most alarming circumstance in our position is the state of affairs in India where we are expecting every hour to hear some catastrophe; but as the Government are not responsible for this, it will do them no damage, however disastrous it may be for the country.

March 13th Sunday

. . . Peel brought forward his financial plans in a speech of three hours and forty minutes acknowledged by everybody to have been a masterpiece of a financial statement . . . A few people expected an income tax, but the majority did not. [He reduced import duties on 769 articles and imposed a 7d income tax for three years.] . . . This great measure, so lofty in conception, right in direction and able in execution, places him at once on a pinnacle of power and establishes his government on such a foundation as accident alone can shake . . .

March 14th

The great interest aroused by the Budget has in some degree absorbed that which the melancholy Indian news would otherwise produce . . . It is a grievous thing to lose 5000 men, cut off by a sudden insurrection and perishing because circumstances beyond the controul of man prevented their obtaining succour; . . .

March 19th

This day Lord Hertford[2] is buried at Ragley . . . no man ever lived more despised or died less regretted . . . As Lord Yarmouth, he was known as a sharp, cunning, luxurious, avaricious man of the world with some talent, the favourite of George 4th, (the worst of Kings) when Lady Hertford, his mother, was that Prince's mistress. He was celebrated for his success at play by which he supplied himself with the large sums of money required for his pleasures . . . But after he became Lord Hertford and the Possessor of an enormous property, he was puffed up with vulgar pride . . . and could only endure people who paid him court and homage. After a great deal of coarse and vulgar gallantry, he formed a connexion with Lady Strachan . . . She was a very infamous and shameless woman, and his love after some years changed to hatred; and she, after getting very large sums out of him, married a Sicilian . . . There has been, as far as I know, no example of undisguised debauchery exhibited to the world like that of Lord Hertford, and his age and infirmities rendered it all the more shocking. Between sixty and seventy years old, broken with various infirmities and almost unintelligible from a paralysis of the tongue, he had been in the habit of travelling about with a company of prostitutes . . . generally picking them up from the dregs of that class . . . he got up and posted with his seraglio down to Richmond. No room was ready, no fire lit, nevertheless he chose to dine there amidst damp and cold, drank a quantity of champagne, came back chilled and exhausted, took to his bed, grew gradually worse and in ten days he died. And what a life terminating in what a death! . . . faculties far beyond mediocrity wasted and degraded, immersed in pride without dignity, in avarice and sensuality, all his relations estranged from him and surrounded to the last by a venal harem who pandered to the disgusting exigencies *lassate sed nondum satiate libidinis* . . .

March 23rd

Dined on Saturday at Lady Holland's with Melbourne and a number of Whigs. Much talk of Peel and what would be the conclusion. Melbourne, to do him justice, is destitute of humbug, does not see things through the medium of his wishes or prejudices, but thinks impartially and says what he thinks. He said Peel would carry all his points and that there would be no serious opposition in the country for if any public meetings were called, the Chartists would be sure to outvote any resolutions against the Income-tax . . .

On Sunday Lord Munster [eldest son of the long liaison between William IV, as Duke of Clarence, and Dora Jordan] shot himself. He had been in low spirits for some time and tainted with the hereditary malady. He was a man not without talent, but wrongheaded . . . he fell into comparative obscurity and real poverty and there can be no doubt that the disappointment of the expectations he once formed, together with the domestic unhappiness of a dawdling, ill-conditioned, vexatious wife, preyed upon his mind and led to this act. The horror of the deed excited a momentary interest, but he will soon be forgotten . . .

June 5th

I have not written one line since March 23rd – a longer interval (I think) than has ever passed since I began to journalise . . . The racing and racehorses and all things appertaining thereto, the betting, buying, selling, the quarrels and squabbles, the personal differences and estrangements, the excitement and agitation produced by these things have had the effect upon my mind of diseasing it, of withdrawing my attention from public affairs, from literature, from society, from all that is worth attending to and caring for . . .

September 1st

. . . Peel began the session with his great financial measures which were received on their first appearance with considerable applause by the Opposition and with a sulky acquiescence on the part of the Tories . . . John Russell not only showed no disposition to lead the party to regular attacks on the Government, but he very soon became impatient to go and seek rural recreation . . . Before his departure, however, a sort of guerrilla warfare had begun which afterwards became more desultory, but more brisk and incessant . . . and Palmerston taking the post of leader, they all kept up an incessant fire on the Treasury Bench. The Whigs were exceedingly provoked with John for quitting his post, and equally delighted with Palmerston for retaining his with such constancy and taking such an active part . . .

Parliament was no sooner up than the riots broke out, [a response to wage cuts, people were killed in Preston and the Potteries. These *were* 'the Hungry Forties'.] [The riots were] sufficiently alarming but for the railroads which enabled the Government to pour Troops into the disturbed districts and extinguish the conflagration at once . . .

September 3rd

One of the topics on which Palmerston attacked the Government with the greatest bitterness was the supposed abandonment of Auckland's policy with respect to Afghanistan, and the withdrawal of troops from the country . . . and he thundered away on the disgrace of a retreat, the advantages of permanent occupation, asked (without eliciting a reply) what Government meant to do . . . A few days ago I met Sir Charles Metcalfe, [later Baron, former provisional Governor-General] the greatest of Indian authorities. He was decidedly opposed to the expedition originally . . . But he thinks that we have now no alternative and must re-occupy Cabul [*sic*] and re-establish our authority. When we have done so, he says, we ought to leave to the Afghans the choice of their ruler, and then make a treaty with him, whoever he may be . . . such a one as it is his interest to keep, for he will not keep any other . . .

October 5th

I have been at Woburn for a couple of days . . . The Duke [Bedford] is well and wisely administering his estate and improving his magnificent place in every way . . . The management of his estates is like the administration of a little Kingdom. He has 450 people in his employment on the Bedfordshire property alone, not counting domestic servants. His pensions amount to £2000 a year. There is order, economy, grandeur, comfort and general content.

October 29th

Melbourne has had an attack of palsy, very slight, and he is recovering, but it is of course alarming. He is not himself aware of the nature of the seizure and asks if it was lumbago. This shows how slight it was. Macaulay's book, which he calls *Lays of Ancient Rome*, came out yesterday, and admirable his ballads are. They were composed in India and on the voyage home . . . He has been addicted to ballad writing . . . He is a wonderful fellow altogether . . . Canadian affairs . . . have lately preoccupied the world for want of something better . . . Sydenham turns out to have been a man of first rate capacity[3] with great ability, discrimination, judgment, firmness and dexterity . . . Though of a weak and slender frame and his constitution wretched, he made journeys which would have appeared hard work to most robust men. On one occasion he travelled without stopping from — to —, and the moment he got out of his carriage, he called for his papers and went at the business as if he had only returned from a drive. This is something very like greatness; these are the materials from which greatness is made: indefatigable industry, great penetration, powers of persuasion, confidence in himself, decision, boldness, firmness, and all these jumbled up with a finikin manner and a dangling after an Old London harridan; . . . [but] 'the world knows nothing of its greatest men' . . .

November 2nd

At Windsor yesterday for a council; almost all the Cabinet went together in a special train. A Whig engineer might have produced an instantaneous and complete change of Government . . . Lord Wharncliffe and Kay Shuttleworth, who are both come from the North, have given me an account of the state of the country and of the people which is perfectly appalling. There is an immense and continually growing population, deep distress and privation, no adequate demand for labour, no confidence, but universal alarm, disquietude and discontent. Nobody can sell anything . . . Kay says that nobody can conceive the state of demoralisation of the people, of the masses, and that the only thing which restrains them from acts of violence against property is a sort of instinctive consciousness that, bad as things are, their own existence depends upon the security of property *in the long run* . . .

November 25th

I went last night to a place called 'the Judge and Jury Court' – Bingham Baring, Charles Buller, Freddy Leveson, and myself . . . It is difficult to imagine anything more low and blackguard than this imitation of a parody on a Court of Justice . . . there is a long low room opposite Covent Garden Theatre (in Bow Street), lit with tallow candles and furnished along its length with benches; opposite these benches is a railed-off space for the Bar and the Jury, and an elevated desk for the Judge. You pay one shilling entrance which entitles you to a cigar and a glass of rum or gin, and water, or beer, a privilege of which almost every man availed himself . . . The room was pretty well filled and in a cloud of smoke

... The Judge, the Counsel and the Jury all had their cigars and gin and water, and the latter, as a recompense for their public services, were entitled to call for what they pleased gratis. Here they try such notorious cases as have been brought in any shape, complete or incomplete ... They deal in very gross indecencies, and this seems to amuse the audience which is one of the most blackguard-looking I ever saw congregated ...

November 30th
Ellenborough's Proclamation which has just appeared, has been fiercely attacked by the Whig Palmerstonian press. But the purport of it seems to be pretty generally approved ... In the midst of all our successes, however, the simple truth is that Akbar Khan and the Afghans have gained their object completely. We had placed a puppet King on the throne, and we kept him there and held military possession of the country by a body of our troops. They resolved to get rid of our King and our troops and to resume their barbarous independence; they massacred all our people, military and civil, and afterwards put to death the King. We lost all hold over the country except the fortresses we continued to occupy. Our recent occupation was undertaken merely to get back the prisoners who had escaped with their lives from the general slaughter, and having got them, we have once and for all abandoned the country ... There is, after all, no great cause for rejoicing and triumph in this.

1843

January 16th
... It is curious to look at the sort of subjects which now nearly monopolise public general interest and attention. First and foremost is the Corn Law and the League; the Corn Law which Charles Villiers (I must do him the justice to say) long ago predicted to me would supersede every other topic of interest, and so it undoubtedly has. Then the condition of the people, moral and physical, is uppermost in everybody's mind, the state and management of the workhouses and prisons, and the great question of education ... And last but not least come the Church questions – the Church of Scotland, the Church of England, the Dissenters, the Puseyites ...

The circumstances attending the termination of the war in Afghanistan have elicited a deep and general feeling of indignation and disgust. Ellenborough's ridiculous and bombastic proclamations and the massacres and havoc perpetrated by his armies, are regarded with universal contempt and abhorrence. A fate seems to have attended this operation from first to last ...

January 19th

I went to Apsley House yesterday ... [The Duke of Wellington] was in very good spirits and humour and began talking about everything, but particularly about Eyre's book,[1] the recent Indian campaign, the blunders committed and Ellenborough's strange behaviour ... I told him what Castlereagh had told me, that he had seen a letter from Ellenborough in which he gave an account of the review he was going to have, when he meant to arrange his Army in the form of a star with the Artillery at the point of each ray, and a throne for himself in the centre. 'And he ought to sit upon it in a strait waistcoat' said the Duke.

January 24th Tuesday

Went to the Grove on Friday, returned yesterday; Auckland, Emily Eden, John and Lady J. Russel, C. Buller and C. Villiers; pleasant enough ... We talked a good deal (of course) about Ellenborough and his proceedings. Auckland told us that he had been convinced he was mad from the moment of his landing, for he seemed to have worked himself up during the voyage to a pitch of excitement, which immediately broke forth. The Captain of the ship he went in was so shocked at the violence he occasionally exhibited and the strange things he said that he on several occasions sent his youngsters away that they might not hear him, and he was strongly impressed with the conviction that he was not in his right mind. He said to Auckland 'that he should come Aurungzebe over them' [(1618–1707) magnificent, despotic and ultimately ruinous Moghul emperor] ... [Ellenborough] told Auckland he intended to turn out the royal family from the Palace at Delhi and convert it into a residence for himself. Auckland suggested to him that this fallen representative of the Moghul Emperors had long occupied this vast habitation which was rather the portion of a town than merely a Palace; that there the family had increased until they amounted to nearly 2000 souls, beside their numerous followers and attendants, and it would not be a very easy or advisable process to disturb them. Ellenborough answered that it did not signify, but they must go, for he should certainly install himself in the Royal residence of Delhi ...

... It was just as I was starting for the Grove that I heard of the assassination of Edward Drummond, [Peel's secretary] one of the most unaccountable crimes that was ever committed, for he was as good and inoffensive a man as ever lived ... It quite baffles conjecture to account for such an enormity ...

January 26th

... When the Queen went to Scotland, Peel went with Aberdeen, [Foreign Secretary] or in some other way, no matter how, but not in his own carriage. He sent Drummond in his carriage *alone*. In Scotland Peel constantly travelled either with the Queen, or with Aberdeen, and Drummond continued to go about in his carriage. I well remember his telling me this, and laughing at the idea of being taken for a great man. It has been proved that this man [McNaghten, the assassin] was in Scotland at the time . . . If therefore he saw, as he must have done, Drummond constantly passing between Peel's house and Downing Street, and recognised in him the same person he had seen in the carriage in Scotland and whom he believed to be Peel, he would think himself so sure of his man as to make it unnecessary to ask any questions . . .

January 29th

The man who shot Drummond (It now appears) acknowledged that it was his intention to shoot Peel and thought he had done so . . . He has certainly been under a sort of delusion that the Tories have persecuted him, but in no other respects is he mad . . . It will be a very serious thing if he escapes and Graham agrees with me that if this happens sooner or later some dreadful catastrophe will occur.[2]

Brighton March 19th

. . . In the course of Conversation with Arbuthnot [minor Tory politician],[3] the other day on various matters he told me something about Ld. Spencer's taking office in '30 which I thought rather curious. Lord S. told it him himself. When Lord Grey was sent for by K. Wm. to form an administration, he went to Althorp [Spencer's then rank, a courtesy title] and asked him what place he would have. Althorp said he would not have any. Lord Grey said 'If you will not take office with me, I will not undertake to form the Government, but will give it up.' 'If that's the case' said the other, 'I must; but if I do take office I will be Chancellor of the Exchequer and lead the H. of Commons' 'Lead the H. of C.?' said Lord Grey; 'but you know you can't speak.' 'I know that' he said 'but I know that I can be of more use to you in that capacity than in any other, and I will either be that or nothing.' He became the very best leader of the H. of C. that any party ever had.

Good Friday April 14th

Came back from Brighton on Sunday evening. The same night [John] Allen died, after a week's illness, much regretted by all the friends of Holland House. He was seventy-two years old and lived for forty years at Holland House . . . He was originally recommended to Lord Holland as a Physician . . . Allen became one of the family, was in all their confidence, and indispensable to both Lord and Lady H. Lord H. treated him with uniform consideration, affection and amenity; she worried, bullied, flattered and cajoled him by turns. He was a mixture of pride, humility and independence; he was disinterested, warm-hearted and choleric, very liberal in his political still more, his religious opinions, in fact an universal sceptic ... Though not, I think, feeling quite certain on the point, he was inclined to believe that the history of Jesus Christ was altogether fabulous or mythical and that no such man had ever existed. He told me that he could not get over the total silence of Josephus[+] as to the existence and history of Christ ...

May 14th

Lord Fitzgerald [the former Vesey Fitzgerald] died on Friday morning, 12th inst., suddenly, inasmuch as he was at the Cabinet on Tuesday, but having long been in a very bad state of health. He ought never to have taken office, for his constitution was unequal to its anxieties and fatigues, and he was too nervous, excitable and susceptible for the wear and tear of political life. He did not contemplate when he took Ellenborough's place,[5] that his Predecessor would render it one of the most troublesome, embarrassing and important in Government ... I remember that Wharncliffe at the beginning of the session said to me in joke. 'Ellenborough will be the death of Fitzgerald,' and this turned out in earnest to be very near the truth ... In history he will be for ever associated with that famous Clare by-election when O'Connell turned him out and got himself returned, that great stroke which led immediately to Catholic Emancipation ...

June 6th

Nothing written for a long time, and for the old reason, racing, the Derby, etc ... On Tuesday in Epsom week went to B[ingham] Baring's at Addiscombe: the Clanricardes, Damers, Ben Stanley, Levisons, Poodle Byng: very agreeable, but the women brimful of ill-nature. Clanricarde and his wife excellent members of society; both of them extremely clever, quick, light in hand. He, with the blood of 20 generations of De Burghs in his veins, what in his own country would be called a big blackguard, and she, descended from a footman and gambler, towering with dignity ...

The political world is all out of joint. Peel is become very unpopular. Ireland is in a flame. The whole country is full of distress, disquiet and alarm. Religious feuds are rife. The Church and the Puseyites are at loggerheads here, and the Church and the Seceders in Scotland; and everybody says it is very alarming and God knows what will happen, and everybody goes on just the same, and nobody cares except those who can't get bread to eat.

June 14th

The Duke of Bedford told me the other day that Prince Albert talked to his brother, Lord Wriothesley[6] (with whom as one of their chaplains he is in the habit of conversing), about the future education of the Prince of Wales, and he said that 'the great object must be to make him as unlike as possible to any of his great-uncles'. This was an imprudent and ungracious speech, and not at all justifiable ... His grandfather [Edward, Duke of Kent][7] was by far the worst of the family, and it will be fortunate if no portion of that blood is eventually found flowing in his veins and tainting his disposition.

Liège Monday June 19th

I set off at eleven o'clock on Saturday morning, from London Bridge by the *Earl of Liverpool* steamer which was loaded with passengers and machinery and a slow, bad boat so that we were seventeen and a half hours crossing over. The weather was very fine, and it was pleasant enough going down the river. All the people were very merry and very hungry during this part of the voyage, but most of them very sad and very sick when they got out to sea ... It was a foggy, misty night, but suddenly, at break of day, the fog was drawn aside like a curtain and we ran into the harbour on a fine morning at half past four o'clock ... [At Ostend] the sands are excellent and there is a magnificent promenade overlooking the sea half a mile long. We started at eleven o'clock on the railroad and came to Liège. The carriages and arrangements are superior to ours and much cheaper as to fare, but very dear in the article of luggage ...

Cologne

... Certainly nothing can be more agreeable than this voyage on the Rhine. The boats spacious and comfortable, an excellent dinner very cheap[8] ... The beauties of the Rhine are not near so striking as I fancied they were; the scenery of the Wye is infinitely finer; in fact there is not a single object of grandeur, but it is all excessively pretty; the river itself is noble, and the constant succession of towns, villages, Palaces, ruins and the various objects which the Rhine presents, render the voyage very interesting and enjoyable ...

... On the whole I am delighted with the expedition and with all I have seen, though the banks of the Rhine are not to be compared to the scenery of Monmouthshire or N. Wales. 'The Castled crag of Drachenfels' is not so striking a ruin as the castle of Dinas Bran, and Dover Castle is more impressive than Ehrenbreitstein; but then there is the Rhine instead of the Wye – the grandest of rivers instead of a slimy streamlet. It is an intolerable bore not being able to speak German ... one feels miserably stupid and helpless at hearing language clattering around one in every direction without being able to comprehend a word of it ...

Frankfort (June) 23rd

... We reached Mayence [Mainz] about nine o'clock. The next morning early I sallied forth (as usual) and poked about the town. I went into the cathedral, where there are a vast number of monuments, not very remarkable, of the

Archbishops of Mainz – great men in their time ... This [Frankfurt] is an extremely pretty town; gay and prosperous in appearance, the streets are so wide, houses so handsome and shops so smart ...

June 24th

Walked about the town, and went into the shops, where I cannot resist buying prints, Bohemian glass and the deer's horn things ... At three o'clock I got on the railroad, and went over to Mainz, to hear the Military bands which play every Friday. The music is really magnificent. It was an Austrian band, about sixty or seventy in number, admirably conducted. The garden in which they play, just beyond the fortifications of the town, is very pretty, and the people sit at tables drinking chocolate or eating ice; ... It is a fine town and remarkable for the frequent intermixture of handsome modern houses with buildings of a very antique, but generally decayed appearance; the town has a great look of well being, and one sees no beggars and no miserable objects. I understand that there is a good deal of relief for the poor and no pauperism of the miserable and degraded character that shocks one so in England ... The Inns are everywhere superior to ours. Instead of the dirty, vulgar, noisy houses that most of our Inns and Hotels are, they are generally great and fine establishments, very clean, very well furnished, the service very much better performed and incomparably cheaper. The town of Frankfort is divided between Protestants and Roman Catholics, but the only religious squabbles or dissensions seem to have been those among English residents and were raised by the English Clergymen ...

Baden-Baden July 2nd

Set off from Mannheim by railroad on Friday morning about ten and got to Heidelberg in under an hour ... The town is swarming with students, wild-looking creatures with long hair, open collars and every variety of beard in cut, colour and length. Their practice of duelling, though forbidden, still goes on, but the combats don't seem to be very dangerous as the first wound or scratch decides it ... I went to see the castle. The library is, I believe, fine and curious, but it is mere waste of time to look at the outside of books, or hear their titles enumerated ...

At eleven o'clock the railroad took me to Carlsruhe [Karlsruhe] where I was obliged to hire a carriage to bring me here. Nothing could exceed the indignation of my servant at seeing the deplorable old rattle-trap which was procured for my use. It seemed to be dropping to pieces, and could not have been clean, within or without, for many years ... At Rastadt (the last stage) Thomas implored me to demand a more presentable vehicle, and piteously remonstrated on the disgrace it would be to make my entry into Baden in such an equipage.

July 3rd

... There was a concert in the great room, and the whole thing was gay and amusing. It was totally unlike anything that can be seen in England, or I suppose anywhere but at some of these Baths. The society is extremely promiscuous and completely democratic in its character, nevertheless perfectly respectable in appearance and behaviour.

July 5th

Yesterday went to dine at Gersbach, a small village just below the castle of Eberstein ... Returned by a new and beautiful road over the mountain. My companion in the carriage, M. de Porbeck, an officer in the Baden army, a well-conditioned and intelligent man, gave me some scraps of what may be called German politicks, some of which I was not prepared for ... The particulars of the discussions of a Baden parliament are not very interesting, but he told me that there is a great and growing desire on the part of the smaller states to form one nation with one or other of the great powers and that before long they would all be absorbed by their own desire. I said surely none of them could desire to belong to Austria. He said this feeling was more prevalent in the North, and he thought eventually all the Rhenish and Protestant states, Baden, Nassau, Württemberg, Saxony would be united to Prussia ...

But as to Austria, he was convinced that the death of Metternich would be the signal for a great movement in that country; that everything was preparing for it, and that event would bring the projects which were spreading more and more every day, to maturity. While this desire to make Germany a nation or to merge the petty independencies in one or two great powers, is according to him, becoming strong and general, there is also a great wish to have Colonies and a Navy, all of which he deems feasible and says Prussia is already beginning to build ships of war ... as I had never before heard of such aspirations I was struck by what he told me. We had a great deal of talk beside about the condition of the people, and he expressed with some pride his satisfaction that while they had nothing of English opulence to boast of, they had not the afflicting spectacle of English misery and destitution ... the subdivision of land (the effects of which I saw in the minute strips of cultivated land on the hill-sides) caused all the agricultural population – much the greatest part of Baden – to be removed above want, and he assured me that the whole of the people were tolerably educated. No soldier, for instance, was allowed to enlist without being able to read and write ... There is certainly a degree of social equality which is very foreign to our habits, and yet it is not subversive of the respect which is due from persons in one station to another. To me it has nothing offensive.

... Go where one will it seems to me that one finds a more satisfactory and harmonious state of things with regard to religion than in England. There is more intolerance, bigotry, obstinacy and *dereason* at home than in all the world besides.

July 7th Friday

The life here is the most idly luxurious I have ever led, but however enjoyable and much as I delight in the scenery, I begin already to feel that it would not do for long. It seems as if everybody was enjoying one vast holiday and had nothing to do but enjoy themselves. I get up between six and seven, walk for a couple of hours ... then go into a cold bath, and dress, breakfast and read and write for about two hours; go to the room to read the newspapers, make visits and stroll about till dinner, dine at some of the tables d'hôtes or in my own room at something between four and five, then drive wherever I fancy to go, returning home when the Sun is gone down and the moon and the stars are out, and repair to the garden. There I sit with any friends I find at a little round table, in the cool of a delicious evening, eating ice and drinking what I please, a band of music playing, and the odours of new mown hay, Orange Trees, limes and roses wafted on every gale ...

London August 1st

I staid on at Baden to meet the Granvilles who arrived from Switzerland on Friday 14th to my great joy. I remained till Wednesday 19th when I took the diligence to Iffetsheim, steamed down the Rhine, embarked at Ostend on Saturday 22nd, had a rough, disagreeable passage to Dover, and got to London on Sunday morning ... the interest and pleasure produced by this short excursion confirm my resolution to do something of the same sort in some direction or other every year, and always (if I can) to avoid *the season* in London ...

I left the Irish Arms Bill in the House of Commons, and there I found it on my return in the packet going out. I read John Russell's first speech with regret and indignation, and I afterwards read all the debates and speeches on both sides with extreme disgust ... the low tone taken by Peel, and the determination announced by him and Stanley to maintain the Irish Church, are both very distasteful to me ... The only man who spoke sense and truth was Rous [MP for Westminster] who (Tory as he is) told them they never would do any good till they settled that question, but that they did not dare attempt it, because the bigotry of England and Scotland were opposed to it ... and none of them would venture to encounter the unpopularity of proposing to reform the Protestant, and establish the Catholic Church ...

August 6th

This year is distinguished by many marriages in the great world, the last and the one creating the greatest sensation being that of [the Earl of] March to my niece,[9] a wonderful elevation [March was heir to the Duke of Richmond] for a girl without beauty, talents, accomplishments or charms of any sort – an enormous prize to draw in the lottery of life. All the mothers in London consider it as a robbery, as each loses her chance of such a prize ...

August 11th

... Peel made a pretty good speech [on the third reading of the Irish Arms Bill], considerably better than he has lately been doing ... The remarkable thing was the bitterness and insolence of his so-called friends and the civility of his adversaries. More O'Farrell and Morgan John O'Connell were even complimentary in what they said on the landlord question. While D'Israeli and Smythe, who are the principal characters (together with John Manners), of the little squad called 'Young England,' were abusive and impertinent.

September 11th

... The Duke of Bedford has been in Ireland, and has conversed, he tells me, with people of all descriptions and done his utmost to procure information on the country ... [The Chief Secretary for Ireland, Lord Eliot] told the D. that the temper of England would not allow of any provision for the R.C. clergy ...

October 16th

I went to breakfast with George Lewis to meet [Leopold von] Ranke[10] ... I went prepared to listen to some first-rate luminaries as Ranke and Macaulay, but there never was a greater failure. The Professor, a vivacious little man, not distinguished in appearance, could talk no English, and his French, though spoken fluently, was quite unintelligible ... On the other hand, Macaulay could not speak German, and he spoke French without any facility and with a vile accent ... He began in French, but very soon could bear the restraint no further and broke into English, pouring forth his stores to the utterly unconscious and uncomprehending Professor. This Babel of a breakfast, at which it was impossible for seven people to converse in a common language, soon came to an end, and Ranke was evidently glad to go off to the State Paper Office, where he was working every day ...

October 31st

I was laid up for two or three days in London, and then went to Riddlesworth [near Newmarket, house of a Mr Thornhill] for two or three more. I arrived at night, and on going into the drawing room, I found four people playing whist, eight others at a round game and one asleep in an armchair. And this is called Society; and among such people I have lived, do live and shall live – I who have seen, known and had the choice of better things. Eating, drinking and amusement is the occupation of these people's lives, and I am ashamed to say such has been mine ... I was reading Charles Lamb's letters in the carriage, and very remarkable they are, among the very best I ever read. I was struck by one passage which I applied to myself: 'I gain nothing by being with such as myself; we encourage one another in mediocrity.' This is it. We go on herding with inferior companions until we are really unfit for better company ... On Sunday (week) I went to Newmarket, where there was an unusual quantity of racing.

November 14th

... I broke off to go to the funeral of my aunt [Lady Mary Bentinck] who was buried in the most private way possible at Kensal Green. I never saw the place before and liked the appearance of it, for I have never seen any reason why none but gloomy images and symbols should be accumulated around the graves of our departed friends ... For the last two years she was afflicted with a cancer, and under the exhaustion produced by this disease she at last sank. She dies full of devout sentiments and uttering that language, at once self-accusing, humble and grateful which the orthodox forms of religion indiscriminately prescribe. God only can judge how far we are sincere.

December 13th

All the people who have been at the Royal progress say that there never was anything so grand as Chatsworth; and the Duke, albeit he would have willingly dispensed with her visit, treated her right royally. He met her at the station and brought her in his own coach and six with coach and four following and eight outriders. The finest sight was the illumination of the garden and the fountains; and after seeing the whole place covered with innumerable lamps and all the material of the illumination, the Guests were astonished and delighted when they got up the following morning to find not a vestige of them left. And the whole garden as trim and neat as if nothing had occurred. This was accomplished by Paxton[11] who got 200 men, set them to work and worked with them the whole of the night till they had cleared away everything belonging to the exhibition of the preceding night.

1844

January 10th

Gout in my hand prevented my writing anything more, and now I forget what else Melbourne let drop, except that it had been all along a grievance with Albert that he was not sufficiently exalted, and that he wanted to have the title of King.

January 16th

Yesterday I heard that it is reported in the City that the Queen's mind is not in the right state. This is the same notion which Mr Drummond imparted to me but which I have never heard of in any other quarter. It is curious; these are slight appearances, nothing in themselves very remarkable, but which indicate restlessness, excitement and nervousness.

Everybody is full of the trial in Dublin – this unhappy trial [of O'Connell for conspiracy] which has been one continual course of blunders and mismanagement from first to last. There is now an immense uproar about the Jury list, and, as if fate had determined that the worst appearance should be given to the whole proceeding, Shaw, the Recorder, is implicated in a manner which can easily be made to look very suspicious. [Frederick Shaw, as Tory MP, was a fervent opponent of parliamentary reform as benefiting Irish Catholics.]

The sheriff sent a list of some seventy-eight names to the Recorder; instead of remaining in Dublin as he ought to have done, he must needs come to England to visit Lord Talbot. He went over for one day to Drayton [Peel's country house] and it happened that on the same day he received the Sheriff's list; he returned it but by some mistake did not return two slips (as they are called) containing sixty and odd names. The list therefore from which the Jury was taken was an imperfect list and they will say, and all the Irish will believe, that the mutilation was a concerted affair between Peel and Shaw ... Then the striking off of all the Catholics from the Jury is inveighed against here as an act of madness, there as an intolerable injustice and insult ... It would be a thousand times better to have O'Connell acquitted by a mixed Jury than convicted by one all Protestant. I do not know whether such an acquittal would not be on the whole the best result; if he should be convicted, the whole process would be considered as a monstrous outrage against justice and the Government will be terribly puzzled to know how to deal with him.

If he is acquitted by a Protestant jury, the triumph of the Catholicks will be much greater, their resentment not much less ... In short it is an inextricable *mess*, and how they will get out of it God only knows. They have missed the great opportunity that was affording them of giving a convincing proof to the Irish people that they wish O'Connell to have a fair trial ... If the Catholick jury had cast their mantles over him, it would soon have been known; the Irish might have sung universal jubilations and lit bonfires on every hill; but it would have been no real triumph and the value of a moral conviction in the eyes of the people of England would have been unappreciable. All of this has been overlooked in a stupid, narrow-minded, short-sighted professional eagerness to *ensure* a conviction ...

... The Duke of Wellington inveighs against 'the licentious press' both in India and here! He hates the press everywhere, but he knows that it is (if an evil) a necessary and unavoidable evil; but in such a country as India, he cannot forgive those who introduced the pernicious anomaly of a free press, and in this I entirely agree with him ...

February 8th

The session has opened favourably enough for Government. The first night Peel made a decided speech, and he has taken a decided attitude. He declared that he did not mean to make any alteration at all in the present Corn Law, either as to duty or scale ... Peel evidently means to give up the notion of appealing to the reason of the country and the moderation which he hoped would help him through his *juste milieu* course and thinks only of wrapping the great Tory body round him and exhibiting himself as the master of certain and willing majorities. As long as this Parliament lasts, it makes him as firm as a rock, after which God knows what will happen ...

February 15th Thursday

Nothing could exceed the satisfaction of the Government at the result of the trial in Dublin which, after all the blunders and accidents, ended very well for them, and far better than they ever expected. The unanimity of the judges they scarcely hoped for; then the jury were unanimous and determined and yet considerate and not violent. The poor devils were locked up (without any necessity) from Saturday night until Monday morning for there would have been no risk in taking the verdict on Sunday ...

... This verdict [of 'Guilty'] arrived very opportunely for the debate [on Ireland and the Church there] which began on Monday and was a heavy blow and discouragement to the Opposition. [The verdict would soon after be reversed on technical grounds.] Most people regard it with satisfaction and think it will do the world of good. The agitation which has been suspended will not now be renewed. The notion of O'Connell's infallibility which had got hold of the people has been destroyed, and the Irish have seen that the Government is resolved to put the law in force and that the law is able to smite those who violate it ...

February 17th Saturday

The debate has moved on heavily. The most remarkable speeches have been Howick's, Sir George Grey's, D'Israeli's and Stanley's. Howick spoke out and declared at once he would make the Catholic the established religion of Ireland. D'Israeli made a very clever speech, not *saying* so much, but implying it, and under the guise of compliment making an ingenious and amusing attack on Peel, Stanley and Graham ... The Opposition however are still divided and subdivided into many shades of opinion ... There is a long interval between Howick and John [Russell]. The fear is that this new Catholic question will be met by a new 'No Popery' cry; though the Tory leaders will prevent this if they can, still it is clear that their declarations must draw them closer to the Church and cement the alliance between them . . .

February 22nd

The debate is still going on. By far the most remarkable speech that has yet been made was Macaulay's – an essay perhaps it may be called, but still a brilliant oration and the end of it, with his reply to Stanley and his appeal to Peel, admirable. He reserved himself for another occasion to speak about the Church which meant that he was in dread of his constituents . . . Stanley's speech a few nights ago, which was delivered in his best style, and much praised by his adherents, is severely censured by all but his adherents. It seems to have exhibited all that acrimony and disposition to bigotry which it is so desirable to get rid of, and though it may have been more exhilarating to the spirits of his friends, it was much less suitable to his station . . .

Sunday (February) 25th

On Friday night after nine nights debate (the longest since the Duke of York's case) the division took place – (99 majority) . . . O'Connell spoke well, temperately, becomingly, was well received, and made a favourable impression; Peel, an able speech of nearly four hours, very successful in repelling his opponent's attacks, a very good party speech, but in my opinion not well argued as to the Church question and certainly containing nothing definite or satisfactory . . . There has been a great display of ability on both sides; . . . The best speeches have been those of John Russell, Sir G. Grey, Howick, Macaulay, Wilde and Shiel: Peel Graham and the two Attorney-Generals [for England and Ireland]; D'Israeli very clever and original, full of finesse, in some respects the most striking of all. I think that on the whole it will do good: as far as the Government are concerned, it will strengthen them for a time; but from this moment a new Catholic question will begin, though it will be indeed rash to predict when it will end . . .

I dined at Palmerston's yesterday; Melbourne was there. He could not say O'C had not had a fair trial; and Luttrell [Whig politician, wit and Holland House regular] said (which seemed to hit off M's own notion) that he had had a *fairish* trial . . .

March 16th

I must mention an anecdote [Mr Grenville] told me the other day illustrating the facility with which Pitt gave Peerages to anybody who had a fancy for the honour. Mr G. one day asked his cousin, Lord Glastonbury, what had induced him to get made a peer for he could not think he had ever cared much for a title. He said 'God, Devil' (for such was his queer habit of expressing himself), 'I'll tell you. I never thought of a Peerage; but one day I took up the newspaper, and I read in it that Tommy Townshend was made a Peer. Confound the fellow, I said, what right had he to be made a Peer I should like to know? Why, I am as rich again as he is and have a much better right. So I resolved to write to Pitt and tell him so. So I wrote, and was made a Peer the following week.'

March 31st

I never remember so much excitement as has been caused by Ashley's Ten Hours Bill[1] nor a more curious political state of things, such intermingling of parties, such a confusion of opposition; a question so much more open than any question ever was before; yet not made so or acknowledged to be so with the Government; so much zeal, asperity and animosity, so many reproaches hurled backwards and forwards.

The Government have brought forward their measure in a very positive way, and have clung to it with great tenacity, rejecting all compromise; they have been abandoned by nearly half their supporters, and nothing can exceed their chagrin and soreness at being so forsaken. Some of them attribute it to Graham's unpopularity, and aver that if Peel had brought it forward, or if a meeting had been previously called, they would not have been defeated; again, some declare that Graham had said they were indifferent to the result, and that people might vote as they pleased, which he stoutly denies; then John Russell voting for 10 hours, against all he professed last year, has filled the world with amazement, and many of his own friends with indignation. It has, I think, not redounded to his credit, but, on the contrary, done him considerable harm.

The Opposition were divided, Palmerston and John one way, Baring and Labouchere the other ... Melbourne is all against Ashley; all the political economists, of course; Lord Spencer is strong against him. Then Graham gave the greatest offence by taking up a word of the *Examiner*'s last Sunday and calling it a *Jack Cade legislation*, this stirring them to fury, and they flew at him like Tigers. Ashley made a speech as violent and factious as any of O'Connell's, and Old Inglis was overflowing with wrath. Nothing could be so foolish as Graham, who ought to have known better and how much mischief may be done by words, and how they stick by men forever. Lyndhurst rubbed his hands with great glee and said 'Well we shall hear no more of Aliens now, people will only talk of Jack Cade for the future,' [Lyndhurst had been pursued by his reference to the Irish as 'aliens'] too happy to shift the odium if he could from his own to his colleague's back ...

Government will carry their bill now, and Ashley will be able to do nothing, but he will go on agitating session after session; and a Philanthropic agitator is more dangerous than a repealer, either of the Union or the Corn Laws. We are just now run over with philanthropy, and God knows where it will stop, or wither it will lead us ...

May 1st

Interval passed at Newmarket (two weeks) ... On arriving in town I found the world had been rattled by the astounding news of Ellenborough's recall by the Court of Directors [of the East India Company], admitted by Ministers in both Houses, in reply to questions asked of them.

... the Duke of Wellington is particularly incensed. He has all along taken Ellenborough under his especial protection, and encouraged and supported him with his praise and approbation. All his irritability is therefore stirred up, and he expressed himself in the House of Lords the night before last in reference to the Directors in very strong terms which was not very becoming and still less prudent ...

May 4th

... Yesterday Reeve[2] told me that Aberdeen sent for Delane and told him the Government and the Directors were going to make their matters up; that he was much satisfied with the line *The Times* had taken (suspending its judgment) and that the Duke of Wellington's speech had been a great cause of embarrassment and annoyance; that they had begged him not to say anything strong, and he had engaged not to do so. The papers will not be produced because they are not producible. Aberdeen owned that Ellenborough's conduct and language to the Directors had been such as it was impossible for them to endure, and he said both they and the Government were sensible how inexpedient it would be to publish such a correspondence. Accordingly these belligerents will agree to bury the past in oblivion, and make it all up. The greedy and curious public and the eager and malicious Opposition will both be cheated of the banquet of public scandal they are both so anxiously expecting.

June 10th

For the last week the town has been kept in a fever by the brief and unexpected visit of the Emperor of Russia [Nicholas I, an unreserved despot] ... Nobody knows now what was the cause of this sudden and rapid expedition, for he travelled without stopping, from, and with extraordinary rapidity, Petersburg with the exception of twenty-four hours at Berlin and forty-eight hours at the Hague. He alighted at the palace, embraced the Queen ... The Duke attired himself in the costume of a Russian Field Marshal to receive the Emperor. On Monday he went to Windsor, Tuesday to Ascot, Wednesday they gave him a review ... It was a mighty small concern for the Emperor who reviews 100,000 men and sees 15,000 mount guard every day; but he expressed his satisfaction, and when the Queen said her troops were few in number, he told her that she must consider his troops at her disposal exactly the same as her own ... His appearance on the whole disappointed me. He is not so tall as I had heard, he was about 6ft 2, I should guess; and he has no remains of the beauty for which he was once so celebrated and which at his age (forty-eight) need not have faded entirely away; but the cares of such an empire may well have ravaged that head, on which they sit not lightly. He is become bald and bulky, but nevertheless is still a very grand looking personage ... he does not bear the highest aristocratic stamp; general appearance is inferior to that of Lord Anglesey or Lord Granville (both twenty-five years older) and to others. He gives me more the idea of a Thracian Peasant raised to Empire than of the descendant of a line of Kings; ...

As he moved round the circle all smiling and urbane, I felt a sensation of awe mixed with that of curiosity at reflecting that I saw before me a Potentate so mighty and despotic, on whose will and pleasure or caprice depended the fortune, the happiness and the lives of millions of creatures; and when the condition of those subject millions and the frequent exercise of such unbounded power flitted over my mind, I felt a pleasant sensation of consciousness that I was beyond the sphere of its influence, free as the birds in the air, at least from him ...

June 21st Friday

... They say he is excessively disgusted with the dullness of the court, and well he may be. The Queen has no conversation, and no attempt was made to amuse him. Lady Clanricarde, to whom he paid a visit, told me that she was struck with his saying not one word expressive of admiration or satisfaction with anybody or anything at court – not a syllable in praise either of the Queen or Prince ...

July 5th

... Tom Duncombe [(1796–1861) Yorkshire squire and radical Whig], indefatigable for mischief and grand jobman of miscellaneous grievances, brought forward the case of M. Mazzini, whose letters had been opened by Graham's warrant. This matter, in itself most ridiculous, inasmuch as Graham had done no more than what every other Secretary of State did before him, soon acquired a great and undue importance.[3] The press took it up; the Whig Press was a good ground of attack on the Government, and especially Graham; and *The Times* merely from personal hatred of Graham whom they are determined to write down if they can on account of his honest support of the Poor Law ... When Graham found himself thus attacked and reviled, he resolved to cast off all the official reserve in which he had at first wrapped the question ... so he moved for a Select Committee who are to take evidence and make a report. He has composed it of five Whigs and five Tories, excluding all who are or have been in office, and Tom Duncombe, the accuser. This concession has by no means disarmed his opponents and *The Times* particularly has continued to attack him with the utmost virulence, but so coarsely and unfairly as quite to overshoot the mark.

Bretby September 8th

... During the recess, the dispute which had some time before begun between us and France took a threatening aspect, and for some time it was a toss-up whether we went to war or not. Peel had announced to the Commons in very lofty language that Government would exact an ample reparation for the outrage perpetrated on Pritchard at Tahiti.[4] While Guizot evinced no disposition to make any ... What we wanted (not demanded) was that some *act* should be done to mark the sense of the French Government of what was due to us – the recall of D'Aubigny or of Brûat [local French officials, civil and military] or of both; but Guizot said 'Je ne rapellerai personne' and all he offered was to express 'regrets et improbation'. This, which was a mere scintilla of an apology, we could not accept as a sufficient reparation for so gross an outrage, and at one moment up to the day (Thursday last) ... it looked very bad ... But when matters appeared most desperate, a suggestion was thrown out ... that besides the verbal apology, a compensation of money should be made to Pritchard. On Wednesday, the Cabinet met to decide whether they should accept the final offers of France (to the above effect) or refuse them; and the result was that they agreed to accept them ... It is, I think, not impossible that the decision of this Cabinet was in some degree quickened by the reversal of O'Connell's judgment. [On legal grounds the House of Lords on 4 August reversed the conviction and sentence of O'Connell which took place the same morning, much to their disgust.] I think they were right, especially as we have certainly done enough to make the French Government see that we do not intend to submit any more impertinence on their part.[5] ... I called one day at Apsley House, saw the Duke and found him in a talkative humour on this affair ... The Duke said that the disposition of the French was to insult us whenever and wherever they thought they could do so with impunity, and that the only way to keep at peace with them was to be stronger in every quarter of the globe than they were; ... Wherever they had ships we ought to have a naval force superior to theirs; and we might rely on it, that as long as that was the case we should find them perfectly civil and peaceable; and wherever it was not the case, we should find them insolent and troublesome.

The Judgment in O'Connell's case came like a clap of thunder; though ministers were aware of it, for Lyndhurst told them it would be so. Wharncliffe had the greatest difficulty in preventing the Tory peers from voting; Redesdale and Stradbroke were especially anxious, and the former in the highest possible dudgeon ...

The Grange Saturday September 14th

... This has certainly been a most unfortunate business from the beginning to the end. Between the blunders and the accidents, the various untoward circumstances in the course of the trial, the unavoidable fact of a wholly Protestant jury, the undoubted partiality of the Chief Justice; then the division of opinion among the Judges and the political character of the Judgment itself displays, all ending with the triumph of the criminals and the mortification of the Government ...

1845

January 18th

... I came a few days ago from the Grange where I met Dr Buckland and A.D. Wilberforce;[1] the latter a very quick, lively, agreeable man who is in favour at court and has the credit of seeking to be preceptor to the Prince of Wales, an office to which I should prefer digging at a canal. Or breaking stones on the road ... Lord Ashburton[2] in great force, and droll to see the supreme contempt which He and Palmerston entertain for each other.

I went there from Broadlands [Palmerston's estate], where I left the Viscount full of vigour and hilarity and overflowing with diplomatic swagger. He said we might hold any language we pleased to France and America and insist on what we thought necessary without any apprehension that either of them would go to war, as both knew how vulnerable they were, France with her Colonies, and America with her Slaves, a doctrine to which Lord Ashburton by no means subscribes. Before these places I was at Woburn and at Ampthill [both Russell estates] where the D. of Bedford told me a good deal about his communications with Albert who seems to talk to him very openly ... He told me that A. complained of the manner in which the proceedings and motions of the court were publicly known and discussed, and how hard it was; that on the Continent the Government knew by its secret agents what the people were about, but here they knew nothing about other people's affairs, and everybody knew about theirs; that whatever they did, or were about to do, was known ... The Duke told him he wondered he had discovered that everything was and must be known here about them, and that it was the tax they paid for their situation; that the world was curious to know and hear about them, and therefore the Press would always procure and give the information ... all conspicuous people were brought into public notice in the same manner. He owned this was true and seemed struck by it. It is the misfortune of these people never to hear the language of truth and sense ...

January 30th

Yesterday Wharncliffe told me he had a secret to tell me. This was Gladstone's resignation which has been in agitation nearly a year, ever since Peel gave notice that he would do a great deal more for Irish education and improve Maynooth [the Catholic seminary in Ireland, already given limited financial support by central Government]. Nor does Gladstone really object to these measures; but he thinks that he has so deeply and publicly committed himself to the opposite principle that he cannot without a great appearance of inconsistency be a party to them . . .

Thursday February 6th

On Tuesday night for the first time for some years I went to the H. of Commons, principally to hear Gladstone's explanation . . .

. . . Gladstone's explanation was ludicrous. Everybody said that he had only succeeded in showing that his resignation was quite uncalled for.

Peel put an end to any mystery about his measures, and stated (in general terms) all he intended to do. The Government, however, expect a good deal of opposition and excitement from the religious part of the community, from Dissenters and Scotch. Ashley has put himself at the head of the Low Church party, and will make a great clatter. Sandon [later Lord Harrowby] did not dare accept the Board of Trade and seat in the Cabinet for fear of disgusting the Liverpool Protestants . . .

Hatchford February 25th

Here I am come to recruit my strength after being confined for a fortnight with gout and fever, more than usually severe. While I was laid up, the parliamentary campaign proceeded very briskly: first with Peel's financial statement in a very able speech, more than three hours long, which was admired for its clearness and force. [It involved the repeal of duties on more than five hundred articles and renewal of Income Tax for a further three years.] His financial reforms are considered very bold and skilful, but the Tories hail them with anything but satisfaction, though they are too crestfallen to resist, or even to murmur, except an odd agriculturalist here and there. Everybody regards this measure as a great wedge thrust in, and as the forerunner of still more extensive changes, and above all that the Income tax is to be permanent . . .

April 5th Saturday

Peel brought in Maynooth [a grant of £30,000 to the Irish Catholic seminary in Ireland] on Thursday . . . He made an excellent and judicious speech, and had a majority of 102, but a queer one, for above 100 of his own people voted against him, and above 100 of the Whigs with him . . . The Carlton Club was in a state of insurrection afterwards and full of sound and fury; In the minority were Inglis, and the zealots of course, – Hastie and some of the Scotch, Tom Duncombe, D'Israeli – a motley combination. It is a very odd combination and may be productive of great events before long. The disgust of the Conservatives and their hatred of Peel keep swelling every day, and what Ministers expect is that on some occasion or other they will play Peel a trick, stay away and leave him to be beat on some trumpery occasion . . .

April 6th

Everybody is talking of the great stir that is making in the country against the Maynooth grant and the large increase in Peel's unpopularity which it has produced . . . it disgusts the Tory party and creates fresh sources of dislike and disunion between the great body of the Conservatives and the Government is indubitable, and Peel and his colleagues are so well aware of this that they think that something must before long occur to break up the Government . . . [Wharncliffe] showed me a paper which he drew up last year on the situation and prospects of the Government which is very sensible and very true. It was to the effect that they could not possibly go on much longer, as they clearly had not the confidence of the mass of those who were called their supporters; that they were placed in a false position, and that their measures appeared to be more suitable to the principles of their opponents than to those of their own party; that in all the great questions – agricultural, fiscal, educational and Irish – this was evidently the case, and that on all of them, the Tories or Conservatives were years behind their Leaders. The truth is that the Government is Peel, that Peel is a Reformer and more of a Whig than a Tory, and that the mass of his supporters are prejudiced, ignorant, obstinate and selfish . . .

April 22nd

. . . The steam had been getting up in the country, and the table of the H. of C. was loaded with petitions against the Bill from all parts. *The Times* newspaper kept plugging away at Peel in a series of articles as mischievous as malignity could make them, and by far the most disgraceful that ever appeared on a political subject in any journal; the Ultra-Tories grew more and more rabid, and D'Israeli made one of his bitterest attacks on Peel which was widely cheered in the House and well be-praised out of it by Whig and Tory papers and all the Haters of Peel who now compose a large majority of the world . . .

. . . On the last night John Russell and Peel spoke. The former made a speech which has excited universal admiration and applause. It was perfect, not for its eloquence or any remarkable display of ability, but for its tone, temper, discretion and propriety. It was exactly what it ought to have been, neither more nor less; it was calculated to do good, and it has raised him immensely in public estimation . . . [Peel] declined noticing any of the attacks on himself, and with much gravity and seriousness, urged the necessity of passing the measure . . . His speech too was considered as clearly indicative of a consciousness that his party was broken up and the termination of his term of office approaching. The division gave him a better majority than was expected (147).

I came to town on Friday, and on Saturday morning I saw Wharncliffe and asked him what he thought of it. He said it was a large majority, and so far well, but that it made no difference in their position. And he did not think they

should be in office a month hence ... Everybody knows that the Tory party
has ceased to exist as a party; that Peel's unpopularity is at the moment so
great and so general that there is no knowing where to find any interest
friendly to him, scarcely any individual. On the other hand, his disgust at the
position in which he finds himself, and at being made thus the object of so
much obloquy and reproach are equally strong, and no one doubts that he
really contemplates, and anxiously wishes to resign. But then what is to come
next? ...

May 10th

These are my holidays – exclusively devoted to the turf, passed in complete
idleness without looking into a book or doing one useful or profitable thing,
living with the merest wretches whose sole and perpetual occupation it is,
Jockies, trainers, betters, blacklegs, blackguards, people who do nothing but
gamble, smoke and talk everlastingly of horses and races ... I was at Newmarket
all last week, and have been at Horton for Chester all this. One day I did give
up the races, and Stradbroke and I went over to Birkenhead to occupy the
whole day ... Not many years ago the ground was an unprofitable marsh.
They showed us a small white house which was the first that was built and
which stood alone for some time. The property belonged to a Mr Price, and
when first the notion of speculating in building there occurred to the late Mr
Laird[3] ... £50,000 was the sum offered Mr Price for his property. Not long
after, he was offered £100,000, and this time a bargain was nearly completed,
and the only difference between the parties was whether it should be pounds
or guineas. Luckily for Mr Price, it went off upon this, and such was the rapid
increase in the value of the land, that he has since sold it for considerably above
a million. We went to see the pier, the place where the docks are to be; then
to Mr Laird's ship building establishment, and saw the iron steam frigate they
are building ... the present population is 16,000, but they are building in every
direction.

Ghent June 16th

... At last I escaped from racing and politics, left London by the mail train,
arrived at Dover at half past twelve, crossed at four and reached Ostend at a
quarter past nine, came on to Bruges at twelve, spent the day there ... spent
yesterday and today in seeing Bruges and Ghent, and whatever is best worth
visiting in both, and a good deal there is of one sort or another; but I am too
sleepy now to go on with the subject.

Wiesbaden June 22nd

Bruges and Ghent are both fine Old towns, particularly the latter, containing
many and curious buildings particularly the new Palais de Justice and the

theatre which, with its saloons, is the most magnificent *salle de spectacle* I ever saw ... From Ghent I came to Cologne, thence to Coblentz [Koblenz], and then here on Thursday last, this being Sunday. The Rhine which disappointed me the first time, appeared to the last degree tiresome, and a more languid and uninteresting journey I never made. There is nobody here I know and I am bored to death. If I were not ashamed I would throw myself into the steamboat and go home directly ...

London August 7th

I was in great disgust at Wiesbaden, the first days of my abode there, but I soon fell into the way of life, and made up my mind to it more easily and more completely than I ever expected to do. This was in fact rendered more easy by the growing disinclination which is creeping over me for society and by the almost dread and dislike I feel more and more for conversation ... One great cause undoubtedly is my deafness which prevents my hearing what passes around me, makes me slow of apprehension and is productive of both melancholy and embarrassment. However to return to my history. I remained at Wiesbaden till the latter end of July, making no acquaintance and doing nothing but read such books as I got from Frankfort, going nowhere ... I went to see Worms, a decayed old town full of historical recollections, and I gazed at the great tree, under which, according to tradition, Luther took shelter on his way to the Diet. From Wiesbaden I went to Ems for two nights, which was as full as Wiesbaden was empty ... I came on to Malines where I diverged to Antwerp and spent half a day there looking at the pictures and was well repaid. The fine Rubens's in the Cathedral are in such bad light that it is difficult to see them satisfactorily, but the pictures in the Museum are very grand; crossed the water in one of the old boats, eight hours, and arrived in town on Tuesday morning, July 22.

Broadlands August 21st Thursday

I went last Saturday to the Grove; very pleasant party. Palmerstons, Lady Morley, Lady Holland, Macaulay, Bessborough, Luttrell, Henry Bulwer. Macaulay subdued in talk but still talking more and better than anybody else ... Melbourne by way of being very well, but there are only gleams left of his former self. He seems to bear on his face a perpetual consciousness of his glory obscured, and looks grave and stern while he sits for hours in silence ... In talking over the Post Office affairs of this and last year and the attacks on Graham, he said that he remembered having signed warrants for opening O'Connell's letters, and Freeling[4] bringing him the warrants back and saying he thought the best thing to do with them was to thrust them into the fire, which was done. He said they never found anything in them; ...

... Everybody expects that [Peel] means to go on, and in the end to knock the Corn Laws on the head and endow the R.C. Church; but nobody knows how and when he will do these things ...

September 3rd

I read in the newspaper the day before yesterday an account of a lad brought up for not supporting his child. The Father was fifteen or sixteen years old, the mother a year or two less, and the Grandmother of the child — the girl's mother — appeared, who was twenty-nine years old and had fourteen children. This seems to me to be curious enough to be worth recording ...

On Saturday (14th) we went to Osborne House, Isle of Wight, to a Council. Special train to Gosport in about two hours and a quarter, *Black Eagle* steamer to E. Cowes, very agreeable trip. Osborne a miserable place and such a vile house that the Lords of the Council had no place to remain in, but the entrance Hall before the Council. Fortunately the weather was fine so we walked about looking at the new house the Queen is building; it is very ugly, and the whole concern wretched enough. They will spend first and last a great deal of money here, but it is her own money and not the nation's ... We hear of nothing but the dissatisfaction which the Q. gave in Germany, of her want of civility and graciousness, and a great many stories are told which are probably exaggerated or untrue. It is clear however that the general impression was not favourable. Nothing can exceed the universal indignation felt here by people of every description at the brutal and stupid massacre of the deer which Albert perpetrated, and at which she assisted ... the truth is, her sensibilities are not acute and though she is not at all ill-natured, perhaps the reverse, she is hard-hearted, selfish and self-willed.

September 7th

A complete absence of events till a few days ago when, after a very short illness, Lord Spencer died at his House near Doncaster. [Spencer, as Althorp, had been the pivot of the Grey Ministry as it took the Reform Bills through the Commons] ... Without one showy accomplishment, without wit to amuse or eloquence to persuade, with a voice unmelodious and a manner ungraceful, and barely able to speak plain sense in still plainer language, he exercised in the House of Commons an influence and even a dominion greater than any Leader either after or before him ... His friends followed this plain and simple man with enthusiastic devotion, and he possessed the faculty of disarming his political antagonists of all bitterness and animosity; ...

November 16th

... It has been during the last two months that I have been too idle to write that the rage for railroad speculation reached its height, was checked by a sudden panic in mid-career, and is now reviving again ... I met one day in the middle of it the Governor of the Bank [William Cotton] at Robarts' who told me that he never remembered in all his experience anything like the present speculation; that the operations of '25 which led to the great panic were nothing to it; and that there could not fail to be a fearful reaction … It is incredible how people have been tempted to speculate; half the fine Ladies have been dabbling and the men most unlikely have not been able to refrain from gambling in shares, even I (though in a very small degree), for the warning voice of the Governor of the Bank has never been out of my ears. Simultaneously with all this has grown up to a gigantic height the evil of the potato failure, affecting in its expected consequences the speculations, and filling with fear and doubt every interest.

… All the world went last night to the St James's Theatre to see the second representation of [Ben Jonson's] *Every Man in his Humour* by Dickens and the *Punch* people. House crammed full. I was in a bad place, heard very ill and was so bored by that at the end of the Third Act, I went away. Dickens acted Bobadil very well indeed and Douglas Jerrold (the Author of the Caudles), [Douglas Jerrold, editor of *Punch*, was also well known for *Mrs Caudle's Curtain Lectures*] Master Stephen also; the rest were very moderate and the play intolerably heavy …

I have said nothing about Newmarket. My horse Alarm proved himself the best going (to all present appearance) and won the great Stake of the Houghton meeting [the Cambridgeshire]; but I won very little, not daring to back him. I had the mortification of seeing it proved that he would, beyond all possibility of doubt, have won the Derby but for his accident. That would have been worth winning; it would have rendered me independent, enabled me to relinquish my office when I pleased, be my own man, and given me the power of doing many an act of kindness, and assisting those I care for. Such a chance will probably never occur again.

Worsley November 22nd Saturday

… I have passed a few days in seeing this place and some of the manufacturing wonders of Manchester … On Wednesday I went through the subterraneous canal, about a mile and a half long, into the coalpit, saw the working of the mine and came up by the shaft; a black and dirty expedition, scarcely worth the trouble, but which I am glad to have seen. The colliers seem a very coarse set, but they are not hard worked, and in fact, do no more than they chuse … On Thursday to Manchester and saw one of the great cotton and one of the great silk manufactures. Very curious to me who am ignorant of mechanicks and could only stare and wonder without being able to understand the niceties of the beautiful and complicated machinery by which all the operations in these trades are performed … [The recreation ground] is a large piece of ground, planted and levelled about, what is called the paying-House where the men are paid their wages once a fortnight. The object is to encourage sports and occupations in the open air and encourage them not to go to the Ale House. There are cricket, quoits and football, and ginger-beer and coffee are sold to the people but no beer or spirits. This has only a partial success . . .

In Birley's (cotton) factory 1200 are employed. The majority are girls, who earn from ten to fourteen shillings a week. At Nasmyth's the men make from twenty to thirty-two shillings a week . . . In the hot factory rooms the women look very wan, very dirty and one should guess very miserable. They work eleven hours generally, but though it must be thought domestic service must be preferable, there is the greatest difficulty in procuring women-servants here. All the girls go to the factory in spite of the confinement, labour, close atmosphere, dirt and moral danger which await them. The parents make them go because they earn money which they bring home, and they like the independence and the hours every evening and the days from Saturday to Monday of which they can dispose.

Worsley November 24th

. . . The day I came here Lady Holland died, that is she died at two o'clock on the preceding night . . . She evinced during her illness a very philosophical calmness and resolution and perfect good humour, aware that she was dying and not afraid of death. The religious people don't know what to make of it. She seems never to have given the least sign of religious belief . . . Though she was a woman for whom nobody felt any affection and whose death therefore will have excited no grief, She will be regretted by a great many, some from kindly, some from selfish motives . . . Lady Holland continued to assemble around her until the last a great society, comprising almost everybody that was conspicuous, remarkable and agreeable . . . She was often capricious, tyrannical and troublesome, liking to provoke and disappoint and thwart her acquaintance, and she was often obliging, good natured and considerate to the same people.

London December 5th

I came to town yesterday, and find political affairs in a state of the greatest interest and excitement. The whole town has been electrified in the morning by an article in *The Times* announcing, with an air of certainty and authority, that the discussions (and disputes) in the Cabinet had terminated in a resolution to call Parliament together early in January and propose a total repeal of the Corn Laws . . . It appears that before the appearance of John Russell's letter [an open letter of 22 November in the *Edinburgh Review* announcing his conversion to Repeal], the Free-Trading ministers were disposed to take the course now determined on, and Aberdeen thinks it was great error and misfortune that they did not do so in November, and so appear to have taken the initiative rather than to be goaded to it. John's letter however (which was written without concert with, or the knowledge of, anybody) fell like a spark in a barrel of gunpowder ... When the [*Times*] article appeared yesterday morning, Wharncliffe was in a great state of agitation ... it was not true ... *The Times* was mystified [had been deluded] and had been all along ...

December 6th
It is impossible to describe the agitation into which all classes of person have been thrown by the announcement about the Corn Laws – the doubts, the hopes, the fears which it has excited and the burning curiosity to know the truth of it ... [Wharncliffe] did his best to make me doubt the accuracy of *The Times* statement, telling me nothing, but mysteriously saying a very short time would reveal the truth ...

Friday December 12th
Yesterday all was known. Peel had resigned on Saturday and John [Russell] was sent for the same day ... John was at Osborne yesterday, and has called his friends together today. The Whig talk at Brooks's is that the Government about to be formed cannot stand, that they will be able to do nothing with the House of Lords ... I doubt whether [Tory] rage and fury against Peel will be the least diminished by his resignation; on the contrary they will think he has cast them into the Lion's mouth ...

Saturday December 13th
At John Russell's in the morning, no one was present but Palmerston, Cottenham, Clarendon and Macaulay who came in at the end ... Clarendon came to me afterwards and told me what had passed. The Queen wrote to John and summoned him to her presence. She said Sir R. Peel had resigned and she had thought it expedient to ask him to assist her. He asked her why Peel had resigned. She said that since November last He had been satisfied that the time was arrived when the Corn Laws must be repealed, but that the difficulty he had found with his Cabinet had at length induced him to resign. John then said that before he could undertake anything, he must know what would be Peel's course in respect to the measures he should propose and what chance there would be he should have of being able to carry them ...

The Queen began [*sic*] to John immediately about Lord Palmerston, and expressed great alarm at the idea of his returning to the F.O., and her earnest desire that he would take the Colonial Office instead and that John would propose it to him. She had already talked to Aberdeen [Peel's Foreign Secretary] who told her she must make up her mind to P's returning to the F.O. as he would certainly take nothing else ...

Tuesday December 16th

Nothing settled L. [Lansdowne] and J. R. went to Windsor on Saturday, the first novelty that struck them was the manner of their reception; all changed since they went out of office. Formerly the Queen received her Ministers alone; with her alone they communicated, though of course Albert knew everything, but now the Q. and Prince were together, received Lord L. and J. R. together and both of them always said *We* – He is become so identified with her that they are one person, and as He likes and she dislikes business, it is obvious that while she has the title he is really discharging the functions of the Sovereign. He is King to all intents and purposes . . .

Afternoon

. . . John had written to the Queen and begged her to obtain a more positive answer whether the Protection part of the Cabinet would or could form a Government; and the Queen wrote to Peel accordingly . . . After stating positively that the dissentients would not make the attempt, he went on to say that he was disposed to support the measures of the new Government, but he thought it better that there should be no direct communication between them, that it would give offence to many people, and not be relished by Parliament; that he could say that there were many Peers who, whatever their opinions might be about Corn Laws, would be anxious that any measure which passed the H. of C. should pass the H. of Lords and would do all in their power to assist it . . .

Friday December 19th

Yesterday morning the die was cast. John Russell accepted the Government . . . On Wednesday morning [Peel] sent his reply . . . It was very cold, declined to enter into any discussion or to give any pledges, and expressed a hope that H.M. would not think him wanting in respect if he referred her to his former letter . . . Then ensued a quantity of conversation and discussion, all the pros and the cons, Peel's peculiar character and position, and, in short, whether they should go on or give it up. At length John, who had stood with folded arms and let this go on for some time in silence, said, 'If you wish to know my opinion. I think we ought to take the Government.' . . .

December 20th Saturday

No novel or play ever presented such vicissitudes and events as this political drama which has for ten days been enacted before the public . . . Yesterday morning they met at John Russell's as usual . . . Then J. R. said 'Now if you please, I want to see you singly and I will begin with Howick'⁵ . . . He had offered Howick the Colonies. H. accepted, but begged to know the other arrangements, and particularly the F.O. He told him 'Palmerston.' 'Then,' said H. 'I will not be in the Cabinet.' . . .

... In the afternoon J. R., finding Howick would come to no terms, declared that he would throw the whole thing up, that he could not do without Grey in the Lords, and that the breach with him would produce difficulties and embarrassments that would materially impair his chance of success. Peel was to go down to Windsor to resign, and J. R. wrote to the Queen to inform her of what had occurred, and begged her to put Peel off until the afternoon, and meanwhile he would himself go down to Windsor where he is, in fact, gone, to resign ... The Government is really like a halfpenny whirling in the air, with J. Russell's head on one side and Peel's on the other.

Sunday December 21st

J. Russell went down at eleven o'clock, resigned, and the Queen accepted his resignation ... At two, Peel resigned and upon her informing him that J. R. had resigned, giving him the minute to read, and requesting him to retake the Government, he immediately, without making any difficulties, consented to do so, saying, however, that he would have supported John Russell if he had formed his Government. The Queen immediately wrote to J. R. and told him what had passed which he announced to us at dinner at Palmerston's. I never saw people so happy, as most, perhaps all of them, are to have got out of their engagement ...

Monday December 22nd

... I have been so engaged in the narration of passing events that I have not said a word on the sudden death of Lord Wharncliffe, who, after an illness of ten days, was struck on Thursday last by a stroke of apoplexy, and died on Friday morning, none of his family having supposed him in any danger. He was not a popular man in general society; his manners were rude and ungracious, and to those who knew little of him, or who had occasional relations with him, he generally gave offence; but he was deservedly loved and esteemed by his family and friends ... He was very far from being a man of first-rate capacity, but he had good strong sense, liberal opinions, honesty, straightforwardness and courage – rather more, I think, of physical than of moral courage, for a braver man never existed ... he showed a want of moral courage in submitting so meekly to join the Tories in their mad attempt upon the Reform Bill, after the second reading had been carried when Lyndhurst proposed to postpone Schedule A, one of the greatest political blunders that was ever made ... On Peel's Government being formed in '35, he came into office; and again in 1841 Peel invited him to join ... In public life thus playing a secondary, but an honourable and useful part, in private life he was irreproachable, amiable and respected ...

At night I met Morpeth[6] at Miss Berry's who talked it all over and acknowledged his disgust and disappointment. He said he could not help thinking that the state of Lady John's health had had a considerable effect on John's mind, and unstrung his nerves; that when he had seen him after the finale he (M.) had expressed himself rather strongly; and the next day he called on John and said he was afraid he had done so. Lord John said he felt a little hurt, and then pulled out of his pocket a letter, and desired him to read it. It was from his wife saying she had not long to live. He burst into tears, and said that he rejoiced for himself to be out of it. [She died in 1898, he in 1878] ... Le Marchant, wishing to extract sweet from bitter, said, 'Well, after all, it may do us good. It will show that the Whigs are not so greedy after office, and it will wipe out the recollection of those two years when we staid in too long.' Macaulay replied 'I don't know that at all, it may only increase the blame. We staid in when we ought to have gone out, now we stay out when we ought to have gone in.'

London December 24th
Yesterday Council at Windsor; Stanley out and Gladstone in ...

1846

January 13th
... Clarendon received Henry Pierrepoint [a relative by marriage to the Duke of Wellington] at the Grove a few days ago who came from Strathfieldsaye [Wellington's Hampshire estate] and his account of the Duke and what he says is not without interest, so I transcribe it from his letter ... It is clear the D. of W. resents the whole of Peel's conduct, that he dislikes him, feels that he has never had his whole confidence, and has foreseen for the last six months that he was preparing to overthrow the Corn Laws. Pierrepoint considers this to be the cause of the unapproachable state of irritation in which he has been during the Autumn. The Duke says 'rotten potatoes have done it all; they put Peel in his d——d fright'; and for both the cause and the effect he seems to feel equal contempt ...

When they all shuffled back to their places at the Queen's command, he looked on himself as one of the rank and file, ordered to *fall in*, and he set about *doing his duty* and preparing for battle. He has written a great many letters to Tory Lords such as Rutland, Beaufort, Salisbury, Exeter and has received some very stiff and unsatisfactory answers. Particularly from Beaufort '... [that] they had for their Leader a man who had violated every principle and pledge, and in whom no man could put any trust'. I have no doubt that Alvanley, who has long been laid up at Badminton, dictated this letter, for he is very violent, and says 'Peel ought not to die a natural death'.

There has been a curious scene with Melbourne at Windsor ... It was at dinner when M. was sitting next to the Queen ... M. suddenly broke out, 'Ma'am it is a damned dishonest act' and then he continued a tirade against abolition of the Corn Laws, the people not knowing how to look and the Queen only laughing. The court is very strong in favour of Free Trade and not less in favour of Peel ...

January 14th

I saw Bessborough last night, just come from Ireland, talked over present affairs ... He says there will be no deficiency of consequence in the potato crop, none of the potatoes are *entirely* spoilt; the state of Ireland very bad in parts and requires coercive measures ...

January 22nd

Parliament meets today, and the truth will soon be out ... During these last days the Whig and Peelite (for now we have Peelites, as contradistinguished from Tories) whippers-in have been making lists, and they concur in giving Peel a large majority. They reckon Protectionists 200, Peelites 180 and then there are the Whigs and Liberals 200 or 300 – but Bessborough, who is very experienced, says these lists are very loose and not to be depended on at all ...

January 23rd

Went to the H. of Commons last night ... Immediately after the seconder, Peel rose and spoke for about two hours. A very fine speech in a very high tone. He owned to a change of opinion which had been going on for two years; was confirmed by the statistical result of his Free Trade experiment and urged on to action by the potato failure in November when he wanted to call Parliament together and open the ports, but was overruled in the Cabinet when he had only three others with him ... He did not get a single cheer from the people behind him except when he said that Stanley had always been against him and never admitted either the danger or the necessity, and then the whole of those benches rang with cheers ... he talked of 'a proud aristocracy' which was an unlucky phrase though clear from the context that he did not mean anything offensive in it. It was certainly not a speech calculated to lead to a reconciliation between him and the Tories; and it is difficult to see how he will be able to go on after this session, supposing him to settle the Corn Bill.

John rose after him and spoke very well; ... very civil to Peel, and altogether proper and well done. Then came an hour of gibes and bitterness, all against Peel personally, from D'Israeli with some good hits, but much of it tiresome; vehemently cheered by the Tories, but not once by the Whigs who last year used to cheer similar exhibitions lustily. I never heard him before; his fluency is wonderful, his cleverness great and his mode of speaking certainly effective though there is something monotonous in it ...

January 28th Wednesday

Last night Peel brought forward his plan amidst the greatest curiosity and excitement: House crammed and Prince Albert there to mark the confidence of the court ... On Sunday I had seen Charles Villiers [a Whig member and close friend of Greville] and Bessborough who both told me there was a bad disposition among the Whigs, many indisposed to attend, and many anxious only to embarrass the Government, and they both thought the difficulties were increasing. C. V. moreover told me that John Russell had asked him whether he meant to propose the *immediate abolition*, supposing Peel did not make it part of his plan, adding that if he would not, He himself should; and C. V. thought that Peel should be made aware of this.

I accordingly went to Graham [see *supra*] and told it him. He seemed struck by it, and said he could not conceive what J. R. wanted; that he might have taken the Government before, and would have had his and Peel's support. He then talked of the measure; that at all events they would not die in a ditch, 'but would put before the world a great scheme to do by legislation what Mr Pitt had attempted to do by commercial treaties', and a great deal more in the same strain expressive of his opinion that the plan ought to be taken to the country, and his confidence that however it might be received now, hereafter it would be regarded with admiration and applause and that its principles could not fail in the end to be adopted ...

January 30th

... In all this affair so far and since his speech the first night, which was very good, John Russell does not shine; but he is a very clever, ingenious, but *little* man, full of personal feelings and antipathies, and not, I suspect without something of envy, which galls and provokes him and makes him lose his head and temper together.

February 2nd Monday

I called on Graham and had a long conversation with him, telling him precisely what had passed. I was not prepared for what he said in reply, inasmuch as it indicated a possibility at least of their adopting the immediate repeal instead of their own plan.

... [He talked about] Stanley [Lord Stanley, the most energetic opponent of the measure] and his bitterness, thought that he would be disposed to advise the Lords to pass the Bill if it went up to them, but that he would hardly be able to restrain himself from making strong speeches and that, if he got warmed up and poured forth all his feelings and opinions, he would find an audience ready to sympathise with him, and that without intending it he would become the Leader of a Protectionist party ... He said Stanley disliked the manufacturing interest and its progress and power in Lancashire and all round about him at Knowsley [House and estate accompanying the Earldom of Derby, to which Stanley was heir] where his territorial power was diminished by the contact. Asked him why they had not resigned (He and Peel) early in November which would have been much better as it turned out. He said that it would but that He had been acting for twenty years with Stanley, and Peel for a longer time with the Duke, and they could not break up the Government without making an attempt to bring them round to their views and giving them time for consideration ...

February 16th

The debate in the H. of Commons (the dullest on record) lasted all last week and will probably last all this. Meanwhile affairs grow daily more uncomfortable and perplexed. The Government measure will certainly pass the Commons by a majority under one hundred, and most people think it will pass the H. of Lords ... Though the Tories have made up their minds to be defeated, they show no symptom of mitigated feelings towards Peel and the Government. The debate presents hardly any argument on their side, but bitter lamentations and reproaches and quotations from former speeches or addresses by Ministers who are now abandoning them ...

February 18th

The night before last Peel made a very grand speech vindicating himself in a very high tone ... Charles Villiers told Clarendon that it was one of the finest speeches he ever heard in Parliament. It served however to widen the breach between himself and the Tory party ...

While Peel was making this great speech in the H. of C., Stanley was making a very different sort of speech in the Lords. There he denounced the measure in strong terms, exhibited a bitter feeling and a disposition to put himself at the head of the Protectionists and throw out the measure. Such was the impression he gave, and his speech was rapturously hailed both there and elsewhere. It filled with alarm all the moderate people and encouraged the violent ... As for his forming a Government, he is himself as unfit as the rest are incompetent. There is probably not a public man in the country who enjoys so little consideration and inspires so little confidence. His speech has however made the cauldron boil more hotly than ever, and increased the doubt whether the measure will pass.

February 25th

... the Protectionists' great hero, D'Israeli, spoke on Friday for two and half hours cleverly and pointedly ... there was little of his accustomed bitterness and impertinent sarcasms on Peel, but a great deal of statistical detail and reasoning upon it. The Protectionists thought it very fine, but in reality it was

poor and worthless; and on Monday night, Sir George Clerk, who is no orator,
made a very complete exposure of the fallacy of his arguments and the inac-
curacy of his facts . . .

. . . these last few days we have been occupied with the Indian news which
has superseded the interest of the debate. Nobody knows what to think of it;
the slaughter so dreadful, the success so equivocal [not equivocal at all: the
Battle of Aliwal, won by Sir Harry Smith on 28 January 1846, effectively gave
Britain the Punjab] and the conduct of the authorities so questionable. At all
events it was a great feat of arms as far as bravery and resolution go . . .

March 1st Sunday
On Friday night at three o'clock, after twelve nights debate, the House divided
and the Government measure was carried on first reading [at this time a first
reading was not the token affair it has since become] by 97; . . . Cobden
[Richard Cobden, intellectual inspiration of the Anti-Corn Law League] made
an extraordinary speech last night, but one of the ablest I have ever read, and
it was (I am told) more striking still to hear, because so admirably delivered.
The general opinion at Brooks's yesterday was that this division would make
the Lords pass the Bill.

March 18th
In the H. of Commons the Protectionists are bent on delay, and are not allowing
the Bill to go up to the H. of Lords before Easter. They are now *the* Opposition;
they have elected G. Bentinck leader and Beresford and Newdegate Whippers-
in. Stanley, by all accounts, declares himself more and more their leader in the
Lords; and means to urge them on . . . Meanwhile, as the debates go on, the
arguments which go forth to the country, the statistical details and the progress
of famine and pestilence in Ireland, strengthen Government's case and produce
effects on the public mind . . .

March 21st
The Tariff was got through last night, G. Bentinck making a speech of two
hours and a quarter. From never having spoken he now does nothing else. And
he is completely overdoing it, and like a beggar on horseback riding to the
devil . . .

March 29th
Everything here is in a disturbed, doubtful and uneasy state; people angry,
perplexed and dissatisfied . . . [Peel] said that he knew that with 112 men he
could not go on, and they could turn him out when they would . . . Tonight
there is the devil to pay about the Irish question. The Whigs and Irish are
going to move the previous question and postpone the Coercion Bill. If the

Protectionists stay away in any numbers (much more if they vote) the Government will be beat ...

April 4th

The Government would have been beat on the Irish question if the vote had taken place earlier than it did ... the delay that the Protectionists have contrived to make in the Free Trade measures is proving fatal to their cause, for it is now past a doubt that a great change has been reproduced over all the country *among the farmers*. They do not care for, do not dread, the repeal of the Corn Laws, but they do most particularly wish to have the question settled. The evidences to this change are not to be mistaken, and many of the Protectionists admit it. They find to their astonishment that there is no depreciation in landed property, that there is no difficulty in letting farms, and that rents are generally rising rather than falling ...

April 23rd

... The Duke of Bedford gave me some information the other day which exhibits the present views and animus of the different parties. The Peelites and Protectionists equally contemplate the speedy advent of John Russell, and both have made overtures, direct or indirect, to him. Aberdeen called on John the other day about some private business, after which he talked on politicks. He said that it was impossible to go on, that Peel was aware of it, and quite determined not to dissolve Parliament; that he did not know on what issue they would have to go out; that he was told it would not be on the sugar duties, and that they should carry them; but that it was clear they should be beat on something else if not on that; that a Whig Government must be formed which must rely upon Peel and his friends for support, and would receive it ...

May 21st

... Last week the debate in the H. of C. came to a close at last, wound up by a speech of D'Israeli's, very clever, in which he hacked and mangled Peel with the most unsparing severity, and positively tortured his victim. It was a miserable and degrading spectacle. The whole mass of the Protectionists cheered him with vociferous delight, making the roof ring again; and when Peel spoke, they screamed and hooted at him in the most brutal manner. When he vindicated himself and talked of honour and conscience they assailed him with shouts of derision and gestures of contempt. Such treatment in a House of Commons, where for years he had been an object of deference and respect, nearly overcame him.

The Speaker told me that for a minute and more, he was obliged to stop, and for the first time in his life probably, he lost his self-possession; and the Speaker thought he would have been obliged to sit down and expected him to burst into tears. They hunt him like a fox, and they are eager to run him down and kill him in the open, and they are all full of exultation at thinking they have nearly accomplished the object ... Meanwhile the greatest doubt and anxiety prevail among the friends of the Bill in the Commons, and the Protectionists are full of confidence that they shall succeed in making the alterations they intend. There is an active attempt going on to bring about this end by a coalition of a part of the Whigs with the whole of the Protectionists ...

June 1st

So entirely occupied with Epsom last week that I had not a moment to attend to politicks, nor could write anything but bets nor look at any book but my betting book. I must therefore, now that I have an interval of leisure, narrate briefly what I ought at the time to have recorded in more detail.

On May 21st, I mentioned the sanguine hopes and expectations of the Protectionists which were suddenly and entirely overthrown by a bold, judicious and successful move of John Russell's. It reached his ears from various quarters that certain proceedings very like intrigues were going on, principally hatched at Palmerston House and that it was confidently asserted ... that a coalition would certainly be brought about, to which he (John R.) would be a party. He resolved at once and decisively to crush these hopes, and put an end to such reports. He accordingly begged Lord Lansdowne to convoke a meeting of Whig Peers at Lansdowne House ... John made a very stout speech announcing his intention to support the measure in toto, saying he had once been for a fixed duty [the compromise measure upon which the proposed deal would have been based] ... but would not do so now; and after the course Peel had taken, it would be inconsistent with his personal and political honour to be a party to any attempt to alter or mutilate it ...

Melbourne made a bitter speech against Peel, and said that as he saw everybody was resolved to take what he considered a very mischievous course, he should not separate from his friends but would not assist in doing the mischief. There was some discontent evinced but little or no disunion ... This meeting and the result of it was speedily bruited about the town and nothing could exceed the despair and mortification of the Protectionists at the news. It at once extinguished the hopes of the most sanguine. The Duchess of Beaufort, of all men and women the most violent, owned to me that the game was up ...

June 14th

All last week at Ascot at a house of Lady Mary Berkeley's with a racing party. I won the Emperor's Cup with Alarm, but won little more than £2000 on it ... Ibrahim Pacha was at Ascot the Cup day, and desired to shake hands with me when I won the Cup. He is a coarse-looking ruffian, and his character is said not to belie his appearance.

The past week has been characterised by the Coercion Bill in the H. of Commons on which George Bentinck made a furious and outrageous speech, attacking Peel with a coarseness and virulence which disgusted all but those to whom scurrility and insolence are particularly palatable ... The gist of it was (besides the old charges of treachery, etc) an accusation of his having 'hunted Mr Canning to death' nineteen years ago.[1]

Stanley got a tremendous dressing on Friday night from Grey, and still more from Brougham who spoke, they say, in his best H. of Commons style, cutting up Stanley with admirable wit and keeping the H. of Lords in a roar at his expense for three-quarters of an hour, the very thing that would annoy him the most. He had been very arrogant about his own speech, talking about nobody having answered it though the many fallacies it contained had been exposed and refuted over and over again.

May 19th

A day or two after Peel's speech in reply to G. Bentinck, D'Israeli came down and renewed the fight, not without effect ... It was a labour of love to him, and he accordingly delivered a bitter philippick against Peel, renewing the charge of G. B. and supporting it with a mass of fresh evidence culled out of *Hansard* ... it was to the last degree virulent but very able and considerably effective. Peel rose (as it was said very much annoyed), begged the House to suspend its judgment and promised a future and full explanation. The Protectionists have ever since been uproarious, and their papers have teemed with articles abusive of Peel. The Whigs though more reserved and decorous in their language ... whisper to the same effect as the Protectionists go bawling about ...

June 20th

Though ill with the gout, I made shift to hobble down to the H. of C. to hear Peel's defence last night. It was very triumphant crushing G. B. and D'Israeli and was received with something like enthusiasm by the House. G. B. rose in the midst of a storm of cheers at the end of Peel's speech which lasted some minutes, in a fury that his well-known expression revealed to me, and with the dogged obstinacy which super-eminently distinguishes him and a no-less characteristic want of tact and judgment, against all the feelings and sympathies of the House, endeavoured to renew and insist upon his charges. Nothing could be more injurious to himself and his party ... John Russell spoke handsomely of Peel, and so did Morpeth, which was very wise of them and will be very useful. Nothing could be more miserable than the figure which the choice pair, G. B. and Disraeli, cut ... this affair has been of great service to Peel and sheds something of lustre over his last days ...

July 4th

The day after I went to the H. of C., I was much worse and an attack of fever and gout came on, such as I never had in my life before ... [I] am still miserably crippled and weak, and can only be moved from my bed to my sofa and wheeled from one room to another. It was during the worst of my illness that the divisions took place in both Houses and Peel's resignation.[2] Such a transfer from one Minister to another the world has never seen – no rivalry, no mortifications, no disappointment, no triumph, no coldness; all has been civility, cordiality and the expression of feelings, not merely amicable but cordial ... Aberdeen told [Clarendon] that they might count upon both his support and Peel's; that though it was impossible to foresee every political contingency and necessity that might occur, both he and Peel quitted office with a resolution never to take it again;[3] ...

The Protectionists don't seem to know what to do; they are more indignant than ever with Peel; they are disgusted at their overtures not being accepted by the Whig Government; they are provoked exceedingly at places having been offered to Dalhousie, S. Herbert and Lincoln, thus marking more strongly the determination of John Russell to look for support to Peel and his friends, and not to them. Nevertheless their organ and whipper-in, Major Beresford, told one of the Whig people (to be told to Lord John) that after having contributed to drive Peel out, and thereby forced the Government on Lord John, they should not feel justified in raising any opposition to his Government, so that in fact, for the present, there is no Opposition of any sort or kind; everybody seems to be acquiescent, and the swords are universally sheathed. So curious a change in so short a time was never seen.

July 14th

... Meanwhile the Queen is evidently out of humour and in various little ways evinces her sentiments. There has been a sort of squabble about some of the appointments. Not that anybody has been forced upon her, but she took umbrage at some intention She chose to fancy there was to propose someone disagreeable to her, which in fact was only an ebullition of ill-humour. The simple truth is she can't bear any of these people, J. R. especially, and is miserable at losing Peel, and still more Aberdeen ...

Brighton July 18th

I am come here to recruit my strength if possible after my severe illness, but I find cold wind and rain ... [Court appointments] are such trifling matters that they are totally unworthy of attention, except just for this, that in their details they exhibit a good deal of want of candour and sincerity on the part of the Q. and P. As for example, after insisting on the dismissal of Arbuthnot [an equerry, son of Wellington's friend, 'Gosh'] and exposing John R. to all the odium thereof, they had him down to Osborne to finish his waiting and loaded him with civilities, thereby confirming his belief that it was John's doing and not theirs . . .

August 13th

. . . It seems that He [Palmerston] has an incurable and violent dislike and distrust of Clarendon. The evidence of this comes from Lady Palmerston who abused Clarendon violently to him the other night, though I could not make out on what specific grounds. Then the French complain that Palmerston has already begun to disturb the harmony which subsisted in Aberdeen's time and to alter the amicable relations which the latter had established . . .

One of those [things] which worries the Government most is the ridiculous and unbecoming liaison of Bessborough [Lord-Lieutenant] and Mrs Maberley [Irish lady novelist married to the Secretary of the Post Office] which they think will prove seriously mischievous and which they do not know how to deal with. He was not in the House of Lords the other night when they were in danger, having gone, according to custom, with her to Worthing . . .

Very bad accounts of potatoes all over the country, nearly total destruction in Ireland, and now the disease is ravaging Scotland and England.

Wilberforce, (Bishop of Oxford) made a very brilliant speech a few nights ago on the Sugar Bill. As his father's son [his father was William Wilberforce] he thought it necessary to make an anti-slavery oration; it was very able and eloquent . . . He is certainly a remarkable man full of cleverness and vivacity, very unlike a Churchman in society and Parliament . . .

The Grove Sunday September 7th

. . . There was an *Alliance* [group of Christian sects] at Hertford on Tuesday with some French and German orators who harangued in English. I did not go.

Came here on Friday; half the Cabinet are here. John Russell, Woods [Charles Wood, later Lord Halifax, Chancellor of the Exchequer], Greys, Macaulay, very agreeable, capital talk . . . Nothing is so rare as to find something he does not know; and he was not aware that there had been a contest for ecclesiastical supremacy between the Archbishops of Canterbury and York . . . We have been doing our best to persuade John R. to let the Queen go to Ireland, but he is very obstinate and will not hear of it; he gives the worst reasons in the world, but there is no moving him.

London November 4th

. . . The state of Ireland is meanwhile most deplorable, not so much from the magnitude of the prevailing calamity as the utter corruption and demoralisation of the whole people from top to bottom; obstinacy, ignorance, cupidity and idleness overspread the land. Nobody thinks of anything but how they can turn the evil of the times to their own advantage. The upper class are intent upon jobbing, and the lower on being provided with everything and doing nothing . . .

There was a great disposition to open the ports and convene Parliament. John R. was himself inclined that way, but he was persuaded to give up the idea; and it is very well it was given up. I was desired to find out what the Protectionists would say to such a measure, and I reported that they would view it with great wrath and disgust. This contributed in some degree to the resolution to which the Cabinet came.

December 19th Saturday

On Thursday evening at seven o'clock Mr Grenville died after a week's illness which was no more than a severe cold or influenza. If he had lived till the 31st of the month he would have completed his 91st year. I had only known him with any intimacy for the last five or six years.

During which I saw a good deal of him . . . He was certainly the most amiable and engaging specimen of an Old man I ever beheld. I do not conceive that his abilities were ever first rate, and latterly (whatever may have been the case early in life) he entertained very strong prejudices and often very unreasonable ones . . . He never could endure the Reform Bill or forgive its authors; he never would set foot in Holland House after that measure; and he estranged himself from all of his political friends . . .

He was a scholar and a well-informed man and he retained until the last all his literary tastes and habits; he loved the society of literary men, and to the last entered with zest and spirit and unimpaired intelligence into all questions both of literature and politics.

It is difficult to say what the exact colour of political opinions was. He used to be a Whig; but he was, at all events, latterly, a moderate Anti-reforming Whig, with a horror of organick changes and not fond of any changes, disliking free trade and disliking Cobden more; favourable to Catholic Emancipation and the establishment of a Catholic Church, but abhorring O'Connell who was his bête noire, and in his eyes the incarnation of all evil and mischief.

He never was married, but when he was young he was desperately in love with the Duchess of Devonshire, and he never married because her image was enthroned in his breast, and he never could find any woman to compare with her.

. . . His greatest expense was in books; and he had collected a library of extraordinary value, and which for the size of it was reckoned the most complete of any private collection . . . He had constantly dinners, and very agreeable ones, and it was wonderful to see him at ninety years old doing the honours of his table with all the energy, gaiety and gallantry of a man in the prime of life . . .

A life so tranquil and prosperous was terminated by a death no less easy and serene; his indisposition was not such as to interfere with his usual habits; he rose at his accustomed hour and dressed himself to the last, even on the day of his death. He had always a book, latterly the Prayer Book, before him, and his mind was undisturbed and unclouded. He dined and went to sleep in his chair, and from that sleep he never woke up.

1847

Thursday [25 February]
I met Sir Robert Peel yesterday and walked with him some time. I have not had so much conversation with him for years. He praised the Budget, lamented the state of foreign affairs, and talked of Palmerston as everyone does. I said we were always in danger from him, and he must know how difficult it is to controul him. He said 'I am only afraid that Lord John does not exert all the authority and determination which, as Prime Minister, he ought to do.' I said he did it by *flashes*, but not constantly and efficiently.

Yesterday Young Walter [John Walter II, owner of *The Times*] was brought to the office and introduced to me. Old Walter is dying, and he is about to succeed (in fact has succeeded) to the throne of *The Times* and all the authority, influence and power which the man who wields that sceptre can exercise. He seems mild, sensible and gentlemanlike.

Sunday 28th
At court yesterday to make Grey Lord-Lieutenant of Northumberland. They were in high spirits at the Prince's election at Cambridge. [He had been elected Chancellor of the University, but by only 122 votes over Lord Powis.] . . . there have been reports abroad of a dissension in the Cabinet about the Irish Poor Law [over payments of outdoor relief since the workhouses could not cope with the victims of famine], but it is not true. They have all been agreed, and in fact there has been no disagreement on any subject hitherto . . .

March 13th Saturday
The Government are going on here. John speaks excellently; the Speaker says he never saw any Government do their business so well. Charles Wood is an immense thing for them, a good Chancellor of the Exchequer is a tower of strength to a government. Goulburn was only Peel's chief Clerk, Wood is taking a flight of his own . . .

Sunday

Saw Graham yesterday and had a long talk with him. He said John Russell's speech on the Irish Poor Law was the best thing he had done since he was Minister and proved his competence for the office itself; that he viewed with the deepest alarm the measure itself, but that in the temper of the H. of C. and the country it was inevitable . . . He thinks the consequence will be a complete revolution of property, the ruin of the landed proprietors and the downfall of the Protestant ascendancy and of the Church. He expects that the first to abandon the Church will be the Protestant proprietors themselves; that a tremendous ordeal is to be gone through, involving vast changes and social vicissitudes, but that on the whole, and at a remote period, it will produce the regeneration of Ireland . . . I do not pretend to enunciate any opinion as to the solution of this tremendous problem which gives rise to so many thoughts – social, political and religious – perplexing the mind upon all. How those devout people who are supposed to find in everything that happens manifestations of divine goodness and wisdom, and are always overflowing with thanksgiving and praise, accommodate this awful and appalling reality with their ideas and convictions I do not divine . . .

Tuesday March 23rd

Last week (I forget which day) the political and commercial world were struck with astonishment at the sudden and unexpected announcement of the financial arrangement between the Emperor of Russia and the Bank of France, of which nobody, either Politicians or Financiers, could make head or tail, nor up to this moment has any light been thrown upon it. Excursive and eager political minds, however, instantly jumped to vast conclusions, and beheld deep political designs, a monstrous union between France and Russia, French divisions crossing the Pyrenees, and Russian the Balkan.

For the last week the accounts from Ireland have been rather better, but the people are, without any doubt, perishing by hundreds.

March 31st

G. Bentinck made another exhibition in the H. of Commons the night before last in the shape of an attack on Labouchere more violent and disgusting than any of his previous ones. He seems to have lost all control over his temper and his indiscretion and arrogance have excited a bitterness against him to be described. The Protectionists are overwhelmed with shame and chagrin, and they know not what to do: he has ruined them as a party; he was hooted even by those who sat behind him, and all the signs of disapprobation with which he was assailed have only excited and enraged him the more. The Government are now anxious to dissolve as soon as they possibly can, justly thinking the time is ripe for them . . .

April 2nd

... I dined with David Dundas (Solicitor-General) the day before yesterday at the Clarendon Hotel: splendid banquet; twenty miscellaneous friends. Labouchere there told me that Hatherton [the former Edward Littleton, himself a (reticent) diarist] had not long before shown him Dudley's diary which is very curious. It was very regularly kept, and told details of everything he did, giving minute details of his amours both in high and low life and especially of his connexion with [name deleted] ...

... Moxon [Edward Moxon, 1801–58, publisher] told me on Wednesday that D'Israeli had some years ago asked him to take him into partnership, but he refused, not thinking he was sufficiently prudent to be trusted. He added he did not know how Dizzy would like to be reminded of that now.

April 10th

Just before I left town last week I saw Arbuthnot who entreated me, if I had any influence with the Government, to get them to take up the subject of the defence of the country. He said it haunted the Duke of Wellington and deprived him of rest, and night and day he was occupied with the unhappy state of our foreign relations, the danger of war and the defenceless state of our coasts ...

London April 30th

Troubles and difficulties of various kinds have not diminished since I wrote last. The state of Ireland continues not only as bad, but as unpromising as ever, and, in addition, there is the great misfortune (publick and private) of the approaching death of the Lord-Lieutenant [Bessborough]. His illness was very sudden, at least the dangerous symptoms were, and he is dying amidst universal sympathy and regret. John has made his mind as to his successor, but without telling his colleagues his intentions; he may have told some, but certainly not all, for he has not told Clarendon with whom he is on very confidential terms [perhaps because Clarendon was to get the job].

Sunday June 7th

... The principal events which have occurred have been the deaths of Bessborough and O'Connell [very ill for some time, O'Connell died in Genoa] which took place at almost the same time within a day or two of one another. The departure of the latter, which not long ago would have excited the greatest interest and filled the world with political speculations, was heard almost with unconcern so entirely had his importance vanished; he had been for some months morally and politically defunct. And nobody seems to know whether his death is likely to prove a good or an evil or a mere matter of indifference ...

[Bessborough] had almost always been on good terms with O'Connell, indeed he was never on bad terms with anybody; and, as an Irishman, he was agreeable to the people . . . and he conciliated the good will of those to whom he had been all his life opposed . . . It was his misfortune to be always under the dominion of women; under that of Mrs Fox for 25 years, and much more unhappily under that of Mrs Maberly for the last two; the first was very harmless, the last as mischievous as possible. What is most extraordinary but which I believe to be beyond all doubt, is that in neither the new nor the old liaison was there ever any carnal connection. He was a modest, if not a chaste man and, singular as it is, he made himself the devoted Slave of those Ladies without exacting the usual wages of such service . . .

July 13th

The session is drawing to a close, but far from satisfactorily for the Government who have lost ground in publick estimation. Bill after Bill has been thrown over, and, after a great deal of time entirely wasted, the session will end with hardly anything having been done. The two measures given up have been the Health of Towns and the Irish Estates . . . The vexatious opposition to the Health of Towns Bill by G. Bentinck, Hudson [George Hudson, 'the Railway King', railway financier and MP for Sunderland, whose empire would collapse with great consequences in 1849] and Co., made it very difficult to carry it, but the truth is they were wrong to bring in such measures so late in the season, and the measures were not framed in a manner to get through with short discussions . . . the publick does not analyse, but looks to result and therefore sees in the whole conduct of affairs proofs of weakness, vacillation and mismanagement . . . All this is very deplorable.

Then John does not make up by his personal qualities for his political mistakes or shortcomings; he is not conciliatory and he sometimes gives great personal offence . . . He is miserably wanting in amenity and in the small arts of acquiring popularity which are of such incalculable value to the Leader of a party, still more of a Government; then while he has a reputation of being obstinate, he is wanting in firmness . . . In short, on the whole, the Government is not in good odour: they don't inspire confidence; they are neither popular nor respected, but they are indispensable and have the strength of circumstances . . . matters are in the sort of lock which prevents any other combination and any change, but which renders the present Government very powerless . . .

London October 23rd

After many weeks or months during which from idleness or unexplainable repugnance I have never written a line, I at last resume my pen . . . Stirring weeks they have been and full of interest of the most general and lively description . . . we have been absorbed in the great panic in the money market which is still at its height, and of which no man ventures to predict or thinks he can

see, the termination. Men are indeed pretty well agreed as to the cause of the
present distress and in admitting it is the result of over-speculation and of the
Railway mania which fell upon the country two years ago. But the great contest
is to the share Peel's Bill of '44 had in aggravating and keeping up the state
of distress and difficulty in which trade and commerce are involved and whether
this Bill ought to be relaxed by the authority of the Government or not. [Peel's
Bank Act of 1844 had limited the issue of country banks, held responsible for
the panic of the early 1820s, and begun a process of concentrating credit
policy.]

... Charles Wood has, however, been stout and resolute from the first and
quite determined not to consent to any interference ... the most remarkable
circumstance is the intense interest and curiosity which are felt about Peel's
opinions and intentions. Every body asks with anxiety what he says, what he
thinks, what he will do ... his power seems to be as great out of office as it
ever was in office; nothing was ever so strange or anomalous as his position.
Half the commercial world attributes the distress and danger to his Bill; he is
liked by nobody. The Conservatives detest him with unquenched hatred and
abuse him with unmitigated virulence. The Whigs regard him with a mixture
of fear, suspicion and dislike, but treat him with great deference and respect ...
All eyes are turned upon him as by a sort of fascination. If the country could
be polled to decide who should be Minister, he would be elected by an immense
majority ... the notion is that the present men are weak and the publick necessities and perils are great, and if a crisis of difficulty and danger should arrive,
that Peel is the only man capable of extricating the country from it ...

Newmarket November 1st Monday

... On Friday I believed it to have been *settled* that nothing should be done by
the Government to relieve the panic. On that day, however, G. Glyn and other
bankers had an interview with John Russell and they came from it with a
persuasion that he would do something. The same evening Peel came to town
in his way to Windsor. Charles Wood went to him, laid before him the state
of affairs, telling him all the accounts they received from the country, all the
pressure they were undergoing and explained their views and intentions.

On the next day (Saturday) still more urgent demands were made, and still
more alarming representations arrived. On Sunday, a Cabinet, or half-Cabinet,
was held and there it was resolved to grant the relief that has been seen.
[Permission for the Bank to issue paper in excess of the 1844 limits.] ...

November 21st Sunday

State of Ireland awful. I have written to Clarendon repeatedly, urging him to
ask for great powers. He was reluctant and wanted to try the force of the law
as it is, and the Cabinet were not disposed to adopt coercive measures; but the

public voice loudly demands coercion and repression ... Parliament never met in more difficult and disturbed times: complete disorganisation, famine and ruin in Ireland, financial difficulty, general alarm and insecurity here, want of capital, want of employment. It requires all one's faith in the general soundness and inherent strength of 'the thing', as Cobbett called it, to silence one's apprehensions ...

December 1st

I went to the H. of Lords the night Parliament opened and heard Stanley's speech. It lasted above two hours, was a declaration of war, very slashing and flashing, and drew forth vehement cheers from the Lords behind him. It was a regular Stanleyan speech, just like himself and exhibits all his unfitness for the great functions of government and legislation ... The next day G. Bentinck bellowed and gesticulated for two hours in the House of Commons with the same violence but without the same eloquence as Stanley. Everybody looked with impatience for the Irish measures and everybody expected ... that they should be as strong as they could be made ...

December 7th

The Irish measures were introduced, and everybody was surprised they were not stronger. Peel supported the Government and there was hardly any opposition ...

December 15th

... Hampden's[1] bishoprick has made a great stir: thirteen protesting Bishops, a stout answer from John, a long, very clever rejoinder from the Bishop of Exeter and a sensible protest the other way from Bishop Stanley. There never was a greater piece of folly than John's bringing this hornets' nest about his ears, nothing could be less worthwhile. It is not over yet, and there will be more kicking and clamouring; but John, however foolish he was in making the appointment, must of course go through with it now, and then, like everything else, it will be soon forgotten.

December 24th

... I went yesterday to St George's Hospital to see the chloroform [the first experiment with chloroform had been made by Joseph Simpson seven weeks earlier] tried. A boy two and a half years old was cut for a stone. He was put to sleep in a minute; the stone was so large and the bladder so contracted the operator could not get hold of it and the operation lasted above twenty minutes with repeated probings by different instruments; the chloroform was applied from time to time and the child never exhibited the slightest sign of consciousness, and it was exactly the same as operating on a dead body ... I have no words to express my admiration for this invention which is the greatest blessing ever bestowed upon mankind, and the inventor of it the greatest of benefactors, whose memory ought to be venerated by countless millions for ages yet to come ...

It is a great privilege to have lived in the times which saw the production of steam, of electricity and now of ether – that is of the development and application of them to human purposes to the multiplication of enjoyments and the mitigation of pain. But wonderful as are the powers and feats of the steam engine and the electrick telegraph, the chloroform transcends them all in its beneficent and consolatory operations.

VOLUME V ENDS

VOLUME VI

1848

January 1st

The Hampden affair [the appointment of Renn Hampden as Bishop of Hereford] is still on with prejudicial effects to everybody concerned in it. Dean Merewether [the Dean of Hereford], who is piqued and provoked at not having got the Bishoprick himself (Which Wm. IV once promised him) wrote a foolish, frothy letter to J. R., who sent an equally foolish because petulant reply – only in two lines ...

Last week after a few days' illness, without pain or trouble, Lord Harrowby died at Sandon [the family estate] having just completed his eighty-fifth year ... He was at the top of the second-rate men, always honourable and straightforward, generally liberal and enlightened, greatly esteemed and respected ... He was very well informed. Madame De Staël speaks of him somewhere as 'Lord Harrowby qui connaît notre littérature un peu mieux que nous mêmes'; but his precise manner and tart disposition prevented his being agreeable in society.

Bowood Friday January 7th

... Great talk here of G. Bentinck's resignation from the leadership of the Opposition [the rump Conservative Party after the departure of Robert Peel and his following]. John Russell and his colleagues are very sorry for it; nobody can think of a successor to him, and, bad as he is, he seems the best man they have. It seems they detest D'Israeli, the only man of talent, and in fact they have nobody ...

The Hampden war has been turning greatly to the advantage of the Doctor; his enemies have exposed themselves in the most flagrant manner ... The P. [Prince Albert] writes to John every day very violent and urges him to prosecute Dean Merewether, which of course John is too wise to do. That Dean is a very paltry fellow, and has moved heaven and earth to get made a Bishop himself; besides memorialising the Queen, he wrote to Lord Lansdowne and suggested to him to put an end to the controversy by making him a Bishop now and Hampden one at the next vacancy. The whole proceeding reflects great discredit on the great mass of Clergymen who have joined in the clamour against Hampden, and on the Oxonian majority who condemned him, for it is now pretty clear that very few if any of them had ever read his writings. Now that they are set forth and people see his unintelligible jargon about dogmas themselves unintelligible, there must be some dispassionate men who will be disgusted and provoked with each other and at the ferocity with which these holy disputants assault and vituperate each other about that which none of them understands, and which it is a real mockery and delusion to say that any of them really believe; it is cant, hypocrisy and fanaticism from beginning to end ...

Brocket January 22nd

Came here this afternoon, Melbourne having at last invited me. I have been intimately acquainted with him for thirty-five years and he never before (but once to dinner) invited me into his house ... He is well and in good spirits and ready to talk by fits and starts, very anti-Peel and anti-Free-trade, rattled away against men and things, especially against the Denisons [The Denisons, Evelyn, Edward (of Salisbury) and mile-high George, were heavy-duty Christians best avoided] and the Bishop of Salisbury in particular. I asked 'Why then did you make him a Bishop?' He said 'It was the worst thing I ever did in my life.' ...

Lady Beauvale [Melbourne's sister-in-law, married to his brother Frederick] told me some anecdotes of the Royal children which may some day have an interest when time has tested and developed their characters. The Princess Royal [Victoria, later briefly Kaiserin of Germany] is very clever, strong in body and mind; the P. of Wales weaker, more timid, and the Q. says he is a stupid boy; but the hereditary and unfailing antipathy of our Sovereigns to their Heirs Apparent seems this early to be taking root, and the Q. does not much like the child ... She is certainly an odd woman; her devotion and submission to her husband seem to know no bounds. When first she married, Melbourne told her she must not expect her domestick happiness *never* to be ruffled. She did not like this at all. But it never has. Albert never looks at her handsome Ladies and Maids of honour. He is absorbed with other objects, full of ambition and the desire of governing and having political influence.

February 8th

On Monday we received news of the revolution in Sicily, of the concessions extorted from the King, and the promulgation of a constitution at Naples ... There was a meeting yesterday at Stanley's to chuse a leader, but they parted without doing anything. Stanley said it was not for him to point out a Leader to the Members of the H. of C, and he eulogised G. Bentinck (who has taken his place on the back benches). They are to meet again tomorrow and it is supposed that Granby [Marquess of, heir to the Duke of Rutland] will be their choice! Except his high birth, he has not a single qualification for the post; he is tall, good looking, civil and good humoured, if these are qualifications, but he is heavy, dull and ignorant, without ability or knowledge, destitute of ideas to express and the art of expressing them if he had any; and yet this great party can find no better man.

Friday 13th Sunday

On Friday was with Graham for a long time, talked of everything, affairs at home and abroad ... talked a good deal of colonial matters, and said the change in our commercial policy [free trade] brought about the necessity of a great one in our Colonial policy, that we ought to limit instead of extending our colonial empire, that Canada must soon be independent. He condemned the Caffre War [more usually Kaffir War, one of several, this example brought about during the expansion of the Cape of British rule by the Governor to the Orange River] and extensions of Cape Colony, that we ought to have a *Gibraltar* there, a house of call; condemned [expansion in] New Zealand and Labuan and Hong Kong, considered the West Indies interest as gone ... He is all for 'defence', but says the only way is to draw our troops home which are scattered over our useless and expensive dependencies ...

London February 28th

The French Revolution has for the time being driven every other subject out of thought and so astounding has the event been, so awful and surprising its inconceivable rapidity and the immensity of the operation, that every mind has been kept in a restless whirl and tumult incompatible with calm reflection ... no human being dreamt of a revolution and the dethronement of the King ... At Paris from the King downwards, all seem to have lost their presence of mind and judgment ... then came Thiers and Odilon Barrot, Ministers of a few hours, who, deluded by the deceptive applause of the rabble, fancied they could command and restrain the people of Paris and who persuaded the King to withdraw the troops, telling him they would answer for the people. This fatal advice cost him his crown which perhaps he could have kept on his head. The tide swept on; a host of people, among them Émile Girardin [important press proprietor, owner, *inter alia* of *La Presse*], rushed to the Tuileries, told the King his life was menaced and advised him to abdicate; he refused. The people about him ... pressed him, and he signed the act of abdication. Still the crowd pressed on, and the Palace was unprotected. He resolved or was persuaded to fly; ... They proceeded to Dreux [west of Paris], where they separated, and as yet no one knows where the King is, or where those of his family are who have not yet arrived in England ...

There is a strong impression that if they had unsparingly used the military means at their disposal while it was still time, the Monarchy would have been saved and the tumult suppressed ... But between blunders, bad advice and delay, the insurrection sprang at once into gigantic proportions, and the world has seen with amazement who was considered so astute and courageous with sons full of spirit and intelligence sink without striking a blow for their Kingdom, perishing without a struggle and consequently falling dishonoured and un-regretted . . .

In all this great drama Lamartine stands forth pre-eminently as the prin-cipal character; how long it may last God only knows, but such a fortnight of greatness the world has never seen; for fame and glory with posterity it were well for him to die now. His position is something superhuman *at this moment*; . . . on him almost alone the hopes of the world are placed. He is the principal author of this Revolution; they say that his book has been a prime cause of it, and that which he had the glory of making, he has the far greater glory of directing, moderating, restraining. His labour has been stupendous, his eloquence wonderful. When the new government was surrounded by thousands of armed rabble, bellowing and raging for they knew not what, Lamartine contrived to appease their rage . . . he has acted like a man of honour and of feeling too. He offered the King an escort . . . he sent to Guizot [Prime Minister since 1840] to say if he was not in safety where he was he might come to his house. When he first proposed the abolition of the penalty of death, he was overruled; but the next day he proposed it again and declared if his colleagues would not consent, he would throw up his office, quit the concern and they might make him, if they pleased, the first victim of the law they would not abolish.

March 4th
Called on Guizot yesterday . . . [he said that] 'you English cannot conceive what our lowest class is; your own is a mere mob without courage or organi-sation, and not given to politicks; ours on the contrary, the lowest class, is eager about politicks and with a perfect military organisation, and therefore very formidable.'

March 14th
The Government had a capital division last night, and John [Russell] made a very good and stout speech. In France everything is going downhill at rail-road pace. This fine revolution, which may be termed the madness of a few for the ruin of many, is already making the French people weep tears of blood. Hitherto there has been little or no violence and fine professions of justice and philanthropy . . . They have got rid of a King and a royal family and the cost thereof; they have got a reform (so to call it) so radical and complete that it can go no further; . . . They have got a government composed of men who have not the slightest idea how to govern, albeit they are men of energy, activity and some capacity . . . Ruin and bankruptcy are stalking through the streets of the capital. The old revolutionary principles and expedients are more and more drawn forth and displayed by the present rulers; they are assuming despotick power and using it without scruple; . . . Carnot [Hippolyte, son of

Lazare, father of Sadi, he instituted free universal primary education⌝ instructs the people to elect for their representatives (who are to be the unchecked Masters of the Empire) not men of property and education, but any men who have republican ideas ... All the letters that arrive here, whether they come from Legitimists or Liberals or Orléanists, or indifferent to all parties, tell the same tale of disgust, distress and dread ...

March 25th

Nothing is more extraordinary than to look back at my last date and see what has happened in the course of *five days*. A tenth part of any one of the events would have lasted us for as many months with sentiments of wonder and deep interest; but now, we are perplexed, overwhelmed and carried away with excitements ...

Within these last few days there has been a desperate battle in the streets of Berlin between the soldiers and the mob; the flight of the Prince of Prussia; the King's convocation of his States; concessions to and reconciliation with his people; and his invitation to all Germany to form a federal state; and his notification of what is tantamount to removing the Imperial Crown from the head of the wretched cretin ⌜Ferdinand I, Emperor of Austria 1835–48. He was, in fact, mentally retarded.⌝ and placing it on his own.

Next a revolution in Austria; an émeute ⌜a riot⌝ at Vienna; downfall and flight of Metternich and announcement of constitutional regime; émeute at Milan, expulsion of Austrians and Milanese independence; Hungary up and doing, and the whole empire in a state of dissolution. Throughout Germany all the people stirring, all the Sovereigns yielding to the popular demands; the King of Hanover submitting to the terms demanded of him; the King of Bavaria abdicating ... France rides on with giant strides to confusion and ruin, Germany looks better; ... and the passion for reconstituting a German nationality may yet save her from anarchy. It is very surprising that in no country has a single master-mind started forward to ride on these whirlwinds and direct the storms. In the midst of the roar of the revolutionary waters that are deluging the whole earth it is grand to see how we stand erect and unscathed. It is the finest tribute that has ever been paid to our constitution, the greatest test that has ever been applied to it and there is a general feeling of confidence and a reliance on the soundness of the public mind ...

Our most difficult task has been to deal with Irish disaffection and Irish distress: the former has never been so bold, reckless and insolent ... In plain language they ⌜followers of Mitchell, Meagher and O'Brien, Irish leaders⌝ not only used the same seditious language the first had used, but broke out with greater fury and indecency; in plain language, they called on the people to arm for the purpose of overturning the Constitution, and they said they would have no more Kings and Queens. I thought this must amount to High Treason, but

George Grey [Home Secretary] told me yesterday that the lawyers here hold that to make it treason it must be followed by some overt act. However whether Clarendon [Lord-Lieutenant] was right or wrong in attacking the rebel Repealers ['Repeal clubs' had been formed to agitate for repeal of the Act of Union 1801], it is clear he ought now to throw away the scabbard, and war having been declared to wage it vigorously and unflinchingly.

March 31st

At Northampton races. Nothing new these last few days; Ireland getting more serious and a strong feeling gaining ground that there will be an outbreak and fighting, and that this will be on the whole a good thing, inasmuch as nothing will tame the Irish agitators but a severe drubbing ... Last night I met Delassert [Louis Philippe's Prefect of Police] ... [He] gave an opinion of his countrymen which he said he was ashamed to give, but it was the truth. He said they were not to be governed, for they had no sense of religion or morality or any probity among them ... [But Guizot's] unpopularity was immense and he had committed the great fault of staying in spite of it and for so many years when the French could not bear anything that lasted long ...

April 9th

... All London is making preparations to encounter a Chartist row tomorrow: so much that it is either very sublime or very ridiculous. All the clerks and others in the different offices are ordered to be sworn in special constables and to consti-tute themselves into garrisons ... We are to pass the whole day at the office tomorrow, and I am to send down all my guns; in short, we are to take a warlike attitude. Colonel [actually a mere *captain*] Harness of the Railway Department is our Commander in chief; every gentleman in England is become a special constable; and there is an organisation of some sort in every district.

Newmarket April 10th

Monday passed off with surprising quiet, and it was considered a most satis-factory demonstration on the part of the Government and the peaceable and loyal part of the community. Enormous preparations were made, and a host of military, police and special constables were ready if wanted; every gentleman in London was sworn ... The Chartist movement was contemptible but every-body rejoices that the defensive demonstration was made, for it has given a great and memorable lesson which will not be thrown away, either on the disaf-fected and mischievous, or the loyal and peaceful; and it will produce a vast effect in all foreign countries and show how solid is the rock on which we are resting ...

The Chartists, about 20,000 in number, assembled on Kennington Common. Presently Mr Mayne [Richard Mayne, Metropolitan Police Commissioner] appeared on the ground ... Feargus [O'Connor, leading Chartist; four years later he would be certified insane] thought he was going to be arrested, and was in a terrible fright; but he went to Mayne who merely said he was desired to inform him that the meeting would not be interfered with, but the procession would not be allowed. Feargus insisted on shaking hands with Mayne, swore he was his best of friends and instantly harangued his rabble, advising them not to provoke a collision, and to go away quietly – advice they instantly obeyed and with great apparent alacrity and good-humour. Thus all evaporated in smoke ...

May 3rd

John [Russell] is very much annoyed with the Queen ... she has chosen (without consulting him) to issue an order for everyone's appearing in her drawing room in garments of British manufacture. This was done directly by herself and the Prince, and is taken up eagerly by the protectionists, especially the Ladies. It is so directly contrary to the principles of free trade and such a miserable clap trap that John is disgusted ...

I had a long letter from Clarendon yesterday and saw Southern [former secretary to Clarendon before he became Lord-Lieutenant] in the morning, just come from Dublin where he has been staying several weeks ... Clarendon says not an R.C. in Ireland is to be trusted; and S. gives a deplorable picture of the condition of landed property and proprietors; the inveterate habit of selfishness and indifference to the state of the masses which has long distinguished the landowners makes it impossible to get them to act on the principles which regulate the relations of landlord and tenant here; and he assures me that there are many who contemplate in the most cold-blooded way the relief from a starving and redundant population by the operation of famine ... He complains that Clarendon's plans and schemes for employing the people and developing the national resources do not meet with the attention he has a right to expect from the Government and he doubts if John Russell comprehends or even reads them ...

May 30th

The account of [John] Mitchell's conviction [sentenced to fourteen years' transportation to Tasmania. He escaped.] has given great satisfaction here ... The good of it is that the Government has proved to the Irish and the world that they have the means of punishing these enormous offenders. And that they will not be able to pursue their turbulent and factious course with impunity ... So far as the system of terror is concerned, which is the only one we can now employ, it is a great and happy event, but it will not contribute to the regeneration of the country and will probably augment the fund of hatred against English connexion. Still, anything is better than political impotence ...

June 3rd

... the Government are now getting seriously uneasy about the Chartist manifestations in various parts of the country, especially in London, and at the
repeated assembling and marchings of great bodies of men ... the wide-
spreading disaffection of the people ... the enormous increase of cheap publi-
cations of the most mischievous and inflammatory character which were
disseminated among the masses and eagerly read ... The speeches which are
made at the different meetings are remarkable for the coarse language and
savage spirit they display ... [But] there appears to be a fatal security amongst
the majority whose sluggish minds cannot be awakened to the possibility of a
great convulsion here, not withstanding the continental conflagration that stares
them in the face ...

June 10th

At Ascot all last week ... These demonstrations are getting a great bore
besides being very mischievous ... Lord Londonderry told the Duke of
Wellington he was sure that if a collision took place, the officers of his Regiment
would not be able to restrain their men. Many people think that a severe chas-
tisement of these mobs will alone put a stop to their proceedings and that it
will be better if the Troops should be allowed to act and open fire on them.
This is an evil which must be avoided if possible, but anything is better than
allowing such an evil as this to go on increasing.

June 11th

The Duke of Bedford told me yesterday that he has had a letter from Clarendon
in which he gives him an account of his mode of proceeding which appeared
to him so dangerous and unwise that he has written to him on the subject and
spoken to John about it, who agrees with the D. It is the employment of spies
he objects to and which he says Clarendon is carrying on to an extent as great
as the old system of Sidmouth [Henry Addington, Viscount Sidmouth, Home
Secretary 1812–21, instituted during the distress and unrest of that period a
hated system of spies and *agents provocateurs* on the Russian/Austrian model]
which excited so much indignation ...

June 18th

... Lord Barrington asked me the other night if was true that his [Clarendon's]
opinions had undergone a great change and that he was now convinced that
Ireland could only be governed with and by the support of the Orangemen. I
told him there was, I apprehended, much exaggeration in this, but some truth
... but was convinced he would not suffer the ingratitude and misconduct of
the Catholics to interfere with his determination to render equal justice to all.

May 24th

We are on the brink of a crisis and one of the most fearful nature. The sugar question is going to destroy the Government ... I went to see Graham; I found him in a great state of alarm at the state of affairs and the prospect of the country. He said that he expected the Government would be beat, and that he did not see how they could go on if they were ... He looked on Stanley's coming into Government as inevitable. I asked him what the Cabinet would be: he supposed principally Peel's old Cabinet with G. Bentinck and D'Israeli; ...

June 25th

Everybody was full of the scene [the debate on reduction of sugar duties] in the House of Commons which seems to have been in the last degree deplorable and disgraceful ... nothing could exceed the virulence and intemperance of G. Bentinck's attack on Grey and Hawes [Benjamin Hawes, MP for Lambeth, under-secretary, Colonial Office] accusing them in terms not to be mistaken of wilful suppression of documents, and then the most disgraceful shuffling and lying to conceal what they had done and escape from the charges against them. On the other hand, John lost his temper; and as gentlemen in that predicament usually do, at the same time lost his good taste and good sense. He twitted G. B. with his turf pursuits ...

This brought D'Israeli to the defence of his friend, and he poured forth a tide of eloquent invective and sarcasm which was received with frantic applause by his crew; they roared and hooted and converted the H. of C. into such a bear-garden as no one ever saw before. When Hawes got up to defend himself they would not hear him and attempted to bellow him down with groans and 'Ohs', spurning all sense of justice and decency. It was grief and scandal to all reasonable men. Peel sat it out and never uttered a word, but he cheered Hawes when he was speaking ...

June 30th

... In the meantime however the division on Pakington's motion [Sir John Pakington Bt., MP for Droitwich 1837–74, had proposed an amendment condemning the Government's scheme] was generally known to be safe, and accordingly there was a majority of fifteen against it last night ...

July 5th

Since the division on Pakington's motion the Government stock has considerably risen, and they are now considered safe for the present and for some considerable time to come; they will probably get their sugar bill through ... Then the Chancellor of the Exchequer's announcement that the deficit of £2,000,000 will be reduced to £500,000 and that no new taxes will be wanted, has put people in better humour. The funds are rising, the harvest promises to be good, the Continent is in a better state . . .

London July 21st Friday

. . . The disgust felt here at the state of Ireland and the incurable madness of the people constantly worked on by the Agitators is now so great that most people appear to think that the sooner the collision takes place the better and that nothing is now left to be done but to fight it out and reconquer the country . . . no political measures can now avail to restore peace and to cement the union which in point of fact exists only in name. What makes the Irish question the more dreadful is that the potatoes are again failing, and starvation will be the inevitable lot of the people. In that emergency, when it arrives, the Irish will look in vain to England for no subscriptions or parliamentary grants or aid of any sort will they get; the sources of charity and benevolence are dried up; the current which flowed last year has been effectually checked by the brutality and ingratitude of the people, the rancorous fury and hatred with which they have met our exertions to serve them. The prospect, neither more nor less than that of civil war and famine, is dreadful, but it is unavoidable. [On 22 July 1848 the Commons suspended Habeas Corpus throughout Ireland.] . . .

July 31st

. . . The leaders are skulking about no one knows where; the [Repeal] clubs are either suppressed or self-dissolved; the people exhibit no disposition to rise; the sound and fury, which were echoed and re-echoed from the clubs and the meetings and through the traitorous press, have been all at once silenced. The whole thing is suddenly become so contemptible as to be almost ridiculous . . .

September 28th

I was about to record my own proceedings and such scraps as had occurred to me when my mind was diverted from all other topics by the intelligence of the death of George Bentinck. He had never studied political economy and knew very little on the subject, but he was imbued with the notions common to his party that the repeal of Corn Laws would be the ruin of the landed interest; he therefore hated the Anti-Corn Law League.

And considering that the first and most paramount of duties was to keep up the value of the Estates of the order to which he belonged, and that Peel had been made Minister and held office mainly for this purpose – he considered Peel's abandonment of protection and adoption of Free Trade as not only an act of treachery but of treason to the party which claimed his allegiance, and he accordingly flung himself into opposition with all his customary vehemence and rancour . . .

He brought into politics the same ardour, activity, industry and cleverness which he had displayed on the turf ... He brought the mind, the habits and the arts of an Attorney to the discussion of political questions; having once espoused a cause and espoused a party, from whatever motive, he worked with all the force of his intellect and a superhuman power of application in what he conceived to be the interest of that party and that cause.

... I have not the least doubt that, for his own reputation and celebrity, he died at the most opportune period; his fame had probably reached its zenith, and credit was given him for greater abilities than he possessed ...

November 29th

Melbourne died on Friday night at Brocket without suffering pain, but having had a succession of epileptic fits the whole day, most distressing to his family collected about him ... His taste for reading and information ... continued to the end of his life unbroken, though unavoidably interrupted by his political avocations. He lived surrounded by books ... he could converse learnedly upon almost all subjects and was never at a loss of copious illustration, amusing anecdotes and happy quotations ... he was often paradoxical, and often coarse, terse, epigrammatic, acute, droll, with fits of silence and abstraction from which he would suddenly break out with a vehemence and vigour which amused those who were accustomed to him and filled with indescribable astonishment those who were not ... From education and turn of mind, and from the society in which he was bred and always lived, he was Whig; but he was a very moderate one, abhorring all extremes, a thorough Conservative at heart, and consequently he was only half-identified in opinion and sympathy with the party to which he belonged when in office, often dreaded and distrusted his own colleagues, and was secretly the enemy of measures which his own Government originated, and of which he was obliged to take the credit or bear the obloquy ... He hated the Reform Bill which he was obliged to advocate. He saw indeed that Reform had become inevitable, and therefore reconciled it to his conscience to support the Bill; but he had not sufficient energy or strength of will to make a stand against the lengths which he disapproved ... [On Victoria's accession] he found himself placed in the most curious and delicate position which any statesman ever occupied. Victoria was transferred at once from the nursery to the throne – ignorant, inexperienced and without one human being about her on whom she could rely for counsel and aid ... She found in her Prime Minister and constitutional adviser a man of mature age who instantly captivated her feelings and her fancy by his deferential solicitude and by a shrewd, sagacious and entertaining conversation which were equally new and delightful to her ...

It would be rendering imperfect justice to Melbourne's character to look upon him rather as a Courtier than as a Statesman ... The Queen often pressed

him to take the garter, but he never would consent, and it was remarked that
the Prime Minister of England was conspicuous at court for being undeco-
rated amidst the stars and ribands which glittered around him . . .

His mind seems all his life long, and on almost every subject, to have been
vigorous and stirring, but unsettled and unsatisfied. It certainly was so in the
two great issues of religion and politicks, and he showed no profound convictions, no certain assurance on either . . . he never succeeded in arriving at any
fixed belief or anchoring himself on any system of religious faith . . . All his
notions were aristocratic, and he had not a particle of sympathy for what was
called progressive reform. He was a vehement supporter of the Corn Laws,
abused Peel with all the rancour of a Protectionist, and died in the conviction
that his measures will prove the ruin of the landed interest . . .

Bowood December 20th
The result of the French election for president has astonished the whole world.
Everybody thought L. Napoleon would be elected, but nobody dreamed of such
a majority. Great alarm was felt here at the probable consequences of Cavaignac's
defeat and the success of his rival, and the French funds were to rise if Napoleon
was beat and to fall if he won. The election has taken place; Napoleon wins by
an immense majority, the funds rise, confidence revives, and people begin to
discover that the new President is a marvellous proper man . . . And now there
is a pretty general opinion that he will be Emperor before long. The ex-Ministers
and Legitimists who were hot for his election, considering him merely as a
bridge over which the Bourbons might return to power, begin to think the
success greater than is agreeable . . .

1849

London January 2nd
The past year, which has been so fertile in public misfortunes and sorrows,
wound up its dismal catalogue with a great and unexpected calamity, the death
of Auckland, who went to the Grange in perfect health on Friday last, was
struck down by a fit of apoplexy on his return from shooting on Saturday and
died early on Monday morning . . . His loss to the Government is irreparable,
and to his family it is unspeakably great . . . Engaged from almost his earliest
youth in politics and the chances and changes of publick life, He had no
personal enemies and many attached friends amongst men of all parties . . .
His government of India was the subject of general applause till just as it was
about to close when the unfortunate Cabul [Kabul] disaster [it cost the lives
of the entire Kabul garrison] tarnished its fame and exposed him to reproaches
which he did not deserve . . . Lord Auckland bore this bitter disappointment

with the calmness and dignity of a man who felt that he had no cause for self-reproach, probably trusting to an ultimate and unprejudiced estimate of the general merits of his laborious and conscientious administration ...

This 'Annus Mirabilis', as it may well be called, is at last over, and one can't but feel glad at getting rid of a year which has been so pregnant with every sort of mischief. Revolution, ruin, sickness and death have ravaged the world publickly and privately; every species of folly and wickedness seems to have been let loose to riot on the earth ... we have had a general saturnalia – ignorance, vanity, insolence, poverty, ambition, escaping from every kind of restraint, ranging over the world and turning it topsy-turvey as it pleased. Every theory and crotchet have had full swing, and powers and dominions have bowed their necks to the yoke and cowered before the misbegotten tyranny which has replaced them ... They can think of nothing but overturning everything that exists and of reconstructing the social and political machine by universal suffrage! ... Universal suffrage is to pick out the men to frame new constitutions, and when the delegates thus chosen have been brought together – no matter how ignorant, how stupid, how in every way unfit they may be – they expect to be allowed to have their own absurd and ruinous way, and break up at their caprice all the ancient foundations and tear down the landmarks of society; and this havoc and ruin and madness are dignified with the fine names of constitutional reform ...

February 9th

... Ireland is like a strong man with an enormous cancer in one limb of its body. The distress is confined to particular districts, but *there* it is frightful and apparently irremediable. It is like a region desolated by pestilence and war. The people really are dying of hunger, and the means of aiding them do not exist. Here is a country part and parcel of England, a few hours removed from the richest and most civilised community in the world, in a state so barbarous and destitute that we must go back to the Middle Ages or to the most inhospitable regions of the Globe to look for a parallel. Nobody knows what to do; ... and while they are discussing and disputing, the masses are dying. God only knows what is to be the end of all this ... Lord Lansdowne (a Great Proprietor) is filled with horror and dread of the scheme that some propound of making the sound part of Ireland rateable for the necessities of the unsound, which he thinks is neither more nor less than a scheme of confiscation by which the weak will not be saved, but the strong be involved in the general ruin. Charles Wood ... contemplates (with what seems like cruelty though he is not really cruel) that misery and distress should run their course; that such havoc should be made among the landed proprietors that the price of land will at last fall so low as to tempt capitalists to invest their funds therein, and then the country will begin to revive ... it will be at a cost of suffering to the actual possessors and to the whole of the present generation such as was never contemplated by any system of policy. Lord Lansdowne thinks Trevelyan [Sir Charles Trevelyan, a name remembered in Ireland ever after for such thinking] is the real author of this scheme, who, he tells me, has acquired a real influence over Wood's mind.

March 2nd

In the midst of more important affairs the exposure that has just been made of Hudson's railway delinquency [the fall of the 'Railway King', George Hudson], has excited a general sensation and no small satisfaction. In the City all seem glad of his fall, and most people rejoice at the degradation of a purse-proud vulgar upstart who had nothing to recommend him but his ill-gotten wealth. But the people who ought to feel most degraded are those who were foolish or mean enough to subscribe to the 'Hudson testimonial' and all the greedy, needy, fine people who paid abject court to him in order to obtain slices of his good things.

March 30th

At Althorp the last three days for Northampton races. The day before I went there I had two hours with Graham who was very serious and very sad about everything, more especially Ireland and India . . . He is now prodigiously alarmed at the opposition the Rate in Aid [revenue levied at 6d in the pound throughout Ireland to rescue the bankrupt poor law unions] is meeting with from the Northern Irish, and greatly staggered by Twistleton's [chief Poor Law Commissioner in Ireland 1847–9] evidence and resignation, in short he is shrinking from his earlier opinions on this subject . . .

. . . Yesterday came the news of the defeat of the Sardinians [the movement for Italian unity led by the King of Sardinia/Piedmont, Carlo Alberto, was set back by the victory of the Austrian occupiers at Novarra] and the abdication of Charles Albert which was received with universal joy, everybody rejoicing at it except Palmerston . . . Yesterday there was a drawing room at which everybody, the Queen included, complimented and wished joy to Collouredo [Austrian ambassador] except Palmerston who, though he spoke to him about other things, never alluded to the news that had just arrived from Italy . . .

April 6th

Clarendon had a long interview with Peel who received him with the greatest cordiality and even warmth . . . and Peel professed the most earnest desire to do anything in his power to co-operate with C. in doing good to Ireland. They discussed Peel's plans and Clarendon stated to him frankly all his objections to them and why a great part of them was impracticable . . . His [Clarendon's] indignation against his own political colleagues is boundless. He poured it all out to me the other night, and he is equally indignant about the past and hopeless about the future; hopeless because John Russell is so feeble and infirm of purpose that he will not predominate over his Cabinet and prevent the chaos of opinions and interests which prevent anything Clarendon proposes being done. He proposes a great part of the obstacles he meets with to Charles Wood who is entirely governed by Trevelyan ... Then he says the Chancellor is a great mortgagee in Ireland, and on account of his own personal interests he resolutely opposes all the plans (relating to the transfer of property) which by any possibility can affect the mortgagee. [Clarendon wanted to make it easier to sell encumbered estates, something which eventually, under Gladstone, happened with considerable success.]

June 3rd

As usual at this time of year I have been too much occupied with the various races to devote any time to politicks or writing here. However I am always roused to exertion by anything about Palmerston ... The Duke of Bedford told me a few days ago that the Queen had been again flaming up about P. more strongly than ever. This was in reference to the suppressed Austrian despatch which made such a noise. [Palmerston, a major foreign affairs technician and a strong, disrespectful personality, tried not to trouble the Queen's modest head with too much detail and had been known to send a despatch before showing her a copy.]

... She sent for John Russell and told him she could not stand it any longer and he must make some arrangement to get rid of P. This communication was just as fruitless as all her proceeding ones ... But the consequence of not being able to get any satisfaction from her Minister has been that she poured her feelings and her wrongs into the more sympathetic ears of the late Minister, and the Duke told me that he knew that the Queen has told Peel everything, all her own feelings and wishes and all that passes on the subject. This John does not know ...

It is well known that Aberdeen and Stanley have for some time meditated a vigorous and combined attack on the foreign policy of the Government, and one day not long since, Aberdeen discussed the matter in full with Delane. He told him they did mean to make this attack, that He and Stanley and Peel were all agreed on opposition to Palmerston, that of Disraeli they were not so sure, and that Peel, though abhorring the foreign policy, was always in dread of doing anything to damage the Government ... The substance of this conversation D. repeated to C. Wood, and they discussed the possibilities that might flow from an adverse result in the H. of C ... The most curious part of it all is the carte du pays it exhibits and the remarkable and most improper position which P. occupies vis-à-vis the Queen, his mistress, and his own colleagues. I know not where to look for a parallel to such a mass of anomalies, the Queen turning from her own Prime Minister to confide in the one who was supplanted by him; the Chancellor of the Exchequer talking over quietly and confidentially with the editor of *The Times* newspaper by what circumstances and by what Agency his Colleague, the Minister for Foreign Affairs, might be extruded from the Government; the Q. abhorring her Minister and unable to rid herself of him; the whole thing is bad, discreditable and injurious.

July 29th

... Since that there has been a Great Foreign affairs debate, an attack on the F. policy arranged by Brougham, Stanley and Aberdeen. The Government expected to be beat, but by the help of proxies, they got a majority of 12. A day or two after, Palmerston made his devils (Bernal Osborne and M. Milnes) get up a discussion in the H. of Commons to enable him to make a speech. He made one (on a Saturday morning) impudent and clever as usual, skimming over with his usual nonchalance the bad parts of the case against him, and interlarding his speech with some very judicious remarks and very sound principles (the very reverse of his practice) and divers plausible clap traps for his Radical friends; the whole being as usual exceedingly well received by a very select audience; for I understand there were not 50 people present; Peel had left town and Graham went away. This speech and the majority in the Lords are construed into a triumph; and P. and Lady P. are on their high horses in consequence. So much for politics.

London September 15th Saturday

... a summons from John Russell to be at Balmoral on Wednesday 5th at half past two for a Council to order a Prayer for relief against the cholera. No time was to be lost, so I started by the five o'clock train, dined at Birmingham, went on by the mail train to Crewe where I slept; breakfasted the next morning at Crewe Hall, which I had never seen, and went on by the Express to Perth which I reached at half past twelve. I started on Wednesday morning at half past six and arrived at Balmoral exactly at half past two ... The place is very pretty, the house very small. They live there without any state whatever; they live not merely like small gentlefolks, but like very small gentlefolks, small house, small rooms, small establishment. There are no Soldiers and the whole guard of the Sovereign and the whole royal family is a single Policeman, who walks about the grounds to keep off impertinent intruders or improper characters ... I never before was in Society with the Prince or had any conversation with him. On Thursday morning John Russell and I were sitting together after breakfast when he came in and sat down with us, and we conversed for about three-quarters of an hour. I was greatly struck with him. I saw at once (what I had always heard) that he is very highly intelligent and highly cultivated, and moreover he has a thoughtful mind and thinks of subjects worth thinking about ... In the evening we withdrew to the only room there is beside the dining room, which serves for billiards, library (hardly any books in it) and drawing room. The Queen and Prince and her ladies and Gordon [Alexander Gordon, equerry] soon went back to the dining room where they had a highland dancing master who gave them lessons in reels. We (J. R. and I) were not admitted to this exercise, so we played at billiards ...

I had a walk on Wednesday with Aberdeen who came there for the Council ... [He] spoke much of the Q. and P. of course with much praise. They had seen with great satisfaction the downfall of the Hungarian cause, and chuckled not a little at it being a mortification to Palmerston. He said the Prince's views were generally sound and wise, with one exception which was his violent and incorrigible German unionism. He goes all lengths with Prussia; will not hear of the moderate plan of a species of federalism based on the Treaty of Vienna and the old relations of Germany; and insists upon a new German Empire with the King of Prussia for its Head.

1850

January 23rd

If I had not been too lazy to write about anybody or anything, I should not have suffered the death of Alvanley to pass without some notice ... He was the most distinguished of that set of roués and spendthrifts who were at the height of the fashion for some years – consisting of Brummel, Sir H. Mildmay, Ld. Sidney Osborne, Foley, John Payne, Scrope Davies and when all of them were ruined and dispersed (never to recover), Alvanley still survived, invulnerable in his person from being a peer and with the means of existence in consequence of the provident arrangement of his uncle who left him a considerable property in the hand of trustees, and thus preserved from the hands of Creditors ... Many a person has been astonished, after hearing the tale of Alvanley's abominable dishonesty and deceit, to see the Plaintiff and the culprit the dearest friends in the world ... When I recollect his constant treacheries and the never-failing placability of his dupes, I always think of the story of Manon L'Escaut, of whom he seems to me to have been a male prototype. It would be difficult to convey any idea of the sort of agreeableness which was so captivating in him ... he was unlike any of the great luminaries of his own or of bygone times; but he was delightful. He was so gay, so natural, so irresistibly comical, he diffused such cheerfulness around him, he was never illnatured ...

February 10th

The Greek Case [the affair of Don Pacifico, a Portuguese citizen and a Jew, who, having been born in Gibraltar, also claimed British citizenship, sued without success for damages after the burning-down of his house and theft of his wife's jewellery in Athens during a three-hour Easter riot watched by the police, following the banning of the popular festival of burning Judas in effigy. He received support from Palmerston, ultimately in the form of a threat of naval action.] will probably be settled thanks to French mediation, but it was a bad and discreditable affair and has done more harm to Palmerston than any of his greater enormities ... As far as P. is concerned, he will, as usual, escape unscathed, quite ready to plunge into any fresh scrape tomorrow, uncorrected and unchecked; he bears a charmed life in politicks, he is so popular and so dextrous that he is never at a loss, nor afraid, nor discomposed ...

February 22nd

... Last night I met Clarendon at dinner at Bath House ... He dined at the palace on Tuesday. I [had] told him they were sure to talk to him of foreign affairs, but he said that he should avoid it. The moment he came into the drawing room after dinner the Queen exploded, and went with the utmost vehemence and bitterness into the whole of Palmerston's conduct, all the effects produced all over the world and all her own feelings and sentiments about it. He could only listen and profess his own almost entire ignorance of the details. After she had done, Albert began, but not finding time to say all he wished, asked him to call on him the next day. He went and had a conversation of two hours and a half, in the course of which he went into every detail and poured forth without stint or reserve all the pent-up indignation and bitterness with which the Queen and himself has been boiling for a long time past ... The remonstrances and complaints, the sentiments and resentments of other sovereigns – of the King of Naples and of the Emperor of Russia, for instance – directly affected her dignity as the Sovereign and Representative of the Nation; and the consciousness that these sovereigns and all the world knew that She utterly disapproved of all that was done in her name, but that She was powerless to prevent it, was inconceivably mortifying and degrading ...

Tuesday June 18th

The great debate in the H. of Lords [essentially an attack upon Palmerston's conduct over Greece and more generally] came off last night in the midst of immense curiosity and interest. The House was crowded in every part; I never saw so many Peers present, nor so many Strangers. There were various opinions about the result, but the Government was the favourite. Bear Ellice [Edward Ellice, former Whig Chief Whip, acquired the nickname 'Bear' because of his Canadian fur trade connections.] offered to lay two to one they had a majority ... Stanley spoke for two hours and three-quarters. He has made more brilliant speeches, but it was very good, moderate and prudent in tone, lucid, lively and sustained ... I never was more amazed than at hearing the division never having dreamt of such a majority [Government defeated by thirty-seven] *reste à savoir* what Government (and P. especially) will do. If he was disposed to take a great line, he would go at once to the Queen and resign . . .

June 19th

There was a Cabinet yesterday, of course for the purpose of deciding what they should do, and the resolution they came to was *to do nothing*.

June 24th

Nothing of course thought of but the division on Roebuck's motion [pro-Palmerston, anti-Lords' vote]. The general feeling is that there will be a majority of about forty . . . it would be very absurd to make it turn on a mere question of numbers . . .

June 25th

Little progress was made in the debate last night; Graham made a strong speech. In the morning I rode with Brunnow [Russian ambassador] . . . He goes to Petersburg in August. The Emperor, [Nicholas I] (he told me) cannot comprehend our political condition and is at a loss to know why the Queen does not dismiss Palmerston; when he hears of the division in the H. of Lords, he will fancy that the Government will resign in consequence of it.

June 29th

. . . Palmerston came out on the second night with prodigious force and success [this was the famous 'Civis Romanus sum', speech]. He delivered an Oration four hours and three-quarters long which has excited universal admiration, boundless enthusiasm amongst his friends, and drawn forth the most flattering compliments from every quarter. It is impossible to deny its great ability; parts of it strikingly eloquent and inimitably adroit . . . [but] on an attentive and calm perusal, the insufficiency of it as an answer and a defence against the various charges which have been brought against him is manifest; but it is admirably arranged and got up entirely free from the flippancy and impertinence in which he usually indulges, full of moderation and good taste, and adorned with a profusion of magnificent and successful clap traps. The success of this speech has been complete and his position is now unassailable. John Russell may save himself the trouble of considering, when this is all over, how he may effect some change involving the withdrawal of the F.O. from Palmerston's hands . . .

July 1st

The day before yesterday Sir Robert Peel had a fall from his horse and injured himself seriously. Last night he was in immediate danger . . .

I rode with Grey yesterday in the Park . . . he said that it was remarkable that this discussion, which was intended to damage Palmerston, had left him the most popular man in the country; that of this there could be no doubt. [John] Bright had said that his vote had given great offence at Manchester, and that Cobden's vote and speech would probably cost him the West Riding at the next election that amongst all the middle classes Palmerston was immensely popular . . .

July 6th Saturday

The death of Sir Robert Peel (which took place on Tuesday night) has absorbed every other subject of interest . . . When we remember that Peel was an object of bitter hatred to one great party (and one great interest), that he was never liked by the other Party, and that he had no popular and ingratiating qualities and very few intimate friends, it is surprising to see the warm and universal feeling which his death has elicited . . . He scarcely lived at all in society; he was reserved but cordial in his manner, had few intimate friends, and it may be doubted if there was one person (except his wife) to whom he was in the habit of disclosing his thoughts, feelings and intentions with entire frankness and freedom. In his private relations he was not merely irreproachable, but good, kind and amiable . . . Nothing but a careful and accurate survey of his career, and intimate knowledge of his secret transactions of his political life and a minute analysis of his character can enable any one to form a correct judgment concerning him . . .

July 28th

This day week the radicals gave Palmerston a dinner at the Reform Club. It was a sorry affair – a rabble of men, not ten out of two hundred of whom I know by sight . . . The court are just as much disgusted with him as ever, and provoked at his success in the H. of Commons. The end of the Session promises to be more stormy than ends usually are, with the Ceylon Committee, the Irish franchise and Rothschild's seat, all troublesome and difficult. The Jew has behaved very ungratefully to John R., but it serves John right for his weakness in suffering himself to be dragged into a fellowship with him . . .

Brighton, August 25th, Sunday

Here for a week past. On Sunday last the death of Arbuthnot took place at Apsley House where he had been sinking for some time. He is a great and irreparable loss to the Duke who is now left alone in the world. Arbuthnot was almost always with him and had his entire confidence . . . The Duke, who for a long time has been growing gradually more solitary and unsocial, more irritable and unapproachable, is now left without any friend or companion . . . Arbuthnot's career has been remarkable. He had no shining parts and never could have been conspicuous in public life; but in a subordinate and unostentatious character he was more largely mixed up with the principal people and events of his time than any other man ... he had, in fact, a somewhat singular and exceptional position; much liked, much trusted and continually employed with no enemies and innumerable friends ... After the death of his wife [Harriet Arbuthnot, the diarist] he lived at Apsley House when in London, and during a great part of the rest of the year with the Duke at Walmer [as Warden of the Cinque Ports, Wellington had occupancy at, and grew very attached to, Walmer Castle] and Strathfieldsay ... He was buried at Kensal Green, and the Duke is said to have been much affected at the Funeral.

August 27th

Yesterday morning Louis Philippe expired at Claremont quite unexpectedly ... Not long ago his life was the most important in the world, and his death would have produced a profound sensation and general consternation. Now hardly more importance attaches to the event than there would be to the death of one of the old bathing-women opposite my window. It will not produce the slightest political effect, nor even give rise to any political speculation. He has long been politically defunct ... The worst Kings have seldom been destitute of many devoted adherents; but in his day of tribulation, although he may rather be accounted amongst the best than the worst, he was abandoned by all France, and his fall was not only unresisted, but suffered to take place with scarcely a manifestation of sympathy or regard ...

November 10th

But such trifles as these [a royal squabble about the precedence of the Duke of Cambridge], and such serious matters as an impending German war, are uninteresting in comparison with the No Popery hubbub which has been raised, and which is now running its course furiously over the length of the land. The Pope [Pius IX] has been ill-advised [he had created, without consulting the British Government, an English hierarchy of Catholic bishops] and very impolitic, the whole proceeding on the part of the Papal Government has been mischievous and impertinent and deserves the severest censure. Wiseman [see *supra*, now made Archbishop of Westminster and a cardinal] who ought to have known better, aggravated the case by his imprudent manifesto. On the other hand the Protestant demonstration is in the last degree exaggerated and absurd ... [John Russell] wrote a very imprudent, undignified and (in his station) unbecoming letter ... On the one hand it has filled with stupid and fanatical enthusiasm all the Protestant Bigots, and stimulated their rage; and on the other it has irritated to madness all the zealous Catholics, and grieved, shocked and offended even the most moderate and reasonable ... Clarendon writes me word that the effect it has produced in Ireland is not to be told ... Two days ago Bowyer [Sir George Bowyer, Catholic baronet, later MP], came to me from Cardinal Wiseman (who was just arrived) to ask my opinion whether anything could be done, and what. I said ... that now it was too late to do anything, John Bull had got the bit in his mouth and the Devil could not stop him ... This odious situation will continue till it is superseded by something else or expire for want of ailment more solid than fanatical denunciations.

[*November*] *21st*
... The Queen takes a great interest in the matter, but she is much more against the Puseyites [Tractarians, Anglo-Catholics, etc] than the Catholics. She disapproves of John's letter. I find their aversion to Palmerston is rather greater than ever, for to his former misdeeds is now added the part he takes about German affairs, on which Albert is insane; so that they hated him before for all he did that was wrong, and they hate him now for doing what was right ...

November 26th
... The Queen wrote a letter to Palmerston, which was of course Albert's production, in which she talked of Denmark wresting Schleswig from Germany, and that the triumph of Austria [in resisting Prussian primacy] would be fatal to the constitutional cause. P. treats their opinions and interference with great contempt and says 'What can they do?'

December 11th
I could no longer stand the torrent of nonsense, violence and folly which the newspapers day after day poured forth, and resolved to write a letter which was published in *The Times* the day before yesterday and signed 'Carolus' ... Then we see the headmaster of Rugby school petitioning the Postmaster-general to remove a letter-carrier because he is a R. Catholic! ...

At Windsor yesterday for a Council. My letter 'Carolus' has made a decided hit ... I brought Palmerston from the station in my brougham; all very amicable. We talked about popery and Germany, and agreed very well; he mighty reasonable ... I said no doubt it was desirable to see changes and improvements, and for various reasons that Prussia should be powerful but only if her power was acquired by fair means and without trampling on the rights of others, and on all obligations human and divine. He said 'Exactly, that is the real case; but her conduct has been so wanting in prudence, in consistency, in good faith that she has arrayed against her those who wish best to her.' ...

1851

Brocket Sunday (February)
[With the death of the former Prime Minister and the succession as 3rd Viscount Melbourne of his brother Fred, otherwise Lord Beauvale, an old friend of the

diarist, Greville became a frequent visitor to Brocket Hall.] Events have come quickly on us. On Thursday night Locke King brought on his annual motion for extension of the suffrage – leave to bring in a Bill. John opposed it but pledged himself he would bring in a measure next session, if he was still in office. Nevertheless he was beat by two to one, 100 to 52. The Conservatives went away, no trouble was taken, and this was the result ... Hume, Bright etc insisted on dividing, and one of them (I think Bright) insultingly said 'If you don't divide and overthrow him, he will throw over his promise and do nothing.' ... great and general was the consternation on Friday. John got up (just when the Budget was to have come on) and made a statement that was tantamount to resignation. The House dispersed in a state of bewilderment and the town was electrified by the news ...

London February 25th

Came to town yesterday morning – found everything unsettled: Aberdeen, Graham and J. R. trying to agree upon some plan, and to form a Government. At half past four, Delane came into my room, straight from Aberdeen. A. told him he was still engaged in this task, but, he owned with anything but sanguine hopes of success ... Went to Brooks's, found it very full and excited; some persuaded Graham and Co. would come to terms and patch the thing up ... Lord Lansdowne, Carlisle and Labouchere dined here (Bruton Street) [Greville had recently moved from Grosvenor Place to Bruton Street] and about eleven o' clock, a box was brought for Lord L. It was a circular from J. R. announcing the final failure of the Graham negotiation, and that everything was at an end ... Every body goes over the lists of Peers and Commoners whom Stanley can command, and the scrutiny presents the same blank result of men without experience or capacity save only Herries who is past seventy and has been rusting for the last twenty years and more, and D'Israeli who has nothing but the cleverness of an adventurer. Nobody has any confidence in him or supposes he has any principles whatever; and it remains to be seen whether he has tact and judgment enough to lead the H. of C.

[February] 27th

It appears that Stanley was to say yesterday whether he would *try* or not. He is trying ... His rabble are very violent and abuse him for not at once taking the Government. This does not make his position easier. D'Israeli has behaved very well and told S. to do what he pleased with him; he would take any office and, if he was likely to be displeasing to the Q., one that would bring him into little personal contact with her. If he could get anybody essential to his Government to join (Gladstone of course), he would act under him.

Friday February 28th

After another day of curiosity and rather a growing belief that Stanley would form a Government it was announced in the afternoon that he had given it up . . .

March 2nd

I heard last night the result of the Notts election. It was a very foolish thing for Lord Manvers to put up his son at all, but having done so, he ought to have left no stone unturned to secure the victory. The effect of this contest and the breach between Landlords and Tenants, unless it can be repaired, presents the most alarming sign of the times.

March 4th

The last act of the drama fell out as everybody foresaw it would and must. The Duke of Wellington advised the Queen to send for John again. He was sent for, came back with his whole Crew and without any change whatever. Granville [George Leveson-Gower, Earl (1815–91), Liberal statesman] dined at the Palace last night and the Q. and Albert both talked a great deal to him about what was passing and very openly . . . Her first and foremost aversions are Palmerston, whom she seems to hate more than ever, and D'Israeli next. It is very likely this antipathy (which no doubt Stanley discovered) contributed to his reluctance to form the Government . . .

May 10th

Journal in arrear. The day of the opening of the Exhibition [1 May] I went into the Park instead of the inside, being satisfied with insights in the way of procession and royal magnifience, and thinking it more interesting and curious to see the masses and their behaviour. It was a wonderful spectacle to see the countless multitudes, streaming along in every direction and congregated upon each bank of the Serpentine down to the water's edge; no soldiers, hardly any policemen to be seen, and yet all so orderly and good-humoured. The success of everything was complete and exultation of the court unbounded . . . Since that day all the world has been flocking to the Crystal Palace, and nothing but expressions of wonder and admiration . . .

May 31st

I have been too much occupied, even absorbed, by my Derby concerns to trouble myself about anything else, but I have been occupied to some purpose, for I won the largest sum I ever did win on any race – not less than £14,000, the greatest part of which I have received and no doubt shall receive the whole . . . meanwhile the world seems to have thought of nothing but the Exhibition, and all politics have appeared flat, stale and unprofitable. This has turned to the advantage of the Government ... Everybody now admits that they are quite safe for this session ...

July 5th

... Lord Derby's [the 13th Earl (1775–1851), a keen zoologist of whom Greville remarked elsewhere that 'he spent half a million on kangaroos'. Stanley succeeded him] death has taken Stanley out of the field for a time. D'Israeli made a foolish motion and bad speech. Government had a good majority; nobody took the least interest in the proceeding ...

London November 8th

About three weeks ago Kossuth [Lajos Kossuth, Hungarian patriot and revolutionary] arrived in Southampton and Winchester with prodigious demonstrations and a great uproar on the part of the Mayors and Corporations, the rabble and a sprinkling of Radicals of whom the most prominent were Cobden and Dudley Stuart ...

November 16th

At Windsor for a council on Friday. There I saw Palmerston and John mightily and cordial talking and laughing together ... The Queen is vastly displeased with the Kossuth demonstrations, especially at seeing him received at Manchester with as much enthusiasm as attended her own visit to that place. The numbers and the noise that have hailed Kossuth have certainly been curious, but not one individual of station or consideration has gone near him which cannot fail to mortify him deeply ...

Panshanger December 14th

At twelve o'clock yesterday morning the wonderful Electric telegraph brought us word that two hours before the President had established his Coup d'État at Paris with success. Everybody expected that it would happen, nobody that it would happen so soon ...

Panshanger December 14th

Naturally the French Revolution has absorbed all interest. The success of L. N's coup has been complete, and his audacity and unscrupulousness marvellous ... Few can approve of his violent measures and arbitrary acts, but on the other hand there is such a general feeling of contempt for the Constitution and of disgust at the conduct of the Assembly and the parties which divided it that nobody lamented their overthrow or regarded with the slightest interest or compassion the leaders who have been so brutally and ignominiously treated ... it is the object of his adherents to make the world believe that his measures were rendered necessary by a Socialist plot which he has saved the country by putting down; and besides this we hear of an Orléanist plot . . . These seem to be and probably are mere pretences got up to cover his violence with something plausible and which the world may swallow; the truth being that he has done all with singular boldness, secrecy, adroitness, . . . and relying (as it has turned out he could do) upon the Army, by whose aid he has taken all power into his own hands.

Sunday 22nd

. . . On Friday last Luttrell died at the age of eighty-one, having been long ill . . . He never took any part in public life, and was always in narrow circumstances and had the air, and I think the feeling, of a disappointed man. He was in fact conscious of powers which ought to have raised him a higher place than that which he occupied in the world . . . As it was, he never had any but social standing, but that was one of great eminence and success . . . he moved in the very best society, was one of the cherished and favoured habitués of Holland House and the intimate friend and associate of Sydney Smith, Rogers, Lord Dudley and all the men most distinguished in politics, literature and social eminence . . . His contribution to the pleasure of Society was in talk, and he was too idle and too much of a sybarite to devote himself to any grave and laborious pursuit. There are however so many more good writers than talkers . . .

December 23rd

'Palmerston is out' – actually, really and irretrievably out. I nearly dropt out of my chair yesterday when at five o' clock, a few moments after the Cabinet had broken up, Granville rushed into my room and said 'It is none of the things we talked over; Pam is out, the offer of the F. Office goes to Clarendon tonight and if he refuses (which of course he will not) it is to be offered to me.' . . . It now appears that the cause of Palmerston's dismissal (for dismissed he is) is his having committed the Government to full and unqualified approval of N's coup d'état which he did *in conversation* with Walewski [French ambassador] . . . Upon this piece of indiscretion to which it is probable that P. attached no importance, being so used to act off his own bat, and never dreamt of any danger from it, Johnny determined to act . . .

December 24th

To my unspeakable astonishment Granville informed me yesterday that Clarendon had refused the foreign office and that he had accepted it . . .

Brocket Hall Christmas Day

I received a letter from Clarendon yesterday with his reasons for declining. They are very poor ones and amount to little more than his being afraid of

Palmerston, first of his suspecting it was an intrigue to get rid of him, and secondly of the difficulties Pam would throw in his way at the F.O., he had advised John to take Granville but said if it was absolutely necessary, he would accept. I can't help thinking he will be mortified his refusal and advice being so immediately taken.

December 27th

... I have seen today an admirable letter of Guizot's, full of a melancholy and dignified resignation to a state of things he abhors, commiserating and ashamed of the condition of his country. He says if he were disposed to triumph over his enemies il a bien de quoi. Where, he asks, is Thiers, where is the Republic, where is Palmerston? France is now so frightened of Socialism and so bent on averting the peril of anarchy, that she will submit to anything. But this panic will one day pass away, and Government cannot be carried on for ever by Soldiers and Peasants, and in spite of all the intellect and all the elevated classes of the country.

Sunday

Yesterday Granville was with Palmerston for three hours. He received him with the utmost cordiality. 'Ah, how are you Granville? Well, you have a very interesting office but you will find it very laborious; seven or eight hours daily will be necessary for the current business besides the extraordinary and parliamentary, and with less than that you will fall into arrears.' He then entered into a complete history of our diplomacy, gave him every sort of information and even advice; spoke of the court without bitterness and in strong terms of the Queen's 'sagacity'; ended by desiring G. would apply to him when he pleased for any information or assistance he could give him. This is very creditable and (whatever may come of it) very wise, gentleman-like, becoming and dignified ... [Greville adds a later footnote: When G. came out of Pam's room and went into the dining room to get his hat, he found Peter Borthwick waiting; and the next day there was a bitter and malignant article in the *Morning Post.*]

1852

January 8th

Graham came up to me last night (laid up with gout) at a quarter past nine and went away at twenty minutes to one. In the course of four hours we discussed every subject of interest that now engages interest ... He thinks the present Government will not get through the next Session, that weak and unpopular as they are (and still further weakened by the loss of Palmerston), and surrounded by dangers and enemies on all sides, they must fall; and he does not think that his joining them or some of the other Peelites doing so (with or without him) would save them. It will not do to try to patch the old garment ... J. R. ought to go to the Queen and tell her he cannot go on, and then she ought to send for Aberdeen and him together and desire them to set about the formation of a Government. I suggested that it would never do to send for Aberdeen in this way; it would be taken as an insult to Palmerston and exasperate one half of the Whigs and make them unmanageable.

February 5th

... At length the moment arrived. In all my experience I never recollect such a triumph as J. R. achieved and such discomfiture as Palmerston's. [Russell revealed the episode of the previous year when the Queen had complained bitterly of a despatch sent off before she was consulted, also that on that occasion Palmerston had submitted to Cabinet opinion and withdrawn the despatch] John made a very able speech and disclosed as much as was necessary and no more. Beyond all doubt his great *coup* was the Queen's minute in 1850 which was absolutely crushing ... The effect was prodigious. P. was weak and inefficient ... Not a man of weight said a word for him ... [The crushing of Palmerston was a transient one. His amendment to Russell's Militia Bill of 16 February was carried, Russell resigned and Derby formed a Government.]

March 26th

... The new Government is treated with great contempt, and many of the appointments are pitiable; the most striking perhaps is that of Malmesbury at the Foreign Office, so ignorant and so mediocre as he is. But while it is the fashion to exalt Derby himself and treat with great scorn almost all his colleagues, I think Derby himself is quite unfit for the post of Prime Minister as any of them can be for those they occupy. His extreme levity and incapacity for taking grave and serious views, though these defects may be partially remedied by the immensity of his responsibility, will ever weigh upon his character and are too deeply rooted in it to be eradicated ... the notion of his being so high-minded and chivalrous and a pattern of integrity and honour, is a complete mistake. He is not so in private life – that is in his transactions on the turf where he is avaricious and unscrupulous – and it is not likely that a man should be one thing in private, and another in public, life ...

May 2nd

... The Derby Government had been sinking more and more in public opinion ... The Opposition were much elated at seeing the Government in this state and in fact they had a very good game to play when the petulance, obstinacy and imprudence of John Russell brought upon them a disastrous defeat, and set up the Government completely ... [Russell] came down to the House and opposed the second reading of the Militia Bill. The fault was enormous for the inconsistency was glaring. Palmerston immediately fell upon him with the greatest acrimony and lashed him with excessive severity, carrying the House along with him and evidently enjoying the opportunity of thus paying off old scores ... there was a majority of two to one in a full House. Nothing could exceed the exultation of the Ministerialists but the resentment and indignation of the Opposition ... J. R. was denounced as unfit to lead a party; still more again to be at the head of a Government ... Palmerston's conduct in this debate paves the way for his joining Derby if he chuses it, and it is by no means improbable that a large proportion of the Peelites will do the same.

The probability of this is increased by Disraeli's speech the night before last, on bringing in his Budget. This was a great performance, very able, and was received with great applause in the House. But the extraordinary part of it was the frank, full and glowing panegyrick he passed on the effect of the Free Trade measures of Sir R. Peel, proving by elaborate statistics the marvellous benefits which had been derived from his tariffs and reductions of duties – not however alluding to Corn ... It is difficult to say what may be the effect of this speech, but it seems impossible that any sort of Protection in any shape can be attempted after it ...

May 12th

... a studied ambiguity conceals [Ministers'] principles and their policy if they have either. It would however look as if they meant to pander to the No Popery rage which is now so rife, and to make the country believe they intend to give effect to the passionate desire, which no doubt largely prevails, to attack the Catholics in some way. This desire is very strong and general in this country, but in Scotland it is universal. Aberdeen told me the whole country was on fire, and they would like nothing so much as to go to Ireland and fight and renew the Cromwellian times, giving the Papists the option of going to 'Hell or Connaught'. As Ireland is equally furious, and the priests will send sixty or seventy Catholic members equally full of bigotry and zeal, all ready to act on the orders of Cullen [Paul Cullen (1803–78), Archbishop of Armagh, then Dublin, later Cardinal] and Wiseman, we may look for more polemical discussion, and that of the most furious character, than we have ever seen before, even during the great emancipation debates.

Bath July 7th

... The elections are now begun and a few days will disclose whether Derby's Government will be able to stand its ground or not ... Derby himself has shuffled and prevaricated and involved himself in a studied and laboured ambiguity which has exposed him to bitter taunts and reproaches, and Disraeli has been a perfect will o' the wisp, flitting about from one opinion to another, till his real opinions and intentions are become matter of mere guess and speculation. He has given undoubted proofs of his great ability, and showed how he could handle such a subject as finance with which he could never have been at all familiar ... The Opposition have, on the whole, been very moderate and fore-bearing ... [Palmerston] broke out into his old style about foreign politics and Austria and had the assurance to allude to his own Italian policy, and the silly impertinence to say that Austria would have done much better to take his advice and relinquish all her Italian dominions, – all of which was loudly cheered by his Radical friends, but the whole exhibition regretted and blamed by the more sensible of his own adherents ...

London July 23rd

After passing a fortnight at Bath, I returned to town a fortnight ago. The Elections are now nearly over, all indeed except some of the Irish. They have been on the whole unsatisfactory in every respect ... The end has been a very considerable gain to the Government, one with which they profess to be perfectly satisfied ... in this I think they are perfectly right, for they certainly will have more than 300 in the H. of Commons, all Derbyites, staunch supporters and move-able like a regiment. The Opposition will be as many or perhaps rather more but that is counting Whigs, radicals (of different degrees), Peelites and the Irish Brigade – different factions, greatly at variance amongst each other and who will rarely combine for any political object ... The conduct of the Government and their supporters has been just what might have been expected from their language and parliament; they have sacrificed every other object to that of catching votes; at one time and in one place representing themselves as Free Traders, and in another as Protectionists, and everywhere pandering to the ignorance and bigotry of the masses by fanning the No-Popery flame ...

Distinguished men have been rejected for mediocrities by whom it is discred-itable for any great constituency to be represented. The most conspicuous example of this have been Lewis in Herefordshire, Sir G. Grey Northumberland, and Cardwell Liverpool. [Philip] Pusey was obliged to retire from Berks and [Sir Edward] Buxton was beat in Essex, victims of Protectionist ill-humour and revenge. Both were succeeded by far inferior men who have no other merit than those Protectionist longings which they do not pretend they shall ever have the means of gratifying ...

This state of the parliamentary parties has the effect of reviving the resent-ment of the Liberals against J. Russell, as they attribute to him and his misman-agement the defeat they have sustained at the election and the present unpromising condition of the Liberal Party ... Brooks's grumbles audibly against John, and there is an evident indisposition to accept him again as Prime Minister ...

August 2nd

At Goodwood last week; glorious weather and the whole thing very enjoyable; a vast deal of great company – D. of Cambridge, D. of Mecklenberg, D. of Parma, D. of Saxe-Weimar . . . Derby was there – not in his usual uproarious spirits, chaffing and laughing from morning till night, but cheerful enough . . .

G. Lewis, whom I saw yesterday, gave me a deplorable account of the moral and intellectual state of the constituency of Herefordshire, enough to shake the strongest faith in popular institutions . . . the battle was fought entirely upon the question of Free Trade. There was no religious element there. He was beat by the Farmers and the small Proprietors, men with small landed proprietors by whom any diminution or rent was severely felt; and by the Clergy who went against him to a man because their incomes had likewise suffered by the fall in the price of grain on which their tithe commutation is calculated . . . The small freeholders were all for Lewis, and if they had voted for him as they had promised he would have gained his election; but no sort of intimidation or violence was spared towards them by the large farmers and they were frightened and driven to forfeit their pledges and vote against him . . . In many instances the voters did not know whom they were going to vote for, nor even who were the Candidates. They were made to vote against the Free Traders, and sent to the poll with tickets for the three Protectionists. [Lewis would find a seat in 1855 at Radnor and serve in a string of Cabinet posts.]

August 9th

I called on Graham on Friday and found the Duke of Bedford with him. He was exceedingly dejected at the state of public affairs . . . thinks the amount of bribery and violence which have prevailed has given a great stimulus to the question of ballot, for which the desire is greatly extending, and that it will be difficult to oppose it. At the same time he thinks the evil and mischief of the ballot enormous and more dangerous in its democratic tendency than any other measure of reform . . .

August 28th

Went to Bolton Abbey for two days before York races [where, as he tells a friend in a letter, he won £5000 – £250,000 in modern money] then to Nun Appleton for them; since that to Brocket and back to town . . . They don't appear to have so great a contempt for Malmesbury at the F.O. as I should have expected . . . The fact is, he is not a stupid man at all, but ignorant and inexperienced to the greatest degree.

London September 18th, Saturday

It was at Doncaster on Wednesday that I heard of the Duke of Wellington's death . . . in spite of some foibles and faults, he was beyond all doubt, a very great man . . . his greatness was the result of a few striking qualities – a perfect simplicity of character without a particle of vanity or conceit, but with a thorough and strenuous self-reliance, a severe truthfulness never mislead by fancy or exaggeration, and an ever-abiding sense of duty . . . The Duke was a good-natured but not an amiable man; he had no tenderness in his disposition and never evinced much affection for any of his relations. His nature was hard and he does not appear to have had any real affection for anybody, man or woman . . . Domestic enjoyment he never possessed, and as his wife was intolerable to him (though he always kept on decent terms with her, at least, ostensibly), he sought the pleasure of women's society in a variety of capricious liaisons (from which his age took off all scandal) that he took up or laid aside and changed as fancy and inclination prompted him . . .

Although the Duke's mind was still very vigorous and he wrote very good papers on the various subjects that were submitted for his judgment and opinion, his prejudices had become so much stronger and more unassailable that he gave great annoyance and a good deal of difficulty to the Ministers who had to transact business with him. He was opposed to almost every sort of change and reform in the military administration . . . the late Ministers often acted or refrained from acting in deference to his opinions and against their own and took on themselves all the responsibility of maintaining his views and measures even when they thought he was wrong . . .

Notwithstanding the friendly and eulogistic terms in which he spoke of Sir Robert Peel just after his death it is very certain that the Duke disliked him and had a bad opinion of him . . . [and] the Duke (though he sided with Sir Robert when the schism took place), in his heart bitterly lamented and disapproved his course about the Repeal of the Corn Laws, not so much from aversion to Free Trade as because it produced a fresh and final break-up of the Conservative Party which he considered the greatest evil that could befall the country . . .

His position was eminently singular and exceptional, something between the royal family and other subjects . . .

November 12th

The Question of Protection or Free Trade, virtually settled long ago, was formally settled last night, Derby having announced in terms the most clear and unequivocal his final and complete abandonment of Protection . . .

November 16th

Went yesterday to the lying in state of the D. of Wellington; fine and well done, but too gaudy and theatrical, though this is unavoidable . . . These public funerals are very disgusting mia sententia . . .

December 6th

... the world has been in a state of intense curiosity to hear the Budget, so long announced, and of which such magnificent things were predicated ... At length on Friday night Disraeli produced his measure in a House crowded to suffocation with Members and Strangers. He spoke for five and a half hours much too diffusely spinning out what might have been said in half the time. The Budget has been on the whole tolerably well received ... The people who regard it with least favour are those who will be obliged to give it the most unqualified support, the Ex-Protectionists, for the relief or compensation to the landed interest is very far from commensurate with their expectations ... I think it will go down and make the Government safe ... they have got from three hundred to three hundred and fifteen men in the H. of Commons who, though dissatisfied and disappointed, are nevertheless determined to swallow everything and support them through thick and thin ...

... the Duke of Bedford came to me yesterday and told me he had never been so disheartened about politics in his life or so hopeless of any good result for his party ... and Aberdeen, whom I met at dinner yesterday, is of much the same opinion ...

December 9th

Within these few days the Budget, which was not ill received at first, has excited a strong opposition, and tomorrow there is to be a pitched battle and grand trial of strength between the Government and Opposition upon it, and there is much difference of opinion as to the result ... Nobody knows what part Palmerston is going to take.

Panshanger December 18th

... We received the account of the division at Panshanger yesterday morning, not without astonishment; for although the opinion had latterly been gaining ground that the Government would be beat, nobody expected such a majority against them [They were defeated by 19 votes: 286 to 305.] ... [The debate] was closed by two very fine speeches from Disraeli and Gladstone, very different in their style, but not unequal in their merits.

Panshanger December 19th

Went to town yesterday morning to hear what was going on. Derby returned from Osborne in the middle of the day, and the Queen had sent for Lords Lansdowne and Aberdeen. She had been gracious to Derby and pressed him to stay on ... I gathered that they had already resolved to keep together and to enter on a course of bitter and determined opposition ... The language of the Carlton corresponds with this, and I have no doubt they will be as virulent and as mischievous as they can.

Went over to Brocket just now and found the Palmerstons there. He is not pleased at the turn events have taken, would have liked the Government to go on at all events some time longer, and disgusted at the thought of Aberdeen being at the head of it. This is likewise obnoxious to the Whigs at Brooks's ...

December 22nd

... [Lansdowne] had seen Aberdeen who had received no answer from John Russell, and A. was prepared if he did not get his acceptance the next morning (yesterday morning) to give the thing up ... this morning C[larendon] received a letter from Aberdeen announcing that John had agreed to lead the H. of C. but either without office or with a nominal one. And asking C. to take the Foreign Office ...

Hatchford 24th Friday

The great event of yesterday was Palmerston's accession to the Government. Lord Lansdowne had called on him the day before, and had, I suspect, little difficulty in persuading him to change his determination and join the new Cabinet ... he had agreed to take the Home Office. The next thing was Johnny's consent to take the Foreign Office ...

December 28th

It is singular that I have never attended a Council during the nine months Derby was in office, not once [Malmesbury, about whom Greville is so cutting, had his revenge in mutual ignorance, writing in *his* memoirs that Derby 'had not noticed his absence, as he never knew whether it was John or Thomas who answered the bell']; consequently there are several of his Cabinet whom I do not know by sight – Pakington, Walpole and Henley. With my friends I resume my function.

December 29th

Council yesterday at Windsor. I went down with the *ins* and we saw nothing of the *outs* who went by another train and Railway. Palmerston there looking very ill. They all seem on very cordial terms ...

1853

January 5th

The elections are all going well except Gladstone's who appears to be in very great jeopardy. Nothing could exceed the disgraceful conduct of his opponents, lying, tricking and shuffling as might be expected from such a party.

January 30th

Yesterday morning F. Lamb (Lord Beauvale and Melbourne) died at Brocket after a short but severe attack of influenza, fever and gout ... He was not so remarkable a man in character as his Brother William, less peculiar and eccentric, more like other people ... He never was in Parliament, but engaged all his life in a diplomatic career, for which he was very well fitted, having been extremely handsome in his youth and always very clever, agreeable and adroit. He consequently ran it with great success, and was in high estimation at Vienna where his brother-in-law Palmerston [married to Lady Cowper, sister of the two Lamb brothers] sent him as ambassador. He was always much addicted to gallantry and had endless liaisons with women, most of whom continued to be his friends long after they had ceased to be his Mistresses, much to the credit of all parties. After having led a very free and dissolute life, he had the good fortune at sixty years old to settle (as it is called), by marrying a charming girl of twenty. This Adine, who was content to unite her May to his December, was to him a perfect Angel, devoting her youthful energies to sustain his valetudinarian existence with a cheerful usefulness which he repaid by a grateful and tender affection, having an air at once marital and paternal ... He nominally belonged to the Liberal Party, but in his heart he was strongly Conservative, and he always dreaded the progress of democracy, though less disturbed than he would otherwise have been by reflecting that no material alteration could possibly overtake him ...

February 25th

The Jews and Maynooth question [the rights of those unlike Disraeli, professing the Jewish religion to sit in the Commons, and further money for the Maynooth seminary] have been got over in the H. of C. without much debate, but by small majorities ... Disraeli voted for the Jews but did not speak which was base of him. Last night I met Tomline [Member with Disraeli for Shrewsbury 1841–6] ... he says he [Disraeli] dislikes and despises Derby, thinks him a good 'Saxon' speaker and nothing more, has a great contempt for his party, particularly for Pakington whom they seem to think of setting up as leader in his place. The man in the H. of C. whom he most fears as an opponent is Gladstone. He has the highest opinion of his ability and he respects Gladstone as a Statesman ...

March 1st

... Last night the Marquis Massimo D'Azeglio [a major figure in the Risorgimento] came here. He was Prime Minister of Piedmont till replaced by Count Cavour and is come to join his nephew [Vittorio D'Azeglio, known unkindly as 'Minimo'] who is Minister here. He is a tall, thin, dignified looking man with very pleasing manners. He gave us a shocking account of the conduct of the Austrians at Milan in consequence of the recent outbreak.

Their tyranny and cruelty have been more like deeds in the Middle Ages than those in our own time; wantonly putting people to death without trial or even the slightest semblance of guilt, plundering and confiscating, and in every respect behaving in a manner barbarous and impolitic. They have thrown away a good opportunity of improving their own moral status in Italy, and completely played the game of their Enemies by increasing the national hatred against them tenfold. If ever France finds it in her interest to go to war, Italy will be her mark, for she will now find the whole population in her favour, and would be joined by Sardinia who would be too happy to revenge her former reverses with French aid ... [As all this actually happened at the end of the decade, Greville was fully entitled to add a footnote 'Remarkable prediction, verified in 1859.'] ...

March 3rd

Aberdeen has gained great credit by making Mr Jackson, Rector of St James, Bishop of Lincoln. He is a man without political patronage or connexion, and with no recommendation but his extraordinary merit both as a Parish Priest and a Preacher ...

March 10th

I met Flahaut [formerly French ambassador in Vienna, later in London] last night, just returned from Paris. He said that he found there a rancour and violence against us among all the Austrians, and Russians and Prussians no less, quite inconceivable ... Madame de Lieven writes to me in this strain, and even Liberal and intelligent Foreigners like Alfred Potocki [later Prime Minister of Austria] (who has been accused of being a rebel in Austria) writes that we ought to expel the [Italian] Refugees. At Vienna the people are persuaded that there is some indirect and indefinable participation on the part of the British Government in the insurrectionary and homicidal acts of Milan and Vienna, and they have got a story that the Assassin Libeny [executed for stabbing at Franz Josef] had a letter of Palmerston's in his shoe ...

March 24th

... [Aberdeen] said that the best thing for them to do was to bring forward a measure of so Liberal and popular a character as to make any serious opposition impossible. Clarendon agreed to this, and I told him that this had long been my own idea, and that what they ought to do was to throw open the civil and military appointments to competition, and to grant appointments after examination to qualified Candidates, just as degrees are given at the Universities ... [The Northcote–Trevelyan report of 1854 would successfully recommend exactly this procedure – for the Civil Service] ...

April 21st

[Gladstone's Budget] came off on Monday night. He had kept his secret so well that nobody had the least idea what it was to be, only it oozed out that the Income Tax was not to be differentiated. He spoke for five hours, and by universal consent it was one of the grandest displays of and most able financial statements that ever was heard in the H. of Commons; a great scheme, boldly, skilfully and honestly devised, disdaining popular clamour and pressure from without, and the execution of it absolute perfection . . . It has raised Gladstone to a great political elevation, and, what is of far greater consequence than the measure itself, has given the Country assurance of a *man* equal to great political necessities and fit to lead parties and direct Governments . . .

May 15th

. . . While I was at Newmarket came out the strange story of Gladstone [he had been talking in his customary improving way to a prostitute in Coventry Street] and the attempt to extort money from him before the police magistrate. It created for the moment great surprise, curiosity and interest, but has almost certainly passed away already, not having been taken up politically, and there being a general disposition to believe his story and to give him credit for having had no improper motive or purpose . . . it is very fortunate that G. was not tempted to give the man money, but had the courage to face the world's suspicions and meet the charge in so public a manner . . .

May 30th

Great alarm the last two or three days at an approaching rupture between Russia and Turkey as, if it takes place, nobody can pretend to say what the consequences may be . . . Still though matters look very black, Clarendon [who had become War Secretary] is not without hopes of war being averted and some means found of patching up the affair, the [Russian] Emperor having promised that he will in no case resort to *ulterior measures* without giving us notice of his intention. The difficulty for him now is to recede with honour, as it would be to advance without danger . . . Brunnow is in mortal agony, dreading above all things the possibility of his having to leave this country . . .

June 13th

. . . the great event has been the sailing of our Fleet from Malta to join the French Fleet at the mouth of the Dardanelles . . . The Emperor of Russia will be deeply mortified when he hears of this junction; or besides that it will effectually bar the approach of his Fleet to Constantinople, if he ever contemplated it, there is nothing he dislikes or dreads so much as the intimate alliance of France and England.

July 9th

For the last fortnight or three weeks little has occurred which is worth noting. The Eastern Question drags on, as it is likely to do. Aberdeen, who ten days ago spoke very confidently of its being settled, now takes a more desponding view . . .

July 12th

. . . All along Palmerston has been urging a vigorous policy, and wished to employ more peremptory language and stronger measures towards Russia while Aberdeen has been very reluctant to do as much as we have done and would have been well content to advise Turkey to accept the last ultimatum of Russia and so terminate what he considers a useless and mischievous quarrel.

London August 8th

Ever since last Monday when Clarendon made a speech in the H. of Lords on which a bad interpretation was put in reference to the question of peace or war, there has been a sort of panic, and the public mind, which refused at first to admit the possibility of war, suddenly rushed to the opposite conclusion, and everybody became persuaded that war was inevitable . . .

Sunday 28th

Charles Villiers told me last night that [Palmerston's] influence and popularity in the H. of C. are greater than ever, and if this Government should be broken up by internal dissension, he would have no difficulty in forming another and gathering around him a party to support him. This is what the Tories are anxiously looking to, desiring no better than to serve him, and flattering themselves that in his heart he personally dislikes his Colleagues and in political matters agrees with them, (Tories) . . .

September 3rd

The most important question now pending is what to do with the Fleets. They cannot remain much longer in Besika Bay, and must either retire to Vourla or enter the Dardanelles. The Emperor Napoleon wishes they should enter the Dardanelles, but only just, and not go on to Constantinople; and Clarendon takes the same view, proposing a mezzo termine . . .

Sunday 8th Thursday . . .

[Clarendon] said he would lay two to one the Emperor does not accept the modified Note; it will be a contest between his pride and his interest, for his army is in such a state of disease and distress that he is in no condition to make war; on the other hand, he cannot without extreme humiliation accept the Turkish Note. What will happen if he refuses, nobody can possibly divine.

September 20th

At Doncaster all last week [races] saw Clarendon yesterday very much alarmed at the prospect in the East. He thinks it will be impossible to restrain the Turkish war party ... the Russian Generals had actually received orders to prepare for the evacuation which the Emperor would have commanded the instant he heard the Turks were willing to send the Vienna Note. The Emperor Napoleon has again given the strongest assurances of his determination in no case whatever to separate his policy from ours, his resolution to adhere to the English alliance, and to maintain peace à tout prix which he frankly owns to be indispensably necessary to the interests of his country ...

Monday September 26th

At Hatchford all last week. Saw Clarendon on Thursday before I was there and heard that two ships of each Fleet were going up the Dardanelles, and that the rest would probably soon follow, as the French were now urging the measure. He was then going to Aberdeen to propose calling together the Cabinet, the state of affairs becoming more critical every hour, and apparently no chance of averting war ... He showed me a letter from Palmerston in which he spoke very coolly of such a contingency as war with Russia and Austria, and with his usual confidence or flippancy of the great blows that might be landed on both Powers ... Meanwhile the violence and scurrility of the Press here exceeds all belief. Day after day the Radical and Tory papers, animated by very different sentiments and motives, pour forth the most virulent abuse of the Emperor of Russia, of Austria, and of this Government, especially of Aberdeen.

October 4th Tuesday

Yesterday morning a Messenger arrived, bringing the telegraphic despatch from Vienna which announced the determination of the Turks to go to war, and that a grand Council was to be assembled to decide on the declaration, news which precluded all hope of adjustment ...

... Granville told me last night he thought P. was not at all displeased at the decision of the Turks, and as he still clings to the idea that Turkey is powerful and full of energy, and he is quite indifferent to the danger to which Austria may be exposed, and would rejoice at her being plunged in fresh difficulties and threatened with fresh rebellions and revolutions, he will rather rejoice than not at the outbreak of hostilities ... Palmerston is sixty-nine years old and it is too late for him to look out for fresh political combinations and other connexions ... He will therefore go on as he does now, but accept such popularity as is offered him as a means of enhancing his own importance in this

Cabinet, and in the event of anything happening to it, making his own pretensions available ...

October 18th

... In a letter this morning from my brother he says 'Lady Palmerston goes
crowing on at all the blunders of the Government and the luck that it is for
Palmerston.'

October 26th

Delane was sent for by Ld. Aberdeen the night before last when they had a
long conversation on the state of affairs, and A. told him that he was resolved
to be no party to a war with Russia on such grounds as the present, and that
he was prepared to resign rather than incur such responsibility ...

November 2nd

All last week at Newmarket, during which nothing of moment occurred but
the renewed attempts at negotiation and the consent of the Turks to defer the
commencement of hostilities ... Clarendon told me that he was heartily sick
of the whole question, in which the double trouble and difficulty were cast
upon him of reconciling the Russians and the Turks and of preserving agreement in the Cabinet where Aberdeen was always opposing measures of hostility
towards Russia, and Palmerston for pushing them forward.

November 10th

All attempts at settling the Eastern Question by *Notes* have been rudely interrupted by the actual outbreak of hostilities. Meanwhile the notes sped on their
way, but at Vienna it was deemed no longer possible to settle it in this manner,
and that there must now be a regular treaty of peace, the terms of which the
Allies might prescribe, and there is now a question of having a Conference to
carry on the affair ... Reeve [Greville's former assistant, see *supra*] is just
returned from the East, having spent some time in Constantinople, and came
home by Vienna ... Reeve has a very poor opinion of the power, resources and
political condition of Turkey, and does not doubt the military success of the
Russians. He says the corruption is enormous – everybody bribes or is bribed
... The whole state is rotten to the core.

November 27th

... Heard the particulars of the Reform Bill which (if there is to be one) seems
as little mischievous as can be. It appears to have encountered little or no opposition in the Cabinet, and John considers it as having been accepted and settled
there ... after criticising the Bill (ably as I am told) [Palmerston] ends by
announcing that he shall consent to it ...

I brought Clarendon from the Station to Downing Street when he told me that he had begun some fresh attempt at renewing negotiations ... He said nothing could exceed the difficulties of the case nor the embarrassments of his own position. The Turks are now indisposed to agree to anything, or to make any concessions whatever, and of course the E. of R. neither will nor can make peace and withdraw, without some plausible satisfaction. Then at home ... John Russell is very reasonable and agrees almost entirely with him; but whenever he thinks he is going to be outbid by Palmerston, is disposed to urge some violent measures also ...

December 12th Monday

This morning the Duke of Bedford came here and told me he had called on Clarendon on Saturday when he said to C. that he was very uneasy about Palmerston and thought he was meditating something, though he did not know exactly what he was at. C. interrupted him − 'Certainly, he is meditating breaking up the Government; in fact he has told me so.' ...

Panshanger December 14th

It turned out that Palmerston had struck on account of Reform and not (ostensibly at least) about foreign affairs ... John Russell was indignant ... saying he was absolutely faithless, and no reliance [was] to be placed on him ...

The news of the Turkish disaster in the Black Sea is believed [in fact, on 30 November, the Russians had destroyed Turkish ships in the harbour at Sinope] ...

December 24th

On Thursday at the Cabinet the resolution was taken which amounts to war. The French sent a proposal that the Fleets should go into the Black Sea, repel any Russian aggression and force any Russian ships of war they met with to go back to Sebastopol, using force in case of resistance. He [Aberdeen?] assented to this proposal and orders were sent accordingly. This must produce hostilities of some sort and renders war inevitable. It is curious that this stringent measure should have been taken during Palmerston's absence, and that he had no hand in it ...

Bowood December 26th

... Clarendon received a letter from Cowley [British ambassador in Paris] (while I was with him) in which he said he sent him a paper which tended to show that the E. of R. was bent upon the destruction of Turkey, and prepared to run every risk, and encounter any Enemy in pursuit of this object. This, I think, very likely; and what is equally likely that per damna ad caedes, and with much more danger and damage to himself, he will accomplish the ruin of the

Turk. But all speculation must be vague and fallacious as to the results of such a war as is now beginning.

VOLUME VI ENDS

VOLUME VII

1854

January 5th

Dined on Tuesday with the Chancellor: an array of Lawyers, the Chancellor of Ireland (a coarse, vulgar-looking man with twitchings in his face), Ld. Campbell, Alderson, Coleridge, and the Solicitor-General (Bethel); besides these Aberdeen, Graham and one or two more men.

I sat next to Graham and had much talk. He said the Cabinet that morning had gone off early, and he thought matters would go on quietly now. Palmerston quite at his ease and just as if nothing had happened, which was exactly like him ... In discussing the probability of Russia and Turkey being brought to terms we agreed that the conditions accepted by the Turks formed a sufficient basis. When I asked him whether this would not satisfy even Palmerston, and whether he would not be desirous of making peace if it could be brought about, he said he thought not, that Palmerston's politics were always personal, and that nothing would satisfy him now but to *humiliate* the Emperor ... The alterations in the Reform Bill (proposed on Tuesday) were principally these: to extend somewhat the disfranchisement and to give more of the seats to the counties (which was what both Lord Lonsdale and Lord Palmerston wished) and to reduce the county franchise from 20 to 10 ... the town franchise to be 36 with three years rating as originally proposed. This is intended to admit the working classes; as Clarendon said the *principle* of the last Reform Bill having been to *exclude* them, and to *admit* them ...

January 15th

I never yet noticed the extraordinary run there has been for several weeks past against the court, particularly the Prince ... It began a few weeks ago in the Press particularly in the *Daily News* ... and was immediately taken up by the Tory papers, the *Morning Herald* and the *Standard* and for some time they have poured forth article after article, letter after letter, full of the bitterest abuse and all sorts of lies ... the charges against him are to this effect: that he has been in the habit of meddling improperly in public affairs ... that he is German and not English in his sentiments and principles ... Then He and the Queen are accused of having got up an intrigue with foreign powers, Austria partic-ularly, for getting Palmerston out of office last year ... Charges of this sort, mixed up with lesser collateral ones, have been repeated day after day with the utmost virulence and insolence by both the Radical and Tory journals . . . those who come up from distant parts of the country say that the subject is the universal topic of conversation in the country towns and on railways. It was currently reported all down the North Road, and actually stated in a Scotch paper, that P. Albert had been committed to the Tower . . . It only shows how much malignity there is amongst the masses, and which a profligate and impudent mendacity can stir up . . .

January 16th

. . . There can be little doubt that the Tory Leaders got alarmed and annoyed at the lengths to which their papers were proceeding and have taken measures to stop them. The Radical papers nothing can stop, because they find their account in the libels; the sale of the *Advertiser* enormously increased since it has begun this course, and, finding perfect immunity, it increases every day in audacity and virulence . . .

February 1st

Parliament met yesterday; a greater crowd than usual to see the procession. The Q. and P. were very well received, as well as usual, if not better; all the *enthusiasm* was bestowed on the Turkish Minister, the mob showing their sympathy in his cause by vociferous cheering the whole way . . . In the Lords Derby made a slashing speech, but very imprudent which played into Aberdeen's hands who availed himself of it very well and made a very good speech . . . Derby was put into a great rage by Aberdeen's speech and could not resist attacking *me* (whom he saw behind the Throne). He attacked my letter [to *The Times*] in which I had pitched into the Tories for their attacks on the Prince. I saw his people turn round and look towards me, but I did not care a fig and was rather pleased to see how I had galled them, and struck home . . .

February 9th

Nobody now thinks of anything but of the coming war and its vigorous prosecution. The national blood is up, and those who most earnestly deprecated war are all for hitting as hard as we can now that it is forced upon us . . . The war is certainly very popular, but I don't think its popularity will last long when we begin to pay for it unless we are encouraged and compensated for our sacrifices by some very flattering successes . . .

February 20th

. . . The H. of Commons as well as the Country are so excessively warlike that they are ready to give any number of men and any amount of money, and seem only afraid that the Government will not ask enough. I expect we shall all have had enough of it before we have done with this question, and that our successes and the effect produced upon Russia will not be commensurate with the prevailing ardour and expectation here ...

March 6th

After a great struggle, John was persuaded to put off his Reform Bill, but only till the end of April, so that in a few weeks the same embarrassment will begin again. The satisfaction at it being deferred at all is great and general, and everybody thinks that some expedient will be devised for putting it off again, when the time comes so that we shall be rid of it for this year [reform did not come until 1867 at the instigation of Disraeli] ...

March 13th

The only event of recent occurrence was the dinner given last week to Sir C. Napier at the Reform Club with Palmerston in the chair ... [Graham] made an excessively foolish, indiscreet speech which has been generally censured ... [Henry Reeve's footnote quotes as follows: 'My gallant friend (Napier) says that when he goes into the Baltic he will declare war. I, as First Lord of the Admiralty, give my free consent to do so. I hope that the war may be short, and that it may be sharp.'] ...

March 29th

The die is cast, and war was declared yesterday ... We are already beginning to taste the fruits of it. Every species of security has gone down, and everybody's property in stocks, shares etc, is depreciated from twenty to thirty per cent. I predict confidently that before many months are over, people will be as heartily sick of it as they are now hot upon it. Nobody knows where our fleets and armies are going, nor what they mean to attempt, and we are profoundly ignorant of the resources and power of Russia to wage war against us. As the time for action approaches, Austria and Prussia grow more reluctant to engage in it. The latter has declared her neutrality and ... I do not believe the former will ever be induced to *act* with us against Russia.

May 3rd

... The death of Lord Anglesey, which took place a few days ago, has removed one of the most conspicuous of the comrades of the Duke of Wellington, who all seem to be, following very rapidly their commander. He distinguished himself greatly in the command of the Cavalry in Sir John Moore's retreat ... In the Waterloo campaign he again commanded the cavalry, not, (as was supposed) entirely to the Duke's satisfaction ... He lost his leg at the battle of Waterloo, being close to the Duke at the time when the few brief words that passed between them were characteristic. When the ball struck him, he turned

to the Duke and said 'B.G. I have lost my leg'; the Duke rejoined, 'Have you
by G?' For this wound Lord A. was entitled to a very large pension of which
he never would take a shilling. He was a great friend of George 4th ... but
their friendship came to an end when Lord A. connected himself to the Whig
Party, and when he went to Ireland as Lord-Lieutenant he deeply offended the
King by his open advocacy of the R. Catholic cause in 1829 ...

When the regiment of Guards became vacant ... King William sent for
Lord Anglesey and announced to him that he was to have it; he of course
expressed his acknowledgements, but early the next morning he went to the
King and said to him that he felt it his duty to represent to him that there was
a man worthier than himself to have this regiment, that Lord Ludlow had lost
his arm at their head, and that he could not bear to accept that to which Lord
L. was so justly entitled ...

May 7th
It is scarcely a year ago that I was writing enthusiastic pangyricks on Gladstone,
and describing him as the great ornament and support of the Government and
as the future Prime Minister ... but a few months seem to have overthrown
all his favour and authority. I hear nothing but complaints of his rashness and
passion for experiments; and on all sides ... that the City and the monied men
have lost all confidence in him ...

May 10th
Gladstone made a great speech on Monday night ... His speech was certainly
very able, was well received, and the Budget pronounced an honourable and
creditable one ... I do not yet know whether his defence of his abortive scheme
has satisfied the monetary critics. It was certainly very plausible and will probably be sufficient for the uninformed and half-informed who cannot detect any
fallacies which may lurk within it ...

May 12th
... E. Mills [Edward Mills, partner in the bank, Glyn, Mills & Co.] tells me
Gladstone's recent speech has immensely raised him, and he stands very high
in the City ... said he had lately met [Spencer] Walpole who told him he had
the highest admiration for Gladstone and thought he had more power than
ever Peel had at his highest tide.

June 25th
There never was such a state of things as that which now exists between the
Government, the party and the House of Commons ... Last week John Russell
opposed the motion for the abolition of Church rates in a flaming High Tory
and Church speech. The motion was rejected by a slender majority, but his

speech gave great offence to the Liberal Party and his own friends. Immediately afterwards came on the motion (in the University Bill) for admitting Dissenters to the University. This John Russell opposed again, although in his speech he declared he was in favour of the admission of Dissenters, but objected to the motion on various grounds. The result was that he went into the lobby with Disraeli and the whole body of Tories, while the whole of the Liberal Party and all his own friends and supporters went against him and defeated him by a majority of 91 . . . I think he has completely put an extinguisher on himself as a Statesman and as the leader of a party; they will never forgive him or feel any confidence in him again . . .

The people are wild about this war, and besides the general confidence that we are to obtain very signal success in our naval and military operations, there is a violent desire to force the Emperor to make a humiliating peace . . . and all sorts of stories are rife of the terror and dislike of the war which prevail in Russia, and of the agitation and melancholy in which the emperor is said to be plunged. But the authentic accounts from St Petersburg tell a very different tale . . .

September 4th

. . . They are not all satisfied with Raglan [formerly Fitzroy Somerset, subsequently Field-Marshal, Commander in Chief in the Crimean campaign] whom they think old-fashioned and pedantic . . . and are still more disgusted with his discouragement of the Indian officers who have repaired to the army, and who are, in fact, the most efficient there are . . . It is very curious that neither the Government nor the Commanders have the slightest information as to the Russian force in the Crimea nor the strength of Sebastopol . . .

September 11th

. . . So certain are they of taking Sebastopol that they have already begun to discuss what they will do with it when they have got it. Palmerston wrote Clarendon a long letter setting forth the various alternatives and expressing his own opinion that the Crimea should be restored to the Turks . . .

October 2nd

. . . On Saturday came the news that Sebastopol had been taken which we did not believe a word of, but after dinner came the telegraphic account of the victory gained on the 20th on the heights above the Alma . . .

October 8th Sunday

The whole of last week the newspapers without exception (but the *Morning Chronicle* particularly) with *The Times* at their head, proclaimed the fall of Sebastopol in flaming and triumphant article with colossal type, together with divers victories and all sorts of details, all of which were trumpeted all over the town and circulated through the country. I never believed one word of it and entreated Delane to be less positive and more cautious, but he would not hear of it, and the World swallowed the news whole and believed it ... When the bubble burst, the rage and fury of the deluded journals knew no bounds and *The Times* was especially sulky and spiteful ...

November 4th

... In *The Times* of yesterday appeared a very able letter of Bright's with his view of the war and the faults committed by our Government in respect to it, which as nearly as possible expresses my own opinion on the subject. I never agreed with those who fancy that by mere bluster we might have averted the war, but I think by more firmness towards not only Russia but towards Turkey and still more towards the press and public excitement here, together with a judicious employment of the resources of diplomacy, we might have prevented it. However we are in for it and I not only see no chance of getting soon out of it, but I do not feel the same confidence that everybody does, that we are certain to carry it to a successful end.

London, November 13th

At Worsley all last week; nothing thought of but the war, its events and vicissitudes. The tardiness of intelligence and the perplexity and agitation caused by vague reports and telegraphic messages drive everybody mad; from excessive confidence, the public, always nose-led by the newspapers, is fallen into a state of alarm and discouragement ... There does not seem at the moment more reason to doubt that we shall take Sebastopol than there ever was, but the obstinate defence of the Russians indicates that its capture will not be effected without a tremendous struggle and great sacrifice of life ... there is no disguising from ourselves that we have got a much tougher job on our hands than we ever contemplated ... We are now talking of sending every soldier we possess to the scene of the action and expending our military resources to the last drop, leaving everything else at home and abroad to take care of itself ...

November 14th

Yesterday morning news of another battle from which we may expect a long list of killed and wounded [the Battle of Inkerman, 5 November 1854]. The affair of the 25th [the charge of the Light Brigade at Balaclava], in which our light cavalry was cut to pieces, seems to have been the result of mismanagement in some quarter, and the blame must attach either to Lucan, Cardigan, Captain Nolan (who was killed) or to Raglan himself. Perhaps nobody is really to blame, but if anyone be, my own impression is that it is Raglan. He *wrote* the order and it was his business to make it so clear that it could not be mistaken and to give it conditionally ... [to] prevent its being vigorously enforced under circumstances which he could not foresee, or of which he might have no cognisance.

November 16th
Telegraphic despatch from Raglan with account of the battle of the 5th, from which we learn only that we were entirely successful at repulsing the Russian attack, but that our loss was very great. Another long interval of suspense to be succeeded by woe and mourning ...

November 23rd Thursday
Last week at Savernake and at the Grange; came back on Tuesday; and yesterday morning arrived the despatches with account of the furious battle of Inkerman in which, according to Raglan's account, 8000 English and 6000 French resisted the attack of 60,000 Russians and eventually drove them back with enormous loss, our own loss being very great ... admitting that there may be some exaggeration in estimate of the numbers of the Russians and their loss, it still remains one of the most wonderful feats of arms that was ever displayed ... My brother lost his youngest and favourite son [Cavendish Hubert Greville, second son of Algernon Greville] in this battle – a boy of 18 who had only landed in the Crimea a few weeks before and who was in a great battle for the first and last time ... This is only one of innumerable instances of the same kind, and half England is in mourning ... But the Nation is not only as warlike as ever, but if possible more full of ardour and enthusiasm, and thinking of nothing but the most lavish expenditure of men and money to carry on the war ...

November 29th
In the evening I met Clarendon at the Travellers' and had a long talk with him about all sorts of things ... We talked over Raglan and his capacity for his command, and we both agreed that he had given no proofs of his fitness for so mighty a task. C. said that he was struck by the badness of his private letters, and he had been from the beginning by those from Varna, and that he had evidently not a spark of imagination and no originality. We both agreed that it would never do to express a hint of a doubt about his merits or capacity ... His personal bravery is conspicuous and he exposes himself more than he ought ... C. says there is no chance of taking Sebastopol this year, nor of taking it at all till we have an army strong enough to drive the Russian out of the Crimea ...

December 11th

At Middleton on Saturday. There I saw a letter from Stafford who is at Constantinople tending the sick and wounded ... He says he had heard so much about the sufferings and privations of the Soldiers, and of the bad state of the hospitals, that he resolved to go there and judge for himself the truth of all that had been written and asserted on the subject; that he did so and found the very worst accounts exceeded by the reality, and that nothing could be more frightful and appalling than it all was. It has greatly improved, but was still bad enough ... He says that while nothing could exceed the heroism of our soldiers, the incapacity of their Chiefs was equally conspicuous, and that the troops had no confidence in their leaders; he adds, it is essential to give them a good general if the war goes on ... Bright has published his letter in a penny form (or somebody has done it for him) with pièces justicatives extracted from the Blue Books and from other sources, and, in my opinion he makes out a capital and unanswerable case. He does not indeed prove, (nor attempt to prove) that the Emperor of Russia is in the right absolutely, but he makes out that he is in the right as against England and France, and he shows up the conduct of the Western Powers very successfully. But in the present temper of the country, and while the war fever is still raging with undiminished violence, all appeals to truth and reason will be totally unavailing ... I do not dare to avow them myself; and even for holding my tongue, and because I do not join in the senseless clamour which everywhere resounds, I am called 'a Russian' ...

December 18th

The dislike of the Foreign Enlistment Bill [it provided for the recruitment of 15,000 non-British nationals in the British Army and was denounced as unconstitutional, especially in the House of Lords, before finally passing] is very general, but nobody can give any reason for their opposition to it.

The Grove December 31st

The last day of one of the most melancholy and disturbing years I ever recollect. Almost everybody is in mourning, and grief and despair overspread the land. At the beginning of the year we sent forth an Army amidst a tumult of joyous and triumphant anticipation and everybody full of confidence and boasting and expecting to force the Emperor Nicholas in the shortest possible time humbly to sue for peace, and the only question was what terms we should vouchsafe to grant him, and how much of his dominions we should leave him in possession of. Such presumptuous boasting and confidence have been signally humbled, and the end of this year sees us deploring the deaths of friends and relations without number, and our Army perishing before the walls of Sebastopol which we are unable to take and after bloody victories and prodigies of valour, the Russian power hardly yet diminished or impaired. All last week I was at Hatchford with Grey ... Grey's idea is that there has been much mismanagement here and still greater on the spot, and that Raglan is quite incompetent and, as far as we can see, nobody any better ...

1855

January 14th

... The court exceedingly annoyed and alarmed at Raglan's failure; Prince showed Clarendon (or told him of) a letter from Colonel Steele [Raglan's secretary] who said that he had no idea how great a mind Raglan had, but that he now saw it, for in the midst of distresses and difficulties of every kind in which the Army was involved he was perfectly serene and undisturbed, and his health excellent!! Steele meant this as a panegyrick, and did not see that it really conveyed a great reproach. The conviction of his incapacity for so great a command gains ground every day ...

January 22nd

Every day one looks with anxiety to see and to hear whether the chances of peace look well or ill, and at present they look very ill ... Parliament meets tomorrow, and I think a very short time will elapse before the fate of the Government is decided by some vote about the conduct of the war. I think the Government themselves desire it and ... would not be sorry to be driven out in a respectable way of ending than by those internal dissensions which, like a cancer, are continuously undermining them ...

January 24th

The Government is at an end, or at least probably will be before the end of the day. The Duke of Bedford has just been to me to tell me that last night after returning from the H. of C. John [Russell] wrote a letter to Aberdeen to resign his office, and he will not attend the Cabinet today. Nobody knows it but A. himself and I am not permitted to tell Granville even, but it will be announced to the Cabinet this evening. The immediate cause of John's resignation is Roebuck's [John Arthur Roebuck, Radical MP for Sheffield] motion ... which would have been turned into a motion of censure and want of confidence ... Accordingly, he said he could not and would not face this motion: Graham and Sidney Herbert might defend the conduct of the war, but *he* could not ... Nothing can in my opinion, justify John, and his conduct will, if I am not mistaken, be generally condemned and deprive him of the little consideration and influence he had left ...

January 26th

Yesterday morning the Cabinet met, and after some discussion they resolved unanimously not to resign, but to encounter Roebuck's motion . . .

January 31st

The division was curious: some seventy or eighty Whigs, ordinary supporters of Government, voted against them, and all the Tories, except about six or seven who voted against the motion; Cobden and Bright staid away.

John Russell's explanation, had he spoken the truth, would have run in these terms 'I joined the Government with the greatest reluctance, and only at the earnest entreaty of my friends, particularly Lord Lansdowne. From the first I was disgusted at my position, and I resolved unless Lord Aberdeen made way for me, and I again became Prime Minister, that I would break up the Government. I made various attempts to bring about such a charge, and at last, after worrying everyone to death for many months, I accomplished my object, having taken what seemed a plausible text for doing it.'

February 2nd

The Queen herself decided to send at once to Derby, and the result proves how wise her decision was, for She is relieved from the annoyance of having him, and he is placed in such a position that he cannot embarrass her new Government when it is formed. Derby went to Palmerston, invited him to join and bring Gladstone and Sidney Herbert with him. On their declining, he gave it up and H.M. then sent for Lord Lansdowne.

Sunday February 4th

. . . It has been seen how Derby failed; she then sent for Lansdowne whom she desired to go about and consult different people and see what their opinions and inclinations were, and report them to her. This was on Friday. He did so and made his report after which, on the same principle which had decided her to send for Derby, she resolved to send for John Russell, his supporters having been the strongest element in the victorious majority. Accordingly, on a Friday night or early yesterday morning, she placed the formation of a Government in his hands . . . However the result of his applications was so unfavourable that last night he considered his attempt virtually at an end though he had not actually given it up this morning, and some further communication was taking place between him and Clarendon, which was to be decisive. As soon as this is over, the Queen will play her last card and have recourse *to the man of the people!* – to Palmerston, whom they are crying out for, and who (they fondly imagine) will get us out of all our difficulties . . .

February 7th

Yesterday Aberdeen and Newcastle, particularly the latter, renewed their endeavours to prevail on Gladstone to give up his scruples and to join the Government, and at last they succeeded, and in the evening Palmerston was able to announce that he had succeeded in his task and the Government was formed . . .

February 17th

Palmerston presented himself to the H. of C. last night for the first time as Minister, and not apparently with a very brilliant prospect of success . . . The great point he had to handle was the disposal of Roebuck's committee [of enquiry into the conduct of the war] which he is determined (if he can) to get rid of. The success of this seems very doubtful. One man after another got up and declared he should vote for its going on. Roebuck insists on it; and Disraeli announced his determined opposition to any attempt to quash it . . .

February 19th

The Government have determined to knock under about Roebuck's Committee, and would have done very much better (as I told Granville) to have done so at first. But the state of the House of Commons is such that nothing but some very unexpected turn can enable them to go on long . . . For the first time in my life I am really and seriously alarmed at the aspect of affairs and think we are approaching a period of real difficulty and danger. The Press, with *The Times* at its head, is striving to throw everything into confusion and running amuck against the aristocratic element of society and of the Constitution . . .

February 23rd

Graham, Gladstone and S. Herbert have resigned, greatly to the disgust and indignation of their colleagues, to the surprise of the world at large, and the uproarious delight of the Whigs and Brooks's Club, to whom the Peelites have always been odious. These stupid Whigs . . . are entirely indifferent to the consideration that the greater part of the brains of the Cabinet is gone out with these three, that it is exceedingly difficult to fill their places, and that we exhibit a sad spectacle to all Europe . . .

March 2nd

News just arrived that the Emperor of Russia is dead . . .

March 10th

It is remarkable that though seven days have elapsed since the news of the E. of R's death reached us, and that we heard it by an electric telegraph the very day it happened, we are still without authentic and detailed information of what has since occurred at St Petersburg . . . so that we have no means of

judging whether the chances of peace are improved by the accession of
Alexander II . . .

[Palmerston] finds great difficulty in filling the vacant offices and evinces
much want of tact and good management in his endeavours to do so, offering
and retracting his offers in a very loose way. For example he offered Sir R.
Peel [the late Prime Minister's easygoing eldest son] the Clerkship of the
Ordnance which he accepted; and then he found Monsell did not mean to
resign it, so he had to withdraw the offer. Then he told him he should be
Colonial under-secretary if J. Russell [Russell, who had been made plenipotentiary to the peace negotiations in Vienna, had been recalled after the resignations to be Colonial Secretary] would consent. J. R. would not consent, and
then he offered him a seat at the Admiralty. Sir R. in some dudgeon demurred,
and P. inferring from his ill-humour that he would not take this place, offered
it to Henry Brand [later, 1872–84, Speaker] who accepted, desired his writ
might be moved for, and went to the railway station to go down to the place
he represented [Lewes]. Just as he was starting, a Messenger arrived with a
letter for P. saying Sir R. Peel had taken the Admiralty, so he could not have
it and the gentleman had to return home without any office at all.

March 31st

Having no public events nor any secret information to record, I must put down
my own private concerns, uninteresting as they are. I am busy on the task of
editing a volume of [Tom] Moore's correspondence . . . and finishing the
second article upon Joseph [Bonaparte]'s Memoirs. These small literary occupations interest and amuse me . . . it is well I can amuse myself with them; and
now that I am growing old (for I shall be sixty-one the day after tomorrow)
it is my aim to cultivate these pleasures more and more, and make them my
refuge against the infirmities which beset me, and the loss of youth. My great
fear is lest my eyesight fail, and I earnestly hope I may die before such a
calamity should befall me.

April 14th

. . . for the last fortnight all interest in peace and war and in all political questions has been absorbed in the dreadful catastrophe of Frank Villiers, [Tory
MP for Rochester] which has created a sensation in society just like that of
poor De Ros's affair some years ago.

Everybody who knew him well was aware that his reckless extravagance
and the system of borrowing at enormous interest with the security of friends
must sooner or later come to an end and produce a fearful smash. But nobody
imagined or suspected the dreadful reality and that, besides the money, for
which he had got the names of Lords Glasgow, Bath, Clifden and a host of
others who were foolish enough to become his securities, he had raised enor-

mous sums upon bills, the acceptances of which were all forgeries. This appalling discovery has overwhelmed his family with grief and horror, and the whole of society with astonishment and disgust. It is not yet known when he began these practices nor who were his accomplices except that he had one in the person of a Mrs Edmunds, already famous as a whore, bawd and usurer, and who was more than suspected of having been a party to certain forgeries upon the late Ld. Lichfield.

It is now about a month or five weeks ago that he suddenly disappeared. He never was seen in the H. of Commons and much surprise was excited when he did not attend the Spring races at Epsom. It began then to be surmised that there was something wrong; and when the week after at Northampton races, he was neither seen nor heard of, the matter began to be generally talked about, and mysterious hints were whispered that he had been obliged to abscond for good and all. Soon he became the talk of London and a report was circulated that he was not only overwhelmed with debt but concerned in some cases of forgery. These reports continued to spread and in a very short time, the whole truth became known and was communicated to his family. Lord Jersey placed the whole matter in the hands of his solicitor (Frere) who advised him to wash his hands of it altogether.

But Disraeli who was apprised of the whole matter, went to Lord Jersey and strongly advised him to prevent if possible the cases of forgery being brought out in a Court of Justice and to employ Padwick to ascertain the amount of the forged bills and buy them up. After some hesitation Jersey consented to do this and Ly. J. agreed to produce the money. Padwick set to work having a written authority from Lord J. to buy up the bills, which are said to amount to about £40,000, the whole of the debts, good and bad, amounting to £80,000 or £100,000. Meanwhile nothing was heard of F. and nobody knew where he had gone nor anything about him. The only letter (so far as I know) that he wrote was one to Lawley without dates or place or time in which he said that he had been compelled to keep out of the way for a time, having been the victim of an atrocious conspiracy got up for political motives; that he should have a most extraordinary story to tell him when he returned which should be quite soon. That he was employed in sifting this conspiracy to the bottom and should cover the conspirators with confusion and bring them to justice.

For what purpose this tissue of lies and absurdity was written it is difficult to guess ... very soon the accumulating evidence put an end to all such hopes. So matters stood up to the Craven meeting, and it was generally known that the Jerseys were preparing to make a great pecuniary sacrifice and that the forged bills at least would be bought up and perhaps a part, if not the whole, of the good liabilities be provided for. But in the middle of last week Padwick received a communication from Lord Jersey or his Solicitor withdrawing the

authority that had been given him and announcing that they had resolved to
pay nothing and let the affair take its course ... the consequence of it will
inevitably be that the whole thing will come out in some Court and criminal
proceedings will be taken against F. if they can only catch him. It is supposed
that he has taken refuge in some country with which there exists no treaty of
extradition ... there is now a run against the aristocracy and though without
just cause a case of such enormous villainy is sure to be commented on in
terms calculated to heighten the prevailing and growing prejudice. [In fact,
the Jerseys did pay up, not least because of the solicitous attentions of Disraeli,
one of whose own bills had once fallen into the hands of Mrs Edmunds. The
episode would bring Greville and Disraeli together, (see *post*), 12 November
1855. Francis Villiers did not return to this country, but died a few years later
in that classic resort of English delinquency, Spain. Henry Reeve suppressed
this story from his edition of the *Memoirs*. Strachey and Fulford restored it.]

April 17th

Yesterday I went out 'with all the gazing town' to see not the least curious of
the many curious events I have lived to witness, the entry of the Emperor and
Empress of the French into London.

April 20th

The visit of the Emperor has been one continued ovation, and the success of
it complete. None of the Sovereigns who have been here before have ever been
received with such magnificence by the court or by such curiosity and delight
by the people. Wherever and whenever they have appeared, they have been
greeted by enormous multitudes and prodigious acclamations ... Everybody
is struck with his mean and diminutive figure and vulgar appearance, but his
manners are good and not undignified ... When he was invested with the
Garter, he took all sorts of oaths – old feudal oaths – of fidelity and Knightly
service to the Queen.

Paris June 17th

Having resolved to go to Vichy for my health, here I am on the road; crossed
over yesterday morning, a very disagreeable but short passage from Folkestone,
good journey by rail, and got here at nine o'clock, lodged very hospitably at
the Embassy. French carriages on the railway are very much better than ours,
particularly second class; country between Boulogne and Paris looking well
and thriving ...

Paris June 23rd Sunday

I came here to pass through to Vichy, and accordingly on Tuesday last to
Vichy I went. I arrived there in the evening, found a detestable apartment

without a fireplace; the weather was intolerable, it never ceased raining, and the cold was intense. Finding that it was useless to take the waters in such weather, and being disgusted with the whole thing, I resolved to return to Paris which I did on Friday, and here I am comfortably established in the Embassy again ...

Thursday 27th

Yesterday morning arrived an invitation to dine at the Tuileries the same evening. I went there, was ushered into a room with eight or ten men in it, none of whom I knew except Count Bacciochi [First Chamberlain to Louis Napoleon] ... In a few minutes H.M. made his appearance; he immediately came up to me, bowed very civilly and asked me the usual questions of when I came to Paris, etc. In a minute dinner was announced and we went in ... At dinner (which did not last above twenty-five minutes) he talked (a sort of dropping conversation) on different subjects, and I found him so easy to get on with that I ventured to start topicks myself ... After this he asked me to sit down which I did at a round table by his side and M. Visconti [court architect] on the other side of me, and we had a conversation which lasted at least an hour and a half on every imaginable subject. It was impossible not to be struck with his simplicity, his being so natural and totally without any air or assumption of greatness ... It was difficult to bring away all the subjects he discussed and I do not know that he said anything wonderfully striking, but he made a very favourable impression on me, and made me wish to know more of him, which I am never likely to do ... a little while after, when we were talking of the siege of Sebastopol, he asked if I had ever seen a very good engineer's map of the whole thing; and when I said I had not, he said 'Then I will show you one'; and he again went into his cabinet and brought it out. After this long palaver he took leave of me, shaking hands with much apparent cordiality ...

Thursday July 5th

One of my attacks came on this day week and disabled me from going anywhere, doing anything, and still more from writing anything. In the meanwhile we received the news of Raglan's death [from dysentry]. Though they do not care about it here, there has been a very decent display of sympathy and regret, and the Emperor wrote to Cowley with his own hand a very proper letter ...

Friday

Yesterday to the Exhibition in the morning; then to Notre Dame and the Luxembourg Gardens and drove about Paris; dined en trio with Madame de Lieven and Guizot, nothing of course but political talk. G. thinks there has

been not only a series of diplomatic *invention* not to strike out some means of
adjusting this quarrel, in which I agreed with him. This morning Labouchere
and I went to Versailles ... We saw all the apartments in which Louis XIV
lived, and what remains of those of Madame de Maintenon ... We saw too in
minute detail the apartments of Louis XVI and Marie Antoinette, and the
passages through which she fled to escape from the irruption of the mob on
the 5th of October. The whole thing was as interesting as possible.

July 9th

I meant to have left Paris last night, but an invitation arriving to dine with
the Emperor at St Cloud today, I put off going till tomorrow ...

Tuesday 10th

Dined at Villeneuve L'Étang. We went to the Palace of St Cloud in Cowley's
carriage where we found an Equerry and one of the Emperor's carriages which
took us to Villeneuve. A small house, pretty and comfortable enough ... The
Emperor sat between the two Ladies, taking the Duchess [of Hamilton] in to
dinner. It lasted about a quarter of an hour, and as soon as it was over H.M.
took us all out to walk about the place, see the dairy and a beautiful Bretonne
cow he ordered to be brought out, and then to scull on the lake or étang which
gives its name to the place ... we passed about half an hour on the water. On
landing ices, etc, were brought, and the carriages came to the door at nine
o'clock, a char à banc with four Percherons and postillions exactly like the old
French Postboy, and several other open carriages and a pair ... We then set
off and drove for some time through the woods and drives of Villeneuve and
St Cloud, and at last at about ten o'clock we were set down at the Palace ...

Of course in this company there was nothing but general conversation and
I had no opportunity of having any with H.M.; but he was extremely civil,
offering me his cigars which I declined and expressing anxiety that I should
not catch cold. He made the same impression on me as before as to his extreme
simplicity and the easiness of his intercourse; but I was struck with his appearance being so very mesquin [shabby]. More than I thought at first.

July 13th

Left Paris on Tuesday night at 7.30, got to Calais at three; low water and
steamer three miles out to sea; went in a boat amidst a torrent of rain which
lasted the whole journey and all day. Train just gone when we got to Dover,
arrived in town about eleven. Found a precarious state of affairs, all confusion
and consternation, Bulwer having given notice of a motion of want of confidence on account of John Russell, whose affair has brought himself and the
Government to the very brink and almost to the certainty of ruin. [Russell
had said in the Commons on 6 July that, during his time negotiating in Vienna,

the Austrians had made proposals which he was convinced would have been a foundation of peace, but that the British Government refused them] . . . I found Brooks's in a state of insurrection. And even the Attorney-General (Cockburn) told me that the Liberal Party were resolved to go no further with J. R. and that nothing but his resignation could save the Government . . .

Bath July 19th Thursday

Came here on Saturday night. In the course of Friday morning met Drumlanrig who told me the subordinate place men had caused J. R. to be informed that if he did not resign they should, and vote for Bulwer's [elder brother of the novelist and diplomat] motion on Monday. This produced his resignation but in circumstances as mortifying as possibly could be . . . It was no sooner known that he had resigned than the excitement began to subside . . . The motion was withdrawn and the debate took place, and such a debate! – . . . Bulwer's speech was a tissue of foul abuse with the grossest and most wilfull misrepresentations to draw inferences he knew to be false and fallacious . . .

After much consideration of John Russell's conduct, I think it is not obnoxious to the severe censure with which it has been visited, and though he has committed errors, they are venial ones and admit of fair explanation. Had not Buol [Karl-Ferdinand Graf von Buol–Schauenstein, Austrian plenipotiary to the Vienna Conference]'s publication revealed to the world what had passed between them confidentially, nothing of it would have been known . . . The statement about him in Buol's circular naturally led to questions, and then it was necessary to tell everything and lay bare the arcana of Cabinets and Conferences . . . He writes . . . 'I have endeavoured to stand by and support Palmerston, too much so, I fear for my own credit, but had I resigned on my return from Vienna, I should have been abused as wishing to trip him up and get his place: in short, the situation was one of those where only errors were possible. I have acted according to my own conscience; let that suffice.' . . .

September 17th Monday

. . . The Prince of Wales was put by the Queen under Clarendon's charge, who was directed to tell what to do in public, when to bow to the people, and whom to speak to. He thinks the Queen's severe way of treating her children very injudicious and that the Prince will be difficult to manage, as he has evidently a will of his own and is rather positive and opinionated, and inclined to lay down the law; but he is clever and his manners are good. One day in the carriage some subject was discussed when the Prince said something which C. contradicted, to which he replied, 'At all events that's my opinion.' When C. said 'Then Y.R.H.'s opinion is quite wrong' which seemed to surprise him a good deal . . .

October 29th

All last week at Newmarket, and probably very nearly for the last time, at least as an owner of racehorses, for I have nearly got rid of them all, and am almost off the turf, after being on it for nearly forty years – horresco referens, for it is a whole life passed in idleness, folly and bad company . . . The delinquent Bankers were convicted and sentenced to the highest penalty of the law with universal satisfaction [Strahan, Paul and Bates of the Strand having failed in June, the three principles were in October charged and convicted at the Old Bailey of embezzlement and sentenced to fourteen years' transportation].

November 12th

. . . I have occasion to see Dis[raeli] often about F[rank] Villiers' affairs (about which he has been wonderfully kind and servicable), and on these occasions he always enters on some political talk, and in this way we have got into a sort of intimacy as I never thought could have taken place between us.

November 27th

At length there really does appear to be a prospect of putting an end to this odious war . . . Yesterday morning I met G. Lewis [now Chancellor of the Exchequer] in the Park and turned back and walked with him to the door of his office when he told me the exact state of affairs . . . The Austrians have framed a proposal for peace which they offer to send to Russia, and if She refuses it, Austria engages to join the allies and declare war. The Emperor Napoleon agrees with Austria and is resolved not to go with the war if peace can be arranged on the Austrian terms . . . It is in fact a second edition of the Vienna Conference and proposals with this difference that, while on the last occasion the Emperor [of France] knocked under to us and reluctantly agreed to go on with the war, he is determined to go no longer, and requires that we should defer to his wishes.

Our Government are aware that they have no alternative, and that there is nothing for them but to acquiesce with good grace and make the best case they can for themselves here, that case being that the Emperor was determined to make peace, and that we could not carry on the war alone. This was the amount of Lewis's information and, to which he added the expression of his disgust at the pitiful figure we cut in the affair, being obliged to obey the commands of Louis Napoleon and, after our insolence, swagger and bravado, to submit to terms of peace which we had already scornfully rejected; all which humiliation, he justly said, was the consequence of our plunging into war without any reason and in defiance of all prudence and sound policy.

This morning the *Morning Post* has published the terms which are offered by the Allies and are now on their way from Vienna to Petersburg. They were already pretty well known, but it is the first time that Palmerston (for the article is evidently his own) has announced them so openly and distinctly, and they state totidem verbis that it is an *ultimatum* which is to be sent to Petersburg ... [it] is a stretch of arrogance and dictation not justified by the events of the war ...

1856

January 5th

Intelligence arrived yesterday that Esterhazy had presented the Austrian proposal to Nesselrode on the 28th who received it *in profound silence.* Yesterday morning the *Morning Post*, in communicating this fact, put forth an article indecently violent and menacing against Prussia [Prussia had been the most reluctant of the powers over the crisis and had not gone to war] ...

Hatchford January 2nd

The speech which L. N. addressed to the Imperial Guard the day before yesterday, when they marched into Paris in triumph, gives reason for suspecting the manifesto against Prussia in the *Morning Post* was French, for there is no small correspondence between the speech and the article. In the last Prussia is openly threatened and told if she will not join the allies in making war on Russia, the Allies will make war upon her; in the first the Guards are told to hold themselves in readiness and that a great French army will be wanted.

January 15th

Came from Middleton yesterday morning and found on my arrival the Russian answer ... I suspect our Government will have been disappointed that so much was conceded as to make a peremptory rejection so monstrous as to be hardly safe ...

January 17th

Saw Lewis yesterday and for the first time saw something approaching to a *certainty* of peace ...

12 o'clock

Payne has just rushed in here to say that a telegraphic message, dated Vienna, ten last night, announces that 'Russia accepts *unconditionally* the proposals of the Allies'. The consequence of this astounding intelligence was such a state of confusion and excitement on the Stock Exchange as was hardly ever seen before ...

January 18th

Though the account in *The Times* was not exactly correct, it proved to be substantially so ... there was such a scene on the Stock Exchange as hardly was ever witnessed; the funds rose three per cent, making five in the last two days ... the press has succeeded in inculcating the public with such an eager desire for war that there appears a general regret at the notion of making peace ...

January 22nd

What the people of England would really like would be to engage France to continue, and to issue a joint declaration of war against Austria and Prussia.

January 26th

Yesterday morning Disraeli called on me in re F. Villiers, and after we discussed that, he began talking politics. He is very triumphant at his pacific views and expectations having turned out to be true ... He said that he had never stood so well with the *best* men in his party as he did now. He has forty-five (the cream of the Conservatives) to dine with him on Wednesday next. Then he talked of Derby and all the blunders he had made in spite of all the advice he had given ... If Dis. is to be believed, the best of the Conservatives are disposed to go with him rather than with Derby, but I very much doubt this. However it will soon be seen what the state of that party is.

January 31st

Parliament meets today. Who would have thought a few weeks ago that the Queen's speech would announce the preliminaries of peace? Who would have thought that tidings of peace would produce a general sentiment of disappointment and dissatisfaction in this nation? ... The Press is much perplexed; the newspapers don't know what to say. They confidently predicted there would be no peace, and urged the people to go on clamouring for war as long as they could; but since they have seen that their noise is ineffectual, and that peace is inevitable, they have nearly left off inveighing against it, because doing so without any result only exhibits their own impotence, which is just what they most wish to avoid. They therefore now confine themselves to a sort of undergrowl. Muttering abuse against Russia and Austria, calling out for more stringent terms, and still indulging in a desperate hope that some unexpected difficulty may occur to break off the negotiations and plunge us into war again ...

February 21st

... Last night the Evangelical and Sabbatarian interest had a great victory in the H. of C. routing those who endeavoured to effect the opening of the

National Gallery and British Museum on Sunday. The only man of importance who sustained this unequal and imprudent contest was Lord Stanley [Derby's son, a very liberal Tory]. At this moment cant and Puritanism are in the ascendant, and so far from effecting any anti-Sabbatarian reform, it will be very well if we escape some of the more stringent measures against Sunday occupations and amusements with which Exeter Hall [Evangelical HQ] and the prevailing spirit threaten us.

March 1st

I left London [for Paris, where the peace conference was taking place] on Thursday with Flahaut and my brother ... I had hardly arrived before a card came from Morny [Louis Napoleon's illegitimate half-brother, one time Minister of the Interior and inspirer of the cheese sauce] who gave a great evening party with two petites pièces [that is *pièces de théâtre*] ... I was much struck with the ugliness of the women, and the extreme recherché of their costumes. Nature has done nothing for them, their modistes all that is possible ... I made acquaintance with Fleury [equerry, later diplomat] the Emperor's grand Écuyer [riding companion] renewed it with Bacciochi ... as is said, his pimp, and I was presented to Cavour and the Grand Vizier, [Ali Pasha] as little like the beau ideal of a grand Vizier as can well be imagined ... He is a very little, dark, spare, mild-looking man, speaks French perfectly and exceedingly clever, well-informed, enlightened and honourable ...

Orloff [Russian secret policeman, plenipotentiary at the Paris Conference] spoke very frankly about the war and the conduct of the late Emperor, which he had always regarded as insane – his sending Menshikoff to Constantinople. If he had sent him (Orloff) instead, he could answer for it, there would have been no war ... This morning after breakfast I had a long conversation with Cowley. He did not speak despondingly of the peace but spoke of the difficulty of coming to satisfactory terms and such as Clarendon could consent to, which he attributes principally to the French who, having gained all the glory they want for the satisfaction of their national vanity, have no longer any desire to go on with the war. And we are placed by them in a fix ... he said all the objections he had entertained against Paris being the place of conference had been more than realised, and that the thing to have done would have been to have them in some dull German town where there would have been no amusements and occupations and no intrigues, and where they would have applied themselves vigorously to their work in order to get it done as quickly as possible.

March 3rd

Went about visiting yesterday, and at night to the Tuileries, an evening party and play, two small pieces; Emperor very civil to me as usual ... then the

Grande Maîtresse told him the Empress was ready when he went out and came back with her on his arm, Mathilde, Princess Murat and Plon Plon [Prince Napoleon, a relation] following – all so vulgar looking. As the Emperor passed before me, he stopt and presented me to the Empress. She does not look her best of course, but I was much disappointed with her beauty. I was introduced to Orloff and in the course of the evening had a long talk with Brunnow, who said they had made all the advances and concessions they could, and it was for us to move towards peace and not to advance one step and then to retreat two . . .

At night

. . . When I got home found Cowley, . . . He is quite convinced that Walewski [now French Foreign Minister] has played false, and he believes, but cannot prove it, for a bribe; and that he has made clear to Orloff what he must give up, and when he can be stout.

March 6th at night

. . . Cowley seemed very low coming home. His dejection is extreme, and he said this morning that he could not recover from his extreme disappointment at the conduct of the Emperor, that he had always had a bad opinion of Walewski and no reliance on any of the ministers, but he would have staked his life on the Emperor remaining true to us, that he had always assured our Government that they might depend implicitly on him, and it was a bitter mortification to have been deceived himself and deceive them. I asked how Clarendon felt about all this, and he said that Clarendon had never spoken to him about it, and preserved a calmness which astonished him. 'What' I asked 'did the Cabinet at home say?' He said 'they seemed to place entire confidence in Clarendon and leave all power and responsibility to him.'

March 9th

Called on Fould [Achille Fould, recurring Minister of Finance] who introduced me to Mange, Minister of Finance, said to be a great rogue. Everything here is intrigue and jobbery, and Cowley tells me there is a sort of gang, of which Morny is the chief, who all combine for the purposes of peculation: Morny, Fould, Magne and Roher, Minister of Commerce. They now want to get out Billaut, Minister of the Interior, whom they cannot entirely manage, and that Ministry is necessary to them on account of the railroads which are under his management . . .

March 15th

. . . I am myself inclined to think the Russian would have agreed to our terms if those terms had been heartily backed by the Emperor; but except to give something more of a triumph to the English public, I am not of opinion that the difference between what we required and what we shall get is worth much. When the dénouement is before the world, it will appear how insane it was to plunge into such a war, and that the confusion and unsettled state of affairs which will be the result of it are more dangerous to the state of the Turkish empire than the ambitious designs of Russia ever were ... As to forming another coalition for the sake of semi-barbarous nationalities on the coasts of the Caspian, nothing would be more impossible. England herself, who will soon recover from her madness, would not hear of it and France still less. The war was founded in delusion and error, and carried on by a factitious and ignorant enthusiasm, and we richly deserve to reap nothing but mortification and disappointment for all the blood and treasure we have spent ...

April 1st

News of peace reached London on Sunday evening and was received joyfully by the populace, not from any desire to see an end of the war, but merely because it is a great event to make a noise about. The newspapers have been reasonable enough, except for the *Sun* which appeared in deep mourning and made a violent tirade against peace.

May 14th

... Sir Benjamin Hall [First Commissioner of Works], having bethought himself of providing innocent amusement for the Londoners on a Sunday, established a Sunday playing of military bands in Kensington Gardens and the other parks and gardens ... Some murmurs were heard from the puritanical and Sabbatarian party, but Palmerston having declared himself favourable to the practice to the H. of Commons, the opposition appeared to cease. The Puritans however continued to agitate against it in meetings and in the Press (the best part of the latter was favourable to the bands) ... [The Cabinet] were informed if the Government resisted the motion, they would be beat, and moreover that no man could support them in opposition to it without great danger of losing his seat at the next election ... this influence would be brought to bear against every man who maintained by his vote this 'desecration of the Sabbath'. Accordingly it was resolved by the Cabinet to give way, and the only question was how to do so with anything like dignity and consistency. The Archbishop of Canterbury was made the deus ex machina to effect this object. He was made to write a letter to the premier representing the feelings of the people and begging that the bands might be silenced. To this Palmerston wrote a reply in which he repeated his own opinion in favour of the music, but that in deference to public sentiment he would put an end to their playing. For the present the only question is whether the angry public will not vent its indignation and resentment tomorrow in acts of uproar and violence ...

Wednesday May 28th

Yesterday on Epsom course [Derby Day] arrived the news of Palmer's being found guilty of the Murder of Cook. [The Harold Shipman of his day, Dr William Palmer of Rugeley poisoned twenty people. After his execution, Rugeley town councillors who asked Palmerston for permission to change the town's name were told 'Only, gentlemen, if you name it after me!'] This case and the trial have excited an interest almost unprecedented, unlike anything seen since the case of Thurtell about twenty years ago or more. [It was actually thirty-three. The bankrupt squire murdered the bookmaker William Weare, who had swindled him.] . . .

November 19th

The death of Jervis made the office of Chief Justice of Common Pleas vacant. According to established (but I think bad) usage, the Attorney-General, Cockburn [Alexander Cockburn (1802–80) later Lord Chief Justice], had a right to take the place . . . he was much averse to take it, but everybody pressed him to accept it, and after much hesitation and consultation, he has agreed to be Chief Justice . . . He gives up Parliament, for which he is well equipped, where he acts a conspicuous part, being a capital speaker, and which he likes, and feels that it is his element. He gives up the highest place at the bar and makes £15,000, £16,000 [£750,000 or £800,000 today] and sees that he shall be obliged to give up in great measure his loose habits and assume more decorous behaviour which will be a great sacrifice for him, and he becomes a Judge with £6,000 a year, not being a good lawyer . . .

November 23rd

. . . It is said and I believe truly that now Cockburn has taken the irretrievable step he is very sorry for it, and is more struck by the necessary consequences of his promotion than he was at first. He has all his life been a very debauched fellow, but he is clever, good natured and of a liberal disposition and very much liked by his friends. A story is told of him that he was in the habit of going down on Sundays to Richmond or elsewhere with a woman and generally with a different one, and the landlady of the inn he went to remarked that Sir A.C. always brought Lady Cockburn with him, but that she never saw any woman who looked so different on different days . . .

December 7th

Great astonishment has been excited by the appointment of a Mr Bickersteth as Bishop of Ripon, against whom nothing can be said, nor anything for him, except that he is a very Low Churchman. All the vacant Sees have now been filled with Clergymen of this colour which is not very fair or prudent, as it will exasperate the moderate High Churchmen . . . and such a policy will most likely have the effect of encouraging the advocates of those extreme measures of an anti-Catholic or puritanical character which always give so much trouble when they are brought forward in Parliament.

1857

January 20th

Two remarkable deaths, one of which touches me nearly, is that of Madame de Lieven; the other is the Duke of Rutland ... Very different characters. Madame de Lieven came to this country at the end of 1812 ... She had so fine an air and manner and a countenance rather pretty and full of intelligence as to be on the whole a very striking and attractive person, quite enough so to have Lovers, ... Those who were most notoriously her Slaves at different times were the present Lord Willoughby, the Duke of Sutherland ... the Duke of Canizzaro ... and the Duke of Palmella ... and she immediately took her place in the cream of English society, forming close associations with the most conspicuous women in it and assiduously cultivating relations with the most remarkable men of all parties ... George IV delighted much in her company, and she was a frequent guest at the Pavillion ... for although Madame de Lieven was not very tolerant of mediocrity, and social and colloquial superiority was necessary to her existence, she always made great allowances for Royalty and those immediately connected with it ... She became the friend of Lord Castlereagh, of Canning, the Duke of Wellington, Lord Grey, Lord Palmerston, John Russell, Aberdeen and many others of inferior note ...

In 1834 the Lievens were recalled, and she was established at Petersburg in high office about the Empress, but her séjour there was odious to her, and she was inconsolable at leaving England where, after a residence of about twenty years, she had become rooted in habits and affections, although she had never really understood the country ... [Greville added no comment on the Duke of Rutland.]

February 8th Sunday

I am just come from hearing the celebrated Mr Sturgeon ['Spurgeon' actually, Baptist revivalist] preach in the Music Hall of the Surrey Gardens. It was quite full; he told us from the pulpit that 9000 people were present ... He is certainly very remarkable and undeniably a very fine preacher: not remarkable in person, in face resembling a smaller Macaulay, a very fine and powerful voice which was heard through the whole hall ... The text was 'Cleanse me from my secret sins', and he divided it into heads, the misery, the folly, the danger (and a fourth which I have forgotten) of secret sins ... He preached for about three-quarters of an hour, and, to judge of the handkerchiefs and the audible sobs, with great effect ...

February 27th

... Derby made a grand onslaught the beginning of last week on the China question [Bowring, Governor of Hong Kong's response to a supposed insult by the Chinese Commissioner, Yeh, of occupying forts and shelling the city had been endorsed by Palmerston] ... All the speaking with the Opposition, but it is quite curious how afraid people are of seriously shaking the Government. The day the debate in the Lords ended, that in the Commons began on the same question, duce Cobden. The great event of the first night was John Russell's speech and powerful attack on the Government. It was one of his very best efforts and extremely successful with the House, but it was exceedingly bitter ...

... There is in fact a strong feeling, both in Parliament and the country, against all that has been done in Canton ... Granville tells me that [Palmerston and Clarendon] had been under the extraordinary delusion that the Canton affair had been very well done and would be received with great applause and satisfaction here; in point of fact that it was a great *hit* from which the Government would derive considerable advantage ...

Nothing can equal the excitement and curiosity here about the division. All sorts of efforts have been made all ways to influence voices ... everybody expects it to be so near that there are as many opinions as men.

March 4th

Majority of 16 against Government, more than any of them expected. A magnificent speech of Gladstone; Palmerston's said to have been very dull in the first part and very bow-wow in the second; not very judicious, on the whole bad and certainly failed to decide any doubtful votes in his favour. I rejoice that the House of Commons has condemned this iniquitous case for the honour of the country ...

March 24th

Dissolution on Saturday and all the world busy about the elections ... the dinner at the Mansion House the other day to the Ministers was a sort of triumph for Palmerston, who was rapturously received and cheered. He made a very bad speech but which did well for such an audience. [He accused his opponents, the Tories, of being ready to pay for English heads severed by the Chinese!] ...

March 29th Sunday

... The most interesting event was the City election and the return of John Russell ... he fell off and only ended third, but still he had 7000 votes after having been assured by his old adherents ... that he would be 'beat disgracefully' and hardly have any votes at all.

After this the most interesting events were the defeat of the Manchester men and (generally though not universally) of the voters for Cobden's motion, Bright and Milner Gibson, Cobden, Ricardo and Layard all defeated ... I am sorry for the loss of Bright and Cobden, because such able men ought not to be ousted and replaced by mediocrities ... The cry of Palmerston and nothing but Palmerston, has done very well to go to the hustings on, but having accomplished its purpose, other cries much more serious will soon take its place ...

... Old Lady Keith is dead at some prodigious age [ninety-five, born in 1762]. She was the Queeny of Dr Johnson, Mrs Thrale's daughter, and was the last surviving link between those times and our own, and probably the only person living who could remember, certainly who had lived in intimacy with, Johnson himself and his remarkable contemporaries ...

June 3rd

... The House of Lords has been busy with the Divorce Bill, and there has been a good deal of vigorous debating, particularly among Lyndhurst, the Bishops of Oxford and London, and [Lords] Campbell and Wensleydale, who hate each other and have exchanged blows.

June 20th

All this past week the world has been occupied with the Handel concerts at the Crystal Palace ... I went to the first ('Messiah') and the last ('Israel in Egypt'); they were amazingly grand, and the beauty of the locale, with the vast crowds assembled in it, made an imposing spectacle ... But the wonderful assembly of 2000 vocal and 500 instrumental performers did not produce musical effect so agreeable and perfect as the smaller number in the smaller space of Exeter Hall ...

June 28th

Went last Saturday to Strawberry Hill [essay in early Gothic revival created for Horace Walpole]. A large party of people, Persignys [Duc de, French Ambassador], Speaker and femme etc, etc, etc; an enjoyable villa with its vast expanse of grass, profusion of flowers and fine trees affording ample shade. Horace Walpole's ridiculous house unaltered, but furbished up and made comfortable ...

... At Hatchford the past week and when I got to town I was apprised of the disastrous news from India, the most serious occurrence that has ever been in that quarter ... till we receive the details, it is idle to speculate upon it.

The Queen has made P. Albert 'Prince Consort' by a patent *ordered in Council* – a very foolish act, it seems to me. It confers on him neither title, dignity, nor privileges, and I can't see the use of it ...

July 15th Wednesday

For the last three weeks or more all public interest and curiosity have been absorbed in the affairs of India and the great mutiny that has broken out there. And which has now assumed such an alarming character ... certain it is that the East India Company have been in what is called a fool's paradise on the subject ... While the Russian war was going on a clamour was raised against the Government for not calling away *all* the British troops in India, and sending them to the Crimea.

July 19th

... Amidst all the bad news from India the good feature is that so many of the Native Troops, and not only the military but the whole population of the Punjaub [*sic*] have shown so much fidelity and attachment to the British Government. It is the strongest testimony to the wisdom of our rule, and of the capacity of the natives to appreciate the benefits they derive from it, for beyond question, the introduction of European civilisation into the east, and the substitution of such a government as that of England for the cruel, rapacious, and capricious dominion of Oriental Chiefs and dynasties is the greatest boon that the people could have had conferred upon them ...

August 2nd

... Disraeli entered at great length into the causes of the present confusion, and the misgovernment and bad policy which had engendered it, and although his speech was able, and probably contained a great deal that was true, it was deemed (as it was) mischievous and ill-timed and very ill received by the House.

September 6th, Sunday

... They have made some Peers, of whom the most conspicuous is Macaulay and I have not heard any complaints of his elevation. Lord Lansdowne has declined the offered Dukedom which I rather regret ... While Macaulay is thus ascending to the House of Peers, his old enemy and rival, Croker, has descended to his grave, very noiselessly and almost without observation ... He had lived to see his predictions of ruin and disaster to the country completely falsified ... he certainly occupied a high place among the second-rate men of his time; he had very considerable talents, great industry with much information and a retentive memory ... his long acquaintance with the world and with public affairs and his stores of general knowledge made him entertaining, though he was too overbearing to be agreeable ... A few years ago he had a literary fight with John Russell in which John was the aggressor and when Croker had much the best of it – at this moment I can't recollect what it was about ...

September 22nd

. . . I am on the point of starting for Balmoral, summoned for a Council to order a day of humiliation. I was in hopes this miserable cant and humbug would not have been repeated on this occasion, but the pseudo-religious part of the community never lose an opportunity clamouring for such pious manifestations, and the Government never dare to treat their nonsense with the contempt it deserves.

Dunrobin Castle October 2nd Friday

Came here from Gordon Castle by sea from Burghead to Little Ferry . . . a most princely possession and the palace exceedingly beautiful and moreover very comfortable . . . The Indian news of this week is bad and promises as ill as can be and I expect worse by every mail that comes. We are justly punished for our ambition and encroaching spirit, but it must be owned that we struggle gallantly for what we have perhaps unjustly acquired. Europe behaves well to us for although we have made ourselves universally odious by our insolence and our domination, and our long habit of bullying all the world, nobody triumphs over us in the hour of our distress, and even Russia who has no cause to feel anything but ill will toward us, evinces her regret and sympathy in courteous terms . . .

London October 6th

I fell in with Granville and Clarendon at Watford and got into their carriage . . . my first enquiries were about India . . . Clarendon said that if it was possible for Havelock to maintain himself a short time longer, and that reinforcements arrived in time to save the beleagured places, the tide would turn and Delhi would fall; but if he should be crushed, Agra, Lucknow and other threatened places would fall with renewals of the Cawnpore horrors, and in that case the unlimited spread of the mutiny would be irrepressible, Madras and Bombay would revolt, all the scattered Powers would rise up everywhere, and all would be lost . . .

Hatchford October 8th

Granville . . . the most reserved and boutonnée of men, who scarcely ever tells me the most indifferent matter of fact, spoke of his colleagues and of the court with a freedom that he might have deemed imprudent . . .: The Queen is not clever, and everything is done by the Prince who is to all intents King. She acts in everything by his inspiration and never writes a letter he does not dictate every word of. His knowledge and information are astonishing and there is not a department of the Government regarding all the detail and management of which he is not much better informed and more capable than the Minister at the head of it . . .

November 27th

... The Press goes on attacking Canning [Charles, Viscount Canning, Governor-General, son of the late Prime Minister] with great asperity and injustice and nobody here defends him. [*The Times*, which wanted 'death for every mutineer, the destruction of all Muslim mosques and the razing of Delhi and its utter destruction', and opined that 'Every gable end and tree in the place should have its burden in the shape of a mutineer's carcass', added that 'between justice and these wretches steps a prim philanthropist from Calcutta' whom it called 'Clemency Canning'.] Though I am not a very intimate or particular friend of his, I think him so unfairly and unjustly treated that I mean to make an effort to get him such redress as the case admits of, and the only thing which occurs to me is that Palmerston, as head of the Government, should take the opportunity of the Lord Mayor's dinner to vindicate him ...

November 4th

I have been speaking to Granville about Canning ... He replied that *he could not trust Palmerston*, but he meant tonight to speak in his defence at a dinner to be given to the Duke of Cambridge ...

November 8th Hatchford

... I was told it was not well received, but nevertheless it has produced an effect ... It was the first word that has been said for Canning in public and it has evidently been great use to him ... Palmerston pronounced a glowing eulogium on Canning last night at the Ld. Mayor's dinner which will inevitably stop the current of abuse against him. It has already turned *The Times*. He seems to have been induced to do this by the great pressure brought to bear on him ... and he did it handsomely enough. His speech was otherwise bad enough, full of jactance [swagger] and bow-wow ... He told them that we had a military force now embodied as strong as we had before the Indian Mutiny, which I take to be a downright falsehood.

London December 2nd

Yesterday [Viscount] Sydney received a letter from Lady Canning that, although undoubtedly many horrible things had happened in India, the exaggeration of them had been very great and that She had read for the first time in the English newspapers stories of atrocities of which she had never heard at Calcutta ...

Shaftesbury too ... does his utmost to make the case out to be as bad as possible to excite the rage and indignation of the masses to the highest pitch ... [he] complains that the particulars of mutilation and violation have not been more copiously and circumstantially given to the world ... it is no doubt something connected with the grand plan of Christianising India, in the furtherance of which the High Church and the Low Church appear to be bidding against each other; and as their united force will in all probability be irresistible, so they will succeed in making any Government in India impossible.

December 8th

Went to H. of Lords last night and heard Ellenborough speak for the first time – an admirable and measured style of speaking. It was a good night for Canning. *The Times* has ... turned right round and defends him, finding the Government are in earnest in doing so; all this is very disgusting, but it is better that they should be thus inconsistent.

London December 17th

Though the last advices from India were satisfactory as far as they went, it is generally understood that the next mail must bring the account of a bloody battle at or near Lucknow, in which though no one doubts that the British will be victorious, it is certain that there will be gross loss of life ...

Disraeli called on me a day or two ago and we had a political chat ... He said Palmerston's popularity was of a negative character and, rather more from the unpopularity of every other public man than from any peculiar attachment to him ... He don't appear to have made up his mind what course to take on the Indian question, and it is evident that at present the party have decided on nothing ...

December 21st

... [George] Lewis told me that Palmerston had given notice to the Chairs [Council of the East India Company] that the Government had come to a resolution ... to put an end to their domination, and that the plan was to have an Indian Secretary of State with a Council, and the council to have the distribution of the patronage.

December 29th

By the Indian papers just arrived it appears that the relief of the Residency of Lucknow and the deliverance of all who were confined in it was complete, but there was no great battle ... The Mutineers, though always worsted, seem to fight better than they were thought capable of doing ... the suppression of the Mutiny is still far from being accomplished.

1858

January 1st

It is worth noticing that after a year of fine weather, of which nobody can recollect the like, this first day of New Year has opened like one of genial spring. This nearly unbroken course of wonderful weather for about nine or ten months gives rise to many speculations as to its cause, and no doubt there is some physical cause, although it has not yet been ascertained.

January 5th

Today the winter seems to have set in in earnest.

January 7th

Not many days ago *The Times* concluded an article on the Indian war ... 'Thus ends the Indian Mutiny of 1857'; and today we have the news of Wyndham [actually Windham] having been defeated by the Gwalior Force; of Sir Colin [Campbell] having been obliged to quit Lucknow *without having actually captured it* in order to repair this check ... of the death of [Sir Henry] Havelock, the hero of this war ...

   ... Shaftesbury is stirring all the fanaticism of the country, and clamouring for what he calls the *emancipation* of Christianity in India ... The real meaning of the Exeter Hall clamour is, that we should commence as soon as we can, a Crusade against the religions of the natives of India, and to attempt to force Christianity upon them ...

January 16th Saturday

Went to the Grange on Tuesday and returned yesterday morning; met by the news of an attempted assassination of the Emperor Napoleon [the bomb thrown by an Italian nationalist, Felice Orsini] whose escape seems to have been providential.

January 23rd

I received a visit from Disraeli who said he had come to consult me in confidence ... he is meditating on the possible chances of him and his party ... and knowing that some sort of coalition with some other party would be indispensable to form any other government an idea had crossed his mind that this might be practicable with some of the most moderate of the Whigs, especially with the younger ones, such as Granville and Argyll ... if I did not think so, what my ideas were as to the most advisable course in order to avert the threatened Reform ... [The Reform Bill, which Disraeli would enact in 1867, would be more sweeping than any contemplated by the Whigs.]

February 2nd

... It was well known that the French Government had been urging ours to adopt measures ... against the refugees and their machinations in this country; but while the question was under discussion we were astounded ... by the publication in the *Moniteur* [official Government journal] of certain addresses from corps or regiments of the French Army to the Emperor, full of insult and menace to this country . . . We are going to have to do something to soothe them, but as it will be no more than to make that a felony which is now only a misdemeanour, it may be doubted if this will satisfy or appease them . . . and I doubt if even this slight concession will be obtained from Parliament without some strong and indignant remarks on the tone which has been adopted towards England.

February 11th

I never remember Parliament meeting with much greater curiosity and excitement. The situation of the Government is regarded as so precarious and the revolution in Palmerston's popularity, and therefore his power, is quite extraordinary . . .

February 20th Saturday

. . . the public feeling had become more and more exasperated at the Conspiracy Bill, and at the conduct of France. The first reading would not have been carried as it was, perhaps not at all but for the *apology*, as it was called of the Emperor, . . . But this soothing effect was very transitory. It was remarked that while the *Moniteur* continued to insert fresh addresses of an offensive character, the apologetic despatch did not appear at all . . . Milner Gibson [Thomas Milner Gibson, one of the 'Manchester men' defeated at the election, had come back for Ashton-under-Lyne] took advantage of the prevailing temper and a resolution in the shape of an amendment . . . very skilfully concocted which was a direct vote of censure on the Government . . . Great was my astonishment when I read in *The Times* this morning that the Government had been beat on Milner Gibson's motion by 19, and a few minutes later Granville came in and said that this defeat must be conclusive, and nothing left for them but to resign . . .

March 2nd

Last night Derby made his statement . . . a very judicious and becoming speech.

March 12th

It is remarkable how completely the affairs at home have superseded the interest belonging to those of India. Nobody seems to think about what so recently absorbed everyone's thoughts and feelings . . . The apprehensions I had on the subject, and which I have expressed, have been very far from realised, and those who took more sanguine and confident views of the issue of the contest have been justified by the event.

March 21st Sunday

... The other day I got a note from Derby (about a Council) at the end of which he earnestly begged me if I had any influence with *The Times* to get them to abstain from writing any more irritating articles about France, for that these articles provoked the French to madness, and, as matters are, that nothing but the utmost care and moderation on both sides enabled the two governments to go on in harmony. I accordingly sent his note to Delane, who promised to attend to it, though it was hard to leave the French Press without replies ...

March 25th

Pélissier is going to replace Persigny here as ambassador, a strange choice. He is a military Ruffian, who knows no more of diplomacy than he does of astronomy ... The Duke of Bedford has been here, come from Aberdeen who tells him the Peelites are all verging towards a union with John, some more some less; Graham devoted to him, Sidney Herbert and Cardwell perfectly well disposed, the D. of Newcastle gradually becoming so, and Gladstone at present the least friendly, but A. thinks is getting more friendly and will eventually join his standard, and Aberdeen himself doing all he can to bring about this union. [These negotiations, when accomplished, effectively created the Liberal Party.] ...

Hatchford March 30th

On Friday last Disraeli brought on the Government of India Bill which Ellenborough told some of his friends would be 'a great success' and which everyone expected to be an improvement on Palmerston's ...

April 8th

Derby made a striking speech at the Mansion House, which has been severely ridiculed by *The Times*, but which nevertheless contained a good deal of truth. He said that there were very few questions nowadays in which different Governments *could* act differently, and he invited not only every sort of criticism but of suggestion as to the India Bills to measure before Parliament ...

April 24th

The events of the past week have been Disraeli's Budget, which has been received with favour and excited no opposition in any quarter, and the withdrawal of the Government [of] India Bill, which was done by Disraeli, rather unwillingly; but their maxim seems to be 'anything for a quiet life' ... The general notion seems to be that they are safe for this session, but it is a very inglorious safety ...

May 13th

... [Lyndhurst] is particularly disgusted with the state of the Jew question, and with the foolish and obstinate conduct of the Government in the H. of Lords about it, on which he was very eloquent, particularly for their having made a great whip and getting up every man they could lay their hands on to come and vote, instead of leaving it to take its chance, and at least making an open question of it ...

June 7th

The most interesting event of last week was the (virtual) settlement of the eternal Jew question, which the H. of Lords sulkily acquiesced in. It was very desirable for many reasons to put an end to it.

Norman Court June 6th

Every day it appears more and more evident that Palmerston's political career is drawing to a close and he alone seems blind to the signs which denote it ...

June 22nd

... Among the events of last week one of the most interesting was the Queen's visit to Birmingham, where she was received by the whole of that enormous population with an enthusiasm which is said to have exceeded all that was displayed in her former receptions at Manchester and elsewhere ... [This] lends some force to the notion entertained by some political thinkers, that there is more danger in conferring power upon the middle classes than in extending it far beneath them ...

Petworth July 31st

Came here from Goodwood, not having been here for twenty years, and am rather glad to see once more a place where I passed so much of my time in my younger days. I think it is the finest house I have ever seen, and its collection of pictures is unrivalled for number, beauty and interest ...

London November 4th

... I hear the Queen has written a letter to the Prince of Wales announcing to him his emancipation from Parental authority and controul ... She tells him that he may have thought the rule they adopted for his education a severe one, but that his welfare was the only object, and well knowing to what seductions of flattery he would eventually be exposed, they wished to prepare and strengthen his mind against them ... it seems to have made a profound impression on the Prince, and to have touched his feelings to the quick. He brought it to Gerald Wellesley [Dean of Windsor] in floods of tears ...

November 17th

... Montalembert's paper is admirable [the Comte de Montalembert, leader of a Catholic political group in France, had praised British institutions, notably the Commons, applauding the debate on India on the grounds of its freedom] ... especially about the Indian debate and Indian policy and the causes of Palmerston's fall and the loss of his popularity. His prosecution by the Imperial Government is either an enormous mistake and political error, or a stroke of policy so deep and refined as to be beyond my comprehension.

1859

January 14th

All Europe has been thrown into alarm by the speech which the E. Napoleon made to the Austrian Ambassador on New Year's Day ['I regret that relations with your Government are not so good as I could wish.'] and by the announcement which followed it that Prince Napoleon was going to Turin to marry the King of Sardinia's daughter ... the best informed persons and those who are most accustomed to watch the signs of the times are convinced that the time is near at hand when the peace of the world will be broken, that the Emperor is determined upon an aggression on Austria ...

Bretby January 27th

... Reeve said that he had been told that Palmerston was likely to give utterance to some sentiments very anti-Austrian, and in favour of Italian nationality, than which nothing could be more mischievous or more conducive to the objects of Louis Napoleon.

January 31st Monday ...

... Derby told me that the Princess Royal's accouchement was near turning out fatally. Though nobody knows it ... The labour lasted thirteen hours and the child got twisted in the womb and came out with his bottom foremost. [The child lived – and became Kaiser Wilhelm II.]

February 19th

The general complaint is that nothing is done in Parliament and that there is general apathy ... The Chancellor [Chelmsford] obtained a momentary odium by his attempt at perpetrating a very shameless job by making his Son-in-Law a Judge in lunacy without having any qualifications ...

February 27th

... On Thursday morning the world was electrified at reading an article stating that Cowley [Earl Cowley, Wellington's nephew, diplomat] was going on a special mission to Vienna for the purpose of making matters up, if possible, between France and Austria. The day before I had been appraised of the fact by Granville who had heard it from Clarendon to whom Cowley had imparted the secret of his mission ...

... In the midst of the absorbing interest of this great question, the Government Reform Bill is coming on. They appear to have thought it advisable to bespeak the good word of *The Times* and accordingly they sent Delane a copy of their Bill. This morning the heads of it appear in *The Times* with an approving article. Mild as it appears to be, it is too strong for Walpole and Henley [Home Secretary and President of the Board of Trade].

March 1st
Disraeli brought forward his Reform Bill last night in a well-set speech, only too elaborate.

March 3rd
It would be difficult to say how the Government Reform Bill has been received. The night it came out everybody who spoke, spoke against it ...

March 15th
Within the last few days the symptoms from France have been more menacing. At Paris the convention is general that war is meant, and I am obliged to believe it likewise ...

March 22nd
Nothing could be more uninteresting than the first evening of the debate on J. R.'s Resolution [a response to Disraeli's Bill].

March 24th
When I think of the Reform Bill of 1832, and compare the state of affairs at that time with that of the present time, nothing can be more extraordinary. Then the interest was intense, the whole country in a fever of excitement, the Press rabid, the clamour for reform all but universal, party running tremendously high, no doubt or hesitation ... This debate has begun and seems likely to continue, how differently! There are neither zeal nor union on one side or the other, everybody is dissatisfied with the state of affairs, and nobody can see a satisfactory issue from the general embarrassment ...

Gladstone is come back from Italy completely duped by Cavour who has persuaded him that Piedmont has no ambition or aggressive objects, and that Austria alone is guilty of all the trouble in which the world has been plunged ...

March 26th

The debate goes on to the intense disgust of everybody, though enlivened by a few clever and telling speeches ... On Friday Palmerston spoke, with great vigour but not much effect. His speech was very jaunty but very insincere ...

April 1st

The great debate came to an end last night. The majority was greater than either side expected ... and there were several very powerful speeches, but principally on the side of the minority. Gladstone's was particularly good, and Dizzy's reply, with a very effective philippic against John Russell, was exceedingly clever and delivered with much dignity and in good taste.

... This morning the prevalent idea was that they would resign, but this evening, and after Derby's brief notice in the H. of Lords, it is rather that they will dissolve ...

Clarendon came in and we talked of foreign affairs. He thinks war inevitable, and that the French are only gaining time to complete their preparations.

Thursday 7th

The determination of the Government, announced in both Houses on Monday evening, took the world by surprise. Nobody thought there would be a dissolution ... The Opposition Leaders are evidently taken aback; the Derbyites assert that they have reason to expect a gain of forty seats, but nobody believes it ...

April 15th

... I met Disraeli yesterday afternoon, when he told me they had got such satisfactory news from the Continent that he considered the affair as virtually settled and the danger at an end. [A demand made by Britain and France that Sardinia Austria would disarm in Italy. Cavour made the undertaking, hence Disraeli's optimism; two days later Austria refused.] God grant it may be so, but I am far from being satisfied that the danger is over ... I believe the concessions which France expresses herself willing to make to our entreaties to be a part of her game ...

April 27th Newmarket

On Monday we heard that the Austrians had sent their ultimatum to Sardinia, and there was a complete panic in the City ...

May 7th

Another severe fit of the gout, principally in the right hand, has prevented me writing a line for the last fortnight during which war has broken out, and the general election has been begun and ended, and, what is most important to myself, I have resigned my office [on 6 May] ...

May 17th

The elections are nearly if not quite over ... they present a gain of nearly thirty for the Government ... the general election has been eminently satisfactory in this, that it has elicited the completely Conservative spirit of the country ... it has also manifested the indifference of the country to all parties and to all political ties and connexions ... It is remarkable that the Catholics have supported the Government, and that they have done so under orders from Rome. [Cardinal Paul] Cullen is there, and has signified to the priests the pleasure of the Pope [Pius IX] that the Derby Government should be supported. Clarendon told me this yesterday and the reason is because they think this Government more favourably inclined to Austria than any other, especially than either Palmerston or J. Russell would be. The Papal Government have never forgiven the Whigs for the Ecclesiastical Titles Bill ...

June 6th

As I was at Epsom every day this week, I have heard nothing of what is going on except the fact that there is to be a great meeting of the Liberals at Willis's Rooms [in earlier days called Almack's, Willis's would, in 1895, be the place where Oscar Wilde's Algy informed Ernest that he would be giving him supper] this afternoon, called by a list of people which includes Palmerston and John and Milner Gibson, whose signature betokens the ascent of the Radicals to the object of it ...

June 7th

The meeting of the Opposition yesterday at Willis's Rooms went off as well as they could expect or desire. The Two Leaders gave the required assurances that each would serve under the other, in the event of either being sent for. There was a general concurrence in the plan for attacking the Government at once ... there were however some rather ominous manifestations made at this meeting. It seemed to be agreed that the new Government should embrace not only Whigs and Peelites but 'advanced Liberals' ...

June 9th

There is great excitement about this debate ... On the first night Disraeli made a capital speech, and nobody else on their side would speak at all ... Palmerston's speech was in accordance with his declaration at Willis's and with his ancient practice; it was violently pro-French and anti-Austrian, and it was full of gross falsehoods and misrepresentations which he well knew to be such.

In his seventy-fifth year and playing the last act of his political life, he is just what he always was . . .

Sunday June 12th

Derby resigned at eleven o'clock and the Queen immediately after marked her sense of his conduct by sending him an extra Garter [additional to the currently filled quota].

June 26th

While we have been settling our Government for good or evil, the war has continued to pursue its course of uninterrupted success of the Allies, and unless something almost miraculous should occur, the Austrian dominion in Italy may be considered at an end . . .

July 12th

On Friday morning the world was electrified by reading in *The Times* that an armistice had been agreed upon between the belligerent Emperors in Italy . . .

July 13th

We had scarcely had time to begin discussing and speculating on the probable results of the armistice before the news of peace being actually concluded burst in upon us . . . Nothing is more likely than that the King and his Cavour will find, in spite of all they are to obtain, that they will not have a bed of roses to repose upon after their fatigues and labours . . . Whether the Pope will accept the temporal office assigned to him may be doubted, but it cannot be doubted that his supremacy will not be willingly accepted and acknowledged by the Italians generally to whom the Papal rule is already odious. [The idea, which fell down at once, was for the Pope to be a President of a Swiss sort of confederation.] One cannot but feel glad at the deep mortification and disappointment which will overtake the Republicans and Socialists, the Mazzinis, Garibaldis, Kossuths et hoc genus omne at a pacification so ruinous to all their hopes and designs . . .

July 15th

The friends of the Emperor Napoleon say they believe his motives for making peace *on any terms he could* to have been principally that he was so shocked and disgusted at the fearful scene of pain and misery that he had to behold after the battle of Solferino in addition to the other battle fields and at the spectacle of thousands of killed and wounded presented to his eyes, that his nerves could not bear it.

August 7th

Edmond Mildmay [British military attaché in Austria] told me that at Solferino the Austrian loss was 20,000, the French 19,000 and the Sardinians 9000 men ...

Viceregal Lodge, Phoenix Park, August 22nd Monday

I have at last accomplished the object I have desired for so many years and find myself in Ireland. I have seized the first opportunity of being my own master to come here ... Greatly struck by the fineness of the town of Dublin and of the public buildings especially.

August 24th

Yesterday in the morning a review in the Phoenix Park, after which Bagot [a senior Dublin Castle official] took me to Howth Castle which I was curious to see but is not very remarkable, though very ancient ... Dublin is for its size a finer town than London, and I think they beat us hollow in their public buildings. We have no such squares as Merrion [nor, since the depredations of Charles Haughey, does Dublin], nor such a Street as Sackville Street.

August 28th

Went yesterday to Waterford; pretty good town, but looking very foreign.

Viceregal Lodge Wednesday 7th September

Went to Muckross on Thursday last; passed three days there in exquisite enjoyment of the beautiful scenery of Killarney; weather was perfect, and I went over and round the lakes; returned here on Monday, and went yesterday to the Curragh.

Jervaulx Abbey Sunday September 11th

Crossed over from Kingston to Holyhead on Thursday last; beautiful passage. Passed the last day in Dublin with Walter Fitzgerald seeing the town: ... what was once the H. of Commons, now completely altered and not retaining a vestige of the famous locality where Flood and Grattan and Plunkett and Burke once shook the walls with their eloquence. [Not Burke, who was never a Member.] I left Ireland with regret ...

Newmarket October 21st

I gather from [Clarendon] that neither Pam nor John are much in favour with the Queen, but that they cannot have everything their own way in foreign affairs, as the rest of the Cabinet are very vigilant and not at all passive and the Queen likewise. He was lately at Broadlands, and had much talk with Palmerston ... That P.'s hatred of Austria amounted to a Monomania, and this of course produces a divergence between the present policy of France and ours ...

November 18th

... [Clarendon's] confidence has in great measure been produced by a letter from Cowley which he showed me, containing an account of his visit to Biarritz and his communications with the Emperor. He said he resolved not to say a word to H.M. of Italian affairs, thinking the E. would abstain from talking of them to him, but as soon they met, he began to talk and went at length into the whole subject. The upshot was that he found the Emperor in such a state of perplexity and embarrassment, and so fully conscious of the scrape into which he had got himself, that he did not know what to do or which way to turn; his object evidently is to get us to help him out of his difficulty ...

December 25th

... The Government are getting ready for the session which is near at hand, Palmerston with his usual confidence, but Granville ... is conscious of the want of that strength and security which a commanding majority alone can give and, without thinking the danger imminent, anticipates the possibility of their being defeated on some vital question. The Opposition, conscious of their numerical force, but anything but united, profess the most moderate views and intentions ...

Disraeli raised himself immensely last year, more perhaps with his opponents and the H. of Commons generally than with his own party, but it is universally acknowledged that he led the House with a tact, judgment and ability of which he was not before thought capable. While he has thus risen, no rival has sprung up to dispute his pre-eminence. Walpole and Henley are null, and it is evident that the Party cannot do without Dis., ... and I have no doubt that whenever any good opportunities for showing fight may occur the whole party will be found united under Dizzy's orders.

1860

January 2nd

The death of Macaulay is the extinction of a great light ... he used frequently to invite me to those breakfasts in the Albany at which he sued to collect small miscellaneous parties, generally including some remarkable people, and at which he loved to pour forth all those stores of his mind and accumulations of his memory ... I don't believe anybody ever left his society with any feeling of mortification except that which an involuntary comparison between his knowledge and their own ignorance could not fail to engender ... what appears to me most admirable and most worthy of imitation in Macaulay is the sound moral constitution of his mind ... Above all, he was no hero-worshipper ... Macaulay excited much indignation in some quarters by the severity with which he criticised the conduct and character of the Duke of Marlborough ... he would not allow Blenheim and Ramillies to be taken as a set-off against his hypocrisy, perfidy and treason.

January 22nd

... It would really look as if the sole or at least the main object of [Louis Napoleon's] policy was to conciliate English opinion and to ingratiate himself with the present Government ... nobody was at least prepared for the pamphlet of 'The Pope and the Congress'. It fell like a thunderbolt, striking terror into the minds of the Papal supporters and adherents and filling with joy all revolted Italy, and with a more sober satisfaction all the Liberals and ultra-Protestants here.

We ... were still more astonished and pleased by ... his intention to change the whole commercial policy of France, and to make her a country of Free Trade. In thus confronting at once the Clerical body and the Protectionist interest in France, he has certainly acted with enormous boldness ... The Commercial Treaty [extensive slashing or abolition of duties between British and French goods] is in great measure the work of Cobden, ... and as an acknowledgement of his exertions he is to be made joint Plenipotentiary with Cowley in signing the Commercial Treaty ...

Bath February 15th

When I left London a fortnight ago the world was anxiously expecting Gladstone's speech in which he was to put the Commercial Treaty and the Budget before the world ... Clarendon shook his head, Overstone [Loyd, the banker] pronounced against the treaty, *The Times* thundered against it, and there is little doubt that it was unpopular and was becoming more so every day. Then came Gladstone's illness ... His Doctor says he ought to have taken two months' rest instead of two days. However at the end of his two days' delay he came forth and consensu omnium achieved one of the greatest triumphs that the House of Commons ever witnessed ... Clarendon, who has all along disapproved of the treaty, wrote to me that Gladstone's triumph was complete and public opinion in his favour. He says ... '[Gladstone] has a fervent imagination, which furnishes facts and arguments in support of them; he is an audacious innovator because he has an insatiable appetite for popularity, and in his notions of Government he is a far more sincere Republican than Bright ... The two are converging from different points to the same end, and if Gladstone remains in office long enough and is not more opposed by his colleagues ... we shall see him propose a graduated Income Tax.'

February 26th Sunday

On Friday night Gladstone had another great triumph. He made a splendid speech, and obtained a majority of 116 which puts an end to the contest. He is now *the* great man of the day, but these proceedings strikingly displayed the disorganised condition of the Conservative Party and their undisguised dislike for their Leader. A great many of them voted with the Government on Friday night and more expressed satisfaction at the result being a defeat for Disraeli.

March 9th

After all it is not improbable that Palmerston will have the gratification of seeing Tuscany annexed to Sardinia ... Next week the Italian States will severally vote their annexation to Sardinia or their separate existence. If, as is almost certain, the former is their decision, the King will accept their resolution, and Piedmontese troops will march into Tuscany ...

Torquay March 27th

... The triumvirate of Palmerston, J. Russell and Gladstone, who have it all their own way dragging after them the Cabinet, the H. of Commons and the country, will probably be the ruin of this country. They are playing into the Emperor Napoleon's hands, who has only to be patient and abide his time, and he will be able to treat all Europe (including England) in any way he pleases ... Nothing but some speedy change of Government and of system can avert the impending ruin.

April 22nd

... John Russell electrified the House and rather astonished the country by delivering a very spirited speech, denouncing in strong terms the conduct of the Emperor Napoleon and declaring the necessity of cultivating relations with the other Great Powers for the purpose of putting an effectual check upon the projects of French aggrandisement and annexation ...

The accounts from Paris are that this speech has made the French very insolent, and the Emperor more popular than he has been for a long time as even his enemies say they will rally round him to chastise English impertinence ...

April 8th Sunday

On Good Friday morning G. Lewis [now Home Secretary] and I were left alone ... he quite amazed me by the way in which he spoke of his principal colleagues J. Russell, Palmerston and Gladstone – of John and his business and fitness for his post with the utmost contempt ... With regard to Palmerston, he said that P. thought of nothing but his pro-Sardinian and anti-Austrian schemes ... Gladstone G. L. evidently dislikes and distrusts, and his financial schemes and arrangements are as distasteful to him as possible. He is provoked at Gladstone's being able to bear down all opposition, and carry all before him by the force of his eloquence and power of words.

May 17th

The Garibaldi expedition [the departure of the Thousand for Sicily] is supposed to have given great umbrage to France but not without some suspicions that secretly she is not sorry for it ... Everybody believes that Cavour has covertly connived at it, though he pretends to oppose it ...

Talking of Neapolitan affairs ... There is just arrived a new Neapolitan minister, Count Ludolph ... He has replaced [di Carini] who by his own desire was recently recalled, and he had begged for his recall because he had been grossly insulted by Palmerston at the Queen's Drawing Room ... Palmerston had attacked him on the proceedings of his Government and the conduct of the King, telling him that revolution would probably be the result thereof, which would be nothing more than they deserved, and which would be seen in this country with universal satisfaction.

Sunday May 28th

Epsom engaged my attention last week, and I could find no time to notice the debate in the Lords on the Paper Duties and the extraordinary majority [against] ... P. said to Gladstone 'Of course you are mortified and disappointed, but your disappointment is nothing to mine, who had a horse with whom I hoped to win the Derby, and he went amiss at the last moment.'

July 8th

I have been so ill till within the last few days that I have not had energy enough to do anything ... Granville told me yesterday morning that it was a toss-up whether Gladstone resigned or not, and that if he did, it would break up the Liberal Party, to which I replied that I was confident he would not resign, and if he did, it would have no effect on the bulk of the Liberal Party.

Buxton August 11th

I came here for my health and to try and patch myself up ... The session of Parliament was drawing to a close, and it was understood that there was to be one more fight in the H. of C. [on the removal of customs duties on paper] ... The Speaker [Denison] wrote me an account of what passed ... 'the division of thirty-three on the Paper Duties was a surprise to all on the spot ... the Irishmen held off, indignant at Palmerston's having mentioned with approval the landing of Garibaldi on the mainland. This was held to be an insult to the Pope, so More O'Farrell, Monsell, Sir J. Acton and eight or ten more would not vote at all. It seemed doubtful to the last. It is a great thing for the

Government in many ways, not the least in having won the battle without the Pope and his men ... The great result is to give some life to half-dead, broken down, tempest-tossed Gladstone.' ...

London November 13th

At the end of three months since I last wrote anything in this book I take my pen in hand to record my determination to bring this journal (which is no journal at all) to an end ... I therefore close this record without any intention or expectation of renewing it, with a full consciousness of the smallness of its value or interest, and with great regret that I did not make better use of the opportunities I have had of recording something more worth reading.

VOLUME VII ENDS

NOTES

Volume I

1814 (pp. 3–4)

1. George Colman the Younger (1762–1836), playwright, theatre patentee and censor!
2. King of Westphalia was the title Napoleon had given to his brother, Jerome.
3. Sir Henry Halford (1766–1844), physician to King George III.

1815 (pp. 4–7)

1. Lord Stewart (1778–1854), younger brother of the Foreign Secretary, Castlereagh, succeeding him in the title of Marquess of Londonderry, ambassador at Vienna, 1814.
2. The variable spelling of the Emperor's surname, retained here, is Greville's.
3. Jean-Baptiste Drouet died, a Marshal of France, in 1844.
4. Sir Robert Wilson (1777–1849), fought at Dresden and Leipzig, dismissed in 1821 for trying to prevent soldiers from firing on a crowd at Queen Caroline's [qv] funeral.

1818 (pp. 7–9)

1. Prince Talleyrand, former Bishop, revolutionary and key Minister of Napoleon, was to become the chief mover of the 1830 July Revolution in France, before emerging in 1831 ambassador to the Court of St James's.
2. On the 18th Brumaire (revolutionary calendar 9th November) 1799, Bonaparte seized power.
3. Captain Maxwell was defeated at one of the two Westminster seats by the reformer Sir Francis Burdett.
4. Lord Castlereagh, briefly later Marquess of Londonderry, Foreign Secretary, whose cold arrogant manner and sympathy with continental absolutists provoked Shelley, 'I met Murder on the way / He had a mask like Castlereagh'. (*The Mask of Anarchy*).
5. Oatlands Park, Weybridge, at that time the residence of the Duke of York, next in line after the Regent, to the throne.
6. Samuel Rogers, gently mocked by Sydney Smith, a minor poet, man about literature and famous for giving breakfasts.
7. Charles James Fox, defining radical leader of the Whigs died in 1806.
8. The Peace of Amiens, a brief respite negotiated with Napoleon in 1802.
9. The famous (and interminable) address of Sheridan during the Westminster trial of Warren Hastings, the Begums of Oudh had allegedly been mistreated and financially mulcted by Hastings.

1819 (pp. 9–11)

1. Dorothea, Countess, later Princess Lieven (1785–1857), wife of the Russian ambassador, salon-keeper, mistress of Metternich, friend of Guizot, correspondent with many politicians, close to Greville, unofficial spokesman for the Russian Government in London.

2. Princess Charlotte was the only child of George IV and Caroline. Her death left the succession with a range of little regarded royal uncles until the birth of Alexandrina Victoria.

1820 (pp. 11–14)

1. Sir William Knighton was a controversial figure because of his influence; though trained as a physician, he was a close confidant first and in 1822 became George's private secretary.

2. Sir William Tierney, physician to George IV and William IV, is not to be confused with the Whig politician, George Tierney.

3. The Cato Street Conspiracy was almost certainly helped to its extreme objective by Government spies operating as *agents provocateurs*. Five of its members were publicly hanged and beheaded.

4. Caroline of Brunswick was now backed by leading Whig politicians, Denham (future Chief Justice) and Brougham (future Lord Chancellor). Her intention to make trouble would be compounded by George forcing his ministers into a stupendously ill-advised suit for divorce, effectively a trial for adultery.

5. White's, then, as now, the St James's Street club, was a citadel of the highest flying of all Toryism.

6. Bartolomeo Bergami (d. 1841), Caroline's courier when living abroad and with whom she was accused of committing adultery.

1821 (pp. 14–15)

1. The Marchioness Conyngham, George IV's last mistress and companion to whom he was wholly devoted, took, as here, every step to provide for her family and connections.

2. It was settled by a compromise, The Revd Richard Sumner was given instead a private chaplaincy and a splendid house in Windsor, the perquisites of a Dr Clarke, who was given the Canonry. The Curate (Sumner) ended as Bishop of Winchester.

1822 (pp. 15–17)

1. Harriet Greville by this marriage ultimately became Countess of Ellesmere.

2. Georgina Lennox was the daughter of the Duke of Richmond, and later married Lord De Ros.

3. Percy Jocelyn, Bishop of Clogher, was detected in the act of sodomy and only escaped the capital charge it then entailed by flight abroad.

4. George Canning, wit and Tory politician, was Foreign Secretary (1822–7), Prime Minister from February 1827 to his death in August that year.

5. Canning's earlier resignation from the Cabinet in December 1820 followed his steady advice not to start a prosecution of Caroline.

1826 (pp. 17–18)

1. Though things were very bad indeed at the bank, reserves were rather larger than Greville states.

2. The Small Notes Bill was moved by Frederick Robinson, Chancellor of the Exchequer, to confine inflation by issuing no notes worth less than £5 after the end of the financial year.

3. Edward Ellice (1781–1863) originally came from Canada, was later Government Chief Whip in Grey's Ministry.

4. This was the time of events at Missolonghi where Byron died.

5. This famous speech was made when the Government sent a force to Portugal to warn off the Bourbon Government of Spain. Canning also said just before his great trope, 'I resolved that if France had Spain, it should not be Spain with the Indies.'

1827 (pp. 18–21)

1. Lord Liverpool, Prime Minister since 1812, a term of Government second only to Robert Walpole's. A moderate Tory, Liverpool had been able to keep a divided Cabinet together.

2. Charles Watkin Williams-Wynne (1775–1845) was unsuccessful candidate for the Speakership in 1817, the President of the Board of Control (1822–8) and declined the Governor-Generalship of India.

3. Clarence, third son of George III, succeeded as William IV in 1830. He had served (without distinction) as a naval officer.

4. Windsor Castle, where extensive rebuilding and extension work in the Gothick manner had been carried out by Sir Jeffrey Wyattville in close consultation with the King.

5. Frederick Robinson, Lord Goderich (1782–1859), was a very successful Chancellor under Liverpool, briefly and unhappily Prime Minister, failing for party and family reasons after Canning's death.

1828 (pp. 21–23)

1. Huskisson, leader of the Canningite group, had voted for a motion disfranchising two rotten boroughs, offering a *pro forma* resignation to Wellington which the Duke disconcertingly accepted.

2. Daniel O'Connell (1775–1847) was effective leader of Catholic Ireland until his death.

3. James Warren Doyle (1786–1834), was once a volunteer from Coimbra University in Wellington's army in the Peninsular War.

1829 (pp. 23–31)

1. The Minster was fired by a madman named Martin whose brother, John Martin, was a noted artist, on 2 February 1829.

2. The far right, or Ultra wing of the Tory party became known as 'the Brunswickers' because of the patronage of Ernest Augusts, Duke of Cumberland and future King of Hanover.

3. Catholics had the vote but, barred by the need to take a violent anti-papist oath, could not sit in Parliament. At Clare in 1828, something Greville did not report, O'Connell stood, was elected and arrived in Westminster. The impossibility of excluding him at a time when Ireland was close to a general uprising made up Wellington's mind.

4. Edward Burtenshaw Sugden (1781–1875), later Baron then Earl of St Leonards, held

the Great Seal of Ireland (1834 and 1841–6) and later Lord Chancellor of the United
Kingdom (1852). He was also a minimally distinguished Law Reporter.

5. Sir William Horne, Solicitor-General (1830), Attorney-General (1832) resigned
    a judgeship as an opponent of the death penalty.

6. They should not have. Robert Peel, who had offended his electors at the University
    of Oxford by his shift to supporting Catholic Emancipation, stood down to fight
    his seat and lost it to Sir Robert Inglis.

7. Peel was quickly returned unopposed at the closed borough of Westbury.

8. Sir Charles Wetherell (1770–1846), Attorney-General under Wellington, was
    member for Boroughbridge.

9. Colonel Waldo Sibthorpe, super-reactionary, almost Absurdist MP for Lincoln,
    1826–56.

10. Twenty years later, Lady Ellenborough's co-respondent, would, as Prime Minister
    of Austria, restore absolutist government with extensive brutality after the '48.

11. Thomas Creevey (1768–1838), Greville's rival as diarist and chronicler of the
    early part of the nineteenth century. Also a Whig politician.

12. Sir James MacIntosh (1765–1834) doctor, journalist, judge, polymath, his defence
    of the French Revolution, 'Vindiciae Gallicae' was a reply to Burke.

1830 (pp. 31–50)

1. Sir Edward Knatchbull, Senior Member for Kent, was shocked that Wellington
    and Peel had put through Catholic Emancipation without consulting the party.

2. Lord Durham, Lord Grey's son-in-law, was made Lord Privy Seal in Grey's
    Ministry, formed in November 1830.

3. Edward Thurlow was Lord Chancellor, with a brief intermission, over fourteen
    years (1778– 92).

4. Jacob Rothschild, another of the family's five arrows, was running the Paris bank.

5. George Bryan Brummel, setter of style, former close friend of the King when
    Prince of Wales, and after a brief tenure as consul was now destitute.

6. Brummel died in an asylum in Caen.

7. Sir Augustus Foster was British Minister at Turin, then the capital of the Kingdom
    of Savoy/Sardinia (1824–40).

8. Lord Cochrane was one of the most brilliant and least orthodox of English sailors.
    The robbery was a much disputed allegation of a stock market fraud. Cochrane, a
    political radical, had many enemies and his subsequent pardon and reinstatement
    implied a rebuttal of the charges. His career was a quarry from which Patrick O'Brian
    extracted many of the tessellations making up his fictional character Jack Aubrey.

9. The Pope at this time was Pope Pius VIII, Francesco Castiglioni (March
    1829–November 1830), soon after succeeded by Gregory XVI (Mauro Cappellari
    (1831–46), an ironic conservative who would respond to plans for railway building
    with the French epigram 'Chemins de fer? Chemins d'Enfer!'

10. Sir Ferdinand Acton, 7th Baron, father of the 'power corrupting' historian, Lord
    Acton, of the Shropshire Catholic family long powerful in the Government of the
    Neapolitan Kingdom.

11. Albani was Cardinal Secretary of State instrumental in the election of Pius and,
    according to The Oxford Dictionary of Popes, 'openly pro-Austrian'.

12. Peyronnet was an unpopular and repressive Bourbon Minister of Justice (1821)

and now (1830), appointed Minister of the Interior in the extreme right-wing Government of Jules de Polignac.

13. At this time the Austrian Empire, which had influence throughout Italy, directly ruled as its own provinces, both Venezia and Lombardia.

Volume II

1830 (pp. 51–67)

1. John Singleton Copley, Baron Lyndhurst (1772–1863), three times Lord Chancellor, reckoned to be the model for the 'highly susceptible chancellor' in *Iolanthe*.

2. Emily Harriet, Lady Fitzroy Somerset (1792–1881) married as her second husband Lord Fitzroy Somerset, later Lord Raglan.

3. Auguste Frédéric Louis Viesse de Marmont, Marshal Marmont (1774–1852), served Napoleon then the Bourbons and had been commanding officer during the July Days (1830).

4. Sir James Graham (1792–1861), a member of the Whig Cabinet, later associated with Peel rather than Gladstone; Peel's Home Secretary (1841–6) and closest confidant.

5. The assassination of the Grand Duke Constantine, Russian Viceroy of Poland, followed the mutiny of four Polish regiments after he had ordered certain Polish military cadets to be flogged.

1831 (pp. 67–90)

1. Henry Hunt, otherwise Orator Hunt, MP for Preston, was the main speaker at the St Peter's Fields meeting in Manchester in 1819 when a charge of yeomanry into the crowd killed eleven people, injured between four and five hundred, including more than one hundred women or girls. Of these 161 suffered sabre wounds, the rest were inflicted by the feet of the crowd or the hooves of horses. This triumph won itself the name 'Peterloo'.

2. John Calcraft was a former member of the Wellington Government, who had spoken temperately against the Bill, then voted for it. In 1832, distressed at the hostility provoked, he committed suicide.

3. Michael Sadler (1780–1835) was an extravagant traditionalist on constitutional matters, but his eccentricities included passionate and effective campaigning against children working fourteen hours a day in factories.

4. Long Wellesley was a rascally member of the Duke of Wellington's family, later the equally rascally Earl of Mornington. His daughter Catherine was an heiress through her mother, Wellesley's first wife. The matter concerned the Lord Chancellor, but, as Wellesley was an MP, he claimed parliamentary privilege.

5. Harriette Wilson (1789–1846). Starting as the fifteen-year-old mistress of the Earl of Craven, she became her age's leading temptress to the carriage trade, rounding off a spangled career by the discreet blackmail of the aristocracy through memoirs, long and profitably projected and, on subscription, flexible about what should be included.

6. *The Custom of the Country*, by Beaumont and Fletcher, was indecent to the quite worldly Greville because it has scenes in the male brothels of Lisbon.

7. Hugh Fortescue, Viscount Ebrington MP, was heir to Earl Fortescue, and a radical aristocratic Whig, who would appear as a rallier of his party again.

8. Richard Lalor Shiel, was an Irish politician, effective deputy to Daniel O'Connell, and later a friend of Disraeli.

9. The 'Conservative Party'. Greville was using the word 'party' in a non-institutional sense, meaning a loose trend or sympathetic group. 'Conservative' was a new word, only coined that year in an unsigned article in the Tory *Quarterly Review.*

10. The entire bench of Bishops with the exceptions of Hereford and Norwich opposed Reform in the first Lords vote.

11. Schedule A: the part of the Reform Bill depriving fifty-six boroughs of their two members on grounds of very small electorates.

12. Schedule B: the Bill gave the vote to £10 freeholders irrespective of the number of payments made during a year. This was at the insistence of Thomas Attwood of the Birmingham Political Union, making it clear to Ministers that most people paid rates by small sums often. This had led to Charles Wetherell's insulting and riot-provoking remarks about ratepayers in Bristol, where he was recorder, saying that to give the vote to the weekly or fortnightly ratepayer meant a pauper franchise.

13. George Agar Ellis, later Baron Dover.

14. Lord George Cavendish-Bentinck, the leading figure on the turf, later, after twenty years' quiescent membership of Parliament, became Peel's greatest enemy over the Corn Laws.

15. Grey was physically tired and, not wanting to renew conflict immediately, had tried to push the recall of Parliament and the taking up of the Reform question anew until the new year. This, together with Wharncliffe's moves, had greatly alarmed the committed reformers of the party. See *inter alia* the memoirs of Lord Broughton, John Cam Hobhouse, who as a new member of the Cabinet, furiously lobbied his elders and organised resistance to delay.

16. 'Electrical'. This is terribly up to date. Michael Faraday had induced electricity for the first time earlier in 1831!

17. 'Henry V' was the eldest son of Charles X, the legitimist pretender who forty years later would miss an open-goal chance of restoration.

18. Commonly Du Barry (1746–93), mistress of Louis XV, and subsequently guillotined.

19. Nicholas, Baron Luckner, Marshal of France, was charged with treason and guillotined.

20. Charles Lambton, known to art history as 'The Boy in Red', Thomas Lawrence's famous painting, was the gifted and beautiful only son of Durham and thus grandson of Grey, adored by them both. He had died slowly that summer of the family trait of tuberculosis which would kill Durham himself at forty-two.

21. It was a recurring King Charles's head among Tories that Peel could have forced a vote on the first night before opinion in an eclectic House began to swing with the argument in favour of Reform.

1832 (pp. 90–111)

1. Lord Auckland, George Eden, Baron, later 1st Earl, strong Whig, subsequently, as Governor-General of India, was caught up in the first Afghanistan disaster.

2. Sir Thomas Duncombe was ardent for the creation of peers to pass the Bill.

3. Henry Phillpotts was a Tory Ultra of such extreme views that Sidney Smith had remarked that he 'must believe in the apostolic succession as the only explanation of the Bishop of Exeter's descent from Judas Iscariot'.

4. Spencer Perceval the Younger, son of the Prime Minister, demanded (and got) 'a day of penance and fasting' and, when the Commons was busy debating at the approach of midnight before the appointed day, denounced it for blasphemy.

5. Irvingites were followers of Edward Irving (1792–1834), a fashionable preacher who matured into religious mania and founded the Apostolic Catholic or Irvingite community.

6. The Birmingham Political Union was the biggest political union and led the others in agitating for parliamentary and general reform. They had invited the King to respond to the defeat of the Bill by making peers. Non-recognition, preferably the physical suppression of these autonomous bodies, was an obsession of the right wing and particularly of Wellington.

7. The Governor-General of India had issued an order abolishing the live incineration of Hindu widows. A group of Hindus appealed against the order and the learned judges were divided on the subject. But political members of the Privy Council, not then barred by convention from voting on legal questions, sustained the Governor-General's sentimental action.

8. Charles Abbott, 1st Baron Tenterden (1762–1832), son of a Canterbury barber, Lord Chief Justice of the King's Bench since 1827, was a strong opponent of Catholic Emancipation and the Reform Bill.

9. Thomas Denman (1779–1854) was appointed Lord Chief Justice following the death of Tenterden – 1832–50 – after being, with Brougham, Queen Caroline's counsel in the famous trial.

1833 (pp. 111–24)

1. A West Indian in the eighteenth and nineteenth centuries, as in Richard Cumberland's highly successful play of the 1770s, *The West Indian*, meant a white plantation and slave-owner.

2. James Stephen (1758–1833) founded the dynasty of Sir James FitzJames, Sir Leslie Stephen and Virginia Woolf and was under-secretary for the Colonies.

3. Adolphe Thiers (1797–1877), a dominant figure until the fall of the Orléans monarchy, was exiled for a time under the Second Empire and became President of France after its fall.

4. Chambers' *Biographical Dictionary* says of *Sir Charles Grandison*: 'its story is not strong enough to reconcile the reader to the prolix impeccability of its superfine hero'.

5. Edward Irving (1792–1834) founded the 'Holy Catholic Apostolic Church', a sect of extreme evangelicals, attractive to unstable personalities. The Chapel was in Regent Square, London.

6. William Fox (1786–1864), an independent-minded Unitarian minister, later radical MP for Oldham 1847–63, preached at the South Place Chapel of The South Place Ethical Society, a group closely allied to Christian socialism.

Volume III

1834 (pp. 125–38)

1.   Poulett Thompson (later Lord Sydenham) was Vice-President of the Board of Trade, previously prominent in the City, and about whom Greville had earlier been actionably virulent.

2.   Reeves, Greville's first editor, has corrected this John Bullish scorn, pointing out in an earlier footnote that 'the Schloss Meiningen is a handsome German Residenz'.

3.   Duncannon, John William Ponsonby, later 4th Earl of Bessborough (1781–1847), Whig politician: on committee drafting the Reform Bill, *inter alia* Lord Privy Seal, later Lord-Lieutenant of Ireland.

1835 (pp. 138–51)

1.   In 1815 O'Connell had fought a duel with John D'Esterre, an outstanding shot who, probably by intention, missed; O'Connell sought only to wound, but the effort was fatal. Ever after he refused personal action in a duel, but would send one of his sons.

2.   Horace Twiss (1787–1849), the son-in-law of Eldon, whose biography he wrote, was a Tory Ultra, barrister and MP 1820–31.

3.   Miss Cooke, an actress, was probably a daughter of the great George Frederick Cooke.

4.   J. R. Planché, ubiquitous playwright.

5.   Theodore Hook (1788–1841) was a playwright, periodical editor, wit and debtor, also noted for hoaxes.

6.   Sir Charles Grey was one of a Commission of Enquiry of three sent to Canada.

7.   Lord Lincoln, Henry Pelham, was a Peelite liberal Tory, later a Minister and succeeded as Duke of Newcastle.

1836 (pp. 151–6)

1.   Of Saxe-Coburg, King of the Belgians, widower of Princess Charlotte. See *supra*.

1837 (pp. 156–64)

1.   Frederick Thesiger (1794–1878). Later, as Lord Chelmsford, he became Lord Chancellor.

2.   Ernest, Duke of Cumberland, younger brother of William IV, had engaged in extreme reactionary politics in Britain before succeeding by Salic Law to the family's German territories.

3.   Thomas Wakley (1795–1862) was the Radical MP for Finchley, 1837–52, and founder of the *Lancet*.

Volume IV

1838 (pp. 165–77)

1.   Cumberland's first act as King of Hanover was to suspend its constitution and prosecute a number of liberal professors at Goettingen.

2.   Michael Faraday (1791–1867) was the creator of the dynamo and the pre-eminent experimental scientist.

3.   Probably Jonathan Pereira (1804–53), chemist and author of *Polarised Light* (1843).

4.   Charles Wheatstone (1802–75) was co-patenter of the electric telegraph in 1837.

5.   A major part of the fortune made by the father of W. E. Gladstone derived from slavery, not slave ownership or trade, but plantations worked throughout his ownership by slaves.

6.   Lord Sefton, William Molyneux, 2nd Earl, a Regency personality and Whig politician, was probably the legitimate brother of Thomas Creevey.

1840 (pp. 185–95)

1.   Mehemet Ali was the Albanian governor of Egypt who had made himself its hereditary ruler.

2.   The Emir Bechir, Druze leader; as a supporter of Mehemet Ali, he joined the invasion of Syria.

1841 (pp. 196–206)

1.   This was the beginning of 'Carlism,' which plagued Spain for three generations, initially an attempt by the pretender Carlos to overthrow the Regent Maria Christina.

Volume V

1842 (pp. 207–13)

1.   Frederick William IV: acceded 1840, declared insane 1858.

2.   Charles Francis Seymour-Conway, 3rd Marquess (1777–1842), was the pre-eminent rake of the period.

3.   Lord Sydenham, Governor of Canada, who died after a fall from his horse in 1841, appears in earlier volumes of Greville (with a torrent of scorn) under his original name, Poulett Thompson.

1843 (pp. 213–22)

1.   Lieutenant Vincent Eyre, a hostage to Akbar Khan in 1842, wrote a memoir of the campaign.

2.   Daniel McNaghten was found not guilty by reason of insanity, and the judgment, defining two instances of insanity, not superceded for a hundred years, became known as 'the McNaghten Rules'.

3.   Arbuthnot was the husband of the journal-keeping Harriet, Wellington's friend.

4.   Flavius Josephus, Roman chronicler of first-century Palestine, was himself of Jewish origin.

5.   President of the Board of Control, equivalent of the later Secretary of State for India.

6.   The Revd Wriothesley Russell, Canon of Windsor.

7.   Sir John Plumb describes Edward, Duke of Kent, as 'a martinet who caused a mutiny in Gibraltar through the severity of his discipline. His love of savage punishments bordered on mania and made him the most thoroughly hated man in the army.'

8.   Greville's own footnote speaks of himself and his brother, Algernon, enjoying 'soup, beef, cutlets, two sorts of fish, vol au vent, stewed peas, another dish of vegetables besides plain bottle of wine and dessert for seven and a half francs (5 shillings)'.

9.   Frances Harriet Greville was the daughter of our Greville's brother, Algernon.

10.   Leopold von Ranke was the pre-eminent German historian, author of *The History of the Popes in the Sixteenth and Seventeenth Centuries.*

11.   Joseph Paxton (1801–65) was head gardener at Chatsworth and later designer of the Crystal Palace.

1844 (pp 222–30)

1.   The Government was legislating upon hours in factories. Ashley, later and better known as the 7th Earl of Shaftesbury, a country Tory uninstructed in Ricardian economics, brought in an amendment, specifically confining them to ten. Greville's prophecy of his not returning until he won proved true with consequences, the evil of which was apparent only to economists.

2.   Henry Reeve was Greville's chief assistant at the Council Office and subsequently his literary executor and first editor of the *Diaries.*

3.   The letters had been forwarded to the absolutist regime in Naples leading to the arrest and execution of friends of the leading Italian Liberal Nationalist.

4.   Pritchard, a missionary turned British Consul in Tahiti, was suspected by the French of stirring up local unrest, then arrested and deported by way of a passing British ship.

5.   A footnote by Henry Reeve tells us that the indemnity was never actually paid. The British Government had decided that, failing satisfaction, it would send a warship. The despatch threatening this was drafted but never sent.

1845 (pp. 230–41)

1.   Archdeacon Samuel Wilberforce (1805–73), later Bishop of Oxford then Winchester, engaged (and was bruised) in the famous public debate on Darwinian evolution with T. H. Huxley.

2.   Formerly Alexander Baring, head of the bank, he was briefly ambassador and negotiator of frontiers in the United States.

3.   John Laird (1805–74) was the son of William Laird, founder of the shipbuilding company later known as Camel Laird.

4.   Francis Freeling was Secretary to the Post Office in Melbourne's time as Home Secretary.

5.   Strictly this was Grey. The 2nd Earl, identified with the Reform Bill, had died earlier that year, but Greville made a point for a while of continuing to speak of the 3rd Earl by the courtesy title under which he was already well known. He was a much more radical figure than his father and later would indeed serve as Colonial Secretary. Greville was not, however, consistent; as we shall see, he lurches in to 'Grey' in the same sentence as 'Howick'.

6.   George William Frederick Howard (1802–64), later Earl of Carlisle, was a Whig politician and Cabinet Minister.

1846 (pp. 241–52)

1.   This charge, which relates to the motive for Peel's refusal to serve in Canning's Government on the question of Catholic Emancipation and an alleged inconsistent statement, is dealt with and convincingly dismissed in Professor Norman Gash's great *Sir Robert Peel*, Vol. II (Longman, 1972), p. 595 *et seq.*

2.   The Corn Bill passed its third reading in the Lords on 25 June. In the Commons,

the second reading of the Irish Coercion Bill failed (by 292 to 219) on the same night.

3. Peel died in 1850 after a riding accident; Aberdeen became Prime Minister in 1852, holding the office till 1855.

1847 (pp. 252–8)

1. Renn Hampden (1793–1868) was an advanced liberal theologian whose Bampton lectures created a furore among the High Church faction. He was Professor of Moral Philosophy and Divinity at Oxford and from 1847 was Bishop of Hereford. Hampden held mildly heterodox views but was chiefly the object of clerical jealousy.

1848 (pp. 259–70)

1. John Mitchell, for his writings, was convicted of 'Treason-felony', an interesting concept even for a nervous government, and transported to Tasmania (then Van Dieman's land). After his escape in 1854, he wrote a book, 'Jail Journey', and in 1874, though ineligible, was elected, then re-elected for Tipperary, before dying in the same year.

2. Pakington came from a Tory family, old enough for an ancestor to have been suspected in the 1720s of Jacobitism. For a colleague in Stanley's ministries, he had Spencer Walpole, collateral descendant of their persecutor, Sir Robert Walpole.

1849 (pp. 270–5)

1. Gladstone, a better judge of commercial and financial matters than Greville, saw George Hudson for all the corners cut, as an entrepreneur of visionary genius. More than any man, Hudson was the creator of the British rail network; and prophetically for modern travellers, he believed that it could only work properly under a single authority.

1850 (pp. 275–80)

1. John Arthur Roebuck managed in 1849 to become the Radical Member for Bath! He would, more realistically, represent Sheffield for 25 years. His fierce manner produced a verb in Yorkshire use: 'I'll John Arthur Roebuck you.'

1851 (p. 283)

1. Lajos Kossuth had been the very effective head of a revolutionary government in Hungary for a year from autumn 1849.

1852 (pp. 285–2)

1. Edward Cardwell, 1813–86 (later Viscount), would, as Secretary for War in Gladstone's first Ministry, 1868–74, carry through the major re-organisation of the armed forces, known as 'the Cardwell Reforms'.

1853 (pp. 292–300)

1. Henry Cowley (1804–84) [later Earl Cowley], served as ambassador in Vienna, Constantinople, Berne and Frankfurt (the Germanic Confederation), before Paris (1852–67).

1854 (pp. 301–9)

1. John Bright would at this time, in his bitter opposition to the Crimean war and its slaughter, make one of the great parliamentary speeches, a single sentence of

which, 'The Angel of Death has been about in the land; I think I hear the beating of his wings' epitomised wider public revulsion.

1855 (pp. 309–19)

1. Sidney Herbert would be the chief political contact (and punchball) of Florence Nightingale in her demands for field hospital reform and funds.
2. Disraeli's devotion in the Villiers affair is demonstrated, as Robert Blake's great biography points out, by a large cache of documents in his archive relating to it.

1856 (pp. 319–25)

1. Alexis Orloff, head of Nicholas 1st Secret Police, came from a family accustomed to brisk ways. Two earlier members had strangled Czar Peter III in 1762.
2. 'Big Ben' clock tower is named after Sir Benjamin Hall.

1857 (pp. 325–31)

1. Queeny Thrale made a second marriage to the much younger Count Flahault ['Flahaut' in Greville's text].
2. Croker, venomous editor of the 'Quarterly', has been credited, as has the less well known John Miller, with coining the word 'Conservative'.

1858 (pp. 331–6)

1. 'Ruffian' hardly says it. Amable! Jean-Jacques Pélissier (1794–1864), had in 1845, suffocated 500 fugitive Arabs in the caves in the Dahra.

1859 (pp. 336–42)

1. Giovanni-Maria Mastai-Ferretti, Pope since 1846, would soon undertake a self-imposed imprisonment (and sulk) at the loss of his temporal power, lasting until the end of his life in 1878.

1860 (pp. 342–6)

1. Overstone, originally Samuel Jones Loyd, [correct] did, however, get other things right. On his death in 1883, he left a fortune in excess of £2,000,000.

INDEX